Cambridge Studies in Chinese History, Literature and Institutions
General Editors
Patrick Hanan and Denis Twitchett

BUDDHISM UNDER THE T'ANG

Buddhism Under the T'ang is a history of the Buddhist church during the T'ang dynasty (618–907), when Buddhist thought reached the pinnacle of its development. The three centuries spanned by the T'ang saw the formation of such important philosophical schools as the Fa-hsiang and Hua-yen, the consolidation of the T'ien-t'ai school, the introduction of Esoteric Buddhism from India, and the emergence of the Pure Land and Ch'an schools as the predominant expressions of Buddhist faith and practice.

Professor Weinstein draws extensively upon both secular and ecclesiastical records to chronicle the vicissitudes of the Buddhist church. The main focus is on the constantly changing relationship between the Buddhist church and the T'ang state. Among the topics discussed in detail are the various attempts to curb the power of the Buddhist monasteries, the governance of the Buddhist clergy, the use of Buddhism to promote secular political ends, and the violent suppression of Buddhism by Emperor Wu (840–846) and its formal restoration under the last T'ang emperor.

Other books in the series

GLEN DUDBRIDGE: The *Hsi-yu Chi:* A Study of Antecedents to the Sixteenth-Century Chinese novel

STEPHEN FITZGERALD: China and the Overseas Chinese: A Study of Peking's Changing Policy 1949–70

CHRISTOPHER HOWE: Wages Patterns and Wage Policy in Modern China, 1919–1972

RAY HUANG: Taxation and Government Finance in Sixteenth-Century Ming China

DIANA LARY: Region and Nation: The Kwangsi Clique in Chinese Politics, 1925–37

CHI-YUN CHEN: Hsün Yüeh (A.D. 148–209): The Life and Reflections of an Early Medieval Confucian

DAVID R. KNECHTGES: The Han Rhapsody: A Study of the *Fu* of Yang Hsiung (53 B.C.–A.D. 18)

J. Y. WONG: Yeh Ming-ch'en: Viceroy of Liang Kuang (1852–8)

LI-LI CH'EN: Master Tung's Western Chamber Romance (*Tung hsi-hsiang chu-kung-tiao*): a Chinese *Chantefable*

DONALD HOLZMAN: Poetry and Politics: The Life and Works of Juan Chi (A.D. 210–63)

C. A. CURWEN: Taiping Rebel: The Deposition of Li Hsiu-cheng

P. B. EBREY: The Aristocratic Families of Early Imperial China: A Case Study of the Po-Ling Ts'ui Family

HILARY J. BEATTIE: Land and Lineage in China: A Study of T'ung-Ch'eng County, Anhwei, in the Ming and Ch'ing Dynasties

WILLIAM T. GRAHAM: The Lament for the South: Yü Hsin's 'Ai Chiang-nan fu'

HANS BIELENSTEIN: The Bureaucracy of Han Times

MICHAEL R. GODLEY: The Mandarin-Capitalists from Nanyang: Overseas Chinese Enterprise in the Modernization of China 1893–1911

CHARLES BACKUS: The Nan-chao Kingdom and T'ang China's Southwestern Frontier

JOHN W. CHAFFEE: The Thorny Gates of Learning in Sung China: A Social History of Examinations

Buddhism under the T'ang

STANLEY WEINSTEIN
Professor of Buddhist Studies, Yale University

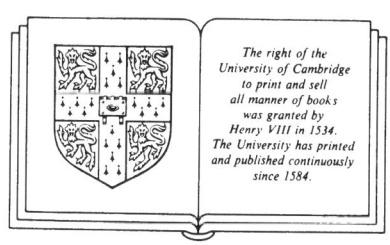

CAMBRIDGE UNIVERSITY PRESS
CAMBRIDGE
LONDON   NEW YORK   NEW ROCHELLE
MELBOURNE   SYDNEY

CAMBRIDGE UNIVERSITY PRESS
Cambridge, New York, Melbourne, Madrid, Cape Town, Singapore, São Paulo, Delhi

Cambridge University Press
The Edinburgh Building, Cambridge CB2 8RU, UK

Published in the United States of America by Cambridge University Press, New York

www.cambridge.org
Information on this title: www.cambridge.org/9780521103480

© Cambridge University Press 1987

This publication is in copyright. Subject to statutory exception
and to the provisions of relevant collective licensing agreements,
no reproduction of any part may take place without the written
permission of Cambridge University Press.

First published 1987
This digitally printed version 2009

A catalogue record for this publication is available from the British Library

Library of Congress Cataloguing in Publication data

Weinstein, Stanley, 1929–
Buddhism under the T'ang.
(Cambridge studies in Chinese history, literature, and institutions)
Bibliography.
Includes index.
1. Buddhism—China—History—581–960. I. Title. II. Series.
BQ638.W45   1985   294.3′0951   85-7769

ISBN 978-0-521-25585-1 hardback
ISBN 978-0-521-10348-0 paperback

To the memory of
Professor Hosaka Gyokusen: 1887–1964
and
Professor Masunaga Reihō: 1902–1981
with respect and gratitude.

Ikku no on nao hōsha subeshi.
    Dōgen Zenji, *Shōbōgenzō gyōji*

CONTENTS

Preface	*page* ix
Part One: The Buddhist Church During the First Half of the T'ang (618–762)	1
Introduction	3
Reign of Kao-tsu (618–626)	5
Reign of T'ai-tsung (626–649)	11
Reign of Kao-tsung (649–683)	27
Interregnum of Empress Wu (684–705)	37
Reign of Chung-tsung (705–710)	47
Reign of Jui-tsung (710–712)	49
Reign of Hsüan-tsung (712–756)	51
Reign of Su-tsung (756–762)	57
The Effects of the An Lu-shan Rebellion on the Buddhist Church	59
The Growth of Pure Land Buddhism	66
Part Two: The Buddhist Church During the Second Half of the T'ang (762–907)	75
Reign of Tai-tsung (762–779)	77
Reign of Te-tsung (779–805)	89
Reigns of Shun-tsung (805) and Hsien-tsung (805–820)	99
Reigns of Mu-tsung (820–824) and Ching-tsung (824–826)	105
Reign of Wen-tsung (826–840)	106
The Suppression of Buddhism Under the Reign of Wu-tsung (840–846)	114
The Restoration of Buddhism Under the Reign of Hsven-tsung (846–859)	136
Buddhism in the Declining Years of the T'ang Dynasty	151
List of Abbreviations	151

vii

Contents	*viii*
Notes	152
Glossary of Chinese characters	206
Bibliography	217
Index	229

PREFACE

The present study started out as a chapter for the second of the two volumes devoted to the Sui and T'ang dynasties in *The Cambridge History of China*. Since I was writing for readers whose interests were primarily in the history and institutions of T'ang China, I decided to focus on these two areas, placing special emphasis on the vicissitudes in the relationship between the central government of the T'ang and the Buddhist church at large.

Having been trained as a Buddhologist, I would, ideally, have preferred to treat both the political and doctrinal aspects of T'ang Buddhism in at least equal measure, but practical considerations weighed against this, the most important being the inevitable limitation of space imposed upon the author of a single chapter in a multivolume work. In view of the prominent position that Buddhism occupied in T'ang society and the extraordinary richness of its philosophical and religious traditions, I became convinced that an attempt to cover all of the major aspects of Buddhism under the T'ang would most likely result in a superficial survey.

Obviously some hard choices had to be made. Considering that a growing body of articles, including several books, already existed in English on some of the major T'ang schools – Ch'an, Pure Land, T'ien-t'ai, Fa-hsiang, Hua-yen, and Mi (Esoteric) – it seemed that, personal preferences aside, if the scope of the coverage had to be narrowed as was clearly the case, this was the area in which it could be done with least loss, since the reader who wished to supplement his knowledge of T'ang Buddhist doctrine could do so to some extent with the materials already at his disposal. On the other hand, the reader would not be able to find in any Western language – or in Japanese for that matter – a comprehensive history of the Buddhist church that covered the three centuries of the T'ang.

I am of course not suggesting that no work has been done on the secular side of T'ang Buddhist history. On the contrary, Jacques

Gernet, Kenneth Ch'en, and D. C. Twitchett in the West, Michihata Ryōshū, Yamazaki Hiroshi, and Tsukamoto Zenryū in Japan, to name only a few, have published seminal studies of the economic or institutional aspects of the Buddhist church in T'ang times. My enormous indebtedness to the pioneering efforts of these scholars is evident. What was lacking – and hence what I have attempted to supply in the present volume – is a chronological survey of the Buddhist church, particularly its relations with the central government, throughout the course of the T'ang dynasty. Although discussion of such important subjects as Buddhist doctrine, scripture, ritual, liturgy, and popular beliefs cannot, and should not, be totally excluded from a history of the Buddhist church, the reader should bear in mind that the present study does not seek to emphasize these aspects of T'ang Buddhism.

I began work on the manuscript in the summer of 1969 and finished it in the fall of 1976. I had of course intended that the manuscript be published shortly after its completion, but owing to various circumstances there was an intervening delay of eight years. One who is unfamiliar with the pace of scholarship in the field of T'ang Buddhism could hardly be faulted for assuming that a study whose publication had been held up for so long a time might have been rendered obsolete by other works that have appeared in the interval.

Such, however, is not the case. Only two works on relevant themes have been published in the West during this period: Antonino Forte's brilliant study, *Political Propaganda and Ideology in China at the End of the Seventh Century* (Naples, 1976), which is an exhaustive examination of primary source materials pertaining to Empress Wu's use of Buddhism for her own political ends, and Raoul Birnbaum's *Studies on the Mysteries of Mañjuśrī* (n.p., 1983), which is largely concerned with the cult of this divinity in T'ang China. In Japan only one relevant work has appeared, Osabe Kazuo's *Tō Sō Mikkyōshi ronkō* (*Essays on the History of Esoteric Buddhism Under the T'ang and Sung*; Kyoto, 1982), which, despite the title, deals mainly with Esoteric Buddhism in T'ang times.

In addition to these works mention should be made of four books by Chinese scholars: Fan Wen-lan, *T'ang-tai Fo-hsüeh* (*Buddhism Under the T'ang Dynasty*; Peking, 1979); Kuo P'eng, *Sui T'ang Fo-chiao* (*Buddhism Under the Sui and T'ang*; Shantung, 1980); Yen Shang-wen, *Sui T'ang Fo-chiao tsung-p'ai yen-chiu* (*A Study of the Buddhist Sectarian Lineages Under the Sui and T'ang*; Taipei, 1980); and T'ang Yung-t'ung, *Sui T'ang Fo-chiao shih kao* (*A Draft History of Buddhism Under the Sui and T'ang*; Peking, 1982). It should be noted that of these four recent publications in Chinese the first two are largely polemical, reflecting the strong ideological bias against Buddhism; the third is basically an attempt to trace the specific sectarian lineages in the Sui and T'ang; and the fourth comprises a collection of drafts for lectures given by Professor T'ang in the late 1920s and early 1930s.

There is little in these recent Chinese publications that would have led me to alter radically what I wrote eight years ago, although I certainly would have benefited from the extremely detailed chronology compiled by Chang Tsun-liu covering the years 581–959 that is appended to Fan Wen-lan, *T'ang-tai Fo-chiao*. Two other works that likewise would have facilitated my research and saved me much drudgery had they been available at the time of writing are Volume 29 of the *Taishō shinshū daizōkyō sakuin*, published in 1982, which is the index to volumes 51 and 52 of the *Taishō* edition of the Chinese Buddhist scripture, and the three-volume *Dōkyō (Taoism)*, published in 1983, which contains an eighty-four page index of Taoist names and terms.

No one is more aware of the shortcomings of the present study than its author. In the best of all worlds a history of the Buddhist church in T'ang China would have been written by someone who is at once a historian in the broadest sense of the term and also a Buddhologist. Unhappily few persons, myself included, possess equally valid credentials for both areas. Not being a historian, I think it only fair to alert the reader to the likelihood of errors in my interpretation of T'ang official documents – edicts, decrees, ordinances, legal codes, and the like. I very much regret that volume 3 of the monumental *Cambridge History of China*, which offers a detailed account of the political history of the Sui and T'ang dynasties, was not yet in print when I was undertaking my research.

It hardly needs saying that I do not conceive of this study as being definitive in any sense. Since there was no systematic history of T'ang Buddhism to fall back upon aside from such skeletal Sung and Yüan church chronicles as the *Fo-tsu t'ung-chi* and the *Fo-tsu li-tai t'ung-tsai*, I had to collect my data for the most part from what proved to be an intimidating array of sources. On the secular side there were the Standard Dynastic Histories, the *Tzu-chih t'ung-chien*, Sung encyclopaedias, collections of imperial edicts, and fragmentary legal codes. The Buddhist sources included the several collections of biographies of eminent monks, catalogues of the canon, sectarian histories, apologias, and encyclopaedias of church institutions and practices.

In the course of my research I no doubt overlooked much of significance, but rather than delay publication still further, I have decided to

Preface

release the manuscript, with all its shortcomings and blemishes, in the hope that it will illuminate at least the contours of the Buddhist church in T'ang times and perhaps stimulate others to undertake further studies in this area. It is for this reason that I have allowed the text to be burdened with rather copious annotation, which will identify the sources of most of my material and, I trust, provide leads for more detailed research by others.

I have followed the usual conventions of Sinological writing: surnames of Chinese and Japanese persons precede their given names; ages cited in Chinese traditional sources have been converted to their approximate Western equivalents, which is generally one year less than the age stated in the Chinese source; years given in the traditional era-name (*nien-hao*) system have been equated with the nearest corresponding year of the Julian calendar; the 'moons' of the Chinese year have been uniformly rendered as 'months'; the English translations of titles of rank and office have generally, but not always, followed the French versions in Robert des Rotours, *Traité des fonctionnaires et traité de l'armée* (Leiden, 1947).

Unfortunately it is not possible to name each of the many teachers, scholars, and friends who deserve thanks for their guidance and encouragement over the years. I am pleased, however, that I do have this opportunity to acknowledge publicly my gratitude to the late Professors Hosaka Gyokusen and Masunaga Reihō of Komazawa University, Tokyo, who gave unstintingly of their time and energy to introduce me to the vast riches of the Chinese Buddhist scripture. Kind teachers and devoted scholars, they embodied in their own lives the bodhisattva ideal.

I also wish to express my appreciation to Professor Yūki Reimon, who supervised my studies in Chinese Buddhist doctrine during the two years that I spent as a graduate student at the University of Tokyo. I count myself fortunate to have had the privilege of receiving instruction from so distinguished a scholar. More immediately, I have benefited greatly from the many fruitful discussions that I have had with Professors Hirakawa Akira and Kubo Noritada, both now retired from the University of Tokyo, who were kind enough to meet with me repeatedly during my annual visits to Japan over the past few years. Their moral support, and that of my good friend, Professor Yokoyama Kōitsu of Rikkyō University, have been sources of constant encouragement. I must also acknowledge my indebtedness to the late Professor Arthur F. Wright of Yale University and to Professor Denis C. Twitchett of Princeton University, who both encouraged me to undertake the

Preface

present study. I am grateful to Yale University for granting me two six-month leaves of absence to work on the manuscript and to the National Endowment for the Humanities for making it possible for me to devote an additional uninterrupted year to this project.

Finally, on the personal side, I would like to express my heartfelt thanks to my wife, Lucie, for her sympathetic understanding, unwavering support, and seemingly boundless patience.

PART ONE

THE BUDDHIST CHURCH DURING THE FIRST HALF OF THE T'ANG (618–762)

Introduction

When Li Yüan proclaimed the establishment of the T'ang dynasty in 618, some six centuries had already elapsed since Buddhism first appeared in China. Starting out primarily as a religion within the foreign merchant communities in the larger cities, Buddhism gradually gained a following among native Chinese.[1] Some were attracted by the new philosophical ideas found in the Buddhist scriptures then being translated into Chinese – concepts such as impermanence and non-substantiality, only vaguely hinted at by late Chou philosophers, which were expounded with great precision in the sūtras. Others were drawn to the religious side of Buddhism, with its impressive rituals, its promise of rebirth in a glorious heaven, its talk of a return to this world at some future time, and, above all, its mystical incantations and rites that were believed capable of averting all conceivable disasters.

From roughly the fourth century onward Buddhism began to permeate all sections of Chinese society from the court and the aristocratic families to the peasantry and city-dwellers. Monasteries, often endowed by powerful patrons with extensive tracts of land, were established throughout China in increasing numbers. Tradition-minded Confucian officials, alarmed at the rapid growth of tax-exempt lands, were soon urging their rulers to take steps to curb the great wealth being amassed by the Buddhist church. The often repeated assertion by eminent monks that the clergy, being super-mundane in its concerns, did not owe obedience to either the state or the family likewise outraged Confucian-oriented bureaucrats and scholars who warned that Buddhist monasticism would undermine the foundations of Chinese society if left unchecked. But so overpowering had the intellectual and emotional appeal of Buddhism become that few rulers during the period of the Northern and Southern Dynasties (317–589) could bring themselves to take repressive measures against the church. On the two occasions when an actual suppression was ordered – first, between the years 446–452, during the reign of Emperor T'ai-wu of the Northern Wei, and then again between the years 574–578 during the reign of Emperor Wu of the Northern Chou – the popular reaction in favor of Buddhism was so strong that in each case the next emperor to ascend the throne thought it prudent to rescind the anti-Buddhist legislation of his predecessor. Although these two attempts to eliminate the Buddhist religion occurred under alien Northern dynasties, it would be erroneous to assume that the non-Chinese rulers of the North were generally hostile to Buddhism. It should be remembered that it was the Northern Wei dynasty that sponsored the magnificent statuary carved in the rocks and caves of Yün-kang and Lung-men. Yet despite the unquestionable piety of the majority of Northern rulers, they insisted that the church be subordinate to the state and retained for themselves the prerogative of appointing the hierarchy of the church. In the South, however, the complete autonomy of the church and the right of the clergy not to bow before the emperor or any other lay person had been explicitly recognized since the middle of the fourth century.[2] So intense had the devotion of Southern emperors become by the sixth century that high-ranking ministers on a number of occasions had to go through the motions of paying a huge ransom to the Buddhist church to return to lay life an emperor who had made a vow to become a servant of the clergy.[3]

When Yang Chien, the founder of the Sui dynasty, finally achieved the unification of the empire in 589, he was quick to see the potential value of Buddhism as an ideological force capable of bringing together the country which had been divided for two and a half centuries.[4] Yang Chien, born in a monastery and raised by a nun, was undoubtedly sympathetic to Buddhism from his youth. He had witnessed the suppression of Buddhism initiated in the year 574 by the Northern Chou and saw for himself the deep resentment that it had provoked among the peoples of the North who, for the most part, were devout adherents. Yang Chien lost no time in establishing himself as a firm supporter of Buddhism. One month after assuming the throne in the year 581 he ordered the construction of a Buddhist monastery at the foot of each of the five sacred mountains.[5] Later in the same year he issued a decree that five additional monasteries should be built at sites closely associated with the fortunes of the imperial family.[6] He also took the extraordinary step of dropping all restrictions on ordinations.[7] To encourage the spread of Buddhism each household was required to make a contribution toward the cost of casting images and copying sūtras, causing a Confucian historian to lament that 'the number of Buddhist sūtras circulating among the common people exceeds the Confucian classics many thousandfolds.'[8] Two years later Yang Chien gave permission for the restoration of all monasteries destroyed by the Northern Chou[9] and probably during the same year issued another edict ordering that a state-supported monastery and convent should be built in each prefecture and county (*chou hsien*).[10] In 585 Yang Chien decreed that a Ta hsing-kuo ssu, 'Monastery for the Prosperity of the Empire', be erected in each of the forty-five prefectures that he had visited before ascending the throne.[11] His desire to placate the clergy and win the support of the Buddhist masses can be seen from his decision in the year 590 to legitimize the status of the several hundred thousand monks and nuns who had previously been ordained without government permission and to extend official recognition to every 'mountain temple' with one or more monks in residence.[12] During his twenty-four year rule Yang Chien is said to have authorized the ordination of 230,000 monks and nuns, the construction of 3,792 monasteries, the copying of 132,086 rolls of scripture, and the production of 106,580 images.[13]

Unlike the rulers of the preceding dynasties, the T'ang emperors for the most part did not exhibit much enthusiasm for Buddhism. Although the first two T'ang emperors tended to view the Buddhist religion with disdain,[14] they were sufficiently shrewd to recognize that it had a devoted following on all levels of society and hence could not be totally ignored by the state, much less suppressed, without stirring up great opposition, as was the case with the ill-fated attempts to do away with Buddhism under the Northern Wei in 446 and the Northern Chou in 574. As we shall see, these early T'ang emperors, on the one hand, adopted a policy of conciliating the Buddhist masses by sponsoring the construction of a number of monasteries, especially at the sites of major battles where many soldiers had fallen, and by holding services for the dead – particularly for those who gave their lives in the imperial cause – as, for example, the seven-day mass conducted in the Imperial Palace jointly by sixty-nine Buddhist and sixty-nine Taoist monks during the sixth month of the year 618, when the founding of the T'ang was proclaimed.[15] On the other hand, these same T'ang emperors consistently sought to extend state controls over the Buddhist church and reduce its material power as manifested in both the size and privileges of its clergy as well as in the number of its monasteries. Expedient patronage accompanied by increasingly restrictive curbs characterized the T'ang policy towards Buddhism before the An Lu-shan rebellion in 755.[16]

Reign of Kao-tsu (618–626)

The T'ang is notable as the first dynasty to give precedence to Taoism over Buddhism. In what may have been an attempt to compensate for its relatively low standing among the prestigious clans of North China, the T'ang imperial family claimed, on the basis of its surname, Li, that it was descended from Lao-tzu, the legendary founder of Taoism, who was believed to have had the same surname. During the period that Li Yüan (the future Emperor Kao-tsu) was plotting to seize power, he maintained close relations with Taoist priests who encouraged his political ambitions. One of these, Wang Yüan-chih, persuaded Li Yüan that he (Li) was now the recipient of the Heavenly Mandate, implying that the time was ripe for Li to assert his claim to the throne.[1] It is difficult to say how seriously Li Yüan took Wang's assurances, but two years after ascending the throne, he conferred upon him the honorary title of *ch'ao-san ta-fu* and as a token of appreciation presented him with a gilt-embroidered cap and purple mantle.[2] That the T'ang attached at least symbolic importance to the event can be seen from the fact that three successive rulers, T'ai-tsung, Kao-tsung, and Empress Wu, heaped honors on Wang.[3] Throughout his campaigns against the Sui, Li Yüan continued to draw encouragement from Taoist oracles and prophecies. One such instance occurred in the year 617, when Li Yüan, then engaged in a struggle with the Sui general, Sung Lao-sheng, ordered his army to begin a retreat because of a shortage of supplies due to heavy rains. Suddenly 'an old man in white robes,' who claimed to be a messenger sent by the god of Mt Huo, appeared at Li's headquarters and told the would-be emperor that the rains would end during the next month, at which time the god of Mt Huo would come to the assistance of Li's army. Believing that the old man spoke the truth, Li resumed his campaign against Sung, whom he subsequently defeated and had executed.[4]

The following year (618) Li Yüan is said to have received yet another revelation. A certain Chi Shan-hsing proclaimed that he had met an old man at Mt Yang-chiao (in present-day Shansi province) swathed in white robes and wearing a crown of gold on his head. The man, who was astride a white horse with a red mane – clearly a sign of his divine mission – instructed Chi to inform Li that he (Li) had attained the Principle of Sageliness (*sheng-li*) and that if Li built in Ch'ang-an a Taoist temple (*kung*) enshrining images of the Taoist divinities (*tao-hsiang*), his empire would endure for ages to come. Through the good offices of Li Shih-min (the son of Li Yüan and future Emperor T'ai-tsung) Chi was granted an audience with Li Yüan, who, elated by the prophecy, bestowed an honorary title and various gifts on Chi. In a subsequent meeting with Li Yüan, Chi announced that he had received a further revelation from the god of Mt Yang-chiao, who now identified himself as T'ai-shang Lao-chün (Grand Lord Lao), the chief divinity of Taoism and apotheosis of Lao-tzu. In the revelation conveyed to Li Yüan, T'ai-shang Lao-chün declared that he was the 'Supreme Immortal (Wu-shang Shen-hsien) surnamed Li ... and the ancestor of the Emperor,' i.e. Li Yüan. After the T'ang forces crushed the rebel Liu Hei-t'a in 623, which had been foretold in the revelation, Li Yüan expressed his gratitude toward his illustrious ancestor by converting Lao-tzu's memorial hall in Po-chou (Lao-tzu's reputed birthplace) into a Taoist temple appropriately named Ch'ing-T'ang Kuan (Temple for Celebrating the T'ang).[5]

The question of what policy the newly established T'ang state should adopt toward Buddhism came to the fore in 621, only three years after Li Yüan had proclaimed himself emperor, when the grand astrologer (*t'ai-shih ling*) Fu I presented an eleven-point memorial to the throne calling for the extirpation of Buddhism.[6] Fu I, who had been trained as a Taoist priest and who had served in the T'ung-tao Academy set up after the suppression of Buddhism by the Northern Chou, had been held in high esteem by Li Yüan ever since the latter had held the post of magistrate of Fu-feng under the Sui. After Li Yüan proclaimed the establishment of the T'ang, he appointed Fu I deputy grand astrologer and shortly thereafter promoted him to the office of grand astrologer. The arguments against Buddhism that Fu I advanced in his memorial were largely part of the stock and trade of the anti-Buddhist polemicists of the period of the Northern and Southern Dynasties: Buddhist monks and nuns were economically unproductive and evaded payment of taxes; they showed reverence to neither the throne nor their own parents; they did not give allegiance to the state and were often in rebellion; they were a harmful influence on society and hastened the downfall of those dynasties that patronized their religion; and they were proponents of an alien philosophy.[7] Fu I accordingly urged the new emperor to disband the clergy forthwith and to put the monasteries to uses that served the needs of the state. Kao-tsu promptly transmitted Fu I's criticisms of the Buddhist clergy to a group of monks for rebuttal. A spate of apologias followed, the most famous being Fa-lin's anti-Taoist polemic, the *P'o-hsieh lun* (*The Refutation of Error*).[8] Between the years 621 and 626 Fu I is said to have memorialized the throne seven times, urging the suppression of Buddhism.[9]

Some traditional Buddhist historians have argued that Li Yüan was at first well disposed toward Buddhism because of an auspicious prophecy that he had received from a Buddhist monk, Ching-hui, before launching his rebellion.[10] In their view, his attitude began to change as a result of Fu I's persistent memorials. Yet, as we have noted, Li Yüan was an admirer of Fu I before the establishment of the T'ang, and on assuming the throne promptly appointed him to high office. This would indicate that the anti-Buddhist views of Fu I were well known to Li Yüan before he became emperor and that they did not constitute a barrier to Fu I's immediate promotion to a position of great responsibility. During his campaign to pacify eastern China in 621, Kao-tsu issued his first repressive edict agaist Buddhism, ordering that no prefecture in areas of turmoil should be allowed more than one monastery with the maximum number of resident monks set at thirty. All monks in excess of this figure were to be returned to lay life.[11]

Fu I's steady stream of memorials as well as the polemics and counter-polemics that they touched off between the Buddhists and Taoists led Kao-tsu in 626 to bring the entire matter before the court for consideration.[12] There could be no misunderstanding of Kao-tsu's own feelings regarding the relative status of Buddhism, since in the previous year he had already issued an edict on the occasion of his participation in a Confucian service at the National College (Kuo-hsüeh) in which he pronounced Taoism and Confucianism to be the twin pillars of the state, whereas Buddhism was to be relegated to the status of a foreign religion.[13] Kao-tsu decreed that Taoism would henceforth be accorded first place among the three teachings, Confucianism second place, and Buddhism last place, thereby revoking the privileged status that Buddhism had enjoyed during the three preceding centuries. In the debate that ensued at the court, Kao-tsu's ministers were unable to reach agreement, some endorsing Fu I's proposals, while others, notably Hsiao Yü, came to the defense of Buddhism.[14] Kao-tsu, apparently irritated by the incessant squabbling between the partisans of Buddhism and Taoism, issued an edict in the fifth month of 626 nominally chastizing both Buddhism and Taoism.[15] While the title of the edict, *Sha-t'ai Fo Tao chao* (*Edict to Purge Buddhism and Taoism*), suggests that its purpose was to treat both religions equally, it is in fact almost exclusively concerned with cataloging the real or imagined sins of the Buddhists: monks are arrogant; they evade taxes; they illegally tonsure themselves; they are insatiable in their demands; they accumulate property; they engage in commercial activities in competition with ordinary householders; and so forth. In striking contrast to the detailed listing of the sins of the Buddhists Kao-tsu's criticism of the Taoists is limited to a single sentence: 'Their involvement in worldly affairs is in sharp contradiction to the tenets of their school.' A simple character count shows that twenty-five times more space is devoted to the attack on Buddhism than to the criticism of Taoism.

At the end of the edict Kao-tsu asserts, no doubt with an eye to placating the religious sensibilities of his subjects, that the real intention of the purge that he is ordering is to protect and promote religion! To do this, he explains, it is necessary to separate 'the jade from the pebbles.' Henceforth those monks and nuns, both Buddhist and Taoist, who are able to adhere faithfully to the rigorous demands of the precepts should be moved to large monasteries where they will be fully supported by the state. However, those persons unable to cope with the hardships imposed by the religious life should be laicized and compelled to engage in productive labor. Lest there be any misunderstanding about the ultimate size of the monastic establishment that he envisioned, Kao-tsu stipulated that there should be no more than three Buddhist monasteries and two Taoist temples in the capital cities and only one Buddhist monastery and one Taoist temple in each of the prefectures; all other monasteries were to be closed down.[16] Once again the impression is created that Buddhism and Taoism are being subjected to equal, if harsh, treatment. The fact, however, is that the blow would have fallen heavier on the Buddhists than on the Taoists, because the former possessed a far more extensive monastic establishment. According to a mid eighth-century historian, in the year 605 there were 120 Buddhist monasteries in the capital city, Ch'ang-an, as against only ten Taoist temples.[17] Thus, in Ch'ang-an at least, the Taoist church would be reduced to one-fifth its original size – a reduction drastic enough – whereas the Buddhist church was to be shrunk to one-fortieth of what it had been. Fortunately for the Buddhists Kao-tsu was forced to yield the throne to his second son, Li Shih-min, known subsequently as Emperor T'ai-tsung, one month after he had issued his call for a purge. The new emperor, recognizing the importance of securing the support of the Buddhists for his seizure of power, immediately had his father's decree rescinded.[18]

Although Kao-tsu's plan to reduce the power and influence of the Buddhist church misfired, he did succeed in further weakening its autonomy. Since the early years of the fifth century the Buddhist church, under both the Northern and Southern dynasties, was nominally headed by a single monk appointed by the state.[19] Under the Northern Wei this monk, successively designated controller of the religious (*tao-jen t'ung*), controller of monks (*sha-men t'ung*), and controller of the Office for the Illumination of Mysteries (*chao-hsüan t'ung*), was in charge of a governmental agency established c. 396 called the Office for Overseeing Meritorious Works (Chien-fu ts'ao) – renamed c. 460 the Office for the Illumination of Mysteries (Chao-hsüan ts'ao) – which had jurisdiction over activities relating to the Buddhist church.[20] The Northern Ch'i raised the status of the Office for the Illumination of Mysteries to that of a court (*ssu*), but treated it as distinct from the nine courts that comprised the major branches of government. Headed by a monk who bore the title grand controller (*ta t'ung*), the Court for the Illumination of Mysteries (Chao-hsüan ssu) was staffed by a full complement of ecclesiastical officers and their lay secretaries.[21]

In addition to the clerically dominated Court for the Illumination of Mysteries the Northern Ch'i also created a Bureau for Monastery Administration (Tien-ssu shu) with a subsection known as the Department for the Buddhist Clergy (Seng-ch'i pu) run by a lay official.[22] Despite the establishment of this new civil bureau, which was one of several attached to the Court for State Ceremonials (Hung-lu ssu), the body that had responsibility, *inter alia*, for the conduct of foreign relations, the actual control of the church seems to have remained in the hands of the hierarchs in the Court for the Illumination of Mysteries. Under the Sui the Court for the Illumination of Mysteries was deprived of its semi-autonomous status, lowered in rank, and redesignated the Bureau for the Veneration of Mysteries (Ch'ung-hsüan shu), becoming one of the three constituent bureaus of the Court for State Ceremonials, where it replaced the dormant Bureau for Monastery Administration.[23]

Kao-tsu retained the Bureau for the Veneration of Mysteries established by the Sui, appointing as its director a relatively low-ranking official who was given authority over the Buddhist and Taoist clergies.[24] To bring the monasteries under closer governmental scrutiny, the Bureau for the Veneration of Mysteries placed an overseer (*chien*) in each Buddhist monastery and Taoist temple.[25] Resentment against the presence of an outsider in the monasteries, however, led T'ai-tsung to abolish the overseer system. In an apparent attempt to curtail still further the nominal independence of the church, Kao-tsu, ignoring a two-hundred-year-old tradition, abolished the ecclesiastic post of grand controller.[26] Instead of allowing a single monk to stand as the primate of the Buddhist order, he instituted a novel system of collective leadership by appointing ten eminent monks, designated the Ten Monks of Great Virtue (*shih ta-te*), to administer church affairs and control the clergy.[27] Although the official histories do not refer to this new institution, Tao-hsüan's *Hsü kao-seng chuan* (*Biographies of Eminent Monks: Second Series*), completed in 664, provides us with a number of interesting details. Of the ten monks appointed by Kao-tsu, only seven can now be identified from their biographies in the *Hsü kao-seng chuan*.[28] These seven monks, significantly, share a number of characteristics: six of the seven, for example, were exegetical scholars as opposed to specialists in meditation.[29] The schools represented by the exegetes were all pre-Sui in origin; the T'ien-t'ai, which was founded under the Sui and lavishly supported by it, was not represented,[30] nor were popular movements such as the Pure Land faith or the Three Stages school. The fact that five of the six monks whose geographical origins are known were Southerners suggests that Kao-tsu, a Northerner, felt the need to placate the powerful southern clergy, as had Yang Chien, the founder of the Sui. Given the respect accorded to senior monks, it is not surprising that only aged monks were selected for this office. Of the six monks whose ages are known, one was eighty-one, three were in their seventies, one was sixty-nine, and one was sixty-one. Only one of these six monks, Ming-chan, lived beyond the reign of Kao-tsu, dying in the year 628. T'ai-tsung, who succeeded to the throne in 626, did not fill any of the vacancies that occurred during his father's reign, thereby allowing the institution of the Ten Monks of Great Virtue to peter out. Henceforth no single monk or group of monks was to be accorded primacy over the Buddhist church either in name or in fact; control was to be vested solely in the hands of lay officials appointed by the government.

Reign of T'ai-tsung (626–649)

As we have noted, Kao-tsu's plan to curtail the power of the church in 626 was frustrated because of the *coup d'état* engineered by his second son, Shih-min, who played a crucial role in the establishment of the T'ang. In the sixth month of 626 Shih-min assassinated the Crown Prince and another brother who stood in his path to the throne. Although his major opponents had been eliminated by this single stroke, he no doubt was aware of the risks of alienating the support of the Buddhist community as his father had done.[1] It is not surprising, then, that his first act, after becoming Crown Prince following the murder of his brothers, was to rescind his father's edict ordering a purge of the clergy and reduction in the number of monasteries. By coming to the rescue of the church at a time when its power and prestige were being threatened, Shih-min may have wished to appear as a defender of the faith, from which position he felt he could count on the support of the Buddhist clergy in his attempt to depose his father.[2]

Although little information is available to show Shih-min's attitude toward Buddhism before he compelled his father to relinquish the throne in the eighth month of 626, it seems safe to assume that in fact he was no more sympathetic to Buddhism than his father. When, for example, his armies occupied Lo-yang in 621, he ordered the dismantlement or destruction of the imperial palaces as an indication of his outrage at the extravagance of the Sui rulers.[3] At the same time he closed all the monasteries in Lo-yang that had been supported by the Sui imperial family and defrocked the entire clergy of the city aside from sixty eminent monks and nuns.[4] Another indication of Shih-min's true feelings toward Buddhism can be found in his treatment of Fu I, the Taoist priest who had instigated Kao-tsu's attempted purge of the Buddhist church. Four months after ascending the throne, T'ai-tsung summoned Fu I to the palace to award him a fief in recognition of his prophesy, delivered at a crucial moment some six months earlier, that Shih-min would be the next emperor. When, during the course of their discussion, T'ai-tsung asked Fu I why he did not appreciate the merits of Buddhist doctrine, Fu I replied in familiar polemical language: 'The Buddha was nothing more than a crafty barbarian who succeeded in deluding his own countrymen. Ill-intentioned men in China subsequently perverted the teachings of Chuang-tzu and Lao-tzu to serve the ends of Buddhism and dressed up its doctrines in bizarre and mysterious language in order to mislead the uneducated masses. Buddhism offers no benefits to our people; on the contrary it is injurious to the state. It is not that I do not understand Buddhism, but rather that I despise it and refuse to study it.' T'ai-tsung's reaction to Fu I's diatribe, we are told, was one of wholehearted approval.[5]

Despite T'ai-tsung's distaste for Buddhism, the first few years of his reign are marked by a number of acts which would seem to indicate that the government had embarked on a pro-Buddhist course. To commemorate his first New Year (627) as emperor, T'ai-tsung invited a number of distinguished monks in the capital to the Imperial Palace where they conducted a seven-day service.[6] On the same occasion he authorized the ordination of some thousand monks and nuns and ordered that his father's former residence, the T'ung-i Palace, be converted into a nunnery,[7] an irony that could not have escaped his Buddhist constituency. In 628 T'ai-tsung decreed more such state-supported services: in the third month a memorial service was held for those who lost their lives in the wars leading to the establishment of the T'ang;[8] in the fifth month, a mass was conducted for the deceased rulers of the preceding dynasty;[9] in the seventh month, T'ai-tsung ordered that henceforth nationwide services should be held in the first and seventh months of each year by both Buddhist monks and Taoist priests to pray for the welfare of the people and a rich harvest.[10] The following year a decree was issued stipulating that monks residing in Ch'ang-an should recite for a period of fourteen days each month the *Jen-wang ching* (*Sūtra of Benevolent Kings*) and the *Ta-yün ching* (*Great Cloud Sūtra*), which were believed to have the power to protect the state from calamities.[11]

In the twelfth month of 629 T'ai-tsung ordered the erection of seven monasteries, each at the site of a different battle, where monks could perpetually offer prayers from the repose of those soldiers killed in the early T'ang wars.[12] The construction of the seven monasteries was obviously given high priority, since all were completed by the fifth month of 630.[13] To emphasize the 'state' character of these monasteries T'ai-tsung directed ranking ministers and scholars, regardless of their religious orientation, to compose the texts for the stele inscriptions.[14]

Although a superficial reading of the decrees issued by T'ai-tsung in the first four years of his reign gives the impression that he was personally sympathetic to Buddhism, there is ample reason to suspect that he was merely patronizing the Buddhist church in order not to antagonize the majority of his subjects who were deeply committed to this religion at a time when his own rule was not yet fully consolidated. His edict of the year 628 calling for state-supported Buddhist services on behalf of the war dead and the edict of the following year ordering the construction of monasteries on battlefields can be seen as an expedient attempt to console bereaved families throughout the empire rather than as an expression of T'ai-tsung's own piety. Significantly, the proposal to establish monasteries in areas where major battles were fought originated not with T'ai-tsung, but with Ming-chan, a monk held in great esteem during the Sui dynasty, who had been nominated by Kao-tsu to serve as one of the Ten Monks of Great Virtue.[15] After T'ai-tsung came to the throne, he invited Ming-chan, who was reputed to be well versed in the art of government, to advise him on political matters. It was not difficult for T'ai-tsung to appreciate the practical political gains that would accrue from Ming-chan's suggestion that the state show concern for the war dead by establishing a network of monasteries linked to the rise of the T'ang.

While it is true that T'ai-tsung, during the first four years of his reign, promulgated a number of edicts that seemed to indicate a degree of state support for Buddhism, we can find little evidence that T'ai-tsung himself was moved by feelings of piety. During the early years of his reign, relatively few learned monks appeared at his court. And more significantly, there is no indication that T'ai-tsung sought instruction in the Dharma from monks, took part in religious discussions, or studied Buddhist scriptures, as rulers of preceding dynasties had done. The Buddhist services that he ordered were not concerned with spiritual goals but material ones: the protection of the state from various types of calamities, the welfare of his subjects, good harvests, and the like. Perceptive Buddhists must have had their doubts about T'ai-tsung's commitment to Buddhism. The very year, 627, that T'ai-tsung ordered the ordination of 3,000 monks and nuns to mark the beginning of his reign, he instructed the censor, Tu Cheng-lun, to 'investigate' the Buddhist clergy and purge corrupt elements.[16] It is difficult to say how widely or effectively Tu cast his net, since the post-T'ang Buddhist chronicles, bent on portraying all but the most violently anti-Buddhist emperors as supporters of the church, ignore the event. But in certain areas at least the purge appears to have been rather thorough, as is indicated by a near-contemporary source which states that in one prefecture, Ch'en-chou (in present-day Honan), only thirty monks were allowed to continue in holy orders.[17] T'ai-tsung's main concern at this time *vis-à-vis* the Buddhist church was the very large number of persons who, taking advantage of the turmoil following the collapse of the Sui, had themselves ordained without official sanction in order to escape taxation. Tai-tsung made it clear from the beginning of his reign that such illegally ordained monks would be dealt with harshly, for already in 627 he issued an edict decreeing the death penalty for all such monks.[18] The search for illegal monks seems to have been intensified two years later, when another order was issued to the effect that illegal monks who failed to surrender to the authorities would be beheaded.[19]

As T'ai-tsung consolidated his rule and became more secure in his position as emperor, his criticism of Buddhism became less restrained. From an attack on illegalities within the church, he rapidly moved on to a condemnation of some of the traditional prerogatives of the Buddhist and Taoist clergy, such as the right of monks and nuns to receive homage from their parents. In the Buddhist view of things this practice was perfectly acceptable, since the monk, by renouncing his worldly ties and accepting the precepts laid down by the Buddha, was no longer bound by mundane obligations. To the Confucian who rejected the premises of Buddhism nothing could be more odious than this particular Buddhist tradition, which appeared as an outrage against the basic principle of filial piety, endangering the very foundations of Chinese society. Although Chinese rulers in the past had contemplated the idea of making the Buddhist church subordinate to the state, as far as can be seen from surviving documents, no emperor before T'ai-tsung sought to regulate the relationship between a member of the clergy and his parents. In the first month of the year 631 T'ai-tsung issued an unprecedented decree which read in part: 'The teachings of Buddhism and Taoism are primarily concerned with doing good works. How, then, can we allow Buddhist monks and nuns, Taoist priests, and the like to hold themselves in such esteem and sit back to receive the homage of their parents? This practice is injurious to the customs of Our people and contravenes the *Classic of Rites*. Let it therefore be discontinued. Henceforth ordained persons shall render homage to their parents!'[20] We have no specific information regarding the circumstances that prompted T'ai-tsung to issue this Confucian-sounding edict, nor do we know precisely how the Buddhist church and its followers responded. Apparently pressure was soon brought to bear on the throne in some form, for two years later, in 633, T'ai-tsung withdrew the edict.[21]

Even though T'ai-tsung showed little personal interest in Buddhism during the first two decades of his rule, he followed the customary practice of commemorating the death of his parents by holding Buddhist observances. In particular, he sponsored a number of services and had several monasteries constructed in memory of his mother who had died in 613 when he was fifteen years of age and who, like many women of Northern elite families, was probably a devout Buddhist.[22] Although there is no record of his having ordered masses performed for the repose of his father's soul, he does seem to have been sufficiently moved by the latter's death in 635 to permit the ordination of three thousand monks.[23] On the surface, this might appear to indicate that he was adopting a conciliatory attitude toward the Buddhist church. In fact, however, T'ai-tsung availed himself of the occasion to launch a broadside against the abuses of the clergy. His edict,[24] which opens with the customary eulogy of Buddhist doctrine in flowery rhetoric, points out that the number of monks has greatly declined because of the recent wars. T'ai-tsung laments that Buddhist monasteries now stand empty and urges that ordinations, not to number more than three thousand, be conducted throughout the empire to provide monks to fill the abandoned monasteries. Officials should determine the precise number of ordinations to be allowed in any given area, but they are warned that they will be held accountable if men of bad character are selected for ordination. The clergy is reminded that reverence of 'non-action' is the basis of the Buddhist precepts[25] – no doubt a tactful suggestion that monks should restrict their activities to contemplation and study within their monasteries and not interfere in secular affairs. The edict then proceeds to catalogue the sins of the monks: they spread superstition while pretending to work miracles; they enrich themselves by falsely claiming to be skilled in medicine, fortune-telling, and other such devious practices; they corrupt officials through bribery and mislead the masses by disfiguring their bodies and burning off fingers. Such acts, the edict continues, are not only a violation of the penal code but also constitute a terrible blemish on the 'sacred teachings' of the Buddha. Once again assuming the well-worn guise of the stern defender of the faith who must chastize the misguided for their own good, T'ai-tsung warns that since his intention is to protect the Dharma, he cannot tolerate such behavior. Offenders will be dealt with according to the regulations (*t'iao-chih*) based on the *Vinaya*, i.e. the rules of monastic discipline attributed to the Buddha. The edict concludes with a directive to local officials to purify Buddhism by carrying out the appropriate investigations and indicting all offenders.

If there were any illusions regarding T'ai-tsung's true sentiments toward Buddhism, they must have been dispelled by his edict of 637 which, following the precedent set by his father's edict of 625, ordered that henceforth Taoist monks and nuns would take precedence over their Buddhist counterparts in all ceremonies.[26] As we have seen, T'ai-tsung's earlier criticisms of Buddhism centered around alleged abuses of the clergy, whom he accuses of not faithfully following the injunctions of the Buddha. In his edict of 637 he shifted the thrust of his attack from charges of corruption within the church to criticism of the pre-eminent position that Buddhism, a foreign religion, had come to enjoy in China. The Tao, he noted, had its beginnings in antiquity; it emerged from the Nameless and was beyond all forms; it functioned in accordance with the movement of *yin* and *yang* and nourished all things; through it the empire is properly governed and justice prevails; it enables man to return to simplicity and purity. Buddhism, he pointed out, by contrast is of alien origin and reached China only during the Later Han dynasty. It is much esteemed by those who hope for blessings in the future or fear a calamitous rebirth. Only uncultured men would presume to ridicule the profundities of Taoism, 'whereas those who eagerly seek after the Buddhist Absolute are people who delight in the curious.' The edict then goes on to lament that bulky alien scriptures have taken precedence over the *Tao-te ching*, and that the traditional teachings of China have now been placed behind those of the One Vehicle, i.e. Mahāyāna. T'ai-tsung asserts his desire to rectify these past abuses and provide guidance for the people, as behooves one descended from Lao-tzu. After attributing the success of the new dynasty and the pacification of the Empire to Taoist virtues, T'ai-tsung declares that it is only fitting that the Taoist teachings should prevail over Buddhism and that the Taoist clergy should be accorded precedence over their Buddhist rivals.

No sooner was the edict issued than Buddhist monks began to protest their inferior status.[27] A group of eleven monks headed by Chih-shih,[28] who had already acquired a reputation as an ardent defender of the secular rights of the church, followed the Emperor's cortege to the imperial palace, where Fa-ch'ang, another member of the group who was the precepts master to the Crown Prince and Empress,[29] presented a memorial on behalf of the irate monks denouncing the decision to give priority to the Taoist clergy. While expressing understanding for the Emperor's desire to pay homage to his ancestor, Lao-tzu, the Buddhists cleverly argued that the Taoist monks were not really followers of Lao-tzu, but of the Yellow Turbans, a peasant-based mass religious movement that led an insurrection against the Later Han which ultimately contributed to the collapse of that dynasty. Lao-tzu, the Buddhists pointed out, had nothing in common with the latter-day Taoist church: he wore ordinary garb; he did not establish temples, nor did he accept disciples. Lao-tzu was content to lead an unobtrusive life cultivating his inner nature. The Taoist priests, however, ignore the teachings of the *Tao-te ching*, which they use merely as means to acquire fame and wealth. Since Taoist movements had been the source of various immoral cults and practices, it was this religion, which bore no real relation to Lao-tzu, that was the true obstacle to achieving peace within the empire. Fa-ch'ang concluded the memorial with a plea to the Emperor to rescind his edict, reminding him, with some degree of exaggeration, that since the Han and Wei dynasties Buddhism had always enjoyed precedence over Taoism.

Having by this time consolidated his power, T'ai-tsung apparently felt little need to placate the Buddhist clergy any longer. He immediately dispatched an official with a curt reply: 'The edict has already been promulgated. The state has severe laws to deal with those who will not obey.'[30] The harsh tone of the Emperor's reply was sufficient to silence all the monks in the group except for its leader, Chih-shih, who openly declared his intention to become a martyr to the Buddhist cause rather than to submit to such an outrage. T'ai-tsung was infuriated when he learned of Chih-shih's defiance, and ordered him to be whipped and banished from the capital. The imperial order notwithstanding, Chih-shih returned surreptitiously after becoming ill so that he might spend his last days at the Ta tsung-ch'ih ssu where he began his religious life. He died in 638 at the early age of 37.[31] Two years later, Fa-lin, another prominent monk who had also participated in the protest,[32] was exiled to Szechwan on the charge that he had slandered the imperial family in one of his polemics against the Taoists.[33] Fa-lin's arrest was made the pretext by T'ai-tsung for still another purge of the Buddhist clergy.[34]

In 637, the same year that T'ai-tsung decreed that the Taoist clergy would take precedence over Buddhist monks and nuns, he ordered the promulgation of a new legal code known as the *Chen-kuan lü* that contained a section entitled *Tao-seng ko* (*Regulations Regarding the Taoist* and *Buddhist Clergies*).³⁵ Although neither the complete text of the legal code adopted by T'ai-tsung nor a full list of its various sections survives today, we can get a fairly good idea of the contents of the *Tao-seng ko* from its Japanese counterpart, the *Sōniryō* (*Statutes Pertaining to Buddhist Monks and Nuns*) which were included in the *Yōrō ritsuryō* (*Penal Code and Administrative Statutes of the Yōrō Period* [717–724]).³⁶ It is clear that the *Sōniryō*, which are preserved in full, were in large part based on the *Tao-seng ko*, as can be seen from the quotations of the latter found in two ninth-century Japanese legal commentaries on the administrative statutes, the *Ryō no gige* by Kiyohara no Natsuno and the *Ryō no shūge* by Koremune Naomoto.³⁷ There is some uncertainty regarding the precise date that the *Tao-seng ko* were first adopted, owing to the fact that legal codes were repeatedly revised under the T'ang.³⁸ Since the earliest Japanese collection of *Sōniryō* – those included in the code of the Taihō period (701–704)³⁹ – which were very close to the *Sōniryō* of the Yōrō period, were promulgated in 702, the Chinese *Tao-seng ko* on which they were based must be of an earlier date. Unfortunately we cannot find any clear statement that the *Tao-seng ko* were first incorporated in the legal code of 637, although circumstantial evidence would seem to indicate that this was the case. For one thing, Hsüan-wan, a monk with great influence at the court, sent a memorial to T'ai-tsung in 635 requesting that clerical offenders be dealt with in accordance with Buddhist law rather than be subjected to the secular laws applied to laymen.⁴⁰ Although Hsüan-wan had already died by the time his appeal reached T'ai-tsung, the latter accepted Hsüan-wan's proposals.⁴¹ Hsüan-wan's protest makes it apparent that the *Tao-seng ko* was not yet in existence before 635. In 656, however, Hsüan-tsang, the renowned translator, sent a memorial to the throne expressing his appreciation to Emperor Kao-tsung for reinstituting the 'earlier regulations [regarding the Buddhist clergy]' (*chiu ko*).⁴² Hsüantsang's statement establishes the fact that the *Tao-seng ko* already existed before Kao-tsung's reign which began in 649. Thus it seems safe to conclude that the *Tao-seng ko* were adopted in 637 when T'ai-tsung promulgated a newly revised legal code.

Although our knowledge of the workings of Chinese law as it pertained to the clergy is far from complete, it would seem that under earlier dynasties offences by monks and nuns were generally dealt with in accordance with the provisions of the *Vinaya*. From time to time various dynasties issued sets of 'monastic regulations' (*seng-chih*), but the evidence suggests that these *seng-chih* were based almost exclusively on the *Vinaya* precepts, secular law being brought into the picture only when monks had committed such capital offences as murder or treason. A typical example of this can be seen in an edict promulgated by the Northern Wei emperor Hsüan-wu in 508, which reads in part: 'Since monks and laymen differ from each other, so also must the laws which govern them be different ... Henceforth monks who commit murder or more serious crimes will be judged according to secular law. All lesser offences will be referred to the Office for the Illumination of Mysteries (Chao-hsüan) for disposition in accordance with the provisions of the Vinaya.'[43] Basically the same practice was continued under the Sui. Emperor Wen, for example, decreed in 595 that offences perpetrated by monks and nuns should be dealt with according to the Vinaya and not secular law.[44] To this end he ordered the compilation of a legal compendium known as the *Chung-ching fa-shih*, which consisted of extracts from the canon that were to be used to regulate the behavior of the clergy.[45] The actual administration of justice was entrusted to a monk who bore the title *tuan-shih sha-men*, 'the monk who adjudicates matters'.[46]

The *Tao-seng ko* promulgated during the reign of T'ai-tsung provides still one more example of the severity with which the early T'ang rulers sought to exercise control over the Buddhist church. While nominally based on the *Vinaya*, the *Tao-seng ko* in fact covered a wider range of clerical activity than did the *Vinaya* and invariably prescribed harsher penalties. The *Vinaya* recognized five grades of offenses, of which the most serious were the four *pārājika* (*po-lo-i*) offences – fornication, murder, theft, and pretending to be enlightened – each punishable by permanent expulsion from the order. The four lesser grades of offenses could be expiated by either varying types of confessions or the act of repentance, depending on the particular grade of offense. The *Vinaya* contained no provisions for punishment by secular authorities, nor indeed did it stipulate that monks should be handed over to the state for prosecution in the event that they violated any precepts of the *Vinaya*.

The *Tao-seng ko* by contrast was concerned only with the physical punishment of the offending monk or nun; it made no provision for the expiation of an offense through confession or repentance, which was the method required by the *Vinaya* to deal with the overwhelming majority of transgressions. Depending upon the seriousness of the offense, the *Tao-seng ko* provided for the imposition of one of three possible penalties: (1) hard labor (*k'u-i* or *k'u-shih*), i.e. the forced confinement of the monk for a specified period of time to an empty monastery hall where he was required to make copies of sūtra texts; in the case of an illiterate monk, 'hard labor' signified work as a porter on a monastery-related construction project; (2) simple expulsion from the order (*huan-su*); and (3) expulsion from the order to be followed by denunciation of the monk or the nun to the civil authorities for criminal prosecution (*fu kuan-ssu k'o-tsui*).[47]

Despite the frequent, self-righteous proclamations by the early T'ang emperors that their stern attitude toward the Buddhist church was prompted by their desire to keep Buddhism pure, the *Tao-seng ko* provides abundant evidence that their primary concern was to insure the docility of the clergy. The first article of the *Tao-seng ko* stipulates that monks or nuns who commit any of the four *pārājika* offenses are to be defrocked and referred to the criminal courts. It is significant that this article then proceeds to prescribe the same harsh punishment to those members of the clergy who 'use astrological signs for the purpose of making prophesies,' speak about state affairs with a view to misleading the people, or study books on military arts, none of which are classified as major offenses in the *Vinaya*. Their inclusion in the *Tao-seng ko* follows simply from the fact that they were proscribed under T'ang civil law.[48] Even in the case of the *pārājikas* the defrocked monk often faced harsher penalties than did the laymen for the same offence, as is indicated by the provision that the penalty for monks and nuns guilty of fornication should be two degrees severer than that for laymen.[49] Similarly, theft of a Buddha image by a layman was punished by three years imprisonment; if the offender was a monk or nun the additional punishment of exile was added to the original sentence of imprisonment.[50]

While it might be reasonable to expect that the clergy should live up to a higher moral standard than that of laymen since the former enjoyed privileges not accorded to the latter, under T'ang law monks and nuns were subject to expulsion from the order – the harshest penalty in the *Vinaya* – for a variety of acts that, by the standards of the *Vinaya*, were either not regarded as offenses at all or else constituted exceedingly minor infractions of Buddhist law. Thus according to the *T'ang liu-tien* expulsion from the order was the penalty imposed on monks or nuns who donned lay clothing, wore robes of silk, 'rode on large horses,' engaged in drunken brawling, invited guests to monasteries, told fortunes, presented officials with foodstuffs belonging to the order, or conspired to form cliques.[51] It should be noted that besides forbidding those acts by monks and nuns which were viewed by T'ang officialdom as detrimental to the state, the *Tao-seng ko* also sought to institutionalize certain customary practices that had become widespread in China, even though not required by the *Vinaya*, such as the ban on eating meat, which, if violated, was to be punished by a sentence of 'hard labor.'[52]

The *Vinaya*, which is the highest monastic law of the Buddhist church, explicitly allows members of the clergy to eat meat as long as they are not personally responsible for the slaughter of the animal.[53] The aversion of monks in China toward eating meat is attributable not to any prohibition in the *Vinaya*, but to certain passages in Mahāyāna scriptures which inveigh against the practice.[54]

One of T'ai-tsung's major objectives in promulgating the *Tao-seng ko* was to limit the extent of participation by the Buddhist clergy in Chinese secular life. Basically he sought to have monks and nuns confined to monasteries where they were to devote themselves to daily religious observances. Thus it is not surprising that preaching the doctrine of the Buddha outside the monastery was regarded as an offense[55] as were such secular activities as fortunetelling, playing a musical instrument, etc. Although it was within T'ai-tsung's power to legislate against a monk's meddling in secular affairs, as he did when he adopted the *Tao-seng ko*, there remained the question of the extent to which such legislation was morally binding on the clergy, since the *Vinaya* was often not concerned with those areas of clerical activity that the early T'ang emperors wished to check. In 639, two years after the promulgation of the *Tao-seng ko*, T'ai-tsung decreed that henceforth the Buddhist clergy would be required to conform to the rules of behavior set forth in the *Fo i-chiao ching*,[56] a sūtra of dubious origin purporting to contain the last admonitions of the Buddha uttered on his deathbed.[57]

Although the *Fo i-chiao ching* was by no means an obscure work – it had been circulating since the end of the fifth century – it had never formally served to regulate the activities of the Buddhist clergy as the *Vinaya* did. The appeal of this sūtra to T'ai-tsung, as his edict explicitly states, was in its strict warning to the clergy to keep clear of all worldly affairs. In the opening paragraph the Buddha admonishes his disciples to uphold the precepts (*prātimokṣa*) after he is no longer with them. He specifically forbids them to engage in any commercial transactions or agricultural work, or to own land, buildings, slaves, or animals. Monks are told that they must not prepare medicines, practice divination, astrology, geomancy, or reckon lucky and unlucky days. Rather they should cultivate self-discipline, eat only at the proper time, and lead a life of purity. The sūtra explicitly prohibits monks from interfering in secular affairs, sending emissaries on secret missions, uttering incantations, concocting elixirs, establishing intimate contacts with men of authority, performing miracles, or misleading the masses. They are cautioned that they should be modest in receiving alms and make no attempt to hoard them.[58]

One might think that the adoption of the *Fo i-chiao ching* as a basic work of monastic discipline by T'ai-tsung was superfluous, since many of its prohibitions were also found in the *Tao-seng ko*. But as we have noted, the *Tao-seng ko* was a set of regulations governing the behavior of the clergy that was drafted by government officials. Although it included some of the injunctions of the *Vinaya*, many of its prohibitions such as those against fortunetelling, the practice of astrology, and the perennial 'misleading of the masses,' which were regarded by the state as a threat to its stability, were not treated in the *Vinaya* as grave offences. Hence T'ai-tsung saw the necessity of supplementing the legal strictures of the *Tao-seng ko* with a canonical work like the *Fo i-chiao ching* which similarly inveighed against clerical involvement in secular affairs. His insistence that all monks be bound by the *Fo i-chiao ching* as they were by the *Vinaya* was unprecedented and lacked support in Buddhist tradition. In his edict of 639 T'ai-tsung claimed that he had the right to determine which specific scriptures should be binding on the clergy in disciplinary matters because the Buddha had entrusted the safekeeping of the Dharma in the 'period of decline' to the secular ruler and his ministers. It was incumbent, therefore, upon the emperor to fix the standards of behavior for the clergy.[59]

T'ai-tsung's persistent policy of curtailing the power of the Buddhist church proved at times to be a source of embarrassment in his contacts with the clergy. One such instance occurred in the year 641, when T'ai-tsung participated in ceremonies marking the completion of the construction of the Hung-fu ssu, a monastery he had founded in 634 in memory of his mother.[60] During the ceremony marking the consecration of the Buddha image, T'ai-tsung became overwrought when the abbot of the Hung-fu ssu, Tao-i, delivered a moving eulogy of his mother. Fighting back tears, T'ai-tsung recalled to the assembled monks how he had lost his mother in his youth without even having had the chance to demonstrate his filial devotion to her. Only through religious observances, he concluded, could he now contribute to his mother's spiritual happiness in the world beyond. T'ai-tsung then wrote with his own hand the text of a 'vow' (*yüan-wen*) in which he speaks in very emotional terms of his deep love for his mother and his wish that she should rapidly attain the bliss of enlightenment.[61] To this end he pledges material support for the Buddhist church, describing himself as 'Emperor and disciple [of the Buddha] who upholds the bodhisattva precepts.'[62] Sensing perhaps that in view of his long-standing policy of curbing the Buddhist church his words might sound hollow to the assembly on monks, T'ai-tsung deemed it appropriate to reassure the clergy that he was not really antagonistic toward Buddhism. His decision in 637 to grant Taoist priests precedence over Buddhist monks, he explained, was based upon a perfectly natural desire to venerate his ancestors, who, after all, were descended from Lao-tzu. He reminded the monks of the monasteries that he had founded on battlefields for the repose of the soldiers who had fallen in the early T'ang wars, and of the monasteries that he had built in memory of his mother, pointing out that he had never sponsored a single Taoist temple.[63] Perhaps out of a desire not to antagonize the Emperor, Tao-i expressed sympathy for T'ai-tsung's motives and disclaimed any resentment by the clergy against the throne. On the contrary he asserted – no doubt tongue in cheek – that the Buddhist community was greatly 'overjoyed' at the imperial decree according priority to the Taoists and flattered the Emperor by declaring that the monks could now practice their religion with their minds at rest owing to the benevolence of the throne. When the monks finally stood up to apologize for having so troubled the Emperor, he ordered them to be seated, declaring that he was after all their disciple. Before returning to his palace, T'ai-tsung, noting the cramped, hot quarters of the monks, promised to make a donation which would enable them to enlarge their hall.[64]

While T'ai-tsung may have been sincerely moved by the memorial services for his mother to utter some kind words to the monks of the Hung-fu ssu and to offer to endow their monastery, there is little indication that he had relented in his hostility toward the Buddhist church as a whole. As late as 646, less than three years before his death, T'ai-tsung was still railing against Buddhism. In a handwritten edict denouncing one of his ministers who had sought to take the tonsure but later recanted much to his annoyance, T'ai-tsung bluntly declared that Buddhism was not a religion that he could follow.[65] He denounced Buddhism for encouraging vulgar customs and futile beliefs, pointing out that its adherents neither could be certain about the blessings they were supposed to receive in the future nor had they been about to avert repeated misfortunes in the past. As examples, T'ai-tsung cited the tragic end of the two Liang emperors, Wu-ti (464–549), and his son, Chien-wen-ti, who were lavish patrons of Buddhism. Wu-ti, who was said to have emptied the treasury in support of the church, died of starvation after his capture by rebels; his son, who occupied the throne for two years after the father's death, was likewise murdered by his captors. For T'ai-tsung this constituted proof of the fallaciousness of the doctrine of retribution, one of the central tenets of Buddhism.

It was only in the last year of his life, after having suffered military defeat in his Korean campaign, which also ruined his health, that T'ai-tsung experienced a change of heart toward Buddhism. This was largely attributable to his great personal admiration for the monk-translator, Hsüan-tsang, who had spent some fifteen years studying in Buddhist monasteries in India, where he acquired a knowledge of Sanskrit and Indian civilization probably unequalled by any other Chinese. Three weeks after Hsüan-tsang's return to China in the first month of 645, T'ai-tsung summoned him to the palace at Lo-yang where Hsüan-tsang was questioned in great detail about the climate, products, and customs of India.[66] It was typical of T'ai-tsung that during the interview with Hsüan-tsang which lasted late into the night, the Emperor made hardly any reference to Buddhism. What interested T'ai-tsung was not Hsüan-tsang's great familiarity with contemporary Buddhist thought in India but his first-hand knowledge of foreign affairs. After extracting a promise from Hsüan-tsang to compile an account of the various countries that he had visited, T'ai-tsung tried to induce him to renounce his vows so that he would be free to serve as an adviser.[67] Hsüan-tsang tactfully declined by pointing out that he had studied Buddhist metaphysics since his youth and had received no training in Confucianism, which was the requisite learning for government officials. He also rejected another request that he accompany the Emperor during the forthcoming Korean campaign on the grounds that the *Vinaya* did not permit monks to visit battlefields. Rather, Hsüan-tsang insisted, he could repay his debt to the state by translating the texts that he had brought back from India, and to this end he sought permission to settle in the Shao-lin ssu, a famous monastery located in the mountains about twenty miles southeast of Lo-yang.[68] T'ai-tsung, seeing that he could not bring Hsüan-tsang into the government, persuaded him at least to take up residence in the Hung-fu ssu, the monastery erected in honor of T'ai-tsung's mother, no doubt in the hope that this extraordinary monk, already celebrated in the capital for his remarkable journey, would add further distinction to the monastery. Before leaving on his ill-fated campaign, T'ai-tsung instructed one of his ranking ministers to provide Hsüan-tsang with whatever financial assistance he might require. The two men were not to meet again for more than three years.

After T'ai-tsung's departure for the Korean front, Hsüan-tsang settled in the Hung-fu ssu in Ch'ang-an, where, with the financial support promised by T'ai-tsung, he assembled a large staff of learned monks to help him in his translation projects. This carefully selected group of assistants[69] included twelve 'verifiers' (*cheng-i*) whose responsibility was to check the accuracy of the translations by comparison with

Reign of T'ai-tsung (626–649)

other works in the canon, nine stylists (*chui-wen*), a philologist (*tzu-hsüeh*),[70] a specialist in Indian languages and literature,[71] and an unspecified number of secretaries and copyists. Within a year Hsüan-tsang had completed the translation of five different texts, most of which belonged to the Yogācāra school of Mahāyāna.[72] He sent copies of these translations along with the account of his travels in Central Asia and India, the *Hsi-yü chi*[73] to T'ai-tsung, requesting that the Emperor honor his work with an imperial preface, which T'ai-tsung declined to do on the grounds that his knowledge of the 'intricacies of Buddhism' was insufficient.[74] At this time Hsüan-tsang's value to the Emperor still lay primarily in his extraordinary knowledge of Indian affairs, as can be seen from the fact that when, in 647, Wang Hsüan-ts'e was sent on his second mission to India, T'ai-tsung requested Hsüan-tsang to translate into Sanskrit his letter to King Śīlāditya that Wang was asked to carry.[75] One can easily imagine Hsüan-tsang's discomfort when he was also asked by the Emperor to render the basic scripture of Taoism, the *Tao-te ching*, into Sanskrit, so that it could be circulated in India.[76]

In the spring of 648 T'ai-tsung, who was now ailing, moved to the Yü-hua Palace in the mountains to the north of Ch'ang-an. In the sixth month, with less than a year of life remaining to him, T'ai-tsung summoned Hsüan-tsang from the Hung-fu ssu, where he had been working, to his temporary palace to make a last appeal to him to 'discard the colored robes of Subhūti [a disciple of the Buddha] in favor of the white garments of Vimalakīrti [a famous Buddhist layman]' so that he might participate in the affairs of government.[77] Only after Hsüan-tsang once again turned down the Emperor's request that he renounce his vows did T'ai-tsung display some interest in Hsüan-tsang's religious work. The Emperor for the first time inquired about the texts that Hsüan-tsang was translating, which was a tacit admission that he had not been following the activities of the distinguished translator whom he had been supporting. Hsüan-tsang told the Emperor that he had been working on the *Yogācārabhūmi*, one of the basic treatises of the Yogacara school, and proceeded to lecture him on its contents, which reportedly so interested the Emperor that he dispatched an official to Ch'ang-an to procure a copy of the text.[78] After examining the treatise, T'ai-tsung is reported to have expressed regret that his preoccupation with politics and military affairs had deprived him of the chance to study the doctrines of Buddhism in any detail. Performing a volte-face, he now proclaimed Buddhism to be superior to both Confucianism and Taoism as well as to the other schools of Chinese philosophy. His secretariat was instructed to prepare nine copies of Hsüan-tsang's newly translated texts for distribution to each of the nine divisions (*chiu chou*) of the empire for the edification of his subjects. He also agreed to Hsüan-tsang's request, submitted two years earlier, to grant an imperial preface commemorating the new translations.[79]

During this last year of his life T'ai-tsung seems to have wholeheartedly accepted Hsüan-tsang as his spiritual mentor. Presumably under the guidance of the latter, he undertook a study of the *Bodhisattva piṭaka sūtra* (*P'u-sa-tsang ching*), a sūtra influenced by the Yogācāra school dealing with the practices of the bodhisattva.[80] T'ai-tsung is now described as spending all of his time with Hsüan-tsang discussing the Dharma and praising the merit of Buddhism.[81] As a token of his esteem for the great translator T'ai-tsung increased the financial support for Hsüan-tsang and bestowed on him a precious cassock made of golden thread and a razor for shaving his head, an indication that he now approved of Hsüan-tsang's continuing as a monk. There is also some evidence that T'ai-tsung may have agreed to accord the Buddhists equal status with the Taoists, but died before he could issue the necessary edict.[82] T'ai-tsung's sudden change of heart toward Buddhism at this time was no doubt largely attributable to his failing health.

After resuming contact with Hsüan-tsang in the spring of 648, T'ai-tsung reported that his health had taken a turn for the better now that he was devoting himself to the practice of Buddhism.[83] When T'ai-tsung sought advice on how he might best accumulate merit, Hsüan-tsang at last saw his chance to come to the rescue of the harried church by persuading the Emperor that the most meritorious act was to ordain monks who could disseminate the teachings of the Buddha, thereby contributing toward the salvation of all sentient beings. T'ai-tsung promptly responded in the ninth month of 648 by ordering five monks to be ordained in each of 3,716 monasteries and fifty monks to be ordained in the Hung-fu ssu. By this one stroke more than 18,500 monks were added to the rolls of the Buddhist clergy. The following month T'ai-tsung moved to the Tzu-wei Palace in Ch'ang-an, where he established on the palace grounds an Institute for the Dissemination of the Dharma (Hung-fa yüan) in which Hsüan-tsang was to carry on his work as a translator.[84] In fact Hsüan-tsang's biography reports that he was able to work on his translations only at night, his days being taken up by lengthy discourses with the Emperor about religion. It is little wonder, then, that Hsüan-tsang declined the abbotship of the Ta tz'u-en ssu, the magnificent monastery erected by the Crown Prince, Li Chih (the future Emperor Kao-tsung), in memory of his mother, Empress Wen-te, when it was offered to him in the course of an impressive ceremony at which three hundred monks were specially ordained. The Ta tz'u-en ssu was formally dedicated in the twelfth month of 648 in what must have been one of the most spectacular ceremonies that Ch'ang-an had seen, attended by the Emperor, the Crown Prince, Hsüan-tsang, and a host of high officials. An Institute for the Translation of Scriptures (Fan-ching yüan) as well as a repository for the hundreds of Indian manuscripts that Hsüan-tsang had brought back from India were established within the Ta tz'u-en ssu, where Hsüan-tsang subsequently did most of his work.

In the fourth month of 649, T'ai-tsung, again ailing, left Ch'ang-an for the Ts'ui-wei Palace in the hills to the south of the capital accompanied by the Crown Prince and Hsüan-tsang.[85] Although the Emperor continued to concern himself in a limited way with court affairs, most of his time was now devoted to discussing Buddhist philosophy with Hsüan-tsang. Perhaps sensing that his own end was near, T'ai-tsung frequently asked his mentor about the Buddhist law of cause and effect, the doctrine of retribution, and the earthly manifestations of the Indian Buddhist sages. At one point the Emperor was so moved by religious fervor that he lamented having met Hsüan-tsang too late in life to have really helped in the dissemination of Buddhism. During his last days T'ai-tsung bade Hsüan-tsang to stay with him in the palace, and when death came to the man who had consolidated the T'ang rule and who had done so much to bring the Buddhist church under the control of the state, Hsüan-tsang, perhaps the most celebrated monk of the day, was at his side to give him solace.

Reign of Kao-tsung (649–683)

T'ai-tsung was succeeded on the throne by his ninth son, Li Chih, who is known as the Emperor Kao-tsung. Lacking a forceful personality, the new emperor was generally reluctant to confront the Buddhist church in the headstrong manner of his father. His attitude toward Buddhism, if not one of open hostility, was one characterized by indifference. Kao-tsung, like his father, held Hsüan-tsang in high esteem, keeping him close by his side and providing him with abundant support for his translation activities. Yet there is little solid evidence that aside from the customary religious observances held for the benefit of members of his family, Kao-tsung showed any real interest in the doctrines of Buddhism. Nevertheless he did sponsor the founding of two important monasteries in Ch'ang-an. The first of these, as we have mentioned, was the Ta tz'u-en ssu, dedicated in 648 by Kao-tsung, then Crown Prince, to the memory of his mother. It will be recalled that his father, T'ai-tsung, likewise had built a monastery, the Hung-fu ssu, in honor of *his* mother. The second major monastery built by Kao-tsung was the magnificent Hsi-ming ssu, consisting of thirteen halls and having in all more than 4,000 rooms, commissioned in the year 656 to commemorate the investiture of the new Crown Prince,[1] Li Hung, the first child born to Wu Chao, who had successfully maneuvred herself into the position of Empress during the preceding year.

After the death of T'ai-tsung, Hsüan-tsang returned to the Ta tz'u-en ssu in Ch'ang-an, where he remained until 657, when he was requested by Kao-tsung to accompany him to Lo-yang. During the eight years spent at the Ta tz'u-en ssu, Hsüan-tsang translated thirty-three works in 191 fascicles.[2] Although Kao-tsung provided the financial support for Hsüan-tsang's group, he himself did not participate in its work, nor did he give unqualified endorsement to all of the latter's proposals despite Hsüan-tsang's exhortation to officials to serve the throne loyally.[3] Thus when Hsüan-tsang suggested in 652 that a three-hundred-foot-high stone pagoda should be erected in the Ta tz'u-en ssu to house the manuscripts that he had brought back from India so that they would be safe from loss by fire, Kao-tsung dispatched a court official to inform him that the project that he had in mind was too ambitious. Instead, Kao-tsung suggested a more modest structure, half the size that Hsüan-tsang had proposed, to be built from inexpensive brick, the funds for which were to be raised through the sale of clothing and other property belonging to seven members of the court staff who had disappeared.[4]

As part of the celebrations attending the investiture of the new Crown Prince, a great vegetarian banquet was held in the first month of 656 at the Ta tz'u-en ssu for 5,000 monks.[5] It is possible that the initiative for this banquet originated with Empress Wu rather than Kao-tsung, who did not bother to attend. Nevertheless Hsüan-tsang succeeded in persuading him, through the good offices of two courtiers, to compose an inscription for a stele to be erected on the monastery grounds to mark the occasion. The inscribed stele, completed in the fourth month of 656, was carried to the Ta tz'u-en ssu in a grand procession led by Hsüan-tsang and watched by a crowd said to number one million people.[6]

In the fifth month of 656 Hsüan-tsang, who had been suffering from the rigors of his travels since his return to China, was taken seriously ill.[7] Kao-tsung immediately dispatched two court physicians to look after him. Although the Emperor did not personally visit Hsüan-tsang during his illness, he was apparently sincerely concerned about his health and sent officials to his bedside several times a day to inquire after him. Fearing that this might be his last opportunity to address the Emperor, Hsüan-tsang sent a deathbed appeal to the throne concerning two matters that had long been troubling him. The first was the question of the precedence accorded to the Taoists over the Buddhists by T'ai-tsung in his edict of 637. Hsüan-tsang asserted that he had repeatedly petitioned the throne to have this order nullified, and in fact had received assurance from T'ai-tsung that he would reconsider the issue, only to see him die before he could do so. The second matter that Hsüan-tsang raised pertained to an edict that Kao-tsung had issued during the preceding year which empowered officials in certain cases to by-pass the *Tao-seng ko* and try members of the Buddhist and Taoist clergies in accordance with ordinary secular law. As Hsüan-tsang delicately phrased it, 'officials in border areas, failing to understand the true intent of the imperial order, have greatly humiliated the clergy by putting them in cangues or caning them, regardless of the seriousness of the offense.[8] This 'final' appeal from the pre-eminent monk of the empire (no doubt along with some prompting from Empress Wu) produced a favorable response from the Emperor: his edict allowing the application of secular law in cases involving the clergy would be rescinded forthwith.[9] The question of the precedence of Taoism over Buddhism, however, could not be resolved so quickly, Kao-tsung replied, since it was already an established custom, having been decreed during the preceding reign. The matter would, therefore, have to be referred to the ranking ministers for consideration. In fact, as we shall see, it was only in 674, after the real power had already slipped into the hands of Empress Wu, that the Taoists lost their right of precedence.

When Kao-tsung decided to move to the Chi-ts'ui Palace in Lo-yang in the second month of 657, Hsüan-tsang, who several months earlier had become the spiritual preceptor to Empress Wu's first child by Kao-tsung, was asked to accompany the Emperor to the new palace where he could continue his translation activities. For this purpose Hsüan-tsang was allowed to bring along five assistant translators and their attendants. Kao-tsung appears to have drawn closer to Hsüan-tsang in Lo-yang, expressing for the first time interest in the progress of his work.[10] When Hsüan-tsang, whose home village was in the outskirts of Lo-yang, applied to the Emperor for permission to rebury the remains of his parents whose grave had fallen into disrepair, Kao-tsung declared that the government would meet all the expenses.[11] Although Hsüan-tsang no doubt welcomed such expressions of imperial support, he could not but be troubled by the great demands on his time as a result of his residence in the palace. In the ninth month of 657 he petitioned Kao-tsung, just as he petitioned the latter's father twelve years earlier, for permission to retire to the Shao-lin ssu on the outskirts of Ch'ang-an, where he could devote himself to meditation, which, he claimed, could not be practiced in the bustling surroundings of the capital. Once again his request was denied – this time on the grounds that his presence was necessary for the spiritual welfare of the Emperor. In the first month of 658 Hsüan-tsang returned to Ch'ang-an with Kao-tsung. Shortly after the completion of the Hsi-ming ssu in the sixth month of 658, Hsüan-tsang was instructed by an imperial decree to take up residence in the new monastery.[12] Despite an impressive ceremony held to mark his arrival, Hsüan-tsang did not remain long at the Hsi-ming ssu. By the tenth month he was again back at the Ta tz'u-en ssu,[13] where he had worked until Kao-tsung brought him to Lo-yang the year before.

Since Hsüan-tsang's return from India in 645 he had been repeatedly asked to translate the whole corpus of *Prajñāpāramitā* sūtras, but was reluctant to do because of its bulk. Sūtras of the *Prajñāpāramitā* class were well known and much studied by the Chinese intelligentsia, *Prajñāpāramitā* texts being among the first Mahāyāna works translated into Chinese in the second century. Hsüan-tsang, whose health had been failing, realized that if he did not soon start on this massive work, he would, in all probability, not live to complete the translation. He appealed to Kao-tsung for permission to move from Ch'ang-an, which he said had too many distractions, to the Yü-hua ssu, T'ai-tsung's former country palace in the northern outskirts of the city, which had been converted into a monastery after the latter's death. Kao-tsung gave his consent, and Hsüan-tsang, accompanied by some of his ablest disciples, proceeded to the Yü-hua ssu in the tenth month of 659. It was at this rustic monastery where Hsüan-tsang spent the remaining four and a half years of his life, that he translated some of the most important texts in the Chinese canon: *Ch'eng wei-shih lun* (*Vijñaptimātratā siddhi*),[14] which subsequently became the preeminent Yogācāra text in East Asian Buddhism and the basic scripture of the Fa-hsiang school; the *Wei-shih erh-shih lun* (*Viṃśatikā*),[15] which is Vasubandhu's famous defense of Yogācāra thought; and, the *Ta po-jo ching* (*Mahāprajñāpāramitā sūtra*)[16] in 600 fascicles – the largest scripture in the canon. This last work was particularly esteemed for its magical powers, Hsüan-tsang's safe return from India having been attributed to his possession of the manuscript of this sacred text. After the completion of the translation of the *Ta po-jo ching* in the tenth month of 663 Hsüan-tsang's chief disciple and successor, Tz'u-en,[17] was dispatched to Ch'ang-an to request an imperial preface, which was subsequently granted.

The enormous effort expended by Hsüan-tsang in translating the *Ta po-jo ching* had taken its toll: Hsüan-tsang was left physically and mentally exhausted. He had translated to 600 fascicles of the *Ta po-jo ching* in the incredibly short span of forty-seven months – an average of almost one fascicle every two and a half days. In addition during the same period, which Hsüan-tsang viewed as a race against death, he translated seven shorter works comprising twenty-eight fascicles. Little wonder, then, that he agreed only with the greatest reluctance to an appeal from some monks in the first month of 664 to undertake a complete translation of the *Ta pao-chi ching*, another composite text of considerable size.[18] After translating only a few lines, he declared to his disciples that he was unable to go on. Hsüan-tsang decided to spend his last days in religious devotions – worship, meditation, and sūtra-chanting. Death came to him on the fifth day of the fourth month in the year 664. Kao-tsung no doubt sincerely regretted the loss of this distinguished monk whose presence had graced the two capital cities for almost two decades and who had brought distinction to his imperial patrons. To mourn the loss of the 'Jewel of the Empire,' as Kao-tsung called him,[19] the court was recessed and a state funeral ordered. However, Kao-tsung's behavior following the death of Hsüan-tsang makes it clear that his primary concern was for Hsüan-tsang as an individual – a monk of unusual talent who served the T'ang ruling family loyally – rather than for the Buddhist teachings to which Hsüan-tsang had dedicated his life. Even before Hsüan-tsang's interment in the fourth month of 664 Kao-tsung decreed: 'Now that the Master Hsüan-tsang of the Yü-hua ssu is gone, all translation activities should cease. Those texts already translated should be turned over to the authorities in accordance with established custom so that copies can be made. All untranslated manuscripts are to be sent to the Ta tz'u-en ssu for safekeeping. Disciples of Hsüan-tsang as well as those monks assisting him in the translation of the scriptures who do not properly belong to the Yü-hua ssu are each to return to his own monastery.'[20] This simple, unadorned edict brought to an abrupt close the activities of the most remarkable and productive group of Buddhist translators and scholars ever assembled on Chinese soil. By the time of his death Hsüan-tsang had translated seventy-five works in 1,335 fascicles,[21] an amount roughly equal in size to one fourth of the canon as it existed in his day. Yet this represented only a fraction of the 657 Sanskrit manuscripts that he had brought from India,[22] the bulk of which were to remain untranslated partly as a result of Kao-tsung's precipitate dispersal of the group of translators and scholars that Hsüan-tsang had trained over the preceding two decades.

In the last years of Hsüan-tsang's life an incident took place which clearly showed that despite the efforts of the early T'ang rulers to curb the power of the Buddhist church, the latter remained a powerful force within Chinese society. In 657, the year after Kao-tsung agreed to Hsüan-tsang's request to enforce the *Tao-seng ko*, he issued an edict forbidding monks and nuns to receive the homage of their parents and seniors.[23] Apparently mindful of his father's failure to compel the clergy to do obeisance before their parents in 631, Kao-tsung proceeded cautiously at this time, decreeing simply that monks and nuns were not to receive homage from parents and seniors. Encouraged by the apparent lack of any strong opposition, Kao-tsung then took the next step in the direction of bringing the church within the realm of secular ethics when, in 662, he ordered his ministers to discuss whether the Buddhist clergy should be required to reverence both their parents and the throne.[24] It should be noted that Kao-tsung was sufficiently cautious to call first for a discussion of this question by his ministers rather than to risk a head-on confrontation between the throne and the church, which would have occurred had he issued a direct order to the clergy. The church, attaching enormous importance to the principle that the clergy transcends the mundane world, had long resisted any attempt to subject it to secular authority. Even the despotic Sui Emperor Yang had been forced in the year 609 to admit defeat after four attempts to compel monks to do obeisance before the throne.[25]

Kao-tsung's order to his ministers to begin discussions on whether monks and nuns should be required to reverence their parents and the throne was issued on the fifteenth day of the fourth month in the year 662. The first reaction from the Buddhist community appeared six days later, when the monk Wei-hsiu led a group of more than two hundred other monks to the P'eng-lai Palace to present a memorial. The clerics were told that their protests were premature since the matter was still under discussion. Undaunted, they reassembled at the prestigious Hsi-ming ssu, where they decided that the best course of action would be to drum up support from prominent Buddhist laymen. On the twenty-fifth of the fourth month the abbot of the Hsi-ming ssu, Tao-hsüan, one of the most respected monks of the day, addressed an appeal to Prince P'ei, fourth son of Kao-tsung and governor (*mu*) of Yung-chou. Two days later Tao-hsüan sent a letter of protest to the mother of the Empress, Lady Jung-kuo, which was then followed by a lengthy appeal to the ranking ministers. Tao-hsüan used two types of arguments in his defense of the traditional Buddhist position. First he traced chronologically the devotion of successive emperors to Buddhism – how they patronized monks, built monasteries, accepted bodhisattva precepts, and most importantly, acknowledged the transcendence of the church over secular authorities. Turning his attention next to the Buddhist clergy, Tao-hsüan quoted passages from five canonical texts, including both the *Vinaya* and the *Fan-wang ching*, the basic scriptures used for the ordination of monks in T'ang times, which expressly forbade monks and nuns to do obeisance before any lay person – relative, parent or ruler. A monk who ignored these injunctions, it was pointed out, could no longer regard himself as a member of the order (*saṃgha*). Similarly, if a ruler compelled monks to break their vows by requiring them to do homage to a layman, regardless of his status, he would in Tao-hsüan's words 'burn up the good roots that make his salvation possible and subject himself to endless suffering . . . The arhats, recluses, and sages will leave his country; the denizens of the heavens will shed tears of grief, and benevolent deities will no longer protect his land; ministers will scheme against each other, and bandits will appear throughout the realm . . .'[26] Tao-hsüan's warning was unmistakable: if the state tempers with the prerogatives of the church, it must risk collapse.

On the fifteenth day of the following month over one thousand civil and military officials from the central administration as well as from the prefectural and county governments assembled in the Department of State Affairs (Chung-t'ai tu-t'ang)[27] to make a final recommendation to Kao-tsung. To make certain that the Buddhist viewpoint was heard, a group of over three hundred monks led by representatives of the great imperial monasteries of Ch'ang-an – the Hung-fu ssu, the Ta tz'u-en ssu, and the Hsi-ming ssu – presented copies of petitions as well as extracts from canonical texts in support of their arguments. In spite of their protests, however, the monks were refused permission to participate in the deliberations on the grounds that the Emperor had specifically instructed lay officials to make the decision. Although the monks agreed to withdraw, their cause was far from lost, since they could count on many influential supporters among the officials. When it became apparent after considerable discussion that the group as a whole would not be able to reach a consensus – 539 officials supported the position of the clergy and 354 opposed their stand[28] – it was decided that individual officials should present their views separately. In all, sixty-four statements of opinion were submitted, thirty-two in favor of continuing the traditional practice of excusing monks from doing obeisance to laymen, twenty-nine opposed to this practice, and three supporting a compromise such as excusing aged or particularly virtuous monks but not all members of the clergy indiscriminately.

Failing to secure the unqualified endorsement of his officials, Kao-tsung decided on a compromise of his own. On the eighth day of the sixth month he issued an edict stating that while he would respect the traditional prerogative of monks and nuns not do homage before the throne, they would henceforth be expected to kneel before their own parents.[29] In fact, he had retreated to the position that his father, T'ai-tsung, had taken in 631. Although one might suppose that the Buddhists could find comfort in the fact that their long-standing privilege of being exempt from bowing before secular authorities had been upheld, it was soon evident that the monks felt themselves to be arguing from a position of strength. Thirteen days after Kao-tsung's decree the first of a new series of petitions reached Kao-tsung protesting the unfairness of requiring the clergy to do homage to their parents. Leading monks once again appealed to prominent lay supporters in an effort to bring pressure on the Emperor to rescind his edict.[30] After receiving five memorials protesting his decision within the short span of four months, Kao-tsung decided to end the confrontation completely and nullified the offending edict.[31] The question whether monks should do homage to their parents and ruler remained alive, however, throughout the T'ang dynasty. In the second month of the year 714 Emperor Hsüan-tsung, like his predecessors T'ai-tsung and Kao-tsung, ordered members of the Buddhist and Taoist clergies to kneel before their parents.[32] Two months later, under circumstances that are unclear, Hsüan-tsung was compelled to withdraw his edict.[33] In the tenth month of 733 Hsüan-tsung once again apparently sought to have the clergy reverence their parents.[34] It was not until after the An Lu-shan rebellion in 755 that the clergy was formally excused from the obligation to reverence the throne. In the year 761 Emperor Su-tsung decreed that Buddhist monks and nuns, coming for an audience, need not do homage; in 773, during the reign of Emperor Tai-tsung, another such edict was issued, this time covering both the Buddhist and Taoist clergies.[35] The Japanese monk, Ennin, who travelled in China between the years 838–847, testifies to the fact that members of the Buddhist and Taoist clergies were exempted from doing obeisance before the throne. While visiting Teng-chou in the third month of 840, Ennin happened to witness a ceremony at which an imperial edict was read before an assembly of townspeople. He noted in his diary, no doubt with some amazement, that the prefect, executive officers, secretaries, military men, and commoners repeatedly bowed, whereas the monks, nuns, and Taoist priests did not do so.[36]

Toward the end of the year 660, Kao-tsung, who had been ailing for some time, suffered a paralytic stroke, which left him temporarily incapacitated. Although he recovered from the stroke, his general state of health had deteriorated seriously, which might account for his sudden interest in Taoism that begins to appear about this time. Two years after his stroke Kao-tsung changed the name of the Ta-ming Palace to P'eng-lai,[37] the latter being the name of the fabled mountains in the eastern seas believed to be inhabited by immortals. In the first month of the year 666 he travelled with Empress Wu to the sacred mountain, T'ai-shan, where he worshipped the Supreme Deity (Hao-t'ien Shang-ti) and performed the ancient *feng-shan* sacrifice attesting to the tranquility and prosperity of the empire. Kao-tsung followed up these essentially Confucian rituals by issuing an edict ordering the establishment of three Taoist temples and three Buddhist monasteries in Yen-chou, where T'ai-shan was situated, and one Taoist temple and one Buddhist monastery in each of the other prefectures (*chou*) of the empire.[38] The monasteries in Yen-chou were each to have fourteen monks, while the prefectural monasteries were alloted seven monks each.[39] At first glance it would appear that the emperor envisioned some sort of religious syncretism by bringing together the three great religious traditions at T'ai-shan. This view is reinforced by the fact that the Buddhist monasteries in Yen-chou were given traditional Chinese names rather than purely Buddhist ones.[40] As we have already observed, the establishment of a state-supported monastery in each prefecture, presumably for the purpose of offering prayers at regular intervals for the prosperity of the empire, was not in itself a new idea. What was unique in Kao-tsung's edict, however, was the provision for creating a network of government sponsored Taoist temples throughout the land.

On his return journey from T'ai-shan in the second month of 666, Kao-tsung visited the birthplace of Confucius. To mark the occasion he conferred a relatively simple title on the sage – T'ai-shih (Great Teacher) and ordered that his memorial hall be repaired.[41] The imperial cortege then moved on to Honan to visit the alleged birthplace of Lao-tzu. To show the exalted status that the latter enjoyed as the imperial ancestor, special honors were heaped on Lao-tzu. He was accorded the posthumous title T'ai-shang Hsüan-yüan Huang-ti, 'Supreme Emperor of Mysterious Origin,' and his mother was designated Hsien-t'ien T'ai-hou, 'Great Empress Who Preceded Heaven.' A memorial hall, under the supervision of two government officials, was erected at Lao-tzu's birthplace, and the county in which he was believed to have lived was renamed Chen-yüan hsien, 'County of the True Source.'

It would appear that after the death of Hsüan-tsang Kao-tsung increasingly turned his attention toward Taoist priests, possibly in the hope that they could provide him with the elixir of longevity. For one such priest, Liu Tao-ho, who lived on Sung-shan, located to the east of Lo-yang, Kao-tsung built a Taoist temple, the T'ai-i kuan.[42] When the *feng-shan* sacrifices of 666 were threatened by heavy rains, Kao-tsung appealed to him rather than to a Buddhist monk to offer prayers that the rains should stop. Liu was subsequently rewarded for his part in making the *feng-shan* sacrifice possible. Several years later, during the Hsien-heng era (670–674), a time when the Emperor's health was deteriorating, Liu thoughtfully concocted an elixir for him. Fortunately for the Emperor Liu first drank the potion himself, which resulted in his death. Another Taoist priest who was invited at the same time to the Court at Lo-yang and questioned about Taoism was P'an Shih-cheng, a disciple of Wang Yüan-chih, the Taoist priest who had foretold Kao-tsu's rise to power. Kao-tsung greatly esteemed P'an, who is said to have lived for some twenty years on Sung-shan subsisting only on pine needles and water. Kao-tsung built for him at state expense several temples, the most important being the Ch'ung-T'ang kuan, 'Temple for the Veneration of the T'ang [Ancestor],' a reference to the ruling family's descent from Lao-tzu.[43]

In addition to Kao-tsung's personal involvement with a number of Taoist priests and hermits, he made a strenuous effort in the last years of his life to enhance the intellectual respectability of the Taoist church so that it could compete with the Buddhists. In the year 675 he ordered that the entire corpus of Taoist scriptures, then said to consist of 7,300 fascicles, be copied as a tribute to the memory of his favorite son, Crown Prince Hung, who had died that year at the relatively early age of twenty-three.[44] Both the Emperor and Empress commemorated the event by composing prefaces, although only the one by Kao-tsung survives.[45] Kao-tsung further enhanced the standing of the Taoist church when he decreed in 678 that Taoist priests would be transferred from the jurisdiction of the Court for State Ceremonials (Hung-lu ssu) to the Court of Imperial Clan Affairs (Tsung-cheng ssu).[46] As we have already noted, both the Buddhist and Taoist clergies had been attached to the Court for State Ceremonials at the beginning of the T'ang. To have been put alongside the Buddhists under the jurisdiction of the governmental office whose major responsibility was to look after foreign affairs must have particularly rankled the Taoists with their nationalistic pretensions. By placing the Taoist clergy under the supervision of the Court for Imperial Clan Affairs Kao-tsung now gave formal recognition to the close link between the imperial family and the Taoist church. In the same decree he ordered that the Taoist clergy should henceforth follow princes (*wang*) in the order of precedence and that their basic scripture, the *Tao-te ching*, would be accorded the same status in the civil service examinations as the Confucian classics.[47]

Yet for all of Kao-tsung's support of Taoism he was careful not to antagonize the Buddhists. In the year 659 he made generous grants of cash and silk to the monks of the Fa-men ssu, which housed the famous finger-bone relic of the Buddha that was reputed to have magical properties, and ordered that an image of Emperor Aśoka with Kao-tsu's own features be installed in this popular centre of pilgrimage. The following year he had the relic brought temporarily to Lo-yang, where he worshipped it at the imperial palace before having it carried in a procession through the streets. Empress Wu showed her devotion by providing an elaborate case of gold and silver for the relic.[48] The following year Kao-tsung ordered the repair of monasteries and pagodas in Wu-tai shan, another Buddhist holy place frequented by pilgrims.[49]

Kao-tsung was particularly anxious to avoid any conflict between the Buddhist and Taoist clergies that might threaten the stability of his empire. To this end he ordered, after a debate at the palace in the year 668 between representatives of the two religions, the burning of all copies of the *Lao-tzu hua-hu ching* (*Sūtra on Lao-tzu's Conversion of the Barbarians*), a spurious 'sūtra' forged by the Taoists during the Western Chin dynasty that held that the Buddha was none other than Lao-tzu, who had gone to India after writing his *Tao-te ching*.[50] This 'sūtra' had long been one of the main bones of contention between the two groups. The Taoists used it to show that Buddhism was merely a watered-down form of Taoism intended for barbarians, while the Buddhists either argued that the work was a forgery or else circulated doctored versions of the text which indicated that, in fact, Lao-tzu was merely an Indian disciple of the Buddha. When Taoist priests in the capital protested, Kao-tsung promptly reassured them that he had no intention of favoring Buddhism over Taoism. The Taoists do not appear to have paid too much attention to the ban, for we find a Buddhist monk petitioning Empress Wu in 696 to enforce Kao-tsung's decision to prohibit the text.[51]

Interregnum of Empress Wu (684–705)

Although Kao-tsung nominally remained emperor until his death in 683, actual political power passed into the hands of his consort, Wu Chao, after the Emperor suffered his first stroke in 660.[1] Wu Chao, who was destined to become one of China's ablest rulers, started her career at the age of thirteen as a low-ranking concubine in T'ai-tsung's entourage.[2] Her father, Wu Shih-huo, had been a successful merchant who threw in his lot with Kao-tsu, when the latter began his rebellion against the Sui; her mother, Lady Jung-kuo, who was mentioned earlier, was the niece of Yang Hsiung, an influential member of the strongly pro-Buddhist Sui imperial family. After T'ai-tsung's death in 649, Wu Chao was compelled to shave her head and enter a nunnery, as did other concubines who did not bear children. Normally, such a concubine would have been obliged to spend the remainder of her life as a nun, but fortunately for Wu Chao she was summoned back to Kao-tsung's court as a relatively high-ranking concubine at the instigation of Empress Wang who was hoping to use Wu Chao to lure the Emperor away from another concubine to whom he had become attached. Wu Chao had no intention of serving as anyone's pawn, and soon succeeded through treacherous schemes in having Empress Wang deposed and herself installed in the latter's place. As might be expected, Wu Chao encountered opposition from bureaucrats with vested interests. Relatives of the deposed Empress Wang felt threatened by the loss of their influence over Kao-tsung, and Confucian officials were scandalized by Kao-tsung's choice of a consort who had once been a concubine of his father. Through various intrigues often involving the shedding of blood, Wu Chao gradually eliminated those who opposed her, so that when Kao-tsung was immobilized by his first stroke in 660, she was able to serve as a *de facto* regent. Frustrated in a feeble attempt to depose her in 664, Kao-tsung, whose health was slowly deteriorating, reconciled himself to her dominant position at the court and never again seriously challenged her.

As we have already noted, Wu Chao was born into a family with pronounced Buddhist sympathies. Having lost her father at an early age, she was raised by her mother, Lady Jung-kuo, whose strong attachment to Buddhism is apparent from the appeals addressed to her by Tao-hsüan during the crisis of 662 when Kao-tsung ordered the Buddhist and Taoist clergies to do homage to their parents.[3] A year after Wu Chao became Empress, she requested Hsüan-tsang, the most eminent monk in Ch'ang-an, to administer the lay vows and pray for the safe delivery of her child. As a token of her devotion to Hsüan-tsang she presented him with a stole as well as many other articles of value. Hsüan-tsang was subsequently asked to serve as the spiritual mentor of the child – the future Emperor Chung-tsung – to whom he gave the name Prince of the Buddha's Light (Fo-kuang wang).[4] Another indication of Wu Chao's enthusiasm for Buddhism is the support that she gave to the construction of the famous cave temples at Lung-men. Between the years 618 and 655, i.e. the founding of the T'ang and Wu Chao's designation as Empress, some seventy dated images were produced in the Lung-men caves. During her fifty-year-long reign (655–705), however, the number of such datable images increased more than fivefold to a total of approximately 380 images. The significance of her influence on image making at Lung-men becomes even more apparent when we consider that for the remaining two hundred years of the T'ang only seventy-six datable images have been discovered.[5]

Her piety notwithstanding, Empress Wu provided only modest support for the Buddhist church while Kao-tsung still lived. The Emperor, as we have seen, turned increasingly toward Taoism after his first stroke. Taoist priests frequented the court as never before, government-sponsored Taoist temples were built in each province, and the *Tao-te ching* was introduced into the examination system. As a result, the Taoists were emerging as one more power group within the empire, although they did not command the vast resources and backing that the Buddhists did. Beset with enemies on all sides, Empress Wu carefully consolidated her position in the years preceding Kao-tsung's death, taking pains to avoid antagonizing any of the major groups that might frustrate her ambition to occupy the throne. The Taoists and the Confucians, many of whom were already hostile to the Empress because she had served as a concubine to both father (T'ai-tsung) and son (Kao-tsung), would surely oppose her with even more intensity if she embarked on a program that would strengthen the hand of the Buddhist church. To reassure the T'ang imperial family of her loyalty Empress Wu gave the name T'ai-yüan ssu, to the monastery that she founded in 670 in memory of her mother,[6] T'ai-yüan being the area from which the Li family arose. Needless to say, the name of the monastery was changed after she reduced the T'ang imperial family to impotence.[7] In the eighth month of 674 Empress Wu took a major step toward her goal of openly assuming power by adopting the unprecedented title T'ien-hou, 'Heavenly Empress,' following a serious illness of the Emperor during the preceding year. During the same month an edict was issued, nominally by Kao-tsung, decreeing that henceforth in all religious ceremonies, both public and private, the Buddhist and Taoist clergies would stand on equal footing, neither taking precedence over the other.[8] This edict would prove to be the first step in Empress Wu's calculated policy of establishing Buddhism as the state religion in place of Taoism. As perhaps a subtle indication of things to come, another edict was issued five years later, again in the name of Kao-tsung who was now nearing death, which allowed translators of Buddhist texts to disregard all taboos in the use of characters occurring in the personal names of T'ang emperors (*kuo-hui*).[9] This made it again possible to write such commonplace Buddhist terms as *Shih-tsun*, 'The World-Honored One' – an epithet of the Buddha – and *chiu-chih*, 'salvation,'[10] which previously had to be written *Sheng-tsun* and *chiu-ch'u*, to avoid the characters *shih* and *chih* which occurred in the personal names of T'ai-tsung and Kao-tsung.

When Kao-tsung finally died in 683, Empress Wu allowed the Crown Prince – the former Prince of the Buddha's Light – to ascend the throne as Emperor Chung-tsung, only to have him deposed two months later when he showed signs of acting independently of his mother. Chung-tsung was replaced on the throne by his brother, Li Tan (Emperor Jui-tsung), who was kept as a virtual prisoner within the palace, neither being allowed to participate in the routine activities of the court, nor being accorded the dignity of an enthronement ceremony. In the ninth month of 684 Empress Wu renamed all of the T'ang institutions and set up tablets for her own ancestors in the style of the imperial family. Her heavy-handed methods soon resulted in a large-scale rebellion led by Li Ching-yeh, a grandson of Li Chi, one of T'ai-tsung's most trusted generals. Empress Wu, having mobilized an army of 300,000 men, crushed the uprising within a month. Four years later she removed the last obstacle in the path to the throne when she succeeded in provoking the T'ang imperial princes into an abortive uprising, which ended with the extermination of most of the prominent members of the imperial family.

With the annihilation of the T'ang princes the way was clear, as far as military power was concerned, for Empress Wu to replace the T'ang with her own dynasty, of which she would be the *de jure* as well as *de facto* ruler. The difficulty that she faced in getting formal recognition, however, was formidable, since the Confucian canon did not accept the principle that a woman might rule in her own right, nor, in fact, was there any precedent of a woman founding a dynasty or ascending the throne without a consort. Her dissatisfaction with the Confucian attitude toward women was already evident as far back as 674, when, after assuming the unprecedented title Heavenly Empress, she proposed that the period of mourning for a deceased mother should be the same as that for a father, even though the father might still be living.[11] If Confucian ideology was an obstacle to legitimizing her imperial aspirations, so, too, could she not look for support to the Taoist church, which since the founding of the T'ang had enjoyed an especially favored status because of the claim of the T'ang rulers that they were descended from Lao-tzu. It was not surprising, then, that she turned to Buddhism, which, despite its massive following on all levels of society, had frequently been subjected to repressive measures by the T'ang rulers. Clearly the Buddhist church as yet had no vested interest in the maintenance of the T'ang dynasty.

No sooner had Kao-tsung died than Empress Wu began to encourage people to 'discover' auspicious omens (*fu-jui*) that could be interpreted in such a way as to foretell her imminent ascent to the throne. A Sung source states with reference to the year 684: 'After T'ai-hou (Empress Wu) assumed the regency, people from all over the Empire competed with each other to inform her of auspicious omens.'[12] When Fan Wen, the magistrate of Sung-yang, presented her with an auspicious stone, she ordered that it be displayed at the court. A high-ranking official who suggested that the stone was a fraud designed to mislead the people incurred the Empress's anger and was demoted and transferred to a provincial post. In the fourth month of 688 Wu Ch'eng-ssu, a nephew of the Empress, instructed one T'ang T'ung-t'ai to inform the court that he (T'ang) had retrieved from the Lo river a stone bearing the prophecy: 'The Imperial Cause will forever prosper when the Sage Mother (Sheng-mu) reigns over the people.'[13] Elated by this 'find,' the Empress designated this stone, whose inscription had in fact been forged by her nephew, the Precious Chart (*pao-t'u*), a name suggestive of the prognostication charts and books that supposedly had emerged from the Yellow and Lo rivers during the reigns of the mythical sage emperors Fu-hsi and Yü. The following month, after worshipping at the Lo river and ordering high-ranking officials serving in both the central and provincial governments to do likewise, she formally assumed the title Sage Mother and Divine Sovereign (Sheng-mu Shen-huang). To emphasize the importance of the prophecy Empress Wu, at the beginning of the new year (689), chose two key words from the stone inscription, 'forever prosper' (*yung-ch'ang*), as a new era-name.

The rash of oracles and omens that appeared toward the end of the 680s prompted a group of ten Buddhist monks[14] in the seventh month of 690 to present the Empress with a copy of the *Ta-yün ching* (*The Great Cloud Sūtra*),[15] along with oracles identifying her with Maitreya (Mi-lo), the Buddha-to-come, and asserting that the Mandate of Heaven had now passed to her. It is not possible to determine whether Empress Wu directly ordered the monks to present the sūtra and prepare the oracles.[16] In any event, the *Ta-yün ching*, which, like all other sūtras, was believed to be the word of the Buddha, contained ideas that could be used to legitimize rule by a woman. In the thirty-seventh chapter of the sūtra the Buddha relates the story of a female divinity named Ching-kuang T'ien-nü, 'The Heavenly Lady Pure and Radiant,' who retained her female form, rather than allowing herself to be transformed into a man, so that she could better help sentient beings.[17] The Buddha then uttered the prophecy that 700 years after his death she will be reborn as a princess in a small kingdom in South India, loved by all her people for her great beauty. Because of her devotion to the Buddhist teachings, her country will prosper and be transformed into a veritable paradise, and the kings of the neighboring states will all submit to her. Ultimately Ching-kuang would be asked to ascend the throne after the death of her father, at which time her rule would be accepted throughout the world. She will crush all heresy and annihilate those who slander the True Doctrine, while heaping honors on those who protect and hold fast to the Buddha's teaching. The Buddha goes on to say that Ching-kuang will succor the poor and lead countless sentient beings to enlightenment by teaching them to live according to the *Ta-yün ching*. After her death she will be transformed into a man[18] and reborn in the Pure Land of Amitābha Buddha before finally attaining Buddhahood under the name Ching-pao tseng-chang.

Despite certain apparent contradictions between the prophecy relating to Ching-kuang in the *Ta-yün ching* and events in the life of Empress Wu – the latter was born in North China, not South India, over fifteen hundred years after the death of the Buddha as it was then reckoned[19] – the sūtra contained ideas that could be cited to justify her assumption of the throne and the elimination of her opponents. Just as Ching-kuang, a devout follower of the Buddha, succeeds her father as ruler, so did Empress Wu, herself an ardent Buddhist, take her deceased husband's place on the throne. Both women create prosperous states and emerge as defenders of Buddhism, rewarding the faithful and punishing the wicked, which in Empress Wu's case, of course, includes her political opponents. Ching-kuang ultimately goes on to become the Buddha Ching-pao tseng-chang, whereas Empress Wu, as we shall see, declares herself to be Maitreya, the redeeming Buddha of the future. Judging from subsequent events there can be little doubt that Empress Wu decided to base her rule on the prophecies in this sūtra.[20]

A bare two months after Empress Wu was presented with a copy of this scripture, she announced the termination of the T'ang and the establishment of her own dynasty which was designated 'Chou'. Yet despite the Confucian ring to the name of the new dynasty, no time was lost in showing what its basic religious orientation would be. In the tenth month of 690 Empress Wu ordered that a Ta-yün ssu, 'Monastery for the *Ta-yün ching*,' should be established in each of the prefectures of the

Interregnum of Empress Wu (684–705) 43

empire as well as in the two capitals.²¹ In each of these official monasteries monks were required to lecture on the *Ta-yün ching*, as indeed were monks in ordinary monasteries throughout China.²² A group of sycophantic priests of dubious standing, headed by the infamous Hsüeh Huai-i, who was reputed to have been the Empress's lover, soon produced commentaries and apocrypha boldly proclaiming Empress Wu to be the earthly manifestation of Maitreya as well as the 'World Ruler' prophesied in the *Ta-yün ching*. A fragment of one such commentary found in Tunhuang openly identifies Empress Wu with Maitreya, justifies her extermination of 'brigands' as necessary for the purification of the Empire, and equates fabulous place-names in sūtras with actual places in China connected with events in the life of Empress Wu.²³ It even makes the remarkable assertion that the bodhisattva Maitreya must be a female since the name connotes compassion (*maitrī*), a feminine attribute.

In the fourth month of 691 an imperial edict formally ranked Buddhism above Taoism, thereby reversing the policy of the three preceding T'ang emperors, and ordered that henceforth Buddhist monks and nuns should take precedence over members of the Taoist clergy.²⁴ This action was taken, in the words of Empress Wu, because 'Buddhism opened the way for changing the Mandate of Heaven.'²⁵ A series of pro-Buddhist measures was promptly inaugurated: in 692, the slaughter of animals and catching of fish were forbidden, much to the annoyance of the Confucians who protested that such restrictions interfered with their sacrifices – the ban was finally dropped in 700;²⁶ in 693 Empress Wu assumed the title of Sagelike and Divine Sovereign of the Golden Wheel (Chin-lun Sheng-shen Huang-ti),²⁷ which is an unmistakable reference to the Buddhist concept of the idealized Universal Monarch (*cakravartin*, 'turner of the wheel [of the Law]') who rules in accordance with the high ethical principles of Buddhism; in 694 the status of the Buddhist clergy was raised by transferring jurisdiction over it from the Court for State Ceremonials (Hung-lu ssu), known since 684 as the Court in Charge of Foreign Visitors (Ssu-pin ssu),²⁸ to the Department of Sacrifices (Tz'u-pu) which oversaw the various rites that were performed on behalf of the imperial clan;²⁹ in the first month of 695 Empress Wu formally added the name Maitreya to her title, thereby combining in her person the secular authority of the Universal Monarch and the religious authority of the Future Buddha. The following month, however, she abruptly dropped the name Maitreya after arranging for the murder of Hsüeh Huai-i,³⁰ her reputed lover, who had taken an active role in producing the commentaries and apocrypha deifying the Empress.

Although Empress Wu evidently connived with the pseudo-monk Hsüeh Huai-i to use Buddhism for the enhancement of her image as a divine ruler, there can be little doubt about the genuineness of her piety or her determination to propagate the Buddhist faith. With the important exception of Hsüan-tsang, to whom T'ai-tsung developed a strong personal attachment in the last years of his life, there was hardly a single translator active between the founding of the T'ang and the death of Kao-tsung.[31] The situation changed radically, however, after 683. Empress Wu not only provided the financial support for a number of able translators but also personally participated in their work much as the Buddhist rulers of the fifth and sixth centuries had done. In 680 she ordered Divākara, who had arrived in China several years earlier, to do his translation of scripture in monasteries in Ch'ang-an and Lo-yang that she had established, and assigned ten monks to assist him.[32] For the longest of his translations, a biography of the Buddha in twelve fascicles entitled *Fang-kuang ta chuang-yen ching* (*Lalitavistara*) Empress Wu wrote a preface that still survives.[33] By the time of his death in 687 Divākara had translated a total of eighteen works, most of which had been completed under her patronage.

Similar support was provided for Bodhiruci who arrived in Ch'ang-an in 693.[34] He was installed in the Fo shou-chi ssu (Monastery of the Buddha's Prophecy), which Hsüeh Huai-i had built in Lo-yang two years earlier to commemorate Empress Wu's accession to the throne. Bodhiruci translated fifty-three texts before his death in 727, including most of the *Ta pao-chi ching*, which Hsüan-tsang had been unable to finish. When I-ching returned to China in 695 after his twenty-four year journey abroad in search of Buddhist manuscripts, he was personally greeted at the East Gate of Lo-yang by Empress Wu.[35] Like Bodhiruci, he was ordered to take up residence in the Fo shou-chi ssu, where he deposited four hundred Sanskrit manuscripts that he had brought back from India. In all, I-ching translated sixty-one texts in 239 fascicles, including such important works as the *Vinaya* of the Mūla Sarvāstivāda school and the *Chin kuang-ming ching* (*Sūtra of the Golden Light*; *Suvarṇa prabhāsa sūtra*). In the year 700 Empress Wu honored I-ching with a 'Preface for the Scriptures Newly Translated Under the Great Chou Dynasty' (*Ta Chou hsin-fan san-tsang sheng-chiao hsü*), which was placed at the beginning of the collection of his translations.[36] The importance that Empress Wu attached to translation of scriptures is evident from the large number of prefaces that she wrote for translators whom she patronized as well as from the active role that she played in sponsoring the translation of specific texts. At the urging of Fa-tsang, the systematizer of the Hua-yen school, she invited the Khotanese monk Śikṣānanda in 695 to come to China to assist in the preparation of a new Chinese version of the *Hua-yen ching* (*Avataṃsaka sūtra*).[37] The translation was begun in the imperial palace in Lo-yang with Empress Wu serving as a copyist and was completed four years later, in 699, at the Fo shou-chi ssu.[38]

In the history of Buddhist thought Empress Wu's reign is particularly notable for the official support that was given for the first time to two new schools: Ch'an and Hua-yen. The Ch'an school, which traces its origins to Bodhidharma, a semi-legendary meditation master who arrived in China in the late 470s. By the middle of the next century a number of Indian monks who were skilled in the practice of meditation were active in Ch'ang-an and Lo-yang, where they transmitted their various techniques to Chinese disciples.[39] Although some Ch'an centers, notably those of Mt Huang-mei[40] in Ch'i-chou (in the present-day Hupeh) and Mt Niu-t'ou[41] (in the present-day Kiangsu), had large numbers of monks in residence, they seem to have been ignored by the early T'ang rulers. Empress Wu's contacts with Ch'an masters began several years after she ascended the throne. In 695, the year that she welcomed I-ching back to China, she invited the Ch'an master, Jen-chien, to the court to question him about the Ch'an teaching.[42] The following year Jen-chien's master, Hui-an, who had been a direct disciple of Hung-jen, the Fifth Patriarch of the Ch'an school, was summoned to the court to lecture, for which he was awarded the honorary title National Teacher (*kuo-shih*).[43] Chih-hsien, another of Hung-jen's disciples, who introduced Ch'an into Szechwan, was called to the capital by Empress Wu in 697.[44]

Of all the Ch'an monks patronized by Empress Wu the most important was Shen-hsiu, the founder of the Northern Ch'an school, who had been recognized as the Sixth Patriarch until challenged by Shen-hui in 732.[45] Shen-hsiu, who was the leading disciple of Hung-jen, settled near the famous Yü-ch'üan Monastery in Ching-chou (in the present-day Hupeh) after the death of his master.[46] Here he built a hermitage, the Tu-men Lan-jo, which soon became a leading Ch'an center. Shen-hsiu enjoyed great popularity, as is evident from the fact that he had seventy major disciples and a very large number of lay supporters, many of whom were persons of considerable standing. Among the latter was Sung Chih-wen, a well-known poet holding an appointment at the court. Sung, aware of the Empress's growing interest in Ch'an, urged her to invite Shen-hsiu to the court, which she did in the year 700. The ninety-year old Ch'an master arrived in Lo-yang the following year in grand style, carried aloft into the palace in a palanquin. So great was Empress Wu's respect for Shen-hsiu that when they met in the audience chamber, she did obeisance before him by sinking to her knees while he sat with legs folded in the meditative position. Shen-hsiu gained an enormous following in Ch'ang-an and Lo-yang that included many prominent officials. In recognition of his high standing he was awarded the unprecedented title of Master of the Dharma in the Two Capitals and National Teacher of Three Rulers (*liang-ching fa-chu san ti kuo-shih*).[47] When Shen-hsiu died in 706, he was given the posthumous name Ta-t'ung Ch'an-shih (The Ch'an Master Ta-t'ung), which was the first time that the title Ch'an Master had been bestowed by the court.[48] Secular historians gave formal recognition to Shen-hsiu's influence at the court by including his biography in the official history of the T'ang – an honor accorded to only two other monks.[49]

In contrast to her interest in Ch'an which was expressed by inviting at least eight Ch'an masters to the court, Empress Wu's patronage of the newly arisen Hua-yen school stemmed from her relationship with a single monk, Fa-tsang, who is regarded as the Third Patriarch and systematizer of the doctrines of this school.[50] Unlike other monks who were supported by her at one stage or another of their careers, Fa-tsang enjoyed her patronage virtually throughout his entire religious life. Born in Ch'ang-an of Sogdian ancestry, Fa-tsang began his religious training at the age of fifteen by undertaking a pilgrimage to the Fa-men ssu, where he burnt off a finger as an offering to a relic of the Buddha. It should be noted that this was the same relic that Empress Wu had enshrined in a gold and silver case in 660. After several years' study on T'ai-po shan, Fa-tsang returned to Ch'ang-an, where he eventually became a disciple of Chih-yen, an extremely learned monk who is regarded as the Second Patriarch of the Hua-yen school. Fa-tsang was introduced by two other disciples of Chih-yen to Empress Wu in 670 when she was in search of monks to assign to the T'ai-yüan ssu in Ch'ang-an which she had just established in memory of her mother. Curiously, Fa-tsang, who was then twenty-seven years of age, was still not tonsured despite his long residence in various monasteries. Empress Wu, apparently impressed by his considerable learning, ordered that he should be tonsured forthwith and appointed abbot of the T'ai-yüan ssu, a post that would, of course, keep him close to the Empress. Four years later, ten senior monks of Ch'ang-an, at the command of the Empress, administered the full ordination to Fa-tsang. To commemorate the occasion the Empress bestowed on Fa-tsang the honorific name Hsien-shou, by which both he and his school are commonly referred to today.

Fa-tsang lectured on the *Hua-yen ching* more than thirty times and played an important part in the translation activities sponsored by Empress Wu. It was largely due to his urging that the voluminous *Hua-yen ching* was retranslated by Śikṣānanda. Although basically a man of scholarship – twenty-three of his works still survive – Fa-tsang was frequently called upon by Empress Wu to offer prayers for rain or for the defeat of her enemies.

Fa-tsang continued to be held in high esteem by the court even after the deposition of Empress Wu in the first month of 705. Chung-tsung, who reascended the throne following the coup d'état that removed his mother from power, requested Fa-tsang to pray for the success of the forces fighting for the restoration of the T'ang. As a token of his appreciation of Fa-tsang's support, Chung-tsung commissioned a portrait of the monk bearing a eulogy. Three years later Chung-tsung agreed to Fa-tsang's proposal that 'Hua-yen Monasteries' should be established in Ch'ang-an and Lo-yang as well as in the Wu-t'ai mountains and the Wu-yüeh region, both traditional Buddhist strongholds. These monasteries were to serve as centers for Hua-yen learning, where the basic treatises of this school would be studied. After Fa-tsang offered successful prayers for rain during the same year (708), Chung-tsung granted him still another honorific title, Kuo-i, 'First in the Empire.' Fa-tsang was similarly venerated by Jui-tsung who came to the throne in 710 after Chung-tsung's death. Honors of every sort were heaped upon him, and when he died at the age of 69 in 712, he was granted a posthumous court rank.

Reign of Chung-tsung (705–710)

The deposition of Empress Wu in the first month of 705 had little immediate affect on the privileged position that Buddhism had acquired during her rule. Her son, the Emperor Chung-tsung, who had reigned for a brief fifty-five days following the death of his father, Kao-tsung, reassumed the throne on his mother's forced retirement and promptly announced the re-establishment of the T'ang dynasty. Yet aside from restoring Lao-tzu's honorific appellation, Hsüan-yüan Huang-ti, which Kao-tsung had conferred on the legendary ancestor of the Li family and Empress Wu had subsequently revoked,[1] Chung-tsung, a weak man like his father, did little to restore Taoism to the place it had occupied prior to his mother's usurpation of the throne. Some eight months after becoming emperor he issued an edict prohibiting Taoist temples from exhibiting paintings of Lao-tzu that depicted him as the Buddha converting barbarians.[2] Chung-tsung pointed out that since the spurious

Lao-tzu hua-hu ching had already been banned by earlier rulers anyone who now attempted to circulate the text would be punished. With regard to this text, which was offensive to the Buddhists, Chung-tsung actually took a firmer stand than his mother, who merely ordered her court-scholars to discuss the issue when the Buddhists protested the continued use of the *Lao-tzu hua-hu ching* by the Taoists. It appears that Empress Wu deferred to the opinion of her advisers who held that the *Lao-tzu hua-hu ching* must indeed have some basis in fact since the story of Lao-tzu's transformation into the Buddha was already mentioned in the *Hou Han shu*.[3]

To celebrate the revival of the T'ang, Chung-tsung ordered the establishment of one Buddhist monastery and one Taoist temple in each prefecture, to be designated respectively Chung-hsing ssu and Chung-hsing kuan, the word '*chung-hsing*' signifying 'restoration.'[4] The idea of a network of state-supported monasteries and temples, as we have seen, was not a new one for the T'ang: Kao-tsung had issued a decree in the year 666 calling for the construction of such monasteries and temples in each of the prefectures. Similarly, the Ta-yün monasteries established by Empress Wu to commemorate the new Chou dynasty that she had founded should also be included in this category. As was the case with the Ta-yün monasteries, most of the Chung-hsing monasteries were in fact large local monasteries that were simply redesignated Chung-hsing ssu. In several cases, former Ta-yün ssu had their names summarily changed to Chung-hsing ssu.[5] Shortly after the edict on the creation of the Chung-hsing ssu was issued, Chung-tsung received a memorial protesting the use of the term of *chung-hsing* on the grounds that it suggested that the T'ang dynasty had been interrupted, whereas the main lineage of the Li family had actually survived intact.[6] It was proposed, therefore, that the auspicious-sounding designation *lung-hsing*, 'resurgence' (literally, 'bestirring of the dragon'), replace the term *chung-hsing* with its negative implications. The advice was accepted, and in the second month of 707 an edict was issued redesignating the Buddhist monasteries and Taoist temples 'Lung-hsing ssu' and 'Lung-hsing kuan.'[7] The edict stipulated that the term *chung-hsing* might no longer be used in the names of monasteries.

Chung-tsung, who spent the first eight years of his life under the tutelage of Hsüan-tsang and who had been pledged to enter the Buddhist order, seems to have been the first male T'ang ruler who was a thoroughly devout Buddhist. He began his reign in 705 with a series of pious acts: a visit to a temple at Lung-men,[8] an invitation to a group of monks to spend their summer retreat at the imperial palace coupled with a request to them that he be permitted to receive the bodhisattva vows,[9] the granting of an imperial preface to honor I-ching's translations,[10] and an order that henceforth aspirants to the priesthood would be required to pass an examination on the Buddhist scripture before they could be ordained,[11] which was an attemple to raise the intellectual level of the clergy. Throughout his five years on the throne, Chung-tsung was in all respects a model Buddhist emperor. In 706 he assisted the translator Bodhiruci, serving as a copyist. During the same year he bestowed a posthumous name on Shen-hsiu who had just died, and granted the purple robe to Hui-an, a Ch'an master called to the court in 696.[12] Fourteen of the latter's disciples were permitted to receive ordination at this time. Chung-tsung generously awarded honorary court titles to at least ten eminent monks. In 707 he invited several famous Vinaya masters to the palace to administer the precepts and even praised one of these, Tao-an, for refusing to rise from his seat even in the presence of the Emperor. When Śikṣānanda, the translator of the *Hua-yen ching*, returned from Khotan in 708, the Emperor, following the example set by his mother, personally welcomed him back at the city gates.[13] Later in the same year he had the finger-bone relic brought to the imperial palace for worship and had discussions with the famous Central Asian thaumaturge, Seng-ch'ieh.[14] In 710 Chung-tsung ordered that a great vegetarian banquet for the clergy be held at the magnificent Hua-tu Monastery in Ch'ang-an.[15] Yet for all his piety Emperor Chung-tsung, who had once suffered the indignity of being deposed from the throne and had spent long years in exile, was unable to escape a tragic death. His consort, the Empress Wei, apparently inspired by the example of her mother-in-law, poisoned the Emperor in the sixth month of 710 in an attempt to seize the throne for her own family. A nephew of the murdered emperor, Li Lung-chi, moved quickly to prevent another usurpation. Lung-chi killed Empress Wei and other members of her family involved in the plot and put his own father, the former Emperor Jui-tsung, back on the throne, Lung-chi retaining for himself the title of Crown Prince.

Reign of Jui-tsung (710–712)

Although Jui-tsung's reign lasted little more than two years, it is particularly significant because it was under this Emperor that the pro-Buddhist policies pursued by Empress Wu and her son, Chung-tsung, for over half a century were reversed. No sooner had Jui-tsung ascended the throne in the seventh month of the year 710 than he issued an edict stripping Buddhism of the superior status that had been accorded it over

Taoism in 691.¹ The edict stipulated that the two religions should henceforth be placed on an equal footing, since both Buddhism and Taoism pursued the common goal of redeeming mankind and enlightening the ignorant. The following month an auspicious omen for the T'ang was discovered: a persimmon tree in the garden of Kao-tsu's former mansion which had withered when Empress Wu usurped the throne suddenly began to send forth new blossoms – clearly a sign that the T'ang would spring to life again. Officials were advanced in rank and an amnesty was proclaimed. Although Buddhist sources state the Emperor authorized on this occasion the ordination of thirty thousand Buddhist and Taoist monks, this would appear unlikely, since, as we shall see, one of the major aims of the T'ang after the restoration carried out by Li Lung-chi was to achieve a reduction in the number of monks and monasteries. Probably the thirty thousand persons mentioned in the Buddhist sources as being ordained on this occasion were simply 'illegal monks' (*lan-tu seng*) who took advantage of the amnesty to legitimize their status.²

One year after Jui-tsung assumed the throne, he received a bitter memorial from Hsin T'i-p'i denouncing the hold that the Buddhists had taken on the country.³ Although much of his argument was couched in the stereotyped language commonly found in anti-Buddhist polemics, the reader cannot but be impressed by the picture of the staggering wealth acquired by the church since the time of Empress Wu as well as by the widespread corruption. Hsin observed with irony: 'Nowadays all men with money or power have become candidates for the Buddhist priesthood;⁴ all those who would avoid corvée or indulge in deception are now novices. It is only the poor and the virtuous who have not been ordained ... seventy or eighty percent of the wealth of the Empire is in the hands of the Buddhists.'⁵ In spite of the obvious overstatement, Hsin's description of the church at this time no doubt largely rang true. Jui-tsung issued an edict, perhaps in response to Hsin's memorial, criticizing Buddhist monasteries and Taoist temples for occupying extensive tracts of land and operating water-mills.⁶ He directed local officials to carry out investigations and authorized the confiscation of land that had been illegally acquired. In 712 a still more drastic step was taken to curb the Buddhist church, when it was decreed that all monasteries lacking a tablet of official sanction (*ming-o*)⁷ would be dismantled and their metal images sent to other monasteries in the area.⁸ It seems doubtful, however, that this edict was actually enforced since, as we shall see, Hsüan-tsung was compelled to issue a similar edict some fifteen years later.

Reign of Hsüan-tsung (712–756)

Hsüan-tsung was twenty-seven years of age when he succeeded to the throne upon his father's abdication in 712. During the first half of his reign, which was the longest of any T'ang emperor, Hsüan-tsung, surrounded by a host of able ministers, carried out a series of far-reaching economic and administrative reforms that resulted in great prosperity. Aware of the church's enormous drain on the resources of the state, he acted with greater determination than any of his predecessors to curtail the power of the Buddhist clergy and to bring it firmly under the control of the government. Secure in his position as emperor, he was not loath to adopt strong, innovative measures which antagonized the Buddhists. That he ultimately failed, as did his predecessors, to weaken the church effectively was due as much to the real support that Buddhism enjoyed on all levels of society as to his own loss of interest in the affairs of government during the second half of his reign.

Hsüan-tsung lost no time in tackling the 'Buddhist problem.' In 713, one year after he had ascended the throne, he issued an edict forbidding members of the aristocracy to petition monasteries for permission to establish Buddhist or Taoist temples on their estates.[1] Hsüan-tsung's concern at this time was probably not aimed primarily at bona fide donations of land to monasteries, but rather at the creation of 'merit cloisters' (*kung-te yüan*), a subterfuge commonly employed, especially in Sung times, by the aristocracy and high officials to evade taxes.[2] In the first month of 714, in response to a memorial from Yao Ch'ung denouncing the widespread use of ordinations by powerful families to escape taxation, Hsüan-tsung ordered a massive purging of the clergy, which resulted in the laicization of more than thirty thousand monks and nuns – a figure perhaps equal to one fourth of the Buddhist order at that time.[3] The following month he took a far more drastic step: a ban was placed on the construction of all new monasteries. Existing monasteries could be repaired only when authorized by government officials who had actually inspected the monasteries and ascertained the need for such repairs.[4] As we have already noted, it was during the second month of 714 that Hsüan-tsung attempted unsuccessfully to compel monks and nuns to reverence their parents. In the seventh month of the same year officials were prohibited from associating with members of the Buddhist and Taoist clergies or providing lodging for them in their homes.[5] Finally, later still in the same month, laymen were forbidden to cast images or copy sūtras.[6] As the edict bluntly put it: 'Those who feel the need to venerate sacred images should go to monasteries for worship; those who would recite scriptures should order them to be read at monasteries.'[7] Lest there be any doubt about the place of the clergy in this new order, a series of edicts was issued instructing the clergy to refrain from proselytizing in the villages, misleading the common people with stories of miraculous happenings, soliciting money, or frequenting marketplaces.[8] Monks and nuns were to lecture to laymen only in monasteries, and their discourses were to be restricted to those matters dealt with in the *Vinaya*. Furthermore, the clergy was prohibited from leading laymen in worship in afternoon or evening services on the grounds that the *Vinaya* proscribed all activities by monks and nuns after the noon hour.[9] In 722, after a lapse of eight years, Hsüan-tsung resumed his efforts to curtail the wealth of the Buddhist church. He instructed the Department of Sacrifices (Tz'u-pu), which since 691 had responsibility for Buddhist and Taoist affairs, to investigate the titles to lands allegedly belonging to Buddhist monasteries and Taoist temples.[10] It was specified that all holdings in excess of the land alloted to the clergy – presumably a reference to the thirty *mou* of land granted to each monk and twenty *mou* to each nun under the 'equal field system' – were to be confiscated. Furthermore precise limits were set on the amount of land that might be owned in perpetuity (*ch'ang-chu-t'ien*) by a monastery. A maximum of ten *ch'ing* was to be allowed for a monastery that accommodated more than one hundred persons, seven *ch'ing* for a monastery with between fifty and one hundred residents, and five *ch'ing* for a monastery with less than fifty persons. Five years later, apparently in the hope of turning the Buddhist church into a completely state-dominated institution, Hsüan-tsung ordered the dismantlement of all village chapels (*ts'un-fang*) and small Buddhist shrines (*fo-t'ang*), stipulating that the religious objects that had been installed in them should be transferred to officially recognized monasteries in their vicinity.[11] The larger Buddhist shrines in the villages were to be closed down but not destroyed, presumably so that they could be requisitioned to serve other purposes. While there is no evidence indicating whether the edict restricting the size of monastic estates was ever enforced, it is asserted in a Buddhist source that the ban on village chapels resulted in the loss of many buildings and images.[12]

Having closed down the unofficial village temples, Hsüan-tsung next turned his attention to the monks in the recognized monasteries. He decreed in the year 729 that a complete register of monks throughout the empire be compiled every three years.[13] Each register was to be prepared in three copies: one copy was to be sent to the Department of Sacrifices (Tz'u-pu), which had jurisdiction over the Buddhist and Taoist churches, the second copy was to be submitted to the Court for State

Ceremonials (Hung-lu ssu), which oversaw foreign affairs, and the third copy was to be retained by the local authority.[14] Hsüan-tsung declared that his intention in ordering the compilation of registers of monks was to have some standard for distinguishing true monks from fraudulent ones.[15] It now remained for Hsüan-tsung to undo the last remaining advantage that Buddhism still enjoyed from the reign of Empress Wu. In 736 he ordered that jurisdiction over Buddhist affairs be transferred from the Department of Sacrifices to the Court for State Ceremonials, the government office responsible for foreign affairs that had been in charge of matters relating to the Buddhist church until Empress Wu's intervention in 694.[16] The following year the Taoists were placed once again under the jurisdiction of the Court of Imperial Clan Affairs (Tsung-cheng ssu), a move calculated to restore to the Taoists the prestigious position they had held before Empress Wu's usurpation. In 743, when Hsüan-tsung had already come under the influence of the great esoteric master Pu-k'ung (see below, pp. 56–7), he returned control of the Buddhist clergy to the Department of Sacrifices (Tz'u-pu) and shifted the responsibility for overseeing the Taoist priests and nuns from the Court of Imperial Clan Affairs to the Office for Peerage Ranks (Ssu-feng).[17]

Although none of the T'ang emperors before Hsüan-tsung, with the sole exception of Chung-tsung, could be described as enthusiastic Buddhists and all attempted through one means or another to bring the church to heel, they nevertheless felt obliged to pay lip service to Buddhism and make certain concessions in the realization that Buddhism had a great hold on their subjects. T'ai-tsung, despite his avowed personal distaste for Buddhism, built the magnificent Hung-fu ssu in Ch'ang-an and, even before coming under the influence of Hsüan-tsang, had authorized the ordination of thousands of monks. And Kao-tsung, who stubbornly refused to yield to the deathbed pleas of Hsüan-tsang to grant Buddhism equal status with Taoism and sought to compel monks and nuns to reverence their lay superiors, nevertheless built two of the grandest monasteries in Ch'ang-an, the Hsi-ming ssu and the Ta tz'u-en ssu. Viewed in this light, Hsüan-tsung's extraordinarily long reign is unique in that it does not contain a single outstanding example of imperial support for Buddhism as evidenced in the building of monasteries, mass ordination of monks, or imperial participation in major Buddhist rites.[18] Nevertheless Hsüan-tsung, like his predecessors, could not but be aware of the political advantages that accrued from using Buddhist monasteries to strengthen the tie between the Buddhist populace and the imperial family. In 738 he ordered that still another

The first half of the T'ang (618–762)

network of state-supported Buddhist monasteries and Taoist temples bearing the designation K'ai-yüan after the era-name then in use should be established in the two capitals as well as in each of the prefectures.[19] It should be noted that many of the Buddhist K'ai-yüan monasteries were created by simply redesignating the Ta-yün monasteries established half a century earlier by Empress Wu.[20] The K'ai-yüan ssu were not intended to promote either Buddhist learning or piety but were merely to serve as regional centers where prayers for the well-being of the emperor were to be offered at specified periods in a setting that would appeal to the religious feelings of his Buddhist subjects. The Lung-hsing monasteries founded by Chung-tsung were retained and charged with the responsibility of conducting masses for the deceased T'ang rulers; the K'ai-yüan monasteries celebrated the birthday of the reigning emperor and offered prayers for his longevity.[21] The practice of requiring Buddhist monasteries to commemorate imperial birthdays did not, in fact, begin with the creation of the K'ai-yüan monasteries in 738; already eight years earlier Hsüan-tsung had decreed that all Buddhist monasteries and Taoist temples should assign a hall for services to celebrate the birthday of the emperor.[22] To emphasize the relationship between the K'ai-yüan monasteries and the imperial person, the former were ordered in 744 to install images of the Buddha in the likeness of the emperor.[23]

At first glance it might seem paradoxical that Hsüan-tsung, in spite of his antipathy toward traditional forms of Buddhist doctrine and practice, should have maintained close relations with a number of monks and provided support for the translation of Buddhist scriptures. When, however, we examine the background of those Chinese and Indian monks who enjoyed imperial favor during his reign, it becomes apparent that the Emperor's interest in them stemmed from the fact that they were all practitioners of Esoteric Buddhism (*mi-chiao*).[24] Esoteric texts had been trickling into China steadily since the fourth century, but it was only under the reign of Hsüan-tsung that Esoteric Buddhism first received active encouragement and official recognition. The reason for this emperor's enthusiasm for this new type of Buddhism[25] is readily understandable if we bear in mind Hsüan-tsung's fascination with Taoism,[26] which made use of ritual practices similar to those employed in Esoteric Buddhism such as astrology, incantations, mystical trances, and the like.

Hsüan-tsung's first contacts with monks of the Esoteric tradition came early in his reign. In the year 716 the Indian Tantric master, Śubhakara-siṃha (known in China as Shan-wu-wei) arrived in Ch'ang-an with a collection of Sanskrit texts.[27] According to an early source, he was well received by Hsüan-tsung, who made him compete with a Chinese thaumaturge in a test of magical skills.[28] The following year, with the help of Chinese assistants, the most prominent of whom was I-hsing, Shan-wu-wei began his career as a translator. In 724 he was ordered to accompany the imperial cortege to Lo-yang, where he translated the *Ta-jih ching*,[29] in close collaboration with I-hsing, who compiled the authoritative commentary on the text.

Śubhakarasiṃha, who worked in the great imperial monasteries founded by the early T'ang rulers, was frequently invited to court where he was asked to perform tantric rituals such as praying for rain. By the time of his death in 735, he had translated twenty-one Esoteric texts. So great were his powers believed to be that his mummified remains continued to be beseeched in Sung times in period of drought.[30]

The other important Indian Tantric master who received Hsüan-tsung's patronage was Vajrabodhi, known in China as Chin-kang-chih, who arrived in Canton in 719 after a one-year stay in Sri Lanka, then a center of Esoteric Buddhism.[31] When he reached Ch'ang-an later in the same year, an imperial decree was issued instructing him to take up residence in the Ta tz'u-en ssu, where Hsüan-tsang had worked. The following year he proceeded to Lo-yang for an audience with Hsüan-tsung, who subsequently designated him National Teacher (Kuo-shih). Vajrabodhi frequently accompanied the Emperor on his travels between Ch'ang-an and Lo-yang. As an indication of imperial backing he was permitted to reside and work in the great state-supported monasteries such as the Tzu-sheng ssu and the Ta chien-fu ssu where he established altars for Esoteric ordinations.[32] It is clear that Hsüan-tsung was interested in Vajrabodhi chiefly because of the latter's reputed magical talents.[33] Thus when drought threatened in 726, Vajrabodhi, at the request of the Emperor, performed various Esoteric rites to avert the impending disaster. Similarly his services were called upon when the Emperor's favorite daughter was taken seriously ill. Vajrabodhi's primary contribution to the development of Esoteric Buddhism in China was his transmission in 723 of the *Lüeh-ch'u nien-sung ching*.[34] This work and the *Ta-jih ching* mentioned above are regarded as the two major scriptures of Esoteric Buddhism. In all, Vajrabodhi translated twenty-five texts before his death in 741.

The two monks who were closest to Hsüan-tsung and who contributed most to the development of Esoteric Buddhism in East Asia were I-hsing and Pu-k'ung. I-hsing was one of the most learned monks of his day, having studied under prominent scholars of the Ch'an, T'ien-t'ai, and Lü (Vinaya) schools before being summoned to the Palace in 717 by

Hsüan-tsung, who had heard reports of I-hsing's knowledge of Taoist magical arts, divination, astronomy, and the calendar, which were subjects of particular interest to the emperor.[35] That I-hsing should be so well versed in Taoist learning is not surprising considering that he had studied under a Taoist priest before becoming a Buddhist monk, a fact not mentioned in Buddhist sources.[36] He is even said to have written a number of works, now lost, on Taoist practices, presumably before his ordination. When Vajrabodhi arrived in Ch'ang-an in 719, I-hsing immediately went to him for instruction and was granted an Esoteric consecration (*kuan-ting*).[37] After studying with Vajrabodhi for several years, I-hsing became an assistant to Śubhakarasiṃha, the other great Tantric master active in China at this time, and served as a copyist when the latter translated the *Ta-jih ching*. Basing himself on Śubhakarasiṃha's lectures that were given during the course of the translation, I-hsing wrote what has come to be regarded as the definitive commentary on this extremely important scripture.[38] I-hsing also made valuable contributions in other fields as well, the most noteworthy being his work on the calendar. In 721 Hsüan-tsung instructed him to devise a new calendar to replace the defective Lin-te calendar that had been in use since the year 666. He completed the draft of the new calendar, known as the Ta-yen li, six years later. Officially adopted in 729, the Ta-yen calendar remained in force in China until 757 and in Japan until 858. When I-hsing died in 727 at age forty-four, Hsüan-tsung conferred on him the posthumous name of Ta-hui Ch'an-shih and authorized an outlay of 500,000 cash for the erection of a pagoda in his memory, Hsüan-tsung himself writing the eulogy for the stele.[39]

In contrast to I-hsing who is well known for his scholarly contributions to scriptural exegesis and for his studies of such secular subjects as astronomy and mathematics, Pu-k'ung distinguished himself as a proselytizer, thaumaturge, and translator. Although born in Central Asia of an Indian father and a Sogdian mother, Pu-k'ung, who is also known by his Sanskrit religious name Amoghavajra, must be regarded primarily as a Chinese tantric master since he was brought to China at the age of nine.[40] When Vajrabodhi arrived in Ch'ang-an in 719, Pu-k'ung, then fourteen years of age, became his disciple and subsequently learned Sanskrit from him. It was probably while Pu-k'ung was assisting Vajrabodhi that he first came to the notice of Hsüan-tsung, who apparently was impressed by his potential magical skills. According to one account, when an insurrection broke out in the An-hsi region in 742, Hsüan-tsung summoned Pu-k'ung to court to offer prayers for victory.[41] Pu-k'ung chanted a sūtra dedicated to the protection of the empire and uttered mystical incantations while Hsüan-tsung held an incense burner. In due course the Emperor saw an apparition of an army of heavenly beings who, Pu-k'ung asserted, would crush the rebels in An-hsi. A few months later, the account concludes, Hsüan-tsung received a letter from his field headquarters reporting that the rebels had fled because of divine intervention. Sometime after the death of his master in 741 Pu-k'ung decided to visit Sri Lanka and India to collect tantric texts. Before boarding ship in Kuang-chou, he presided over the first mass Esoteric ordinations in China. Upon his return in 746 he was again invited to the imperial palace, where he built an altar for Tantric rites and performed a high-level Esoteric consecration (*kuan-ting*; *abhiṣeka*) for Hsüan-tsung. During the next few years Pu-k'ung was regularly called upon by the Emperor whenever disaster threatened.

In 750 Pu-k'ung, perhaps sensing the gradual shift of real power to the military governorships, quit the court to accept the patronage of Ko-shu Han, the military governor of Ho-hsi, where Pu-k'ung subsequently gained many lay disciples among prominent army officers. Pu-k'ung reached Ko-shu Han's headquarters by a circuitous route. He first sought permission from Hsüan-tsung to return to Sri Lanka, but after leaving the capital he was taken ill. Somehow Ko-shu Han learned of this and appealed to Hsüan-tsung to allow the ailing Pu-k'ung to recuperate in Ho-hsi, where he could perform the meritorious work of spreading the Dharma.[42] It seems entirely possible that Pu-k'ung's illness was a ruse to mask his decision to establish himself among the military officers whose power was steadily growing. During the year 753, at the request of Ko-shu Han, he translated four tantras, one of which was another version of the *Lüeh-ch'u nien-sung ching*. Instead of imperial princes and ranking ministers serving as copyists, it was now military officials and their civilian advisers who performed this task. During his stay at Ko-shu Han's field headquarters Pu-k'ung administered the Tantric consecration to several thousand persons.[43]

Reign of Su-tsung (756–762)

Soon after the An Lu-shan rebellion broke out at the end of 755, Pu-k'ung was urgently summoned back to the court at Ch'ang-an to pray for the victory of the imperial forces as he is said to have done once before in 742. He reached Ch'ang-an in the fifth month of 756 and took up residence in the Ta hsing-shan ssu, a great monastery founded by Emperor Wen of the Sui in 582, where he erected an altar for esoteric rites and devoted himself to prayer. When the loyalist army was forced to abandon Ch'ang-an during the following month, Pu-k'ung briefly fell into enemy hands, but through secret emissaries maintained contact with the imperial headquarters, to which he sent copies of tantras whose supernatural powers could help the imperial cause along with a prophecy forecasting the precise date of victory. In the tenth month of 757 the new emperor, Su-tsung (reigned 756–762), who had ascended the throne in Ling-wu (in present-day Ning-hsia) in the seventh month of 756 following his father's forced abdication, reentered Ch'ang-an and freed Pu-k'ung, who was asked to undertake the ritual purification of the palace. Pu-k'ung further strengthened the links between the imperial family and the Esoteric school by using tantric rites to consecreate Su-tsung as a Universal Monarch. In 758 Pu-k'ung was permitted to bring together in a single collection the Sanskrit manuscripts brought to China by Hsüan-tsang, I-ching, Bodhiruci and other great translators which had been held in various monasteries in Ch'ang-an and was promised government support for the translation of some of these texts. As an indication of the official position that Esoteric Buddhism now held at the court, Pu-k'ung was allowed to establish a chapel in the imperial palace at which the *homa* (*hu-mo*) ritual could be performed.[1]

The turmoil accompanying An Lu-shan's insurrection and the impending collapse of the social order produced a religious frenzy at Su-tsung's court. No sooner had the new emperor ascended the throne than he was urged to seek the aid of the Buddha in destroying the rebels.[2] One of his first acts was to have the famous finger-bone relic of the Buddha brought from the Fa-men ssu in Feng-hsiang to the newly established chapel in the palace where it could be worshipped throughout the day.[3] Several hundred monks were assigned to the palace chapel to invoke the name of the Buddha in the mornings and evenings which they did with such gusto that a minister was forced to complain that their incessant chanting could be heard even beyond the palace walls.[4] In addition to the almost endless round of religious services at the court, Su-tsung, following the precedent established by Yang Chien when he founded the Sui dynasty, ordered the construction of monasteries on each of the five sacred mountains.[5] Meanwhile, his father, the former Emperor Hsüan-tsung, who had sought so hard to curtail the power and wealth of the church, was sufficiently frightened by the turn of events to make a grant of 1,000 *mou* of land for the construction of an imposing monastery in the city of Ch'eng-tu where he had taken refuge. As an indication of respect for the autonomy of the clergy, Su-tsung decreed in 760 that monks should no longer refer to themselves as *ch'en*, 'Your Subject,' when addressing the throne.[6] The following year the emperor arranged for a bizarre religious drama to be enacted in the newly completed chapel in the Lin-te Hall of the Ta-ming Palace. His ministers were summoned to render homage to palace attendants who were dressed as Buddhas and bodhisattvas, while army officers portrayed the guardian spirits of Buddhism (*chin-kang shen-wang*).[7] It is not surprising, then, that with such fanaticism rampant the Empress should show her devotion by offering prayers for her ailing husband by copying sūtras in her own blood.[8]

The effects of the An Lu-Shan rebellion on the Buddhist church

Although An Lu-shan himself was killed by his own son fourteen months after he rebelled against the T'ang, intense civil wars continued to rage back and forth over North China until 763. The seven years of almost continuous warfare had far-reaching effects not only on the subsequent political, economic, and social structure of China but also on the development of Buddhist doctrine as well as on the status of the church. Despite the staggering losses that the T'ang suffered during the early years of the rebellion, the imperial family did manage ultimately to triumph over its adversaries. But for its victory the T'ang paid a high price: much of the actual military power had passed into the hands of military governors who often acted as independent satraps, ignoring orders from the capital and pocketing tax revenues. The An Lu-shan rebellion with its inevitable disruption of the economy left the government with an empty treasury at a time when it was extremely hard-pressed for funds to meet military expenditures.

Faced with the very real possibility of collapse during the rebellion and in desperate need of money to finance the war, the T'ang rulers sought some means by which they could tap the formidable resources of the church. With the political and military power of the state weakened and strong contenders in the field, clearly an attempt to bully the church into surrendering some of its wealth could prove disastrous. Shortly after the outbreak of the rebellion it became apparent to some officials that a quick way of raising revenue might be to authorize ordinations for all those who could pay the government for the privilege of being admitted to the clergy. The decision to allow unrestricted ordinations signified the reversal of one of the most fundamental policies of the T'ang toward the Buddhist church, since it might open the way for an unchecked growth in the size of the clergy. It was also a course fraught with fiscal dangers, because duly ordained monks and nuns were exempt from taxation. Thus while unrestricted ordinations might bring in much needed revenue in the shortrun, they ultimately would contribute to the financial ruination of the dynasty.

The first large-scale attempt by the government to raise money through ordinations was carried out in 755, immediately after the outbreak of the rebellion, when a ranking minister, Yang Kuo-chung, dispatched an official to T'ai-yüan to raise money through the ordination of Buddhist monks and nuns and, also, Taoist priests.[1] This abrupt change in policy was enormously successful. In the short span of ten days a million strings of cash were obtained through such ordinations.[2] The following year, two high-level officials, P'ei Mien and Cheng Shu-ch'ing, formally proposed the sale of blank letters of appointment (*k'ung-ming kao-shen*), which would enable the holder to assume a specified title or rank or to claim the status of a member of the clergy. In the year 757 more than ten thousand persons in the Ch'ang-an region sought ordination as either Taoist priests or Buddhist monks after paying the requisite sum of one hundred strings of cash.[3] The fee paid to the government for the ordination certificate was euphemistically designated 'money for the purchase of scented water' (*hsiang-shui ch'ien*). It should be noted that although Buddhist sources assert that the sale of ordination certificates began at this time, there are references to the practice as far back as the reigns of Chung-tsung and Jui-tsung.[4] It was only in the reign of Su-tsung, however, that the practice became official policy.

The sale of ordination certificates continued throughout the remainder of the T'ang with disastrous effects for both the government and the church. Although initially authorized as a wartime expedient for raising revenues for the central government, the sale of ordination certificates soon proved to be a lucrative business for local officials. There are a number of instances of provincial officials in the first half of the ninth century lining their pockets with the receipts from such ordinations. Despite the fact that the practice of locally authorized ordinations had been forbidden in 807, it nevertheless persisted in the provinces. A revealing memorial by Li Te-yü dated 824 describes how Wang Chih-hsing, the civil governor (*kuan-ch'a shih*) of Hsü-chou and Ssu-chou (in present-day Kiangsu), acquired great wealth through the sale of ordination certificates in spite of the prohibition against this practice.[5] According to Li, one out of three male adults in Ssu-chou had taken the tonsure to avoid taxation. He estimated that of the more than one hundred monks that he examined daily at a checkpoint at the Yangtze crossing at Suan-shan only fourteen had previously served as novices (*sha-mi, śrāmaṇera*), the remainder being common people with no previous religious training. The ordination itself was little more than a commercial transaction: upon arrival at the ordination platform that Wang had built, the candidate, whose head had already been shaven, would make a payment of two strings of cash for which he would be issued an ordination certificate. Once he had received the certificate, the candidate would return home without even participating in a religious ceremony. Li Te-yü ended his memorial with a warning that if strong action was not taken to enforce the ban on such activities before the forthcoming celebration of the Emperor's birthday – no doubt a suitable occasion for promoting ordinations – six hundred thousand able-bodied males not only from Kiangsu but from the area to the south as well would be lost as taxpayers. When an amnesty was proclaimed in 830, some seven hundred thousand improperly ordained monks are said to have applied to the Department of Sacrifices in the capital for certificates that would legitimatize their status.[6] It seems likely that the majority of these monks had been 'ordained' under the auspices of men like Wang Chih-hsing.

If the An Lu-shan rebellion gravely weakened the authority of the imperial government and undermined its economy, its impact on the Buddhist church was no less deleterious. On the surface, of course, the church might have given the appearance of being in a stronger position than it had been under the early T'ang rulers because the state no longer possessed the power to check monastic landholdings or set limits on expenditures for the construction of monasteries. Nevertheless the rampant issuing of ordination certificates resulted in the inundation of the clergy by a host of nominal 'monks' whose concerns were often exclusively secular. By the year 830 there were at least twice as many legally ordained monks and nuns as there had been a century earlier.[7] As a Buddhist historian of the Sung period observed: 'The corrupt practice of selling ordination certificates has destroyed our religion.'[8]

The debasement of the quality of the clergy was not the only effect that An Lu-shan had on the subsequent development of Buddhism in China. The wars between contending armies were fought in and around Ch'ang-an and Lo-yang, which had been the leading Buddhist intellectual centers. It was in this region that all of the Buddhist schools that emerged during the T'ang – the Fa-hsiang, the Vinaya (Lü), the Hua-yen, the Esoteric, and the Northern Ch'an – were founded and nurtured. The inevitable destruction of monasteries that resulted from seven years of warfare in the area meant not merely a loss of buildings, which in better times could have been replaced, but also a disruption in scholarly traditions, which had far-reaching implications for the subsequent development of Buddhism in China. Many of the most significant Buddhist commentaries and treatises produced in the first half of the T'ang disappeared after An Lu-shan[9] – although it should be noted that they were often preserved in Korea and Japan. Even such a doctrinally important school as the Fa-hsiang with its voluminous literature vanished with hardly a trace after the An Lu-shan rebellion, only to survive in Japan with its elaborate doctrinal system intact.

The decline in the power and prestige of the imperial court at Ch'ang-an after 755 and the subsequent emergence of virtually independent military governors who maintained large armies and possessed considerable wealth beyond the reach of the central government likewise influenced the development of Buddhist doctrine. While it is true that after An Lu-shan prominent Buddhist clerics such as Pu-k'ung, Ch'eng-kuan, and Tsung-mi, continued to serve emperors as Precepts Masters or Imperial Teachers and happily accepted honorary court ranks, the same men carefully cultivated relations with military governors and other local officials, who increasingly appear as protectors of the faith. A typical example is that of Ch'eng-kuan, one of the most outstanding scholars of the post-An Lu-shan period and the author of fourteen surviving works, who is regarded as the Fourth Patriarch of the Hua-yen school.[10] Invited to lecture at the Court in 795 by Emperor Te-tsung, he was granted the honorary name Ch'ing-liang Fa-shih and the title Professor and Master (*chiao-shou ho-shang*). Four years later Te-tsung conferred on him still another title, grand recorder of the clergy (*ta seng-lu*).[11] In 810 Emperor Hsien-tsung appointed him Controller of Monks (*seng-t'ung*),[12] which had been the highest clerical office in the empire until discontinued by the T'ang. Although Ch'eng-kuan served at the courts of no less than seven T'ang emperors,[13] and was accorded the highest honors, he nevertheless frequently accepted the hospitality of military governors, prefects (*tz'u-shih*), and civil governors (*kuan-ch'a shih*), at whose request he wrote a number of works on doctrine.[14]

The emergence of military governors and other high-ranking army officers as patrons of Buddhism after the An Lu-shan rebellion signified the end of the period of the 'elitist' philosophical schools of Buddhism developed by monks like Hsüan-tsang (Fa-hsiang school), Tao-hsüan (Vinaya school), Fa-tsang (Hua-yen school), and Shen-hsiu (Northern Ch'an school), all of whom worked in the great imperially endowed monasteries of Ch'ang-an and Lo-yang. In contrast to the highly complex metaphysical systems that characterized the Buddhist schools founded during the first half of the T'ang, the most significant feature of the Buddhism of the post-An Lu-shan era was its 'popular' character. Inasmuch as Buddhism had a mass following in China before the rebellion, it obviously contained elements that had a broad appeal to the Chinese people. But this popular side tended to be despised or at best ignored by those eminent monks who enjoyed the patronage of the imperial family and the aristocracy.[15] It is no coincidence that as military men and local officials assumed the role of sponsors of leading monks in the capital, the 'popular' elements in Buddhism – particularly as represented by the Ch'an and Pure Land traditions – came to be increasingly stressed.

Of the four 'elitist' schools, one – the Fa-hsiang – disappeared entirely during the post-An Lu-shan era, a surprising fact in view of the central position that this school occupied in Indian Mahāyāna and the vast literature produced by monks associated with this school during the second half of the seventh century and the early eighth century. A second school – the Lü (Vinaya) – managed to survive through the T'ang, although it dropped from prominence. No significant works by monks of this school dating from the post-An Lu-shan period have come down to us. The important literature of the Vinaya school, at least as it is available to us today, was composed either before the An Lu-shan rebellion or under the Sung dynasty. Unlike the two preceding schools, the Hua-yen and the Ch'an flourished during the second half of the T'ang, although they underwent a significant change in their doctrinal orientation. Beginning with Ch'eng-kuan, the fourth patriarch, the Hua-yen school begins to show a strong influence of Ch'an with its particular emphasis upon intuitive awareness and actual practice as opposed to abstract theory.[16] In this respect the syncretic Hua-yen of Ch'eng-kuan is markedly different from the 'pure' Hua-yen doctrines taught by Fa-tsang. The syncretism of Hua-yen and Ch'an reached its pinnacle with Tsung-mi (780–841), Ch'eng-kuan's most prominent disciple, who is regarded by the Hua-yen school as its fifth patriarch and by the Ch'an school as a Ch'an Master in his own right standing in the line of Shen-hui.[17] The heavy admixture of Ch'an ideas in the writings of Ch'eng-kuan and Tsung-mi is no doubt to a large extent attributable to the foothold that Ch'an had secured among military men and powerful local officials who, as we have seen, often patronized leading monks from the capital.[18]

Just as the Hua-yen school was affected by the gradual shift in power from Ch'ang-an to the provinces, so also did the Ch'an school feel the impact of the An Lu-shan rebellion. We have already noted that the Northern School of Ch'an rose to prominence when Empress Wu invited the aging Shen-hsiu to Lo-yang in the year 700. His teachings, which emphasized the use of meditation as a means to attain enlightenment, had a wide appeal among the elite in the capital cities – members of the aristocracy, high officials, and the literati. After the death of

Shen-hsiu in 706 his disciples I-fu and P'u-chi carried on his work and attracted a large following. P'u-chi in particular was able to gain a significant number of influential disciples and was successful in having himself recognized as the seventh patriarch of the Ch'an school in direct lineal descent from Bodhidharma.[19]

As we have already observed, by the end of the seventh century Ch'an Buddhism was divided into a number of contending lines: the Niu-t'ou school, which claimed descent from Bodhidharma through Fa-jung, a disciple of Tao-hsin, the fourth patriarch; the Szechwan school of Chih-hsien; and the Northern school of Shen-hsiu, which had been recognized as 'orthodox' during the reign of Hsüan-tsung as a result of P'u-chi's influence in Ch'ang-an and Lo-yang. However, the type of Ch'an that ultimately superseded all of these lineages was the so-called 'Southern School' of Hui-neng, who is traditionally depicted as an untonsured disciple of Hung-jen, the fifth patriarch. Although lacking formal education and apparently untrained in the subtleties of Buddhist metaphysics, Hui-neng is said to have grasped the essence of Ch'an better than any of Hung-jen's more learned disciples like Shen-hsiu.[20] Only after leaving Hung-jen did Hui-neng receive his formal ordination. He returned to his native Kuang-chou, where he advocated his unique form of Ch'an which held that enlightenment was not dependent upon scriptural study, intellectual attainments, rigid adherence to the *Vinaya*, or carefully graded religious exercises. In Hui-neng's view, enlightenment was something to be realized intuitively, in a flash of awareness, because it was inherent in all men, the ignorant as well as the educated. Formal study and mechanical observance of rituals prevented people from understanding that their own nature was identical with that of the Buddha; ultimate religious experience was to be attained, not necessarily in the study halls of remote monasteries, but in the context of one's daily life. Such 'popular' teachings gained for Hui-neng many followers, especially among laymen, in the Kuang-chou region, some of whom eagerly sought to spread his message to other parts of China. But whatever his success in the South, Hui-neng, during his lifetime, did not attract any notice among either the clerical elite in the North or the ranking court officials who were increasingly drawn to the more sophisticated Ch'an of Shen-hsiu and P'u-chi.

In 732 Shen-hui, a clerical disciple of Hui-neng, openly challenged the legitimacy of the Northern school at a mass religious meeting in Hua-t'ai in Hopei.[21] He argued that his hitherto obscure teacher, Hui-neng, was in fact the true spiritual descendant of Bodhidharma, who, he asserted, rejected the idea that true religious merit could be acquired by building monasteries, commissioning holy images, ordaining monks, and other such ostentatious displays of piety.[22] When a defender of Northern Ch'an asked him why Shen-hsiu should not be regarded as the sixth patriarch since he had already been granted the title Master of the Dharma in the Two Capitals and Teacher of Three Rulers, Shen-hui responded that no Ch'an patriarch since the time of Bodhidharma had ever accepted an appointment as teacher to an emperor,[23] thus stressing the 'popular' character of Southern Ch'an. In 745 Shen-hui was invited to settle in Lo-yang to preach the new doctrines of Hui-neng. Significantly the invitation was extended by an official concerned with military affairs, one Sung Ting, who was vice-president of the Board of War (*Ping-pu shih-lang*).[24] As might be expected, his denunciation of the 'legitimate' Northern school antagonized some influential followers of P'u-chi and I-fu, who denounced him on the grounds that he was 'collecting adherents,' a charge that implied a threat to the security of the state. In 753 Shen-hui was exiled to I-yang in Honan. During the next three years his place of exile was changed three times.

The outbreak of the An Lu-shan rebellion proved a boon to Shen-hui. As a result of the fighting major changes took place within the government catapulting some of his civil and military supporters to positions of great power. At the same time, his principal adversary, the censor (*yü-shih*) Lu I, who had in large part been responsible for Shen-hui's exile, was captured and murdered by the rebels.[25] Shen-hui, who just three years before had been banished because of the success he had in winning adherents, was brought back to Lo-yang, where he was put in charge of the ordination platform that had been hastily erected by the government for use in conjunction with the sale of ordination certificates. His skill as a preacher now was put to the service of the post-An Lu-shan government. As a result of the large number of ordinations that he supervised considerable revenue was raised for military purposes. Su-tsung had him feted at the court and ordered that a meditation hall be built within the Ho-tse ssu in Lo-yang, where he had lived before his exile in 753. Although Shen-hui died in 762, one year before the end of the rebellion which brought him to prominence, he was successful in introducing the teachings of Hui-neng at the court as well as disseminating them among the military men, officials, and literati.[26] The formal vindication of Hui-neng's Southern school was achieved in 796 when Te-tsung issued an edict declaring that Shen-hui was the seventh patriarch,[27] which, of course, implied that his master, Hui-neng, and not Shen-hsiu, was the sixth patriarch and true successor to Bodhidharma.

The growth of Pure Land Buddhism

The post-An Lu-shan era also has special significance for the development of Pure Land Buddhism, because it was during this period that Pure Land practices were first introduced into the court. 'Pure Land Buddhism' is a loose designation applied to a variety of different beliefs that center around the non-historical Buddha known as Amitābha (Immeasurable Light) or Amitāyus (Immeasurable Life) and his realm (Pure Land) called Sukhāvatī (Land of Bliss).[1] Although, technically speaking, Amitābha is only one of hundreds of non-historical Buddhas mentioned in the sūtras, just as Sukhāvatī is merely one of many such Pure Lands, a popular cult had developed around him and his Pure Land by the first century of the Western era, if not earlier, at a time when Mahāyāna was still in its formative stages in India. In contrast to Śākyamuni, the historical founder of Buddhism who passed into *parinirvāṇa* (perfect nirvāṇa) at the age of eighty and hence no longer had a visible physical form, Amitābha/Amitāyus, as his names indicate, was generally believed to be abiding in his Pure Land, from which his radiance could reach all sentient beings.

Mahāyānists were not all in agreement regarding the role that Amitābha was expected to play in the various soteriological systems that they had devised. To some he was little more than a directional Buddha, namely, the Buddha who presided over the western region where his Pure Land was located and hence was essentially on a par with other such directional Buddhas. To others his resplendent body and glorious Pure Land were objects of intense contemplation, which could free the mind from distractions and strengthen one's resolve to press ahead in the quest for enlightenment. But to the majority of his devotees Amitābha appeared as a compassionate, all-embracing savior who created a Pure Land specifically to serve as a refuge for those who were unable to achieve Buddhahood through their own efforts.

Although Amitābha is mentioned in more than two hundred of the six-hundred-odd extant Mahāyāna sūtras,[2] the Pure Land faith in China was inspired principally by four sūtras:

(1) *TD* 417/418 *Pan-chou san-mei ching* (Sūtra on the trance in which all Buddhas manifest themselves), translated by Lokakṣema in 179.

(2) *TD* 360 *Wu-liang-shou ching* (Sūtra on [the Buddha of] Immeasurable Life), traditionally said to have been translated by Saṃghavarman in 252, but probably translated by Pao-yün in 421.

(3) *TD* 366 *O-mi-t'o ching* (Sūtra on Amita [= Amitābha/Amitāyus]), translated by Kumārajīva in 402.

(4) *TD* 365 *Kuan Wu-liang-shou Fo ching* (Sūtra on viewing the

Buddha of Immeasurable Life), translated by Kālayaśas sometime between 424 and 442.

The first two of these sūtras belong to the oldest group of extant Mahāyāna scriptures, as is evidenced by the fact that both had been translated into Chinese at least twice by the end of the third century.[3]

The *Pan-chou san-mei ching*, as its title indicates, was concerned primarily with the practice of a type of trance commonly known as *pan-chou san-mei*, the latter being an abridged Chinese transcription of the Sanskrit *pratyutpanna Buddha saṃmukhāvasthita samādhi* (the trance in which all existing Buddhas stand before one). Although the object of the trance in principle was to enable one to visualize all Buddhas, the practitioner was especially encouraged to concentrate his mind on Amitābha for a period of from one to seven days, after which this Buddha would appear in a vision. The *Pan-chou san-mei ching* also asserts, even though this was not its primary message, that if the practitioner, after seeing Amitābha, gives rise to the desire for rebirth in his Pure Land, he could accomplish this through continuous meditations on Amitābha.[4]

The *Wu-liang-shou ching* may be regarded as the central text of the Pure Land faith. It narrates in great detail the career of Amitābha from the time when he begins his religious life as a monk named Dharmākara through his realization of enlightenment under the name Amitābha. The sūtra contains a vivid description of Sukhāvatī and a list of the forty-eight vows that determine its characteristics and set forth the conditions for attaining rebirth there. As might be expected from a scripture that stands at the heart of the Pure Land tradition, it concludes with an exhortation to all sentient beings to do homage to Amitābha and urges them to strive to be reborn in his Pure Land.

The *O-mi-t'o ching*, which is the shortest of the four Pure Land sūtras, is basically a eulogy of Amitābha and his Pure Land.[5] Doctrinally, its importance is to be found in its insistence that meditation on the sacred name of Amitābha, and not merely the performance of good deeds, is the requisite for entrance into his Pure Land. The *Kuan Wu-liang-shou Fo ching*,[6] like the *Pan-chou san-mei ching*, is primarily concerned with meditational practices that will enable one to visualize Amitābha and his Pure Land. What marks this sūtra as an extraordinarily significant text in the Pure Land tradition is its detailed description of the nine groups of sentient beings, ranging from the most righteous to the most wicked, who all achieve rebirth in Pure Land. Of particular importance to the development of the Pure Land faith is the sūtra's forceful statement that even the most evil man can enter Pure Land by invoking Amitābha's name ten times on his deathbed.

Although Pure Land sūtras were among the first Buddhist scriptures to be translated into Chinese, there are surprisingly few references to the actual worship of Amitābha by either laymen or monks in China during the third and fourth centuries. The beginnings of Pure Land Buddhism as a serious religious movement date from the time of Hui-yüan, one of the most distinguished monks of his day.[7] In the year 402, in what was to become one of the most celebrated episodes in the history of Chinese Buddhism, Hui-yüan, together with 123 clerical and lay followers, vowed before an image of Amitābha to attain rebirth in Pure Land. This event, which is well documented, has been traditionally considered by Pure Land Buddhists to mark the formal establishment of the Pure Land faith in China.[8] Hui-yüan's devotion to Amitābha, particularly his persistent desire to see visions of this Buddha and his vow to be reborn in Pure Land after death, exerted a strong influence on his disciples and friends and through them on other monks in South China.

It is important to remember, however, that Hui-yüan's conception of Pure Land Buddhism was different from that of virtually all later Pure Land adherents in two respects. First, Hui-yüan based his Pure Land faith solely on the *Pan-chou san-mei ching*, that is, he sought to visualize Amitābha by practicing the meditations prescribed in this sūtra, which, he believed, would ultimately bring about his rebirth in Pure Land. Nowhere in his writings do we find any reference to the compassion of Amitābha that is expressed in his vows to save all sentient beings or to the latent power of his name, even though these are crucial themes in the *Wu-liang-shou ching* and *O-mi-t'o ching*, two key Pure Land texts that were almost certainly available to him. By relying exclusively on the *Pan-chou san-mei ching* and ignoring the more central Pure Land sūtras, Hui-yüan sought to gain entrance into Pure Land essentially through his own meditative powers and not through the compassion of Amitābha as revealed in his forty-eight vows. The second respect in which Hui-yüan's Pure Land piety was unique was that it was expressed in the context of a relatively small group of devotees who were united by a pledge to help each other attain rebirth in Pure Land. Contrary to the frequent injunctions in the Pure Land scripture to disseminate the teachings widely, Hui-yüan did not urge the common people to seek their salvation in Pure Land, nor did he attempt to systematize the Pure Land teachings or reconcile them with the prevailing Buddhist doctrines.

Although Hui-yüan himself neither popularized the Pure Land faith nor contributed to the development of Pure Land thought in any substantive fashion, he became an inspiration for later generations of Pure Land Buddhists who embroidered a rich fabric of legends around him. As the seventh-century Pure Land chronicler Chia-ts'ai astutely observed, 'Hui-yüan, Hsieh Ling-yün and the other members of this group all put their hopes in the Western Realm (Pure Land). Yet in the end their religious activities were designed solely for their own benefit. It is for this reason that none of the later scholars of the Pure Land tradition stood in their lineage.'[9] Nevertheless the intense Amitābha pietism generated by Hui-yüan and his cohorts on Lu-shan made an increasing number of monks and laymen in South China aware of Pure Land ideas and led to a slow but steady growth of such religious activities as the carving of images of Amitābha and the copying, chanting, and exposition of the key Pure Land sūtras.[10]

The dissemination of Pure Land Buddhism in North China began a century later than it did in the South, the first dated image of Amitābha at Lung-men having been completed in the year 519.[11] By contrast we know of at least eight such images that were produced in the South during the preceding fifth century.[12] Although Pure Land ideas were steadily gaining acceptance during the sixth century, Śākyamuni remained by far the most widely worshipped Buddha, as the Lung-men statuary clearly shows. During the whole of the sixth century a total of nine images of Amitābha were produced at Lung-men as against fifty images of Śākyamuni and the thirty-five images of Maitreya.[13] The first attempt in China to systematize Pure Land thought was made by T'an-luan,[14] who in his *Wang-sheng lun chu*, laid the foundations for an independent Pure Land faith. T'an-luan taught that those religious practices that had as their object the attainment of higher spiritual states in the present world constitute the path of difficult practice (*nan-hsing tao*), because only the most determined of individuals can overcome the various obstacles and temptations that block the way to enlightenment. Instead he urged his contemporaries to follow what he termed 'the path of easy practice' (*i-hsing tao*), i.e. the path that leads to rebirth in Pure Land by relying exclusively on the power inherent in the vows of Amitābha (*pen-yüan li*). T'an-luan thus rejected the idea of seeking to attain the higher bodhisattva stages in this world through one's own efforts (*tzu-li*), substituting for this traditional goal a total reliance on 'the power of the Other' (*t'a-li*), i.e. Amitābha. Rebirth in Pure Land signified the attainment of the stage of non-retrogression, i.e. a state from which backsliding was no longer possible. The inhabitant in Pure Land, while not yet a Buddha, was assured of the rapid attainment of enlightenment. By entering Pure Land the devotee had attained a state equal to that of Maitreya, the Buddha-to-be. To achieve this rebirth the devotee had to undertake five types of practices: (1) worship Amitābha, (2) invoke his name, (3) vow to be reborn in his Pure Land, (4) meditate on the glories of Pure Land, and (5) strive to help others to enter Pure Land.[15] Although meditation continued to occupy a prominent place in T'an-luan's thinking, great importance was also attached to the invocation of Amitābha's name, which T'an-luan believed had the power to dispel illusion, eliminate evil, and destroy countless kalpas of accumulated karmic residue.

T'an-luan's goal of creating an independent Pure Land faith was further advanced by Tao-ch'o,[16] a native of Ping-chou (in the present-day Shansi) as was T'an-luan. Tao-ch'o's conversion to Pure Land occurred relatively late in life – at the age of forty-seven, in the year 609, during a visit to the Hsüan-chung ssu, the monastery in Fen-chou (in the present-day Shansi) at which T'an-luan spent the later years of his life. After reading the inscription on the stele erected in memory of T'an-luan, Tao-ch'o became an enthusiastic convert to the Pure Land faith, devoting himself to the practice of invoking the name of Amitābha and lecturing on the *Kuan Wu-liang-shou Fo ching*. Unlike T'an-luan whose main efforts seem to have been directed toward the justification of the Pure Land doctrine in the eyes of the Buddhist clergy, Tao-ch'o sought to disseminate the Pure Land teaching, with its espousal of universal salvation, among the common people, urging them to call upon the name of Amitābha incessantly. He won a large following in the Shansi region, so much so, it was said, that as a result of his missionary zeal everyone in Chin-yang, T'ai-yüan, and Wen-shui counties above the age of six invoked Amitābha's name. Devotees were advised to keep track of the number of their invocations by putting aside a bean each time Amitābha's name was recited and were cautioned not to cry, spit, or relieve themselves in the direction of the west, the locus of Amitābha's Pure Land!

Perhaps as a result of his having personally experienced the suppression of Buddhism ordered by Emperor Wu of the Northern Chou in 574 – it was carried out in Ping-chou in 576, the year after Tao-ch'o had been tonsured – Tao-ch'o stressed that a new form of Buddhism, Pure Land, was now necessary, since the world had entered a period of irreversible spiritual decline.[17] Basing himself on the *Yüeh-tsang ching*, which had been translated into Chinese in 566, Tao-ch'o held that Buddhism was destined to pass through five periods, each five hundred years in duration.[18] In the first period, which began with the demise of the Buddha, the cultivation of wisdom was the dominant characteristic; in

The growth of Pure Land Buddhism

the second period the practice of meditation was the chief religious activity; in the third period the study and chanting of scripture became the principal concern of the Buddhists. Using the chronology that was then current, namely, that the Buddha's demise had occurred c. 949 B.C., Tao-ch'o calculated that the age in which he was living corresponded to the fourth period, the distinguishing feature of which was the acquisition of merit and the practice of penance through the construction of monasteries and other such religious works. In the fifth period, which the world would soon be entering, only small vestiges of Buddhism would survive, since the bulk of the teachings of the Buddha will have already been obscured by the incessant squabbling of the clergy.

In Tao-ch'o's view, for a person to attain spiritual benefit he must adjust his religious practices to the particular period in which he lives. Thus, Tao-ch'o argued, Buddhists of his own day should not attempt to seek salvation primarily through the cultivation of wisdom or the study of scripture, which were suitable practices for the preceding periods, but rather through the invocation of Amitābha's name, which alone has the power to destroy the evil karmic residue that has accumulated over countless eons. In accordance with his concept of the relative appropriateness of different types of practice Tao-ch'o devised a twofold division of the Buddhist teachings. On the one side, there was the Path of the Sages (*Sheng-tao*), which included all varieties of Buddhism, both Hīnayāna and Mahāyāna, that sought to eliminate illusions and bring about the attainment of enlightenment in this world. On the other side, there was the Pure Land teaching (*Ching-t'u men*), which opened the way for all beings to achieve rebirth in Pure Land by relying upon Amitābha's vows and invoking his name. Tao-ch'o believed that his contemporaries no longer had any choice about the type of Buddhism they should follow, because the period in which they were living precluded the possibility of anyone's achieving enlightenment by following the Path of the Sages, i.e. through his own efforts. In the present period of spiritual decline the only way for man to escape from the cycle of birth and death was for him to place his faith in the compassion of Amitābha as expressed in his vows.

The Pure Land tradition of the Hsüan-chung ssu that began with T'an-luan and that was further developed by Tao-ch'o reached its pinnacle with Shan-tao,[19] who had become a disciple of Tao-ch'o in the early 630s. After the death of his master in 645, Shan-tao moved to Ch'ang-an, becoming the first major exponent of Pure Land to settle in the capital. Here he energetically spread the Pure Land faith among the city's inhabitants by making thousands of copies of the *O-mi-t'o ching* and painting some three hundred scrolls depicting Pure Land. Although he was successful in attracting 'countless numbers of men and women' including some fanatical converts who hastened their own entry into Pure Land by committing religious suicide, he does not seem to have made any noticeable impact on either members of the court or prominent monks in the capital such as Hsüan-tsang, Tz'u-en, or Fa-tsang, who were his contemporaries, even though he stayed for some time at the prestigious Ta tz'u-en ssu. Significantly, he chose as his main residence in Ch'ang-an the Kuang-ming ssu, which was situated in the commercial district of the city.

In addition to being a highly effective proselytizer Shan-tao contributed significantly to the development and refinement of Pure Land thought and succeeded in laying the foundations for a self-contained, autonomous Pure Land faith that was no longer simply an appendage to one or another of the great philosophical schools. Like his master Tao-ch'o, Shan-tao believed that in the present period of spiritual decline only the Pure Land teaching could rescue man from the cycle of rebirth and guarantee ultimate enlightenment. According to Shan-tao, Amitābha vowed to save all beings, irrespective of whether they were good or evil, provided that they fulfilled two conditions. The first is that they put their faith in the vows of Amitābha after acknowledging their own wickedness and inability to attain enlightenment through their own efforts. The second condition is that they undertake five types of devotional practices in order to give concrete expression to their inner faith.[20] From among these five practices – reciting sūtras about Amitābha, meditation on Amitābha, worship of Amitābha, reciting the name of Amitābha, and praising and making offerings to Amitābha – Shan-tao singles out the fourth practice, the recitation of the name of Amitābha, as the crucial instrument of salvation, 'the act that truly determines [entrance into Pure Land]' (*cheng-ting chih yeh*), urging people to recite the name at all times and in all situations. The fact that the invocations of Amitābha's name could be undertaken by all men, learned and ignorant alike, with equal ease was central to Shan-tao's belief in the universality of Amitābha's vow to save all sentient beings. The enormous impact that Pure Land ideas had on Chinese laymen during the lifetime of Shan-tao and shortly thereafter is eloquently attested in the Lung-men statuary. Between the years 640 and 710 one hundred and eighteen images of Amitābha were produced as against a mere ten images of Śākyamuni and twelve of Maitreya.[21] In the light of this it is little wonder that by the end of the Sung, Shan-tao was viewed as the second patriarch of the Pure Land school – the spiritual successor to Hui-yüan – and was sometimes identified as an earthly incarnation of Amitābha himself.[22]

It was characteristic of the elitist bent that marked the first half of the T'ang dynasty that neither the court nor the leading monks who enjoyed imperial favor paid much attention to the Pure Land faith as it had been defined by its great exponents Tao-ch'o and Shan-tao. Despite the growing fervor with which the common people were receiving the Pure Land doctrines, the court virtually ignored the existence of Pure Land Buddhism before the An Lu-shan rebellion. Although monks of the philosophical or esoteric schools were richly patronized and routinely invited to preach or conduct religious services at the court, monks primarily associated with the Pure Land faith were accorded no such honors.[23] It was only in the second half of the eighth century, after the T'ang rulers had been jolted out of their complacency by the widespread insurrections, that the court took cognizance of the Pure Land faith that had already rooted itself deeply among the common people in both the provinces and the capital cities of Ch'ang-an and Lo-yang.

Pure Land services were introduced into the T'ang court by the monk Fa-chao[24] who was later dubbed a reincarnation of Shan-tao because of his success in popularising the Pure Land faith, especially the practice of the ecstatic intonation of the name of Amitābha.[25] Inspired by the example of Hui-yüan, Fa-chao made a pilgrimage to Lu-shan, where he built a hermitage in which to practice the visualization of Amitābha, i.e. the trance known as *pan-chou san-mei*, as Hui-yüan himself had done three and a half centuries earlier. In 765 Fa-chao had a vision of Pure Land in which he saw an aged monk attending Amitābha. When informed by Amitābha that the monk was none other than Ch'eng-yüan,[26] a well-known Pure Land devotee then living in the Nan-yüeh mountains (in present-day Hunan), Fa-chao immediately left Lu-shan for Nan-yüeh to join the community of monks that had formed around Ch'eng yüan.

The following year Fa-chao claimed to have had yet another face-to-face encounter with Amitābha, who appeared before Fa-chao in a vision and expounded the practice of intoning the name of Amitābha in five different rhythms, i.e. the so-called *wu hui nien-fo*.[27] Calling this the most suitable teaching for the present period, a 'priceless and rare treasure,' Amitābha equated the five rhythms with the five sounds heard in Pure Land that are spoken of in the *Wu-liang-shou ching*.[28] Amitābha further promised Fa-chao that anyone who practiced the *wu hui nien-fo* would be released from suffering and rapidly attain Buddhahood.

Fa-chao spent the next four years in the Nan-yüeh region devoting himself to meditations on Amitābha, during which time he had repeated visions of a monastery, subsequently known as the Chu-lin ssu, which he believed he was destined to build in the sacred Wu-t'ai mountains.[29] Accompanied by several of his disciples, Fa-chao moved north in 770 to Wu-t'ai, one of the major Buddhist centers of the time, to establish a base for his new version of Pure Land devotionalism in a region that drew large numbers of pilgrims from all China. Continuing his northern trek, Fa-chao had located himself by 774 in T'ai-yüan, a city, as we have noted, with close ties to the imperial clan, where he wrote a major treatise on the *wu hui nien-fo* during a stay at the state-sponsored Lung-hsing ssu.[30]

Fa-chao finally reached Ch'ang-an in the late 770s, where, following in the footsteps of Shan-tao, he proclaimed the Pure Land teachings, while soliciting contributions for the construction of the Chu-lin ssu in Wu-t'ai. The practice of rhythmically chanting the name of Amitābha proved extremely popular, making Fa-chao one of the most celebrated monks in the capital. He was invited by Emperor Tai-tsung to lecture at the court and granted the title National Teacher (*kuo-shih*). In Ch'ang-an Fa-chao was domiciled, at least for some time, at the Chang-ching ssu, a monastery founded in 767 in memory of Tai-tsung's mother. Tai-tsung, in fact, so esteemed Fa-chao that he travelled to Nan-yüeh to pay his respects to Fa-chao's master, Ch'eng-yüan.

After Tai-tsung's death Fa-chao moved to Ping-chou, where the great Pure Land masters T'an-luan, Tao-ch'o, and Shan-tao had been active, to proclaim the *wu hui nien-fo* there, but was again summoned back to the court by Tai-tsung's successor, Te-tsung, to teach its officials how to perform this method of chanting Amitābha's name. In recognition of his accomplishments in promoting the Pure Land faith, an imperial decree was issued upon the death of Fa-chao conferring on him the posthumous epithet Master of Great Enlightenment (Ta-wu Ho-shang).[31] That his teachings continued to enjoy support even after his death is evident from the testimony of the Japanese monk Ennin who reports that Fa-chao's disciple Ching-shuang, who like his master resided in the prestigious Chang-ching ssu, was ordered by imperial decree in 841 to teach the practice of intoning Amitābha's name in the monasteries of Ch'ang-an.[32]

PART TWO

THE BUDDHIST CHURCH DURING THE SECOND HALF OF THE T'ANG (763–907)

Reign of Tai-tsung (762–779)

Although it is no doubt true, as Confucian historians have asserted, that Tai-tsung did not at first hold Buddhism in high regard,[1] the fact is that this emperor, within two or three years after his accession to the throne, proved himself to be perhaps the most devout of all the T'ang rulers. When Tai-tsung succeeded his father, Su-tsung, in the fourth month of 762, the civil war, which had begun with An Lu-shan's rebellion in 755, had not yet been terminated. In the first month of 763 Shih Ch'ao-i, the last successor to the mantle of An Lu-shan, was killed, thus bringing the long insurrection to an end. Later in the same year, however, the new emperor was forced to flee once again from Ch'ang-an when the city temporarily fell to marauding Tibetans. The following year the T'ang was faced with yet another rebellion – this time by P'u-ku Huai-en, a general of Turkish stock, who suspected that many of the high-ranking bureaucrats close to the throne were plotting his downfall. P'u-ku Huai-en, whose daughter was married to an Uighur king (*qaghan*), succeeded in raising an army, reputed to have been two hundred thousand strong, with which he menaced Ch'ang-an. Fortunately for Tai-tsung the alliance between the Uighurs and Tibetans came apart when P'u-ku suddenly died at Ling-wu in the ninth month of 765 just before the planned attack on Ch'ang-an was to have begun.

The eminent Tantric master, Pu-k'ung, who had served Tai-tsung's father and grandfather, lost no time in offering his services to the new emperor who was trying to consolidate his rule. On the thirteenth day of the tenth month, which was Tai-tsung's birthday, Pu-k'ung presented the emperor, who had ascended the throne six months earlier, with an image of the powerful esoteric divinity Marīci (Mo-li-chih), which Pu-k'ung himself had carved from a piece of white sandlewood, along with a copy of the *Mahāpratyaṅgirā dhāraṇi* (*Ta fo-ting t'o-lo-ni*) in an Indian script.[2] In the accompanying memorial Pu-k'ung commended the worship of Marīci, who, it was believed, had the power to overcome all obstacles, and reminded the emperor that all Universal Monarchs recited the dhāraṇī that Tai-tsung had just been given.[3] The following year Pu-k'ung received permission from the throne to erect an altar for tantric consecrations (*kuan-ting tao-ch'ang*) at the Ta hsing-shan ssu 'for the benefit of the empire,' where esoteric rituals would be performed four times yearly. In 764, on the anniversaries of the deaths of Su-tsung and Hsüan-tsung, the emperor ordered the ordination of several hundred Buddhist and Taoist monks.[4]

As the threat from P'u-ku Huai-en increased in the early part of 765 Tai-tsung looked increasingly toward Buddhism in the hope of receiving some sort of divine assistance. In the fourth month of 765, when P'u-ku's forces approached Ch'ang-an, Pu-k'ung requested permission to prepare a new 'translation' of the *Jen-wang ching*,[5] a sūtra that promises protection from rebellions, foreign invasion, and other disasters, provided that the ruler demonstrates his support for Buddhism by not placing monks and nuns under the control of state officials (*t'ung-kuan*) or entering their names in government registers (*chi*).[6] Tai-tsung immediately consented, offering Pu-k'ung the use of the facilities in the Ta-ming Palace.[7] The new version, which was basically a reworking of the earlier 'translation,' was completed in fifteen days.[8] Tai-tsung, who is said to have participated in the translation project, wrote prefaces for the *Jen-wang ching* and the *Mi-yen ching* (*Ghaṇḍavyūha sūtra*), which also was translated at the same time.[9] Copies of the *Jen-wang ching* were carried from the court through the streets of Ch'ang-an in a solemn procession and finally deposited in the Hsi-ming ssu and the Tzu-sheng ssu, two of the leading monasteries in the capital, where the sūtra was chanted in elaborate ceremonies attended by prominent members of the court.[10] On learning of the collapse of P'u-ku Huai-en's rebellion after the latter's death in the ninth month of 765, Tai-tsung attributed the victory of the imperial forces to the power of the *Jen-wang ching* and in the following month ordered a new round of lavish celebrations in the capital. Pu-k'ung, who was credited with having secured the intercession of the Buddhas, was rewarded with nine hundred bolts of fine silk, and his attendants with fifteen bolts each. A new chapel (*nei-tao-ch'ang*) was established within the palace, where one hundred state-supported monks, who were accorded the privilege of arriving and departing on horseback, were to perform esoteric rituals.[11] An order was also issued at the same time prohibiting officials from humiliating members of the Buddhist clergy. In recognition of the benefits that Tantric Buddhism had brought to the T'ang, Tai-tsung conferred in the eleventh month of 765 a posthumous rank and title on Vajrabodhi; Pu-k'ung was likewise given the honorary name Tripiṭaka Master of Great and Extensive Wisdom (Ta-kuang-chih San-tsang) and appointed special probationary director of the Court for State Ceremonials (*t'e chin shih hung-lu ch'ing*).[12]

Tai-tsung's faith in Buddhism was greatly encouraged by his leading ministers, Wang Chin, Tu Hung-chien, and Yüan Tsai. Wang Chin, who was the brother of the artist and poet Wang Wei, was an unusually devout Buddhist, who observed the dietary restrictions prohibiting the consumption of meat and such strong-smelling vegetables as onions, leeks and garlic.[13] Together with Tu Hung-chien he spent vast sums of money on the construction of monasteries and used his considerable power at the court to urge others to do likewise.[14] In 769 Wang Chin obtained permission from Tai-tsung to convert one of his residences in Ch'ang-an into a monastery named Pao-ying ssu in memory of a favorite concubine who had died after a long illness.[15] This monastery, which had been granted a tablet by the emperor and housed thirty monks, soon became a symbol of Wang Chin's power. Whenever a military or civilian governor reported to the court, he was invariably conducted to the Pao-ying ssu and urged to make a monetary contribution for its upkeep.

The pro-Buddhist ministers at court succeeded in convincing Tai-tsung that his family had survived the series of upheavals that followed in the wake of the An Lu-shan rebellion only because of the protection afforded by Buddhism. Yüan Tsai is reported to have told the emperor: 'Good fortune and the preservation of the dynasty can be realized only through the accumulation of meritorious deeds [*fu-yeh*, i.e. the support of Buddhism]. Once this is done, the state will suffer no harm in the long run, even though minor crises may occur from time to time. Thus An Lu-shan and Shih Ssu-ming were cut down by their own sons even at the height of their rebellions; P'u-ku Huai-en, who raised an army for insurrection, fell ill and died no sooner than he left his camp; the Uighurs and Tibetans finally retreated without doing battle despite their deep incursions into our territory. None of these events were brought about by the efforts of men. How can one say, then, that there is no such thing as religious merit?'[16] In meeting with his ministers Tai-tsung spent much of his time discussing Buddhism. Ssu-ma Kuang states that Tai-tsung's obsession with Buddhism had a baneful influence on his subjects who increasingly 'neglected the affairs of the world to serve the Buddha with the result that the government was thrown into confusion.'[17]

Taking advantage of the euphoria following the collapse of the forces hostile to the T'ang, Pu-k'ung petitioned Tai-tsung in 766 for imperial support for the completion of a monastery known as the Chin-ko ssu in Wu-t'ai shan.[18] Since the early fifth century these mountains were believed to be the abode of Wen-shu (Mañjuśrī), a popular Mahāyāna bodhisattva who also figures prominently in Esoteric Buddhism.[19] By the mid T'ang Wu-t'ai shan had become one of the most sacred sites in the Buddhist world and was visited by a succession of eminent monks and pilgrims from China and abroad.[20] In 736 a monk named Tao-i began construction of the Chin-ko ssu after seeing a vision of Wen-shu, but the monastery was never completed, probably because of the An Lu-shan rebellion. Before his death Tao-i sent the court a painting of the finished portion of the monastery which at that time already consisted of thirteen halls capable of accommodating some ten thousand monks. To Pu-k'ung, himself a devotee of Wen-shu, the as yet unfinished Chin-ko ssu represented a natural center for his own brand of Tantric Buddhism with its emphasis on the worship of Wen-shu.

In his memorial Pu-k'ung stressed the role that the Chin-ko ssu could play in unifying the country, reminding the Emperor that his subjects, high and low alike, were eagerly looking forward to the day when this monastery would be finished. He asked rhetorically: 'Who but Your Majesty could bring about the completion of the Chin-ko ssu?' For his own part, Pu-k'ung assured the throne that his interest in the Chin-ko ssu stemmed solely from his desire to 'benefit the empire,' and with this noble aim in mind he sought permission to make a modest contribution – his begging bowl and a set of robes – to help defray some of the costs of construction. Needless to say, the support provided by Pu-k'ung's powerful followers at court was more substantial. As the biography of Wang Chin indicates, the Chin-ko ssu was an awe-inspiring sight with the reflection of its 'gold-plated roof tiles illuminating the mountains and valleys.'[21] The total expenditure for the monastery was said to have amounted to 'millions of cash,' part of which, no doubt, came from the ten military governors who had been urged by the court to assist in its construction.[22] Wang Chin, as a prominent lay supporter, secured permission for several dozen monks from the monastery to canvass the surrounding districts in search of contributions. When the monastery was finally finished in 767, Pu-k'ung was appointed abbot.[23] Han-kuang, a very close disciple of Pu-k'ung who had accompanied him to Sri Lanka and who had overseen the construction of the Chin-ko ssu, continued to reside there after the death of his master.[24] When Ennin visited the Chin-ko ssu in 840, it was still a thriving center for the practice of Esoteric Buddhism and the Wen-shu cult.[25]

Perhaps the most outstanding characteristic of the Tantric Buddhism

Reign of Tai-tsung (762–779)

propagated by Pu-k'ung was the veneration of the bodhisattva Wen-shu, who occupied an important place in traditional Mahāyāna literature as well as in the tantras and maṇḍalas of Esoteric Buddhism.[26] Wen-shu's prominence in early Mahāyāna Buddhism was large attributable to his close identification with the *prajñāpāramitā* (perfection of wisdom) doctrine, i.e. the principle that all conditioned dharmas (elements) are non-substantial (*śūnyatā, k'ung*), which underlies all subsequent Mahāyāna thought. Since the attainment of Buddhahood could be achieved only through a mastery of *prajñāpāramitā*, the latter doctrine – and Wen-shu as its propagator and defender in the period after the demise of the Buddha – came to be regarded as the source of enlightenment and salvation. Thus Śākyamuni the historical Buddha is made to say in one sūtra: 'That I have now realized Buddhahood ... and am able to save the countless sentient beings of the ten directions is due to the grace of Wen-shu who was my master. The innumerable Buddhas of past ages have likewise been his disciples, just as future Buddhas will also be created through the force of his divine power ... Wen-shu is both the father and mother of those who follow the path to Buddhahood.'[27] In the esoteric tradition Wen-shu is identified as a Buddha who out of compassion for unenlightened beings assumed the form of a bodhisattva in order to be able to respond to their needs.[28]

Pu-k'ung's determination to disseminate the Wen-shu cult in China is apparent from the tantras that he selected for translation. Of the eighty-three texts said to have been translated by him[29] no less than ten were concerned primarily with the worship of Wen-shu.[30] In 769 Pu-k'ung petitioned for an imperial order requiring each monastery to install an image of Wen-shu above the customary image of Pin-t'ou-lu (Piṇḍola) that was placed in the refectory to receive offerings of food from the monks before they ate their meals.[31] According to a widespread belief, Pin-tou-lu had been an arhat (*lo-han*), i.e. a 'perfected one' in the Hīnayāna sense, who, as a penance for having worked feats of magic, was told by the Buddha to postpone his entrance into Nirvāṇa so that he might, by accepting food offerings, help those who served him to accumulate merit and thereby ultimately contribute to their enlightenment.[32] The practice of making offerings to Pin-t'ou-lu is said to have been initiated by the monk Hui-yüan[33] and was widely performed in monasteries by early T'ang times.[34] In his appeal to Tai-tsung Pu-k'ung asserted that Wen-shu's image should stand above that of Pin-t'ou-lu, as was the practice in India, 'since he is the fountainhead of all esoteric teachings.'[35] The Emperor, responding favorably to Pu-k'ung's request, issued the desired edict, which, to judge from Ennin's testimony, was enforced at least in those monasteries closely associated with Pu-k'ung.[36] By 772 Pu-k'ung had elicited an imperial order directing the establishment of a Wen-shu chapel in every monastery in the empire.[37] Gratified by the unstinting support that he had received from the throne, Pu-k'ung reported to the Emperor a prophecy by Śākyamuni Buddha to the effect that true Buddhism will ultimately flourish in China, which is destined to be ruled by a sage emperor who will govern the country in accordance with the doctrines of Mahāyāna: 'Although China has had many wise emperors during the eight hundred years since Buddhism was first introduced, none could equal Your Majesty in piety. It is my good fortune to have been able to practice Mahāyāna and serve Wen-shu during your reign. I shall always recite the sacred mantras especially for the benefit of the Empire.'[38] The following year, on the anniversary of the passing away of the Buddha, Tai-tsung ordered the construction of a Pavilion for the Protection of the Empire by Wen-shu, the Great Holy One (Ta-sheng Wen-shu chen-kuo chih ko) within the precincts of the magnificent Ta hsing-shan ssu,[39] the Emperor himself becoming its patron (ko-chu) and providing thirty million cash from the treasury.[40]

From the time that Pu-k'ung became prominent at the T'ang court in 741 until his death in 774, he continuously emphasized the role of Buddhism in the protection of the state (chen-kuo),[41] while at the same time stressing the emperor's function as an earthly surrogate of the Buddha: 'Your Majesty has received the mandate of the Buddha to serve as King of the Dharma [fa-wang]; it is Your Majesty who satisfies the aspirations of the people and holds the secret seal of P'u-hsien (Samantabhadra).'[42] Whenever Pu-k'ung proposed to establish a monastery, translate a text, hold a mass, or arrange for an ordination, he would usually make the point that his sole intention was to benefit the empire or to protect the imperial family. Although the idea that Buddhism could afford protection to the state was advocated in one form or another by most leading monks since the fifth century, it reached its pinnacle during the reign of Tai-tsung. As an indication of his total dedication to Buddhism, Tai-tsung ordered in 766 that the spirit tablets of the seven preceding T'ang emperors be transferred from the Imperial Ancestral Temple (t'ai-miao) to the palace chapel (nei-tao-ch'ang) for the annual Yü-lan-p'en hui, a mass held on the fifteenth day of the seventh month for the purpose of securing the release of one's ancestors from hell. Although the Yü-lan-p'en service had been sporadically held in monasteries under imperial sponsorship since the time of Liang Wu-ti (reigned 502–549), this is said to have been the first occasion that the ceremonies were performed within the precincts of the imperial palace.[43] Tai-tsung also revived the practice of inviting distinguished monks to a vegetarian banquet at the palace on the occasion of the emperor's birthday.[44] In 768 Tai-tsung ordered his ministers and army commanders to receive an esoteric consecration (*kuan-ting*) in an elaborate ceremony conducted by Pu-k'ung at the Ta hsing-shan ssu which was attended by some five thousand laymen over a period of fourteen days.[45] The cost of feeding the thousands of participants was borne by the Emperor, who presented Pu-k'ung with brocaded quilts, fine silk pennants, and other subjects valued at millions of cash.

So esteemed were Pu-k'ung's talents that when a comet appeared mysteriously in 770 he was dispatched to Wu-t'ai shan to 'do meritorious works' (*hsiu kung-te*) in the hope that its baleful effects might be averted.[46] En route back to Ch'ang-an Pu-k'ung paid a strategic visit to T'ai-yüan, the ancestral site of the imperial clan, where he held a lavish 'plenary banquet' (*wan-jen chai*) at state expense.[47] Pu-k'ung availed himself of the occasion to propose the construction of a chapel dedicated to Wen-shu at the Chih-te ssu in T'ai-yüan.[48] No sooner had he received a favorable response from the Emperor than he sent a second memorial to the throne in which he described how deeply moved he had been on seeing momentos belonging to Kao-tsu and T'ai-tsung kept at the T'ai ch'ung-fu ssu in T'ai-yüan.[49] He appealed for tax exempt status for this monastery on the grounds that it was closely identified with the rise of the T'ang and urged that regular services be conducted ten days each month for the repose of the deceased T'ang emperors and the preservation of the dynasty. Having now succeeded in establishing a Tantric base in T'ai-yüan, Pu-k'ung resumed his journey back to Ch'ang-an, where Tai-tsung, delighted by Pu-k'ung's success in exorcising the noxious comet, had him escorted to the palace in the imperial carriage to receive various gifts of great value.[50] Until his death in the year 774 Pu-k'ung was routinely called upon by Tai-tsung whenever some natural calamity threatened and was lavishly rewarded for his services. Four days before his death he was given the honorary rank *k'ai-fu i-t'ung san-ssu* and enfeoffed as Duke of Su-kuo with three thousand households assigned for his support.

The vast expenditures on the construction of monasteries undertaken during the reign of Tai-tsung were probably unparalleled in the history of the T'ang, with the exception of the interregnum of Empress Wu. In 767, on the thirteenth anniversary of the An Lu-shan rebellion – a significant year in Buddhist reckoning – Yü Ch'ao-en, one of the most powerful eunuchs at the court, donated one of his estates in Ch'ang-an for the establishment of a monastery to be known as the Chang-ching ssu in memory of Tai-tsung's mother.[51] Construction was immediately begun on a grand scale, and when it became apparent that the supply of timber in Ch'ang-an was insufficient, Yü Ch'ao-en sent a memorial to the throne requesting that several existing government buildings be taken down so that more material could be made available for the construction of the new monastery. The Emperor promptly acceded to Yü's request and permitted the dismantlement of the Ch'ü-chiang Pavilion, a tower belonging to the Hua-ch'ing Palace, a few temporary government offices, and several official residences.

Tai-tsung's extravagance led a young *chin-shih* named Kao Ying who was later to acquire a reputation for uncorruptibility as an examiner[52] to deliver himself of a bitter denunciation: 'The virtues of the deceased Empress Dowager surely do not require the construction of a monastery so that they might shine forth. Rather we must consider the interests of the people first, if the future security of the empire is to be achieved. What merit can result from abandoning the people and running off to monasteries? . . . We can manage without monasteries, but can we survive without people?'[53] In another memorial Kao Ying vividly described the suffering caused by the construction of the Chang-ching ssu: 'The wise rulers of ancient times sought merit through repeated good deeds; they did not seek it by depleting their treasure. They cultivated virtue in order to ward off disasters; they did not exhaust the energy of the people to accomplish this. The construction [of the Chang-ching ssu] is now being pressed with such urgency that people are unable to rest night or day. Those who lack the strength to do the required work are driven on by whips, their anguished cries filling the street. I think that Your Majesty should not expect to gain merit in this fashion.'[54] Kao Ying's protests notwithstanding, the rapid completion of the still unfinished Chang-ching ssu remained a high priority. On the occasion of the New Year in 768, Tai-tsung paid a personal visit to the monastery, where he offered incense and witnessed the ordination of one thousand monks and nuns.[55] Construction of the monastery, which was said to consist of forty-eight buildings (*yüan*) with a combined total of more than 4,130 bays (*chien*), was completed by the seventh month of the same year in time for the observance of *Yü-lan-p'en*.[56] Throughout the remainder of the T'ang dynasty the Chang-ching ssu figured as one of the leading monasteries of Ch'ang-an and housed many of the most eminent monks of the day.[57]

In order to oversee effectively the numerous religious projects sponsored by the government several new institutions were created during the reign of Tai-tsung. About the year 765 an edict was issued calling for the appointment of ten monks and ten nuns to serve as ordination preceptors (*lin-t'an ta-te*).[58] The responsibility of these preceptors was to ensure that all ordinations within Ch'ang-an were properly performed. It was decreed that any vacancies occurring among the prescribed number of preceptors were to be promptly filled so as to satisfy the provision in the *Vinaya* that ten monks be present when the precepts are administered.

Another important post concerned with religious affairs established in the late 760s was that of commissioner of good works (*hsiu kung-te shih*), the primary function of which seems to have been the supervision of Buddhist monasteries in Ch'ang-an. This office is mentioned for the first time in the title of the monk K'uo-ch'ing, who was appointed director of the Department of Palace Affairs (*Tien-chung chien*) in 769, for which reason he is said to have been much feared by other monks in the capital.[59] By the year 774 another new office known as the commissioner of good works for Buddhist monasteries and Taoist temples in the capital (*ching-ch'eng ssu-kuan hsiu kung-te shih*) made its debut.[60] The first incumbent was Li Yüan-ts'ung, who was concurrently the commander of the Lung-wu Palace Army of the Right (*yu lung-wu chün*).[61] Li's appointment as commissioner of good works was no doubt linked to his long and extremely close association with the Tantric master Pu-k'ung, who, as we have seen, had been held in high esteem by both Su-tsung and Tai-tsung.[62] In his will, drawn up one month before his death, Pu-k'ung expressed his satisfaction that his 'lay disciple, Commissioner Li' would continue to supervise the monks and look after their interests as if he (Pu-k'ung) were still alive.

The Buddhist clergy evidently welcomed the appointment of a powerful military figure whom it knew to be sympathetic as an overseer of church affairs instead of the Confucian officials in the Department of Sacrifices (Tz'u-pu) who were apt to harbor misgivings about the large expenditures for religious projects. Thus when Li Yüan-ts'ung died in 776, the monk Hui-lang, who was Pu-k'ung's successor at the Ta hsing-shan ssu, dispatched an urgent appeal to Tai-tsung requesting that Li be replaced immediately: 'If his post remains vacant, there will be no way to continue the good works that have been started . . . Since the office of commissioner of good works was established, blessings have followed one upon another, while misfortunes have declined in frequency . . . The Buddhist clergy has had no fear of being frustrated or humiliated . . . But now that Yüan-ts'ung is dead, monks in the capital gaze at each other in silence, their eyes reflecting their grief . . . I therefore humbly implore Your Majesty to select another man of virtue to take charge of the Office of Good Works.'63 We do not know how long it took Tai-tsung to act on this advice, but by the eleventh month of the year 778 we find another general, Liu Ch'ung-hsün, who had succeeded Li Yüan-ts'ung as Commander of the Lung-wu Palace Army of the Right, occupying the office of commissioner of good works for Buddhist monasteries and Taoist temples in the capital.64 The available evidence suggests that Liu was chosen for this post simply because he fell heir to Li Yüan-ts'ung's command of the Lung-wu Palace Army and not because he either particularly admired the Buddhist faith or coveted the role of a patron of the church. In fact, as we shall see below, shortly after the death of Tai-tsung, Liu himself proposed the removal of military officials from all posts relating to religious affairs.

In the last years of his reign, most likely in the year 778, Tai-tsung established a new office to represent the palace in its dealings with the Buddhist clergy. To this newly created post, known as the commissioner of good works for the palace (*nei kung-te shih*),65 he appointed the eunuch Li Hsien-ch'eng, who, like the first commissioner of good works for the capital, Li Yüan-ts'ung, had been a close disciple of Pu-k'ung. In his will Pu-k'ung had spoken warmly of the support that he had received over the years from Li Hsien-ch'eng, whom he characterized as a man who 'not only has served the Emperor loyally but one who also is a bodhisattva who protects the Dharma' (*hu-fa p'u-sa*).66 Li Hsien-ch'eng's name figures prominently in a very large number of memorials submitted by monks to the throne throughout the 770s,67 which suggests that even before his appointment as commissioner of good works for the palace around 778, he had been designated to be the Inner Palace official with primary responsibility for receiving communications from the clergy for transmission to Tai-tsung. As was the case with Li Yüan-ts'ung, it seems likely that Li Hsien-ch'eng was chosen to act as the liaison between the Buddhist clergy, largely headed by Pu-k'ung's disciples, and the Inner Palace, where Li Hsien-ch'eng served as a eunuch, because of his long association with Pu-k'ung. Although his formal status within the Inner Palace was that of a secretary (*nei-chi-shih*),68 his title in most of the memorials is given simply as commissioner of the Inner Palace (*chung-shih*)69 or commissioner for overseeing [Buddhist affairs] (*chien-shih*).70

A good illustration of how the two commissioners of good works actually functioned is provided by the monk Yüan-chao in his account of the compilation of a new, 'definitive' commentary on the *Vinaya* that was begun under imperial aegis in 778.71 According to Yüan-chao, who was

Reign of Tai-tsung (762–779) 87

one of the participants in the project, Tai-tsung was distressed by the constant wrangling by monks over discrepancies in the interpretations given in the different existing commentaries on the *Vinaya*. Since, as we have already noted, the *Vinaya* was the ultimate authority within the Buddhist church for regulating the behavior of monks, it was evidently desirable to standardize the Chinese commentaries on it so that a uniform interpretation of the rules could be applied in the different monasteries. Much of the confusion resulted from the widespread use during the eighth century of two conflicting commentaries: the so-called Old Commentary (*Chiu shu*) written by the distinguished *Vinaya* scholar Fa-li[72] in 626 and the New Commentary (*Hsin shu*) completed by Huai-su[73] in 682, which criticized the earlier work with respect to sixteen specific points of doctrine.[74] Each commentary had its own devoted group of supporters who criticized their opponents in sharp terms – a situation that was viewed as disruptive to the Buddhist order by Tai-tsung who saw himself as having been entrusted by the Buddha with the safekeeping of the Dharma.[75]

In order to put an end to the squabbling within the clergy regarding the commentaries, Tai-tsung decided to convene a council of *Vinaya* scholars for the purpose of reconciling the old and the new commentaries. On the twenty-seventh day of the eleventh month of 778 he sent Li Hsien-ch'eng, his commissioner of good works for the palace, to Liu Ch'ung-hsün, commander of the Lung-wu Palace Army of the Right and commissioner of good works for Buddhist monasteries and Taoist temples in the capital, with an order directing Liu to summon a group of *Vinaya* scholars, headed by the monk Ju-ching, to the An-kuo ssu, where they were to prepare a definitive commentary. On the morning of the twenty-ninth day fourteen *Vinaya* scholars drawn from both halves of Ch'ang-an gathered at this monastery in response to the imperial directive. The following day an order was issued to the Office of the Palace Commissary (Shang-shih chü) to provide the fourteen monks at the An-kuo ssu with a ninety-day supply of food. On the next day, which was the first day of the twelfth month, Li Hsien-ch'eng, acting on behalf of the Emperor, sent the monks twenty-five 'strings' (*ch'uan*) of tea, one thousand sheets of paper, fifty writing brushes, and five ink-sticks. By order of the Emperor the hall in which the monks were to carry out their deliberations was then sealed off and no one, monk or layman, was allowed to enter without having his name reported to the authorities. The *Vinaya* scholars worked on their commentary in isolation and uninterruptedly, except for the first month of 779, when they were directed to take part in the New Year services held at two monasteries in

Ch'ang-an, where prayers were offered for the prosperity of the empire. Their synthetic commentary was only half finished when Tai-tsung suddenly died in the fifth month of that year.

With the possible exception of Tai-tsung's first two or three years on the throne when he was preoccupied with military matters in the wake of the An Lu-shan rebellion, Tai-tsung provided lavish support – both material and moral – for the Buddhist church enabling it to grow in numbers and wealth. The Emperor made clear his deep personal devotion to Buddhism early in his reign when, in 765, he had a gilded bronze image of the Buddha installed at the Kuang-shun Gate within the Ta-ming Palace, where he personally led his officials in an act of worship.[76] Two years later Tai-tsung ordered that the two 'relics' allegedly coming from the body of the Buddha – a tooth and a lump of flesh – be moved from the Ch'ung-sheng ssu to the Right Yin-t'ai Gate of the Ta-ming Palace so that he could do reverence to them.[77] He gave concrete expression to his piety by frequently sponsoring 'vegetarian banquets' (*chai*) for the clergy on a grand scale. In the year 773 alone he ordered two such banquets: one, in the fifth month, for four thousand monks at the Chao-ch'eng ssu in memory of the anniversary of the death of Tai-tsung; and the other, in the eight month, for ten thousand monks at the Ta tz'u-en ssu for the general well-being of the people.[78] Similarly mass ordinations involving hundreds or even thousands of monks and nuns at state expense were commonplace. In the first month of the New Year of 773 Tai-tsung authorized all Buddhist monasteries and Taoist temples with less than seven clerics in residence to conduct ordinations so that they could reach this minimum number; monasteries and temples with more than seven clerics but less than fourteen were permitted to ordain three new clerics; and those monasteries and temples with more than twenty-one clerics in residence were allowed to add one new cleric.[79]

In view of the partiality that Tai-tsung displayed toward the Buddhist church, it is not surprising that Buddhists and Confucians should assess his reign in sharply contrasting terms. To Yüan-chao, who was one of the scholar-monks who had benefited directly from imperial patronage, Tai-tsung was a ruler who 'showed respect for the Buddhist church, believed in the doctrines of Mahāyāna, and venerated the Esoteric Teachings.'[80] The Buddhist historian Tsan-ning, writing some two hundred years later, looked back with nostalgia: 'The age of Tai-tsung was one in which the Emperor and his subjects, the court and the country at large, all revered Buddhism.'[81] Yet he was forced to concede that 'non-Buddhists [*i-tao*] resented Tai-tsung's bias in favor of

Buddhism.'[82] In the eyes of the Confucian historian, however, Tai-tsung's massive support of religious enterprises portended economic ruin, while his singleminded dedication to Buddhism smacked of fanaticism. Liu Hsü, the compiler of the *Chiu T'ang shu*, probably spoke for the majority of Confucian historians when he gave the following critique of Tai-tsung's reign: 'Most of the fertile land and much of the wealth in the capital region passed to the Buddhist monasteries and Taoist temples, and the officials were powerless to control the Buddhist clergy. Tai-tsung's faith in Buddhism remained unshaken even in the face of recurrent corruption, rebellion, and military defeats.'[83]

Reign of Te-tsung (779–805)

Te-tsung, who had been invested as crown prince in 764, succeeded to the throne upon the death of his father, Tai-tsung, in the fifth month of 779. Having observed at first hand the steady deterioration in the court's fiscal position over the preceding two decades, Te-tsung immediately instituted a number of bold economic reforms in the hope of achieving financial stability for the central government. As we have seen, it had long been recognized by bureaucrats that the heavy expenditures on the construction of monasteries, religious services, and maintenance of monks and nuns were putting a great strain on the treasury. If the economy was to be on a sound footing, restrictions would have to be placed on the size, wealth, and the activities of the Buddhist church.

The opening salvo, fired almost one month to the day after Te-tsung assumed the throne, came from an unexpected source – Liu Ch'ung-hsün, the commissioner of good works for Buddhist monasteries and Taoist temples in the capital. As an army commander, Liu felt it inappropriate that he should be required to concern himself with church affairs. On the twenty-fifth day of the intercalary fifth month Liu submitted a petition, perhaps inspired in part by the new emperor's ideas of reform, requesting that he be relieved of his duties as commissioner of good works.[1] Te-tsung responded favorably, immediately issuing an impromptu decree, technically known as a *mo-chih*,[2] in which he voiced support for Liu's contention that the sole responsibility of a commander of the imperial guard should be the maintenance of security in the capital. 'Since the practice of the Buddhist religion has no relation to military matters,' Te-tsung wrote, 'the supervision of Buddhist monasteries and Taoist temples falls within the jurisdiction of the officials in the civil departments.'[3] The coordinate posts of commissioner of good works for the palace and commissioner of good works for Buddhist monasteries and Taoist temples in the capital were both promptly abolished by an imperial order, which returned control of the Buddhist clergy to the Department of Sacrifices (Tz'u-pu). In the following month Te-tsung served notice that he would not accept any requests for permission either to found new Buddhist monasteries or Taoist temples or to carry out ordinations.[4] By the middle of the year 780 he made clear his intention of loosening the grip that Buddhist (and to a lesser extent, Taoist) monks had on the court since the An Lu-shan rebellion through their use of esoteric rituals designed to bring about the downfall of the enemies of the imperial family. On the fifteenth day of the seventh month, which is the date for the annual Buddhist mass for the dead (*Yü-lan-p'en*), he abolished these services at the court and ordered the dismantlement of the Palace Chapel (*nei-tao-ch'ang*).[5] At about the same time Te-tsung expelled the Taoist thaumaturges (*wu-chu*), some of whom had achieved high office during the reigns of his father and grandfather.[6]

Te-tsung's early decision to curb the Buddhist and Taoist monks at the court was applauded by many officials, both civilian and military, who had watched with alarm the vast expenditures on religion during the preceding reign. Once Te-tsung had indicated his intention of implementing reforms in the religious as well as in the secular fields, he was presented with a number of concrete proposals advising him how he might best check the enormous religious establishment that he had inherited. In the first or second year of his reign Te-tsung received from Li Shu-ming, the military governor of Chien-nan Tung-ch'uan in Szechwan, a memorial calling for an outright purge of the Buddhist and Taoist clergies.[7] Li, who held the degree in classics (*ming-ching*), is described as a man who 'from the outset despised the abuses of Taoism and Buddhism.' His critique of these religions focused on the harm that they did to the economy, which was very much a reflection of the concerns of the court at this time. Li proposed that he be allowed to assign one of three possible grades to each officially sanctioned monastery in the area under his control. According to his scheme, monasteries of the highest grade (*shang-teng ssu*) would be permitted to accommodate a maximum of twenty-one monks, those of the intermediary grade fourteen monks, and those of the lowest grade seven monks.[8] Only men of impeccable conduct would be selected for these monasteries; monks who did not measure up to this high standard were to be returned to lay life and listed in the registers as 'common people.' All small monasteries, chapels, hermitages and the like that did not have official recognition were to be closed down.[9]

Te-tsung was favorably impressed by Li Shu-ming's proposals, but felt that instead of limiting the purge of the Buddhist and Taoist clergies to the Szechwan region as Li had suggested, it should be applied uniformly throughout the empire.[10] Li's memorial was referred in due course to the Department of State Affairs (Shang-shu sheng), where it met with criticism from P'eng Yen, an official in the Bureau of Records (Tu-kuan), who argued that Li's plan did not go far enough toward correcting the harmful effects that the maintenance of a large clergy was having on the economy.[11] P'eng told the emperor that if his reform (*wei-hsin*) was to succeed, he must eliminate abuses stemming from the excesses of the church. Although he recognized, as did Li Shu-ming, that curbs had to be applied to the Taoist as well as to the Buddhist clergies, he asserted that the former existed primarily in name and hence did not have much real importance. Taoist observances, he noted, rarely led to serious trouble, and their effect on government was negligible. The Buddhist clergy, on the other hand, was the source of all sorts of corruption.

P'eng Yen declared that he had no quarrel with Buddhist teachings *per se*. On the contrary, the Buddhist church in China deserved criticism because its true doctrine of 'non-substantiality' had never been put into practice, since too much time had elapsed between the passing away of the Buddha and the actual introduction of Buddhism into China. Most monks and nuns, in P'eng's view, were uneducated persons of questionable moral character who would not shrink from committing criminal acts ranging from tax evasion to fornication, theft, and murder. Although he conceded that a few members of the Buddhist clergy were noted for their virtuous conduct, even they, ultimately, were of little value to the state since they contributed nothing materially. His arguments were couched in the familiar Confucian utilitarian rhetoric: 'Buddhist monks and Taoist priests do not till the fields, yet they consume food; they do not work the loom, yet they wear clothing.'[12] P'eng estimated that the annual cost for supplying a single monk with food and clothing amounted to approximately 30,000 cash,[13] a sum greater than the taxes paid by five male adults (*ting*). In order to put an end to this enormous drain on the economy, P'eng suggested that Buddhist and Taoist monks under the age of fifty be required to pay an annual tax of four bolts (*p'i*) of silk and be liable for the same corvée labor (*tsa-se i*) that was expected of the common people. Nuns of either religion were to be taxed only two bolts of silk annually. P'eng calculated that if these taxes were levied on the clergy, the total yield of revenue for the treasury would be increased by more than one third. Needless to say, members of the clergy would be free to return to lay status if they so desired, and he estimated that when faced with the prospect of a head tax, the majority of monks and nuns would probably choose this option. P'eng proposed that all clerics over the age of forty-nine be exempt from taxation in the hope of raising the average age of people in religious orders. Citing passages from the *Analects* and the *Lieh-tzu* praising the wisdom of the elderly,[14] P'eng wryly commented that men who had passed their forty-ninth year, irrespective of whether they had taken holy orders, were naturally qualified to be spiritual leaders since they were no longer troubled by sensual desires.

An even more radical plan for a purge of the clergy was presented to the throne by P'ei Po, an official in the Board of Justice (Hsing-pu),[15] who held that monks and nuns were violating the laws of the state and making a mockery of traditional Chinese customs through their practice of celibacy, which threatened the continuity of the family. To remedy the situation, P'ei urged a ban on the ordination of all females between the ages of thirteen and forty-eight, which he regarded as their reproductive years. Similarly, no males were to be ordained between the ages of fifteen and sixty-three, at which time the male was believed to exhaust his power of '*yang* transformations' (*yang-hua*), i.e. the ability to father children. All monks and nuns within these age groups were to be immediately laicized, entered in the tax registers, and furnished with land to work. Since a purge on such a grand scale would inevitably result in the abandonment of a large number of monasteries, P'ei suggested that all deserted monasteries should be taken over by the state and used for other purposes.

Although Te-tsung openly expressed his approval for these various schemes to reduce the size of the Buddhist and Taoist clergies, practical political considerations ultimately prevented their implementation. Yang Yen's drastic proposals of 780 to revamp the tax structure in the hope of strengthening the fiscal position of the central administration aroused the suspicions of the virtually autonomous military governors in North China, who kept a sharp eye open for any possible encroachment on their prerogatives. Their doubts about the real intentions of the new emperor were confirmed the following year when Te-tsung attempted to block Li Wei-yüeh's succession to the post of military governor of Ch'eng-te following the death of his father, Li Pao-ch'en. Te-tsung's interference in the internal affairs of a military governorship led to a concerted rebellion by army officers in the North that dragged on for five years. In 783 the situation became so perilous that Te-tsung was compelled to flee from Ch'ang-an to Feng-t'ien in Shensi. The following year, in an effort to mollify the rebellious governors, Te-tsung issued an edict in which he acknowledged his own responsibility for having provoked the crisis.[16] Under these circumstances it is not surprising that Te-tsung decided in the end to accept the advice of more cautious officials who urged him to confine his reforms to correcting only the grossest abuses and to refrain from any precipitate action against the Buddhist and Taoist churches which had enjoyed imperial patronage as well as popular support.[17] The only new measure of control that Te-tsung in fact instituted is found in an order issued in 782 instructing monastic officials to inform the county (*hsien*) office immediately in the event that a resident monk or nun either dies or leaves his monastery to return to lay life.[18] A similar notification, accompanied by the invalidated ordination certificate of the dead or laicized monk, was to be sent to the prefectural (*chou*) authorities as well. Monasteries in Ch'ang-an were told to file their reports directly with the Department of Sacrifices (Tz'u-pu).

To meet the heavy military expenditure necessitated by the outbreak of fighting in 781, the central administration attempted to increase revenue by levying a variety of new taxes on buildings (*shui-chien-chia*), commercial transactions (*ch'u-mo-ch'ien*), and certain commodities like tea and salt as well as by forced loans from merchants. In an effort to replenish the depleted treasury, some officials resorted to outright confiscation of the property of deceased Buddhist monks and nuns.[19] Although members of the Buddhist clergy in early India were ideally supposed to possess only such personal property as was necessary for their subsistence like robes, a begging bowl, and a mat for sleeping or meditation, in China we find numerous instances of individual monks amassing considerable personal wealth in the form of land, buildings, stocks of grain, slaves, animals, precious metals, and cash, even though Buddhist tradition denied monks and nuns the right to hold such property.[20] As early as the year 509 a decree was issued by Emperor Hsüan of the Northern Wei prohibiting monks from using their own capital for money-lending.[21] In the long run, however, such attempts to curtail the financial activities of clerics generally proved unsuccessful, as can be seen from the numerous references in T'ang and Sung times to 'wealthy monks' (*fu-seng*).[22]

According to the *Vinaya*, members of the clergy were not free to bequeath their property at will. The general rule regarding the disposition of property of deceased monks was that articles intended for personal use such as a monk's robes, bowl, or strainer, i.e. the so-called 'light objects' (*ch'ing-wu*, Pāli: *lahuka parikkhāra*), could be distributed among the clerical friends, disciples, and nurses of the deceased monk, whereas property of substantial value such as land, buildings, orchards, etc., i.e. property technically designated 'heavy objects' (*chung-wu*, Pāli: *garuka parikkhāra*), was to be turned over to the monastery to which the deceased monk belonged for use by the entire Buddhist order.[23] However, as documents discovered at Tunhuang have shown, some monks and nuns drew up wills in violation of the provisions of the *Vinaya* bequeathing property in the category of 'heavy objects' to other monks or even to lay members of their own family.[24] If some monks and nuns showed no compunction about disregarding the *Vinaya* with respect to matters of property, so too did government officials not hesitate to seize anything of value that belonged to deceased monks.

In 767 the *Vinaya* master Ch'eng-ju presented a petition to Tai-tsung requesting that officials be enjoined from confiscating such property.[25] Citing the *Vinayas* of various schools, Ch'eng-ju argued that while a monk (or nun) was entitled to derive benefit from his property as long as he lived, this property must pass automatically to the *saṃgha*, i.e. the monastic community as a whole, upon the death of its owner. Ch'eng-ju asserted that random seizure of the property of a deceased monk was an insult to the clergy because it was suggestive of the confiscation of the property of criminal offenders (*chi-mo*). Although Tai-tsung granted Ch'eng-ju's petition, financial exigencies arising from the wars of the early 780s led some overzealous bureaucrats to revert to the earlier practice of expropriating the property of deceased monks. During the first years of his reign when economic reform and restoration of the dignity of the throne were viewed as real possibilities, Te-tsung was willing to turn a blind eye to this practice even though such action contravened his father's edict of 767. Only after it became clear that there was little prospect of winning a decisive victory over the autonomous military governors and re-establishing the authority of the throne did Te-tsung make his first real effort to placate the Buddhist clergy: in 784 he issued a decree reaffirming the traditional Buddhist view that property of deceased monks and nuns belonged to their monasteries.[26] In this decree Te-tsung acknowledged that recent seizures of monks' property had disturbed the tranquility of the church and ordered his officials henceforth to respect the rules of the *Vinaya* regarding the disposal of the property of deceased members of the clergy and to refrain from all attempts at confiscation.

By the time the war with the military governors came to an end in 786 with the death of the usurper Li Hsi-lieh, Te-tsung appears to have given up his hopes of curbing the power of the Buddhist church. Like

T'ai-tsung and Hsüan-tsung who similarly sought to reduce the wealth of the great monasteries at the beginning of their reigns only to finish their lives as lay supporters of Buddhism, Te-tsung too became reconciled to the continued existence of the Buddhist church as a major force within the empire and gradually assumed the role of devotee and patron. His failure to bring the military governors to heel no doubt helped convince him of the wisdom of adopting a more conciliatory policy toward the Buddhist church. Another factor that contributed to the change in Te-tsung's attitude towards Buddhism in the latter half of the 780s was the ascendancy, particularly in military affairs, after 784 of eunuchs like Tou Wen-ch'ang and Huo Hsien-ming, who were themselves devout Buddhists.[27] In 786 Te-tsung visited the *Vinaya* scholar Tao-ch'eng at the Chang-hsin ssu, where he accepted the bodhisattva precepts (*p'u-sa chieh*), an act that symbolized his formal commitment to Buddhism.[28] Later the same year Tao-ch'eng was invited to the court to administer the bodhisattva precepts to the imperial concubines and chief eunuch stewards (*nei-shih*) of the Inner Palace.[29] The annual *Yü-lan-p'en* observance at court, which Te-tsung had ordered discontinued in 780, was revived about this time.[30] Te-tsung's continuing esteem for Tao-ch'eng, who initiated him into Buddhism, is evident from his willingness to visit his former precepts-master at the Chang-hsin ssu again in 789 in order to hear a discourse on the dharma.[31]

The extent of the change in Te-tsung's attitude toward Buddhism after the war with the military governors is perhaps best illustrated by his response to a proposal in 787 from the governor of Ch'ang-an (*Ching-chao yin*), Yü-wen Hsüan, who requested permission to dismantle abandoned monasteries in the area under his jurisdiction in order to make lumber available for the construction of schools.[32] Te-tsung, who, as we have seen, had viewed with favor a similar suggestion from P'ei Po some six years earlier, even though he finally decided against its implementation, now reacted with great anger. In an edict that forced the immediate resignation and retirement of Yü-wen Hsüan the Emperor thundered: 'Your proposal to transform Buddhist monasteries into Confucian schools [*Ju-kuan*] constitutes an act of blasphemy against the Buddha, the Dharma, and the Clergy. Such an offense cannot be pardoned!'[33]

Just as Te-tsung reversed himself on the question of the expropriation of church property and the performance of Buddhist rituals at the court, so too did he revive, in a somewhat altered form, the offices of commissioners of good works that had been abolished amidst the reforms that marked the first years of his reign. In 788 he appointed three commissioners of good works: one from the 'left' (or eastern) half of Ch'ang-an (*tso-chieh ta kung-te shih* or *tung-chieh ta kung-te shih*), another for the 'right' (or western) half of Ch'ang-an (*yu-chieh ta kung-te shih*), and a third for Lo-yang (*Tung-tu kung-te shih*).[34] Although we have no information regarding the status of the holder of the last of these three posts, contemporary documents indicate that only high-ranking eunuch generals were named to the Ch'ang-an commissionerships. The first incumbents were Tou Wen-ch'ang[35] and Wang Hsi-ch'ien,[36] who were, respectively, commanders of the Shen-ts'e Palace Armies of the Left and the Right. Wang was eventually succeeded in the post of commissioner of good works for the right half of Ch'ang-an by another eunuch general of the Shen-ts'e Army, Huo Hsien-ming.[37] After the latter's death in 798, the commissionership passed to Ti-wu Shou-liang, who likewise was a eunuch commander of the Shen-ts'e Army of the Right.[38]

It seems safe to assume that the eunuch generals did not seek appointments as commissioners of good works solely for reasons of piety or because of an interest in religious affairs, even though eunuchs generally appear to have been devout believers. The post of commissioner of good works no doubt was attractive to the eunuch generals, at least in part, because it provided them with an opportunity to enrich themselves, since the commissioners of good works, after the year 788, were specifically charged with the task of overseeing the construction of monasteries and maintaining the registers of monks and nuns (*seng-ni chi*).[39] The latter responsibility could of course prove to be very lucrative for the commissioner, owing to the widespread practice after the An Lu-shan rebellion of selling ordination certificates.

Despite Te-tsung's plans for curbing the power of the Buddhist church early in his reign, Te-tsung eventually emerged, after the unsuccessful wars against the military governors between 781 and 786, as one of the most devout Buddhist rulers. Numerous instances of his support for Buddhism can be cited for the latter part of Te-tsung's reign. In 789, for example, he issued an edict stressing the sanctity of Buddhist monasteries and Taoist temples and forbade laymen from using them as hostels.[40] He further ordered in this edict that all dilapidated monasteries should be repaired. In the eighth month of the same year he decreed that services should be held annually in each of the major provinces (*shang-chou*) on the anniversary of his father's death.[41] Te-tsung, accompanied by his ministers, also paid frequent visits during this period to monasteries, especially at mid-year when masses for the dead were performed.[42] But his deep piety is perhaps best illustrated by his decision in the first month of 790 to have the famous finger-bone relic that had been enshrined in the Fa-men ssu in Feng-hsiang installed temporarily in the newly reopened palace chapel (*chin-chung ching-she*) so that he could do homage to it personally as Kao-tsung and Su-tsung had done.[43] The relic subsequently was exhibited at the major monasteries in Ch'ang-an, where it was worshipped by throngs who donated vast sums of money. So great was Te-tsung's reverence for the relic that when the time had come to return it to the Fa-men ssu one month later, a general from the Palace Army was delegated to serve as an escort.

It is a curious paradox that Te-tsung, who during the first years of his reign looked with favor on various schemes for reducing the economic burdens that the Buddhist church imposed on the state, should have distinguished himself as the last T'ang emperor to use government funds on a lavish scale to support translation of scripture and other literary projects. We have already noted that when Te-tsung ascended the throne in 779, work was in progress on a new, synthetic commentary on the *Vinaya*, which had begun during the preceding year under the sponsorship of Te-tsung. Although, as we have seen, the newly enthroned Te-tsung agreed to Liu Ch'ung-hsün's proposal to abolish the office of commissioner of good works, which had been supervising the compilation of the *Vinaya* commentary, he nevertheless continued to provide financial support for the project. When the completed commentary was presented to him in 780, Te-tsung responded graciously by awarding Yüan-chao, who was one of the principal participants, a purple robe – the highest mark of distinction for a monk – and an honorary court rank in addition to assigning three hundred households for Yüan-chao's maintenance.[44]

Aside from this particular instance, which was in fact a continuation of a project initiated by his father, Te-tsung does not appear to have patronized Buddhist scholarship until 788, when he authorised the establishment of an Institute for the Translation of Buddhist Scriptures (I-ching yüan), which he placed under the supervision of the eunuch general Wang Hsi-ch'ien, who held the post of commissioner of good works for the western half of Ch'ang-an.[45] The principal beneficiary of the Institute was the North Indian monk Prajñā who had arrived in Canton via Southeast Asia in 781.[46] The following year Prajñā moved to Ch'ang-an, where he met the Persian Nestorian priest Ching-ching ('Adam'),[47] who was the author of the famous Nestorian stele there. Since Ching-ching already had considerable experience in rendering Nestorian texts into Chinese, Prajñā sought his assistance in preparing Chinese translations of Sanskrit Buddhist works. The two men collaborated in 786 to produce the *Ta-sheng li-ch'ü liu po-lo-mi-to ching*, a

Mahāyāna sūtra of the *Prajñāpāramitā* class that was especially concerned with the protection of the state, which was of course a topic of particular interest to the ruler. As might be expected, the translation, executed by an Indian Buddhist who at the time knew little Chinese and a Persian Nestorian who could not read Sanskrit, was something of a fiasco.[48] In 788, a distraught official who deplored the confusion of Nestorian and Buddhist ideas in the translation brought the matter to the attention of Te-tsung, who ordered Wang Hsi-ch'ien to select a group of distinguished monks to assist Prajñā in making a retranslation of the sūtra. Eight eminent monks, including Yüan-chao, were instructed to move to the Hsi-ming ssu, where the new translation was to be carried out. The emperor provided one hundred strings of cash to cover the various expenses and in addition donated a generous supply of tea and incense. When the new translation was finally completed later the same year, Te-tsung wrote a preface for it that still survives.[49] Two years later Prajñā was awarded the purple robe and honored with the title Master of the Tripitika (San-tsang), which signified his formal recognition as the leading translator at the court of Te-tsung.[50]

As was the case with Amoghavajra, Prajñā paid a brief visit to his native India to acquire copies of additional texts for translation into Chinese. He returned to Ch'ang-an in 792 with a sizable collection of Tantric scriptures, many of which he subsequently translated. His most important contribution to Chinese Buddhist literature was his translation of the *Gaṇḍavyūha*, a lengthy Mahāyānist work of considerable literary merit describing the quest for enlightenment by a youth named Sudhana (Shan-ts'ai).[51] A copy of the Sanskrit text of the *Gaṇḍavyūha* had been presented to Te-tsung personally in 795 by an envoy dispatched to China specifically for this purpose by the king of Oḍra in East India.[52] A group of ten monks headed by Prajñā and including Yüan-chao and Ch'eng-kuan – two of the most eminent scholars of the day – was ordered to prepare a complete Chinese version of the text. Work on the translation was begun in 796 and completed two years later. It should be noted that in addition to the support that Te-tsung provided for Prajñā's translation activities,[53] he also sponsored the compilation of two new catalogues of the canon: the *Hsü K'ai-yüan lu*, in three fascicles, completed in 794, which supplemented the *K'ai-yüan lu* compiled by Chih-seng in 730, and the *Chen-yüan lu*, in thirty fascicles, completed in 800, which was the last comprehensive catalogue of the Buddhist canon prepared under the T'ang. Another reference work of great scholarly value produced during Te-tsung's reign was Hui-lin's hundred-fascicle *I-ch'ieh-ching yin-i*, which provides glosses for technical terms and Chinese transcriptions of Indic words and names drawn from 1,300 different works in the Buddhist canon.[54] Although the T'ang dynasty continued for another hundred years after the death of Te-tsung in 805, the close of his reign, which spanned a quarter of a century, marked the end of state-supported literary activities that were one of the hallmarks of T'ang Buddhism.[55]

Reigns of Shun-tsung (805) and Hsien-tsung (805–820)

Te-tsung was followed on the throne by his eldest son, Li Sung (known posthumously as Shun-tsung), who was himself already ailing when he was called upon in the first month of 805, at the relatively advanced age of forty-four, to succeed his father. Shun-tsung reigned for a mere seven months before being persuaded to abdicate for reasons of health and clique politics in favor of his own eldest son, Li Ch'un (subsequently designated Hsien-tsung), who was then twenty-seven years of age. There is much evidence that both father and son were seriously interested in Buddhist thought, particularly of the Ch'an variety, which, as we have noted, had spread rapidly after the An Lu-shan rebellion. While still Crown Prince, Shun-tsung commissioned the celebrated scholar Ch'eng-kuan, who is counted as a patriarch in both the Ch'an and Hua-yen lineages, to compose two short commentaries on the recently translated *Hua-yen ching* as well as to prepare a treatise in defense of the Buddhist prohibition against eating flesh.[1] Even before his accession to the throne, Shun-tsung had already established a close personal relationship with Tuan-fu, one of the most learned monks of his day, who frequented the court of Te-tsung and had been granted the purple robe in recognition of his skill in debating the representatives of Confucianism and Taoism at the court.[2] In 797 Tuan-fu was assigned to the palace of the Crown Prince, who subsequently became his patron and admirer.[3] After becoming emperor, Shun-tsung placed Tuan-fu in charge of Buddhist rituals in the Inner Palace, an act that signified the reopening of the Palace Chapel which had been closed by his father.[4] During his brief tenure as emperor, Shun-tsung invited the Ch'an monk Pao-hsiu to the capital to discuss the value of written scripture with some unnamed Indian translator.[5] In addition, Shun-tsung also summoned to his court the Ch'an master Shih-li, who was a disciple of Shih-t'ou, one of the most prominent figures in the history of Ch'an Buddhism.[6] The story of the enigmatic encounter between Emperor and Ch'an master has been preserved in the Ch'an records.[7]

Hsien-tsung, who succeeded his father as emperor in the eighth month of 805, proved himself to be a devout patron of Buddhism throughout his fifteen-year-long reign. Despite his preoccupation with military affairs, he found time to discourse regularly with Buddhist monks, particularly those of Ch'an lineage, and visit monasteries in the Ch'ang-an area to which he made liberal donations. In fact during the first five years of his reign at least one monk was invited annually to the palace to be personally questioned by the Emperor on points of doctrine.[8]

The reign of Hsien-tsung is especially significant for the development of T'ang religious institutions because of certain fundamental changes that were instituted with respect to control over the Buddhist and Taoist clergies. Apparently unable or unwilling to resist the rapaciousness of the eunuch-general T'u-t'u Ch'eng-ts'ui who was appointed commissioner of good works for both halves of Ch'ang-an in 807,[9] Hsien-tsung ordered that henceforth the latter office would have the scope of its jurisdiction broadened to include the Taoist clergy in addition to the Buddhist clergy, which had been under its supervision since 788.[10] To show that the control over the clergy by the commissioners of good works was absolute, the same decree further stipulated that monks and nuns, whether Buddhist or Taoist, were no longer required to register with the Department of Sacrifices (Tz'u-pu) or the Office for Peerage Ranks (Ssu-feng), which had been responsible for keeping records of the Buddhist and Taoist clergies respectively since 743. Thus, in a single stroke, the enormous religious establishment in China consisting of several hundred thousand monks and nuns was detached from the traditional bureaucratic apparatus and transferred to an office that was solely in the hands of eunuch-generals.

In order to give the Buddhist church some semblance of autonomy in this new arrangement Hsien-tsung broke with the established policy of his predecessors by appointing two distinguished monks to be the chief ecclesiastical officers of the empire. These two monks were responsible for maintaining the clerical registers, which had heretofore been the function of lay officials within the Department of Sacrifices, and for overseeing church matters in general. The appointment of two clerics to take charge of religious affairs, even if under the ultimate supervision of lay commissioners of good works, marked a clear departure from the earlier T'ang policy of not permitting a monk to preside over the church, even nominally, as had been the standard practice under previous dynasties. The two newly appointed ecclesiastical officers were called recorders of the clergy (*seng-lu*), a term that was first used under the Later Ch'in dynasty (384–417) to designate the two third-ranking members of the central hierarchy who were subordinate to the head of the clergy (*seng-chu*) and chief administrator (*yüeh-chung*).[11] Although recorders of the clergy were appointed throughout the remainder of the T'ang, the offices of head of the clergy and chief administrator were left vacant. By designating the two highest-ranking monks recorders of the clergy rather than heads of the clergy, the government made it clear that although the church was now under the immediate administrative supervision of monks, its autonomy was something less than absolute.

In 807, the first two recorders of the clergy, each of equal rank, were appointed by imperial decree: one to 'record' (*lu*) clerical affairs for the 'left' (or eastern) half of Ch'ang-an (*tso-chieh*) and the other for the 'right' (or western) half of the city (*yu-chieh*).[12] The monk Tuan-fu, who, as we have seen, had been put in charge of Buddhist rituals at the court of Shun-tsung, was named recorder of the clergy for the eastern half of Ch'ang-an, a post which he occupied for ten years. Just before Tuan-fu's death in 836, he briefly held both recorder of the clergy posts simultaneously, which appears to have been a unique honor accorded to him in recognition of his services to the courts of six T'ang emperors.[13] The first occupant of the post of recorder of the clergy for the western half of Ch'ang-an was Ling-sui, who since 799 was in charge of the administrative office of the commissioner of good works for the western half of Ch'ang-an.[14] Although the titles of the two recorders of the clergy seem to suggest that their authority was limited to the confines of the city of Ch'ang-an, we know from Ennin's firsthand account that they exercised control over monasteries throughout the entire country and regulated Buddhist affairs in general.[15] This, of course, did not prevent a commissioner of good works from issuing his own directives to the clergy if he so desired.[16] In the military governorships, where the authority of the court was relatively weak, control over the Buddhist monasteries continued to be vested in a single locally appointed ecclesiastical official designated rectifier of the clergy (*seng-cheng*),[17] a title which had been used intermittently in South China since the fifth century to refer to the head of the Buddhist clergy within a specified area.

Although, as we have noted, Hsien-tsung was a devout Buddhist, he was nevertheless alarmed by the growing number of peasants who were claiming clerical status to avoid payment of taxes. In third month of 807, he issued a decree reminding his subjects that since the farmer and his family were the primary source of all food and clothing, they could not be allowed to call themselves Buddhist or Taoist monks or nuns at will, thereby nullifying their civic obligations.[18] Local officials were ordered to report the names of all persons claiming clerical status who were not actively pursuing the religious life. Hsien-tsung also criticized at the same time the construction of luxurious monasteries on the grounds that they would ultimately bring ruin to the nation and decreed that the building of large-scale monasteries must observe the limits laid down in an edict especially promulgated to deal with this matter.[19] As we have already noted above, a ban was simultaneously proclaimed in 807 on all 'private ordinations' (*ssu-tu*), which were a means commonly used by local officials to generate revenue for their own purposes.[20] These restrictions designed to keep people on the tax rolls seem to have met with little success, which was doubtless a reflection of the decline in the authority of the imperial court. A mere four years later we read of a memorial from the Secretariat-Chancellery (Chung-shu men-hsia) deploring the large number of men who evaded military service by becoming tradesmen or Buddhist or Taoist monks.[21] According to this source, it was estimated that the productive workers accounted for no more than thirty percent of the total population.

The last years of Hsien-tsung's reign were marked by conspicuous displays of the Emperor's piety. When, for example, he learnt in 815 of the plans of monks in the Hsi-ming ssu to move the image of the popular Buddhist divinity Vaiśravaṇa (P'i-sha-men) to another monastery in the city he ordered that the image first be lodged temporarily within his palace, to which it was carried in a spectacular procession replete with religious banners and canopies under escort of the imperial cavalry.[22] In 817 Hsien-tsung had a monastery built to commemorate his reign and later in the same year he presented a gift of a hundred bolts of fine silk to the Hsing-fo ssu.[23] The following year he bestowed three hundred bolts of silk on the Hsing-fu ssu, a monastery established by T'ai-tsung in 634, and dispatched commissioners of the Inner Palace (*chung-shih*) to make offerings at a vegetarian banquet for monks and laymen (*wu-che seng-chai*) sponsored by merchants from the west market in Ch'ang-an.

By far the best known instance of Hsien-tsung's personal devotion to Buddhism occurred in the first month of 819, just one year before his death, when he had the famous 'finger-bone relic' that belonged to the Fa-men ssu in Feng-hsiang brought to the Imperial Palace so that he could worship it personally. Despite the notoriety that Hsien-tsung achieved among later generations of Confucian scholars because of his confrontation with Han Yü on this occasion, his act of reverence towards the relic was in no way unique, since at least four of his predecessors on the T'ang throne had likewise paid homage to it.[24] The idea of having the relic brought to Ch'ang-an was first broached by one of the commissioners of good works in the eleventh month of 818, when he related to the Emperor a belief, elsewhere unattested, that peace and prosperity would prevail throughout the empire provided that the relic was removed from its shrine in the Fa-men ssu and displayed publicly once every thirty years.[25] Since the monasteries in Ch'ang-an were firmly under the control of the commissioners of good works at this time, it is possible that the latter sought to persuade the Emperor to have the relic brought to the capital because of its potential for attracting from the faithful large donations of money, part of which was likely to find its way into the pockets of the eunuch commissioners.

Whatever the motives of the commissioners of good works, Hsientsung seems to have been genuinely persuaded by the proposal and the following month dispatched a group of monks led by a commissioner of the Inner Palace (*chung-shih*) to fetch the relic from the Fa-men ssu. When the group, on its return journey, reached the post-station at Lin-kao, ten *li* west of Ch'ang-an, it was met by another commissioner who had been especially sent by the Emperor to provide an escort of imperial guards (*chin-ping*) to conduct the procession to the palace, where the relic was enshrined for three days before being exhibited at the various monasteries in Ch'ang-an to frenetic crowds of worshippers.[26] People of all classes 'from the princes and aristocrats at the top to the commoners at the bottom' appear to have outdone one another in paying homage and making monetary contributions. The more fanatical worshipper, a variety of sources tells us, was not content merely to squander his resources on religious offerings, but also mutilated his body by searing the crown of his head (*shao-ting*) or scarring his arms with fire (*cho-pi*). Still others, pretending to be ascetics, set up stalls where they deliberately seared their limbs in the hope of attracting donations from the superstitious crowds that gathered about them.[27] The population of Ch'ang-an was quickly swelled by an influx of farmers from the countryside, which further contributed to the breakdown of order within the city and disrupted, at least briefly, the economy of the surrounding rural areas.

No doubt many of the literati were appalled by the religous frenzy sweeping the capital, especially since it was induced by and had the support of the Imperial Palace. One such scholar was the famed Confucian Han Yü (768–824), who at the time held the post of vice president of the Board of Justice (*hsing-pu shih-lang*). Some years before, Han Yü had already written an anti-Buddhist (and also anti-Taoist) essay entitled *Yüan-tao* (*An Examination of The Way*)[28] in which he repeated a number of familiar Confucian criticisms of these two religions: their clergies, glorifying the concept of purity (*ch'ing-ching*) and quiescence (*chi-mieh*), were idle and contributed nothing of real value to society; they disdained human relationships, preferring instead to withdraw from the world; moreover, Buddhism was an alien doctrine and hence inferior to the civilized teachings of China. Since, in Han Yü's view, Buddhism and Taoism were both harmful to the state, he proposed that their clergies be laicized, their scriptures burnt, and their monasteries converted into secular hostels.[29] Despite the drastic measures advocated to suppress Buddhism, the *Yüan-tao* seems to have been generally ignored by both the pro-Buddhist elements at the court as well as by the Buddhist church, perhaps because the text had not yet circulated widely.[30]

Resentful of the tumultuous reception being accorded the finger-bone relic as it made its rounds of the monasteries in the capital in the first month of 819, Han Yü presented a sharply worded memorial to the throne bearing the blunt title *Lun Fo-ku piao* (*A Memorial Discussing the Bone of the Buddha*), which in time has come to be held up as an outstanding example of prose writing.[31] Questions of rhetorical merit aside, this celebrated memorial by Han Yü attacking Buddhism added little of substance that could not already be found in the stock anti-Buddhist tirades of preceding generations of Confucian-oriented polemicists. What was new, however, was the intemperate language employed toward the Emperor: 'You are ... putting on for the citizens of the capital this extraordinary spectacle which is nothing more than a sort of theatrical amusement ... Now that the Buddha has long been dead, is it fitting that his decayed and rotten bone, his ill-omened and filthy remains, should be allowed to enter in the forbidden precincts of the Palace? ... Without reason you have taken up an unclean thing and examined it in person ...'[32]

If Han Yü's earlier denunciation of Buddhism in his *Yüan-tao* had gone unnoticed, his memorial of 819 produced an immediate response from Hsien-tsung, who was so outraged at its belligerent tone that within a day after receipt of the memorial he announced at court his intention of having Han Yü put to death.[33] Two ministers, P'ei Tu, on whose staff Han Yü had served with distinction two years earlier, and Ts'ui Ch'ün, rushed to Han Yü's defense pleading for leniency on the grounds that although the memorial did indeed contain offensive language for which the author deserved punishment, his motives were nevertheless pure.[34] Hsien-tsung replied that while he was willing to pardon Han Yü for his criticism that it was inappropriate for an emperor to do homage to the Buddha, he could not allow Han Yü to attempt to intimidate the throne by suggesting, as he did in his memorial, that those emperors who had patronized Buddhism in the past either had short reigns or else came to grief. Members of the imperial clan joined the fray by arguing that Han Yü must be punished as a warning to other arrogant subjects, while officials in charge of examining and criticizing government policies (*chien-kuan*) petitioned for his pardon. Eventually, a compromise emerged according to which Han Yü was sent into virtual exile as the prefect (*tz'u-shih*) of Ch'ao-chou. When Hsien-tsung died in the following year, Han Yü was recalled to the capital as chancellor of the Directorate of the State University (*Kuo-tzu chi-chiu*) and shortly thereafter was restored to his previous post of vice president of the Board of Justice. Little did Han Yü suspect, when he died in 824, that the thorough suppression of Buddhism, though not of Taoism, that he advocated in his *Yüan-tao* would be realized only two decades later.

Reigns of Mu-tsung (820–824) and Ching-tsung (824–826)

Hsien-tsung was succeeded on the throne by his third son, Li Heng (known posthumously as Mu-tsung), who was twenty-five years old when his father suddenly died – or was murdered – in the first month of 820.[1] Owing his accession to a clique of powerful eunuchs, Mu-tsung seems to have carried relatively little weight at court. He enjoyed such pastimes as hunting and polo-playing and frequently held lavish banquets, for which he was subjected to much criticism. Although both Buddhist and secular sources depict him as a devout believer and generous patron,[2] he did not particularly concern himself with religious affairs and made no attempt to effect any significant changes in the status of the church. During his first year as emperor Mu-tsung ordered the recorder of the clergy, Ling-chun, to invite Wu-yeh, a much respected Ch'an master living in Fen-chou, to visit the court.[3] Although the letter from the throne carried by Ling-chun made the familiar point that the emperor was entrusted with the safekeeping of Buddhism, the Ch'an master declined to appear before the emperor to receive his homage claiming that he (Wu-yeh) lacked sufficient virtue.

Mu-tsung met with greater success in inducing another monk, Fa-chen, who was held in high regard in Ch'ang-an for his knowledge of Buddhist and Confucian literature, to take charge of Buddhist services in the Inner Palace.[4] Mu-tsung does not appear to have been any more interested in questions of religious doctrine than he was in sustained political activity, although he made frequent and often extravagant gifts to monasteries and individual monks. In 822, for example, on the occasion of a visit to the Shan-yin ssu in Hsien-yang, he presented the monks with one million cash.[5] In the course of the following year he made a gift of 200 bolts of silk to mendicant monks who had gathered at the T'ung-hua Gate in the east wall of Ch'ang-an,[6] sent 250 strings of cash and 250 bolts of silk to the Hung-fu ssu,[7] offered 500 bolts of silk to monks after viewing an image of the Buddhist divinity Vaiśravaṇa (P'i-sha-men) that had been installed at the T'ung-hua Gate,[8] and donated 1,000 strings of cash to the Chang-ching ssu.[9] It is not surprising that one of the many criticisms levied against Mu-tsung by Sung historians concerned his penchant for making 'random gifts' (*lan-ssu*).[10]

In the eleventh month of 822 Mu-tsung suffered a stroke in the course of a polo match on the palace grounds with his eunuch companions which left him, at least temporarily, unable to walk or to receive his ministers. Although Mu-tsung regained his health, he was nevertheless persuaded by Taoist magicians (*fang-shih*), who had previously been introduced into the court, to imbibe elixirs as his father had done. In the first month of 824 Mu-tsung was suddenly stricken again, perhaps as a result of the potions he had taken, and died two days later. The eunuchs of the Inner Palace initially sought to have Hsien-tsung's widow proclaim a regency, which she refused to do recalling the threat to the stability of the empire that occurred when Empress Wu had embarked on this course a century earlier. Instead she insisted, with encouragement from her elder brother who held the post of president of the Court of Imperial Sacrifices (*t'ai-ch'ang ch'ing*), that Mu-tsung's eldest son, Li Chan, who had been invested as Crown Prince two years earlier when Mu-tsung had his first stroke, follow his father on the throne.[11] In fact, Li Chan (posthumously known as Ching-tsung) was the last T'ang emperor to come to the throne without the active intercession of a particular eunuch clique.[12] Ching-tsung's reign was a brief one, lasting not even three years. He is portrayed as being a thoroughly dissolute youth who was preoccupied solely with amusing himself in a seemingly endless round of merry-making. He showed little interest in the affairs of the court and spent vast sums to ingratiate himself with the large number of eunuchs in service in the palace. Eventually, in the twelfth month of 826, some leading eunuchs, fearing that the disorders in the capital brought about by his wild and often capricious behavior would undermine the stability of the government, conspired to have him murdered at a late-night drinking party. Ching-tsung, at the time of his death, was only seventeen years old.

Reign of Wen-tsung (826–840)

The assassins of Ching-tsung failed in their attempt to enthrone their own candidate, the Prince of Chiang, who was a son of the late

Hsien-tsung, because of the quick action by a rival group of eunuchs headed by Wang Shou-ch'eng who supported Li Han, the second son of Mu-tsung and half-brother of Ching-tsung. In a short but decisive stroke Wang and his allies, using the troops in the capital under their command, completely annihilated their opponents, thus clearing the way for the seventeen-year-old Li Han (known posthumously as Wen-tsung) to ascend the throne. The new emperor, unlike his father and half-brother, took the business of government seriously and soon initiated a number of important reforms aimed at eliminating some of the abuses that had weakened the court of his two predecessors. Before coming to the throne he had avidly read the *Chen-kuan cheng-yao* (the record of T'ai-tsung's discussions with his ministers about the art and purposes of government), which no doubt made him sense even more keenly the decline in imperial authority that had occurred, especially in recent decades, because of the enhanced position of the eunuchs.[1]

Within days after being confirmed as emperor, Wen-tsung took the first steps towards curbing the extravagant expenditures of the preceding two reigns. He ordered that some 3,000 women of the Inner Palace be returned to their homes and terminated the service of 1,270 supernumeraries.[2] Even female musicians previously presented to the court and the polo champions so carefully assembled from military units were dismissed in the name of frugality. A small purge was also begun at the court of those clerics, both Buddhist and Taoist, who sought to exert influence through the use of divination or medicine. Among the group of Taoist priests exiled to South China at this time was Chao Kuei-chen, who was to emerge during the subsequent reign of Wu-tsung as the principal instigator of the suppression of Buddhism that occurred in 845.[3] As part of Wen-tsung's program of fiscal restraint, he kept careful watch on the provinces, where local commanders, since the early ninth century, had been authorizing ordinations as a means to increase their revenue. Although, as we have seen, Hsien-tsung issued an edict in 807 specifically banning local ordinations, the practice nevertheless persisted, as Li Te-yü's memorial dated 824 clearly shows.[4] As an indication of how seriously he regarded this matter, Wen-tsung ordered the civil governor (*kuan-ch'a shih*) of Hung-chou (in the modern Kiangsi), Shen Chuan-shih, to forfeit one month's salary when the latter proposed, in 829, to establish an ordination platform to celebrate the emperor's birthday.[5] In decreeing Shen's punishment, Wen-tsung specifically cited the prohibitions of this practice by preceding emperors.[6]

Another problem with which Wen-tsung had to come to grips was the lack of bureaucratic controls over the Buddhist and Taoist clergies that resulted from Hsien-tsung's order of 807 entrusting the maintenance of clerical registers to the eunuch commissioners of good works instead of the officials in the Department of Sacrifices (Tz'u-pu). As long as the eunuchs held exclusive control over the issuance of ordination certificates they had at their disposal a ready means for generating funds for their own purposes. Although Wen-tsung owed his accession to the throne to the eunuch clique under Wang Shou-ch'eng, by the year 830 he had grown resentful of their unbridled power and arrogance and had begun to encourage secretly the Han-lin academician Sung Shen-hsi, who had just been elevated to the rank of a chief minister (*t'ung-p'ing-chang-shih*), to strike at the eunuchs.[7]

It is not coincidental that while these plans were being developed with Sung, some officials in the Department of Sacrifices, possibly at the instigation of Sung who had previously served in the Board of Rites (Li-pu), presented Wen-tsung with a sweeping proposal designed to end the domination of the clergy by the eunuchs and to place effective government controls on the church.[8] The memorial began with the familiar complaint that both the Buddhist and Taoist clergies were parasites that fed on the people; monks and nuns evaded taxes and exhausted the resources of the country. Despite Hsien-tsung's ban on unauthorized ordinations and the construction of monasteries, the church, with the connivance of its powerful supporters, chose to ignore the laws. This situation, the memorial insisted, must no longer be tolerated. Henceforth anyone even submitting petitions for permission to sponsor activities prohibited under previous decrees should be subject to punishment. To bring the unwieldy clergy under regular government supervision, it was proposed that all properly ordained monks and nuns supply the Department of Sacrifices, through the appropriate prefectural offices, with such data as their religious and secular names, places of birth, names of the heads of their families, scholastic records, and the total number of other monks or nuns in their monasteries. In this way the Department of Sacrifices would be in a position to issue credentials (*kao-tieh*) which could be used to distinguish between proper monks and illegally ordained ones.

The memorial of 830 also proposed a resumption of the practice, discontinued by Hsien-tsung in 807, of making the Department of Sacrifices ultimately responsible for keeping the clerical registers (*seng-ni chi-chang*). Instead of having the registers compiled anew every ten years as Hsüan-tsung had decreed in 749,[9] it was suggested that registers be prepared every five years in order to lessen the chances of deception. New ordinations were to be permitted only in specially designated areas. In the event that a monk returned to lay life or died, his ordination certificate was to be forwarded by his monastery to the Department of Sacrifices so that it might be invalidated to prevent fraudulent use. In an extraordinary move to clear the slate once and for all, illegally ordained monks and nuns were to be permitted, in accordance with the terms of a general amnesty proclaimed during the preceding year,[10] to register with the authorities in order to legitimize their status. As we have noted earlier, some 700,000 'monks and nuns' took advantage of the amnesty. The memorial urged, however, that stern punishment be meted out henceforth to any monk who attempted to ordain an adolescent on his own authority or to any monastic officer or lay official who concealed knowledge of such an ordination. Not only was the construction of all new monasteries to be forbidden, but the local authorities were to be required to submit to the Department of Sacrifices a list of all monasteries within their area of jurisdiction as well as the names of the monks resident in each monastery. A host of restrictions were simultaneously to be placed on the clergy: they were to be forbidden to engage in commerce or other secular activities, travel by boat or carriage, leave their monasteries without permission, petition directly at government offices, or visit the homes of laymen to administer vows, draw up charms, utter incantations, practice divination, numerology, and the like. All village chapels, shrines, and hermitages which had been autonomous were to be placed under the jurisdiction of the larger regional monasteries. The memorial concluded with the lament that in recent years the Department of Sacrifices had existed in name only and had not been able to carry out its assigned functions.

Not since the time of Hsüan-tsung a century earlier had such drastic proposals been put forward for curbing the power of the church. One can only speculate on the reasons for Wen-tsung's failure to act on the memorial immediately, since, as we shall see, he was obviously in sympathy with its objectives and may well have inspired it as part of his overall plan for weakening the Buddhist church and undermining the eunuchs who drew considerable political and economic support from the clergy.[11] For one thing, Wang Shou-ch'eng learned of the plot by Sung Shen-hsi to assassinate the leading eunuchs and succeeded in having him transferred from his court post to K'ai-chou in Szechwan where he was rendered harmless. Another factor that perhaps prevented Wen-tsung from implementing all the provisions of the memorial immediately was the stroke that he suffered toward the end of the year 833, which left him temporarily unable to speak.[12] In any event, the emperor moved cautiously and in stages against the church. A year after receipt of the memorial from the Department of Sacrifices an imperial decree was transmitted to all the prefectural centers ordering the compilation of registers of monks and nuns.[13] Two years later, in 833, it was announced that henceforth the custom of inviting members of the Buddhist and Taoist clergies to the court on the emperor's birthday for a banquet and offerings would be discontinued.[14]

By 835 Wen-tsung was ready for his second attempt to rid the court of eunuch domination. His allies this time were the Han-lin scholar, Li Hsün, and an ambitious politician, Cheng Chu, whose reputed medical skills won for him the patronage of the influential eunuch Wang Shou-ch'eng, whose power Wen-tsung hoped to break. It would appear that once again the assault on the eunuchs was to be coordinated with an attempt to weaken the position of the Buddhist church. The prime mover in this effort was to be Li Hsün, who before his elevation to the post of vice president of the Board of Rites (*li-pu shih-lang*) and chief minister (*t'ung-p'ing-chang-shih*) in 835 had been an assistant instructor in the Ssu-men hsüeh,[15] a government school with a Confucian-oriented curriculum that was open to the children of low-ranking officials and commoners. In the fourth month of 835 Li Hsün proposed the dismantling of the Palace Chapel (*nei tao-ch'ang*) and a purge of all illegally ordained monks.[16] On the same day that he received Li Hsün's memorial Wen-tsung ordered the removal of the Buddhist image enshrined in the palace. Fortunately for the Buddhist community, if not for the general populace of Ch'ang-an, a typhoon struck the city that evening doing extensive damage. The word soon spread that the sudden storm was due to the wrath of the Buddha who was angered at the removal of his image from the palace. To placate public opinion, Wen-tsung promptly restored the image and rescinded, at least temporarily, his decision for a purge of the clergy.[17]

After further consolidating his position at the court by effecting the removal of some of his bureaucratic adversaries in the seventh month of 835, Li Hsün resubmitted his original proposal for a wholesale purge of the clergy, a large proportion of which he characterized as degenerate.[18] As a means of weeding out incapable or insincere monks, he suggested that members of the clergy be compelled to sit for examinations in Buddhist scripture.[19] Although successive emperors had required that *bona fide* candidates for ordination, i.e. those not disposed to bribe some official to have their names inscribed on an ordination certificate, pass a qualifying examination,[20] only once previously had an attempt been made to use the examination system as a means to rid the clergy of uneducated monks. In 724, when Hsüan-tsung was in the midst of his program of curbing the size and wealth of the Buddhist church, he issued an edict, unmentioned in Buddhist sources but preserved in summary in the *T'ang hui-yao*, stipulating that all monks and nuns under the age of sixty would be required to recite from memory two hundred pages of scripture.[21] In order to lighten the burden that this suddenly imposed on the clergy, Hsüan-tsung said in his edict that they would be expected to commit to memory only seventy-three pages each year for a period of three years, after which they would be examined.[22] Failure in the examination would mean mandatory laicization.

On the fourteenth day of the seventh month of 835 Wen-tsung at last issued his edict, contemplated since 830, announcing a massive purge of the Buddhist church.[23] Instead of attacking Buddhism primarily on economic grounds, as the memorial from the Department of Sacrifices (Tz'u-pu) had done in 830, Wen-tsung's edict, echoing sentiments expressed by Han Yü some fifteen years earlier while at the same time presaging the onslaught that was to be made on the Buddhist church a decade later, opened on a stridently chauvinistic note. To justify his call for a purge, Wen-tsung cited first and foremost the foreign origins of Buddhism. Was not the age of Yao and Shun, when China was free of alien ideologies, one of great prosperity? Buddhism, he reminded his subjects, had insinuated itself into China only as a result of the mindless comments of a minister who was attempting to interpret the dream of the Emperor Ming of the Han.[24] For 700 years the Buddhist church had unabashedly catered to the superstitious instincts of the commoners and gentry alike, while its magnificent monasteries grew in number until they filled the empire. Wen-tsung candidly noted in his edict what most of his Confucian-minded minsters had no doubt long thought, namely, that successive T'ang governments had too long talked about the 'Buddhist problem,' but did little to solve it. Now, Wen-tsung asserted, the time had come for the authorities to take stern measures against the church.

First, no new ordinations of monks or nuns would be permitted, nor would laymen be allowed to shave their heads to serve as novices. The practice of monks travelling about to hold popular lectures or conduct penances (*chieh-ch'an*) during the three taboo months (*san ch'ang-chai yüeh*)[25] and the custom of visiting the homes of parishioners after the summer retreat, which provided major sources of income, were denounced as devices for fleecing the people and hence proscribed. The clergy would be expected to adhere to the regulations of the *Vinaya* down to the minutest detail or else face prompt laicization. Officials were not to attempt to dissuade those monks or nuns who, uncomfortable with the prospect of such severe discipline, decided to return to lay life. To reduce the total number of monks and nuns in the country, Wen-tsung incorporated in his edict the suggestion of Li Hsün to subject the clergy to an examination in scripture administered by state officials. Monks and nuns were to be allowed only three months to prepare for the examination, which was primarily a test of their ability to read 500 pages of scripture without error or, failing to do this, to recite 300 pages from memory.[26] The harshness of this requirement is evident if we recall that even Hsüan-tsung who, as we have noted, was strongly hostile to the Buddhist church during the first half of his reign, allowed the clergy three years to prepare for an examination that consisted of reciting 200 pages of scripture. Those monks or nuns who were unable to pass the examination as outlined in the edict of 835 were to be defrocked immediately.

That Wen-tsung's plan to purge the clergy was in part economically motivated can be seen from his specific exclusion from the examination of all monks and nuns over fifty years of age as well as those who were physically weak, those who suffered from chronic illnesses, or those who were deaf and dumb, crippled, or otherwise unable to support themselves independently – in short, all members of the clergy who could not be transformed into productive workers. A provision was also included to exempt those monks and nuns 'of universally recognized merit who were free of all secular taint,' presumably to save such respected monks from the humiliating experience of having to submit to an examination which they might fail. As one might have expected, a total ban was placed on the construction of all new monasteries, although repair of older monasteries would be allowed. Wen-tsung's edict closed, as it opened, with a traditional Confucian refrain: monks and nuns, by their celibacy, failed to procreate and thus undermined the foundations of society. The refusal of monks to work the fields meant that others would go hungry; their refusal to weave textiles would cause others to lack for clothing. How, the edict asked, could one justify the acceptance of an alien and non-productive way of life which was detrimental to the people of China? Only through a purge (*su-ti*) of the clergy, it was asserted, could society be radically cleansed and all people receive fair treatment.

In the months following the promulgation of Wen-tsung's anti-Buddhist edict, which was to take full effect toward the end of the year 835, some of the leading eunuchs were gradually eliminated on one pretext or another. In the ninth month of 835 the eunuch Ch'en Hung-chih, who was believed to have been the assassin of Hsien-tsung, was summoned from his provincial post back to the capital. As he approached Ch'ang-an he was set upon by a force of anti-eunuch conspirators and beaten to death. The following month Li Hsün and Cheng Chu, with the connivance of Wen-tsung, arranged to bring about the suicide of the extremely powerful eunuch Wang Shou-ch'eng who as commissioner of good works for the right half of Ch'ang-an had been in a position to afford protection to the Buddhist church. The final blow against the eunuchs was set for the twenty-first day of the eleventh month, when they would be enticed into the palace gardens where they would be massacred in an ambush arranged by Li Hsün.

The plot, subsequently known as the Honeydew Incident (*Kan-lu chih pien*), misfired completely. The eunuchs, at the time led by Ch'iu Shih-liang, were alerted through the inadvertance of a conspirator general, Han Yüeh, and fled back to the safety of the palace, from which they were soon able to order a counterattack by the Shen-ts'e armies under their command that ultimately claimed the lives of several thousand of their bureaucrat enemies. Li Hsün, ironically, fled to Chung-nan shan outside Ch'ang-an, where he sought refuge with the monk Tsung-mi,[27] who had long enjoyed patronage of the court which had conferred on him the purple robe a mere three months earlier.[28] Although Tsung-mi was inclined to shelter Li with whom he had a personal friendship, the other monks on Chung-nan shan would have none of him and forced his expulsion from their sanctuary. Li quickly fled to Feng-hsiang, the stronghold of his fellow conspirator, Cheng Chu, but was captured shortly thereafter and beheaded. Ch'iu Shih-liang, an ardent Buddhist who had several months earlier been elevated to the post of commissioner of good works for the left half of Ch'ang-an, emerged as the new power behind the throne.[29] With Li Hsün and the other conspirators dead, Ch'iu had little difficulty in persuading the intimidated Wen-tsung, whose involvement in the conspiracy was well known to Ch'iu, to rescind his edict issued three months earlier calling for an examination and purge of the Buddhist clergy.[30] Gratified as the monks and nuns must have been at Ch'iu's intercession, the nullification of Wen-tsung's edict was to be little more than a short-lived reprieve.

After the Honeydew Incident Wen-tsung apparently abandoned his hopes of effecting any radical changes on the political or religious scene, although he appears to have retained his distaste for the Buddhist establishment, an attitude in which he was encouraged by some of his ministers who survived the massacre by the eunuchs. In 836, for example, when Wen-tsung asked his courtiers to give their views on what was most detrimental to society, he was once again treated to a denunciation of Buddhism, which prompted him to repeat the earlier bans on monks travelling about lecturing on scriptures for personal gain.[31] The following year he took pains to point out in a decree that the prohibition against slaughter on his birthday was based solely on his respect for life and was not an indication of his faith in Buddhism or a means to secure religious blessings.[32] He cautioned his subjects not to use the occasion to hold vegetarian banquets for the clergy, which had been the custom on imperial birthdays, and as if to underscore his desire to exclude the Buddhist clergy from participating in the festivities, he specifically authorized serving preserved meat at the banquets.

When Wen-tsung learned in 838 that Li Ying, the prefect of Chengchou, had permitted the ordination of 160 monks, he immediately ordered that they be laicized and that Li Ying forfeit three months' salary.[33] A year later, Ts'ui Li, a vice president of the Board of Rites, presented a memorial to the throne in which he asserted that the longstanding custom of observing memorial days for deceased emperors by feasting members of the Buddhist clergy and having officials burn incense at monasteries lacked any basis in the Confucian classics.[34] Wen-tsung readily agreed and sent notification to all prefectural centers prohibiting officials from joining in religious services at monasteries on such occasions. By the time of Wen-tsung's death in the first month of 840, the stage had been set for the brutal suppression of Buddhism that was soon to follow.

The suppression of Buddhism under the reign of Wu-tsung (840–846)

The impending death of Wen-tsung touched off a short but violent struggle between two rival groups of eunuchs, each supporting its own candidate for the throne. Although a son of Ching-tsung who held the title Prince of Ch'en had been formally designated Crown Prince in the tenth month of 839, he was unacceptable to the powerful eunuch Ch'iu Shih-liang, who occupied the office of Commander of the Shen-ts'e Army for the left half of Ch'ang-an. Ch'iu conspired with another formidable eunuch, Yü Hung-chih, to forge a rescript that set aside the Prince of Ch'en in favor of a half-brother of Wen-tsung named Li Ch'an, Prince of Ying, who was at the time twenty-five years of age. Through a well-timed show of force Ch'iu and Yü succeeded in persuading the officials at court to recognize Li Ch'an, known posthumously as Wu-tsung, as the new Crown Prince. Within two days after the death of Wen-tsung Ch'iu convinced the new Crown Prince, who, as later events will show, was himself disposed towards gross acts of violence, to order the destruction of his erstwhile rival, the Prince of Ch'en, as well as his own half-brother, the Prince of An.

For Ch'iu, who no doubt vividly recalled the plots against himself and other eunuchs hatched by Wen-tsung and his courtiers a mere five years earlier, the enthronement of a new emperor provided a golden opportunity to rid the court of anyone who was deemed to be hostile to his own interests. Ch'iu's contempt for the deceased emperor was such that he did not bother even to wait for the end of the period of mourning before beginning his massacre of Wen-tsung's confidants and advisers, with the apparent blessing of Wu-tsung. The official remonstrants made repeated protests over the indecent haste with which the executions were carried out, but to no avail.

The Japanese monk Ennin, who was staying at the time in a monastery in Shantung, noted in his diary that it was reported that Wu-tsung had murdered over 4,000 supporters of the previous emperor in the capital.[1] Even if this figure is an exaggeration, there is little doubt that Wu-tsung and his eunuch allies inaugurated the new reign, called Hui-ch'ang, with a bloodbath of sorts. Although Wu-tsung was well aware that Ch'iu and Yü were trying to manipulate him and was determined to resist them as best he could, he nevertheless felt that the time had not yet come for an open confrontation. Instead he prudently awarded Ch'iu still another honorary title, Great General of the Cavalry (*P'iao-chi ta chiang-chün*) and enfeoffed him as the Duke of Ch'u (*Ch'u-kuo kung*). Yü, meanwhile, was granted the title of Duke of Han (*Han-kuo kung*).

Whereas Wen-tsung, although hostile to Buddhism, was at best indifferent toward Taoism as a religion, Wu-tsung was fascinated by both Taoist lore and rituals. Like other of his predecessors who occupied the T'ang throne in the early ninth century, he was given to experimenting with the various potions and elixirs concocted by Taoist alchemists,[2] a practice that ultimately shortened his life. Already deeply interested in Taoism while still Prince of Ying,[3] Wu-tsung appears to have conceived a deep-seated hatred of all things Buddhist that was not simply derived from the usual political and economic arguments against the church but reflected in large measure the frustrations of the growing Taoist clergy – much admired by Wu-tsung – who had been long overshadowed by the Buddhists. As Ennin observed: 'The present emperor believes exclusively in the Taoist religion and despises Buddhism. He cannot stand the sight of Buddhist monks, nor does he wish to hear anything about our religion.'[4] Within a month after his enthronement Wu-tsung signaled his intention of elevating the status of Taoism by decreeing that the birthday of Lao-tzu would henceforth be known as *Chiang-sheng chieh* (Festival of the Descent of the Holy One) and would be commemorated by suspending all government functions for a period of three days.[5]

In the ninth month of 840 Wu-tsung arranged for a Taoist ceremony to be held in the Palace during which he would formally profess his faith in Taoism,[6] much as T'ai Wu-ti of the Northern Wei had done in 442 before launching his own suppression of Buddhism four years later.[7] For the ceremony, Wu-tsung summoned a group of eighty-one Taoist priests,[8] headed by the notorious Chao Kuei-chen, who, as we have noted, had been banished from the capital by Wen-tsung shortly after he had assumed the throne in the eleventh month of 826. A sanctified area (*tao-ch'ang*) was established within the palace grounds for the performance of the solemn *chin-lu* (golden talisman) ritual, at which prayers are offered for the well-being of the emperor.[9] The following month Wu-tsung himself ascended the Mysterious Platform (*hsüan-t'an*) to receive Taoist talismans (*fa-lu*) directly from the hands of Chao.[10] The new emperor's preoccupation with Taoism prompted a policy monitor (*shih-i*) named Wang Che to issue a warning against excessive zeal in matters of religion, an act which led to Wang's immediate dismissal from his court post and a demotion in rank.[11]

Wu-tsung's intention to eliminate Buddhist rituals and observances at court became more apparent when he greeted his first New Year (841) on the throne as Emperor. No monks were invited to the Palace, nor did he undertake even a *pro forma* visit to a monastery. He did, however, order the Chien-fu ssu to hold a mass on the fourth day of the first month which was the anniversary of the death of his half-brother, Wen-tsung, but did not participate in this himself.[12] On the seventh day he attended services at the T'ai-ch'ing kung, a major Taoist temple dedicated to Lao-tzu, and sponsored a banquet for the priests.[13] Two days later Wu-tsung issued an edict calling for the resumption of the traditional practice of giving popular lectures (*su-chiang*) for laymen at Buddhist monasteries and Taoist temples during the first, fifth, and nine months of the year,[14] i.e. the three taboo months. These lectures, which provided a major source of income for both monks and monastic establishments,[15] were subject to various regulations that specified the times of year and places at which they might be held.[16] Following the abortive coup against the eunuchs in 835, all popular lectures were banned, presumably out of fear that monks might use these occasions to incite the masses.[17] There seems little doubt that Wu-tsung's decision to rescind the prohibition on popular lectures was taken primarily to encourage proselytizing by Taoist priests whose activities had also been circumscribed by the edict of 835.

It had been the custom since the Northern Wei to invite representatives of Buddhism, Confucianism, and Taoism to debate with each other in the presence of the emperor on his birthday. Such debates, called *tan-ch'en t'an-lun*, 'birthday debates,' were discontinued by the early T'ang emperors who, because of their antipathy toward Buddhism, did not deem this an appropriate way to celebrate imperial birthdays, even though they occasionally sponsored debates at court between Buddhists, Taoists, and Confucians known as *san-chiao chiang-lun*, 'debates on the Three Teachings.'[18] The practice of holding debates on imperial birthdays was revived by Kao-tsung and continued by a number of succeeding emperors including Wen-tsung, who in 827 ordered Po Chü-i to argue the Confucian position despite his strong Buddhist sympathies.[19] Since the debates were by this time largely formalized, Po, presumably, was not unduly inconvenienced.

On the eleventh day of the sixth month, which was the date of Wu-tsung's birthday, two Buddhist monks and two Taoist priests were summoned to the court to discuss the relative merits of their respective scriptures.[20] At the close of the debate Wu-tsung presented a set of purple robes – the highest award – to each of the Taoist priests but denied them to the Buddhists. Since it had been customary since the reign of Tai-tsung to conclude the debates by granting the participants purple robes,[21] Wu-tsung's action could be interpreted only as a deliberate attempt to humiliate the Buddhists.[22] During the same month the Taoist priest Liu Hsüan-ching was granted several honorific titles and instructed along with Chao Kuei-chen to prepare Taoist talismans (*fa-lu*) for the Palace.[23] The Emperor's growing involvement with Taoist priests once again led a policy critic (*pu-ch'üeh*) named Liu Yen-mo, to issue a warning about the dangers of being overly concerned with the search for immortality. Liu, like Wang Che who had tended similar advice during the preceding year, was immediately dismissed and sent off to a provincial post.

The first overt move against the Buddhist church occurred in the third month of 842 when an edict was promulgated requiring monasteries to expel all unaffiliated or unregistered monks (*pao-wai wu-ming seng*).[24] It also prohibited monasteries henceforth from allowing either youths or novices to stay (*t'ung-tzu sha-mi*) on their premises. The ban against ordaining adolescents, as we noted above, had originally been proposed in the memorial sent to Wen-tsung in 830 by the Department of Sacrifices but had never been implemented owing to the failure of the Honeydew Plot of 835. Wu-tsung's edict of 842 forbidding monasteries to train novices was in fact issued in response to a memorial calling for a general purge (*t'iao-liu*) of the Buddhist clergy. It is interesting to note that the author of this memorial, which was ultimately to have such dire consequences for the Buddhist church, was not, as one might have expected, some cranky Taoist priest, but the highly influential bureaucrat and scholar Li Te-yü,[25] who had become chief minister in the ninth month of the year 840.

Li, as a leader of one of the two factions of bureaucrats that dominated politics during the 820s and 830s, had been both in and out of favor over the years. Appointed a Han-lin academician in 820 at the age of thirty-seven, Li was forced by factional opponents to leave the capital for an appointment as civil governor of Che-hsi in 823. Six years later, under the reign of Wen-tsung, Li was promoted to the post of vice president of the Ministry of War (*ping-pu shih-lang*) and was elevated to a chief ministership (*t'ung-p'ing-chang-shih*) in 833, only to be driven from that office the following year. After being in disgrace for a short period, he was rehabilitated and, in 837, appointed *de facto* military governor of the strategic Huai-nan province, where he remained until he was summoned back to the capital by Wu-tsung in the seventh month of 840. When Li was asked to assume a chief ministership, his hostility toward folk religion and popular Buddhist practices must have been well known in court circles. In 823, while civil governor of Che-hsi, he closed down over two thousand 'heterodox shrines' (*yin-tz'u*) and mountain cloisters (*shan-fang*).[26] The following year, as we have already seen, he sent a memorial to the throne denouncing the practice of private ordinations and warning of the ruinous effects that these were having on the economy. In 826 he sent still another letter to the throne calling for the suppression of the 'crafty Buddhist monks' of Po-chou whom he accused of swindling the common people through the sale of a miraculous type of water that was supposed to cure all illnesses.[27]

It is clear from Ennin's personal experience that the edict issued in the third month of 842 calling for the expulsion of unaffiliated or unregistered monks was no dead letter, for within nine days of its promulgation Ch'iu Shih-liang, as a commissioner of good works, had to intercede on behalf of Ennin and the other unaffiliated Japanese monks to prevent their ouster from the monastery in which they were staying.[28] At the end of the fifth month of 842, just before the annual imperial birthday debate was scheduled to begin, Wu-tsung ordered the dismissal, without explanation, of forty eminent Buddhist monks who officiated at religious services in the palace.[29]

The suppression of Buddhism under Wu-tsung (840–846)   119

The decree for a general purge of the Buddhist clergy was finally handed down in the middle of the tenth month of 842.[30] It had two clear objectives: the laicization of 'undesirable' monks and the seizure of all property belonging to individual members of the Buddhist clergy. Undesirable monks were defined as those who mutilated themselves with fire, practiced magic, or bore tattoos or lash marks on their bodies, i.e. were ex-convicts. Also to be laicized were monks who were deserters or ex-artisans as well as those monks who failed to keep their vow of chastity. The decree further called for the confiscation of all money, grain, paddy land or estates privately owned by monks or nuns. Members of the clergy, however, were given the option of retaining their property by returning to lay status and having their names entered in the tax rolls.

While there was little radically new in the definition of undesirable monks, the order to seize all private property belonging to members of the clergy must have sent convulsions through the Buddhist community. The commissioners of good works were immediately ordered to prepare an inventory of all property owned by monks and nuns, with similar instructions being sent to the various prefectural offices. Ch'iu Shih-liang, who was commissioner of good works for the left half of Ch'ang-an, announced his opposition to the purge, but the strong-willed Wu-tsung, backed by his two staunchly anti-Buddhist chief ministers, Li Te-yü and Li Shen, would agree only to a delay of one hundred days in implementing the decree and even then only on the condition that during this period all monks and nuns be restricted to their respective monasteries and convents.[31]

When the decree was finally enforced in the first month of the new year, 3,491 monks and nuns residing in monasteries in Ch'ang-an chose laicization and a taxable status rather than suffer the loss of their property.[32] In its final form the decree also limited the number of slaves that members of the clergy might own.[33] Monks were to be permitted a maximum of one male slave (*nu*) and nuns two female slaves (*pi*).[34] Any slaves held by members of the clergy in excess of these numbers were to be returned to their original masters, or in the event that these were no longer alive, were to be turned over to the government for sale. Furthermore, even within the limited number of slaves allotted to the clergy, the latter would not be permitted to retain any slaves with special skills in military matters, medicine, etc. Monks and nuns were specifically warned against trying to conceal their slaves by having them ordained and listed as members of the clergy.[35] All privately owned property, meanwhile, was to be sequestered pending a further ruling on its disposition. That the decree was immediately implemented is evident from Ennin's diary, which reports that the monastery in which he himself was then residing, the Tzu-sheng ssu, after receiving formal notification from the commissioner of good works to expel all clerics who fell within the categories mentioned in the purge decree, promptly dismissed thirty-seven monks.[36] Severe residence restrictions were placed on defrocked clergy, who were henceforth not only prohibited from living in, or even visiting, monasteries but were also not permitted to remain within the city of Ch'ang-an itself.[37]

Wu-tsung's hostility toward Buddhism, as toward other foreign creeds, was further exacerbated by the growing menace from the Uighurs, who began making incursions into North China after their expulsion from their homeland in Central Asia by the Kirghiz in 840. As long as the Uighurs maintained good relations with the Chinese, their Manichaean religion, which was first introduced into China by Persians in 694, was tolerated, although only grudgingly.[38] In 732 Emperor Hsüan-tsung, for example, outlawed the practice of Manichaeism among the Chinese, but allowed 'Western Barbarians' (*Hsi-hu*), i.e. Persians, Sogdians, etc., resident in China the right to observe their Manichaean faith on the grounds that it had been their native religion (*hsiang-fa*).[39] In 762 the third Uighur *qaghan* Bügü (Mou-yü k'o-han), was converted to Manichaeism, which he soon declared to be the state religion of the Uighurs.[40] He subsequently dispatched Manichaean priests to China, presumably to look after the growing number of Uighur merchants living there.[41] The T'ang government, being in debt to the Uighurs for the valuable military assistance that they rendered during the An Lu-shan rebellion, ordered the establishment of a Manichaean temple in Ch'ang-an in 768, which was granted the name Ta-yün Kuang-ming ssu.[42] In 771 the construction of additional Manichaean temples was authorized in other cities with a foreign population.[43]

As relations with the Uighurs deteriorated, the longstanding dislike of the Manichaean religion, which had not succeeded in attracting Chinese adherents in any substantial number, soon came to the surface.[44] In 841, Li Te-yü, who had been trying to stem the southward drift of the Uighurs into Chinese territory, drafted a letter to their *qaghan* in Wu-tsung's name in which he pointed out the demoralized state of the Manichaeans in China following the decline of the Uighur empire in recent years.[45] Since Li hoped that a major offensive against the Uighurs could still be avoided, his tone was relatively moderate. The Manichaean temples in Ch'ang-an, Lo-yang, and T'ai-yüan would be permitted to continue functioning, but Manichaean temples in the provinces would have to close pending the return of the Uighurs to their traditional homeland. When it became apparent in the early part of 842 that this conciliatory approach was not proving successful, the T'ang government launched a full-scale campaign against the Uighurs which culminated in a crushing defeat for the latter in the first month of 843. No sooner had the Uighur power been broken than Wu-tsung ordered retaliation against the Manichaean clergy and their wealthy Uighur supporters in China.

In the second month of 843 an edict was issued calling for the laicization of all Uighur priests (*hsiu kung-te Hui-hu*) at Manichaean temples in Ch'ang-an and Lo-yang and their prompt resettlement in the provinces.[46] An inventory of all property, including land, houses, and money, belonging to Uighur laymen or priests was to be transmitted to the commissioners of good works who, in conjunction with other high officials, would verify the lists and prepare their own inventories. All money and other movable assets were to be confiscated outright by the government and Manichaean scriptures and holy objects burnt in the streets.[47] Although the edict simply called for the expulsion of the defrocked Manichaean priests, Ennin reports that in the fourth month of 843 Wu-tsung ordered the execution of all Manichaean priests throughout China.[48] As a grim warning to the Chinese Buddhist clergy of things to come, the condemned Manichaeans were made to shave their heads in the manner of Buddhist monks and don Buddhist robes before their execution.

It was at this time that Wu-tsung began to toy with the idea of eliminating Buddhism entirely from Chinese soil.[49] He ordered the two recorders of the clergy (*seng-lu*) to prepare a statement regarding the actual benefits that were alleged to accrue from Buddhism and to explain how the decline of Buddhism might bring adverse effects. Even though the Buddhist case was ably presented by the learned monk Hsüan-ch'ang who wrote several essays describing the traditional pattern of imperial patronage under preceding dynasties, the outcome was a foregone conclusion, with the hapless monk being compelled to return to lay life.[50] Another obstacle to the total suppression of Buddhism was removed in the sixth month of 843, when Ch'iu Shih-liang was forced to resign as commissioner of good works for the left half of Ch'ang-an in favor of the eunuch Yang Ch'in-i, a close associate of Li Te-yü when the latter was based in Yang-chou, who had the reputation of being an irreligious man.[51] Ch'iu, for all his intrigues, was regarded as a staunch defender of the Buddhist church from which much of his reputed wealth may have been derived.[52]

Within days after the resignation of Ch'iu, Wu-tsung dismissed Wei

Tsung-ch'ing from his post as supervisor of the household of the Crown Prince (*T'ai-tzu chan-shih*) for having sent the throne a copy of a lengthy commentary on the *Nieh-p'an ching* that he had previously written.[53] Outraged at the audacity of his minister in producing a Buddhist commentary, Wu-tsung ordered that Wei's home be searched for the original draft so that it could be burnt. In an edict laden with Confucian sentiments – and possibly drafted by Li Te-yü – dated the thirteenth day of the sixth month, the Emperor declared that Wei was derelict in his duty as a high official for having succumbed to Buddhist ideas, when in fact it was his obligation to uphold Confucian values. How, he asked, could Wei bring himself to propagate the teachings of a religion that deserved to be outlawed? The toleration of Buddhism could only do damage to China's traditions. Wei, therefore, was to be demoted to a post in Ch'eng-tu, which, the edict asserted, should be regarded as an act of leniency, since support for Buddhism was tantamount to treason.

Anti-Buddhist sentiment, encouraged by the pronouncements of the Emperor and his chief ministers, had grown so steadily that it was only a matter of time before some incident would provoke a physical assault on the Buddhist clergy. The spark that finally touched off the first massacre of Buddhist monks was a relatively minor episode that occurred in the course of the rebellion by Liu Chen, who attempted, in defiance of a decision by the court, to succeed his uncle as governor of Chao-i after the latter's death in the fourth month of 843. When a military campaign was opened against Liu some months later, orders were issued for the arrest of his representative based in the capital, an officer named Chiang Sun.[54] Chiang immediately went into hiding, and it was soon rumored that he had shaven his head and taken refuge as a monk in some monastery in Ch'ang-an. An order was promptly sent to the commissioners of good works in the capital and to prefectural officials instructing them to defrock and return home any monk whose name did not appear in the clerical registers (*ssu-seng kung-an*).[55] According to Ennin, all monks whose credentials were not in order were detained, and in the case of Ch'ang-an more than 300 such monks who attempted to conceal their status by disguising themselves were executed. Monks in the capital were so terrified, Ennin reported, that those who lacked the proper documents dared not appear on the streets.

Having already eliminated Buddhist services at the court, Wu-tsung, at the urging of his chief ministers Li Te-yü and Li Shen, issued a decree at the beginning of the New Year of 844 banning the observance of the three taboo months (*san chai-yüeh*), during which all slaughter was forbidden.[56] In his decree Wu-tsung cited the Buddhist origin of the three taboo months as his reason for discontinuing their observance. The official prohibition against slaughter during these three months can be traced back to 583, when Emperor Wen of the Sui decreed that there must be no taking of life between the eighth and fifteenth days of the first, fifth and ninth months of the year.[57] In 619, one year after the establishment of the T'ang, Kao-tsu issued a decree considerably broader in scope prohibiting the slaughter of animals and fish as well as the execution of criminals on the first nine days of the New Year and on ten specified taboo days (*chai-jih*) of each month.[58] The provision against slaughter on certain days of each month, which proved to be a great inconvenience, was subsequently narrowed in the legal code promulgated in 719 to a period of ten days in the first, fifth, and ninth months, i.e. the Buddhist taboo months.[59] In 734, when Emperor Hsüan-tsung was at the height of his pro-Taoist phase, he ordered that the ban on slaughter be limited to a three day period in the first, seventh, and tenth months, i.e. the *san yüan-yüeh*, which had been regarded as sacred by Taoists since Northern Wei times.[60] In 757 Su-tsung ordered a return to the earlier practice of prohibiting slaughter during the Buddhist taboo months as well as on the ten taboo days in ordinary months.[61]

In his New Year decree of 844 Wu-tsung acknowledged that even though the ban on slaughter during the Buddhist taboo months had been the policy of the T'ang since its foundation, it nevertheless was basically a tradition that had been inherited from preceding dynasties. He pointed out that since it was extremely difficult to enforce so broad a ban on slaughter, corruption was unavoidable, with the result that 'cooks receive generous gifts to overlook the ban, while police officials are secretly being bribed to remain silent.'[62] Probably a more realistic incentive than culinary concerns for switching from the Buddhist to the Taoist holy days was that the former did not allow executions for a full three months of the year, whereas the latter prohibited executions only on three days of the first, seventh, and tenth months, plus the first three days of the New Year and the anniversaries of the deaths of past emperors. The decree ending the observance of the Buddhist taboo months, it will be recalled, was issued at the height of the rebellion of Liu Chen – a time when many executions were being ordered.

In the year 844 Wu-tsung's infatuation with Taoism and his personal involvement with certain questionable members of the Taoist clergy began to presage ill for the Buddhist community. In the second month of 844 rumors were rife in Ch'ang-an that he had established a liaison with a beautiful Taoist priestess from the Chin-hsien kuan, which he had sumptuously refurbished.[63] A road was constructed linking her convent with the Palace to facilitate his visits to her. In addition he attended services during the course of this month at the Hsing-T'ang kuan, which was another major Taoist temple in the capital, and presented it with 1,000 bolts of silk as he had done previously at the Chin-hsien kuan. The following month, much to the chagrin of Li Te-yü, he restored the notorious Taoist schemer Chao Kuei-chen to the post of Scholar and Master of the Taoist Clergy for Both Halves of Ch'ang-an (*Tso-yu-chieh Tao-men chiao-shou hsien-sheng*),[64] an office from which he had been dismissed by Wen-tsung in 826 at the urging of Li. The latter vigorously opposed the reappointment of Chao to the leadership of the Taoist clergy on the grounds that Chao had previously been removed from this office because of criminal activity and therefore should be kept away from the throne.[65] To mollify Li, Wu-tsung disclaimed any intention of consulting Chao on political matters. With respect to affairs of state, he assured Li, the throne would continued to seek guidance from its chief ministers and, of course, from Li in particular. Wu-tsung declared that he was interested in Chao only because of his (Wu-tsung's) desire to spend his leisure hours discussing Taoism and professed not to have been aware that the Chao Kuei-chen that he had just appointed to head the Taoist church was the same person as the 'Alchemist Chao' (Chao Lien-shih) who had been dismissed from this ecclesiastical post two decades earlier.[66] In any event, he told Li, Chao had done no great harm during his service under Ching-tsung.

After becoming the spiritual mentor to Wu-tsung, Chao availed himself of every opportunity to urge the Emperor to proceed with his plans for the total elimination of Buddhism.[67] To demonstrate the necessity of pursuing so drastic a course, he drew upon a variety of arguments, partly Confucian and partly folk-Taoist. The Confucian arguments were of the kind that had been repeatedly made by bureaucrats – Buddhism was an alien creed; it sapped the strength of the country, etc. – and hence could be expected to win support from Li Te-yü, Li Shen, and the other Confucian-minded ministers. On the Taoist side, Chao relied not so much on the hackneyed philosophical or nationalistic critiques of Buddhism as on popular superstitions that could be interpreted in such a way as to make Buddhism seem a threat to the continuity of the T'ang state. In particular he and his Taoist colleagues resuscitated an old belief dating back at least to 643 which held that the T'ang dynasty would come to an end after the reign of its eighteenth emperor.[68] The text that was used to intimidate Wu-tsung was an obscure apocryphal work called the *K'ung-tzu shuo* (Discourses of Confucius) which asserted that after eighteen generations an emperor 'in black robes' would take over the country.[69] Apocryphal works warning against domination by the color black had circulated already under the Northern Chou dynasty. Such texts probably influenced Emperor Wu-ti (560–578) in his decision to prohibit monks from wearing black and may well have been one of the factors contributing to the suppression of Buddhism that occurred under his reign.[70] In any case, the association between black robes and the Buddhist clergy was well established in the popular mind. Although Wu-tsung technically was only the fifteenth T'ang emperor, numbers could be manipulated to make him appear as the eighteenth by including in the list of rulers the father and grandfather of the founder of the dynasty, which was not an uncommon practice, and Empress Wu.

In the third month of 844 Wu-tsung promulgated a series of harsh decrees designed to interdict the traditional modes of lay support for the church.[71] One of the decrees forbade all offerings before tooth-relics (*fo-ya*) enshrined in monasteries in Ch'ang-an.[72] Another decree prohibited pilgrimages to such holy places as Wu-t'ai shan, Chung-nan shan, the P'u-kuang wang ssu in Ssu-chou,[73] and most significantly, the Fa-men ssu in Feng-hsiang, which held the famed finger-bone relic that provoked Han Yü's angry memorial of 819. Believers were not allowed to make any donations, however small, to these holy places, nor were monks at these monasteries allowed to accept even a single coin as an offering. Any infraction of this rule was to be punished with twenty lashes. These decrees, Ennin reported, so terrified laymen that the major Buddhist sites were soon devoid of pilgrims. On the pretext that Liu Chen's fugitive guard officer, Chiang Sun, might have fled to one of these places of pilgrimage, an investigation of all monks was ordered and those who lacked proper credentials (*kung-yen*) were summarily executed. Meanwhile, another order went out requiring all monks and nuns to return to their monasteries and convents before the bell announcing the noon meal, which was an indirect way of preventing the clergy from accepting dinner from lay patrons. Monks were also not permitted to spend the night at a monastery other than the one at which they were registered. All monks who had been assigned to perform the Buddhist services in the Palace Chapel were permanently expelled at this time, and instructions were issued barring monks from ever appearing again within the precincts of the Imperial Palace. The Palace Chapel was cleansed of all Buddhist paraphernalia, the images smashed and the sūtras burnt.[74] In their place were enshrined statues representing the Taoist Celestial Divinity (T'ien-tsun) and Lao-chün, with

Taoist priests assigned to chant scriptures and practice the magical arts (*tao-shu*).

After issuing his ban on pilgrimages to holy sites, Wu-tsung turned his attention to Buddhist festivals, the most popular of which was the *Yü-lan-p'en* celebrated on the fifteenth day of the seventh month, which coincided with the Taoist Chung-yüan chieh.[75] It was customary for laymen on this occasion to make the rounds of monasteries in Ch'ang-an giving offerings to the clergy in order to effect the release of the souls of their ancestors from hell. Angered by the large numbers of devotees flocking to the Buddhist monasteries in the capital, Wu-tsung ordered his officials to seize the flowers, medicines, and other gifts and deliver them to the Hsing-T'ang kuan, a leading Taoist temple, where they were to be set out in honor of the Celestial Divinity. Residents of the capital were asked to visit the Hsing-T'ang kuan on this day, where Wu-tsung himself had gone to worship. If Ennin's account can be believed, few commoners attended the services at the Taoist temple, however, because of the widespread resentment arising from the Emperor's order to seize all of the offerings made at Buddhist monasteries.

In an effort to weaken the traditional ties that the common people had to Buddhism Wu-tsung issued an edict during the *Yü-lan-p'en* festivities[76] requiring the dismantlement of all mountain cloisters (*shan-fang*), hermitages (*lan-jo*), monastery hostels (*p'u-t'ung*), Buddhist shrines (*fo-t'ang*), wells maintained by local Buddhist associations (*i-ching*), village vegetarian dining halls (*ts'un-i chai-t'ang*),[77] and other such popular Buddhist institutions that were less than 200 *ken*[78] in size and lacked tablets according them official recognition. All clergy attached to such places were to be laicized and made subject to corvée.[79] Ennin noted sadly that more than 300 such Buddhist shrines (*fo-t'ang*) in Ch'ang-an alone were destroyed, many of which possessed images and sūtra scrolls by celebrated artists that were easily on a par with those of the 'great monasteries' (*ta-ssu*) in the provinces. In addition, an order was issued for the destruction of all stone pillars bearing the Buddhist 'Tsun-sheng' incantation (*Tsun-sheng shih-ch'uang*)[80] and for the removal of grave monuments to Buddhist monks. It will be recalled that these repressive measures against the popular aspect of Buddhism, although rigidly enforced for the first time by Wu-tsung, had in fact been conceived of more than a century earlier by Hsüan-tsung and in more recent times had had the support of Wen-tsung, who was unable to implement them because of the failure of the Honeydew Plot.[81]

In the eighth month of 844 Liu Chen, whose rebellion had been a source of anxiety to the court, was assassinated by a subordinate, thus removing the last major threat to the throne. With the defeat of the Uighurs in 843 and the collapse of the rebel armies led by Liu Chen in 844, Wu-tsung apparently felt no need for further restraint *vis-à-vis* the church. During the same month in which Liu Chen's rebellion came to an end Wu-tsung was reputed to have arranged for the murder of the Empress Dowager Kuo (Kuo T'ai-hou), who as a devout Buddhist had repeatedly criticized the various edicts against the clergy.[82] As the orgy of reprisals against the erstwhile supporters of Liu Chen was under way in Ch'ang-an in the ninth month of 844, Wu-tsung is said to have commented after inspecting the severed head of Liu: 'Chao-i [i.e. Liu Chen] is now destroyed. The only tasks remaining are the elimination of the Buddhist monasteries and the complete purge of their clergy!'[83] Chao Kuei-chen promptly dispatched a memorial to Wu-tsung asserting that Buddhism with its emphasis on non-substantiality, impermanence, and suffering was a barbarian religion concerned primarily with death, which he expressly equated with the Buddhist ideal of Nirvāṇa, whereas Taoism, whose divine founder was born in China, had as its goal the attainment of absolute freedom and spontaneity.[84] He assured Wu-tsung that longevity could be realized by imbibing elixirs (*hsien-tan*) and that limitless good fortune would follow if he used Taoist talismans (*shen-fu*). To achieve these objectives, he urged the Emperor to erect within the precincts of the Palace a Terrace for the Immortals (Hsien-t'ai) from which Wu-tsung could 'ascend into the mists [*teng-hsia*] and wander freely through the nine divisions of heaven.'

In matters of religion Wu-tsung was by now strongly under the influence of Chao with his promises of immortality. In the tenth month of 844, acting on the advice that he had received from Chao during the preceding month, Wu-tsung ordered the immediate construction of a Terrace for Viewing the Immortals (Wang-hsien t'ai), 150 feet tall.[85] Three thousand soldiers drawn from the two Shen ts'e armies were assigned to the project. Wu-tsung personally went to the site several times to check on the progress of the work, his impatience growing with each visit. On one occasion, angered by the slow pace, he ordered a chief supervisor to assist in carrying earth; another time he apparently became so enraged that he fired an arrow at a guard killing him on the spot.

While the terrace was still under construction, Wu-tsung issued a new edict designed to reduce still further the number of monasteries and size of the clergy.[86] All small monasteries (*hsiao-ssu*) were now to be dismantled and their images and scriptures transferred to the larger monasteries (*ta-ssu*); their bells were to be confiscated and turned over to Taoist temples, presumably because the latter were experiencing difficulty in acquiring sufficient copper for use in casting ritual implements. Monks living in the hitherto officially sanctioned smaller monasteries were now to be screened: those who did not measure up to the standard of the *Vinaya* were to be returned to lay life regardless of age; old monks of good character were to be moved along with their sūtras and images to the larger monasteries. All young monks living in the smaller monasteries, even if they adhered to the *Vinaya*, were to be defrocked and returned to their villages. Ennin reported that thirty-three small monasteries in Ch'ang-an were closed as a result of this edict.

The authorities moved quickly to implement the order to close all smaller monasteries, which constituted the majority of Buddhist religious establishments in China. By the third day of the first month of 845 Wu-tsung was able to report in an amnesty message that even the larger monasteries were now half empty owing to the recent purges of the clergy.[87] Since commercial activities in the smaller monasteries had virtually come to a halt and the buildings were in the process of being dismantled, it seemed unlikely, his message stated, that they could survive much longer. Wu-tsung declared that he was pleased with the pace of the laicization of those members of the clergy whose behavior was reprehensible or who failed to uphold the Buddhist precepts and reaffirmed the earlier policy of transferring monks and nuns of good character to the surviving larger monasteries. Meanwhile the commissioners of good works were to continue their investigation of 'rich monasteries' (*fu-ssu*), confiscating all goods in their shops and warehouses other than those sold only in direct support of religious activities. The object of the seizure of church property was, ostensibly, to put an end to 'the fleecing of the exhausted people' by the monks in their search for monetary gain. The only reservation voiced in the New Year's message was that officials in the provinces tended to be too lax in their treatment of the church.

The suppression of Buddhism entered its final stage in the third month of 845 when Wu-tsung issued two sweeping edicts – one concerned with monastic property, and the other with the laicization of the clergy.[88] The first of these edicts stipulated that Buddhist monasteries would henceforth be prohibited from holding estates and ordered that all monastic wealth in the form of slaves, cash, grain, or cloth be surrendered to the secular authorities for use in paying the salaries of government officials. Ennin reported that the slaves belonging to monasteries in Ch'ang-an were divided into three groups: those with specific skills that were of value to the military, who were instructed to take possession of them; those who lacked such skills but were young and healthy and hence could be resold; and lastly, the old and enfeebled slaves, who were reassigned to government offices. The second edict issued at this time called for the indiscriminate laicization of all Buddhist monks and nuns who were under the age of forty. It should be noted that the principal difference between Wu-tsung's anti-Buddhist edict issued in the tenth month of 842 and the present two edicts was that the former called for the confiscation of the property owned by monks and nuns individually as well as the laicization of 'corrupt' members of the clergy, whereas the latter two edicts decreed the seizure of monastery-owned property and the defrocking of all monks and nuns under forty, whether or not they observed the Buddhist precepts.

It is not accidental that the promulgation of these two edicts, which effectively signaled the end of the Buddhist church, coincided with the completion of the Terrace for Viewing the Immortals. Wu-tsung was delighted with the Terrace, which was crowned with a five-peaked tower and had grottoes and rock paths laid out at its base. Accompanied by a motley group of military commanders, officials, and Taoist priests, the Emperor ascended the Terrace and ordered seven of the priests to mix the elixirs (*fei-lien*) that were to transform the priests into immortals. Several days later he paid another visit to the Terrace, but was disheartened to learn that none of them had yet achieved the state of an immortal. When asked to explain their failure, the priests are said to have declared that as long as Buddhism continued to be practiced alongside Taoism, the color black, which was associated with Buddhism, would predominate, thus obstructing the path to immortality,[89] presumably by overwhelming the weaker color of yellow which signified the Taoist religion in the popular mind. Wu-tsung's response was immediate: he broadened the scope of his previous edict regarding the laicization of monks and nuns to include all members of the clergy under the age of fifty. Another edict specified that all members of the clergy over fifty who lacked proper ordination certificates from the Department of Sacrifices or whose certificates contained any irregularity must immediately don lay garb and return to their homes.

Ennin recorded that the laicization of monks and nuns in Ch'ang-an under forty began on the first day of the fourth month of 845 and proceeded at the rate of 300 persons a day until the fifteenth day of that month, when the last members of this group were returned home. The defrocking of those persons between the ages of forty-one and forty-nine began on the sixteenth day and was completed by the tenth day of the following month, i.e. twenty-five days later. On the eleventh day of the fifth month the purge entered its final phase with the expulsion of all monks and nuns over fifty whose credentials were not in order. According to Ennin's eyewitness testimony, every possible pretext was used to defrock even those monks and nuns over fifty who held valid papers, which were routinely confiscated by the examining officials if they contained the slightest discrepancy or if the writing on the certificate was smudged. In numerous instances valid certificates of monks and nuns over fifty were arbitrarily seized by the authorities, leaving their holders without any evidence of their status as legitimate members of the clergy and hence exposing them to immediate defrocking. During the period when their ordination certificates were being examined, monks and nuns were forbidden under penalty of death from leaving their assigned monasteries.

Rumors were rife that the Emperor had ordered the execution of all monks and nuns in the capital so that he could use their severed heads to fill in the gaping hole that was left after the earth had been removed for the construction of the Terrace. Wu-tsung, it was reported, had been dissuaded from this drastic step by one of his officials who reminded the Emperor that the clergy basically consisted of ordinary men and women who could be productively employed once their laicization was completed and they had been returned to their native villages. Although, as matters turned out, there were to be no mass executions of the clergy, the purge was relentlessly pursued under the watchful eye of Wu-tsung, who received periodic reports on the numbers of monks and nuns already laicized as well as on the numbers of those still remaining in the monasteries.[90] The swift dismantlement of the Buddhist church caused great suffering not only to the whole clergy who were its immediate victims but also to the 150,000 slaves owned by the monasteries at this time. Ennin has provided a graphic description of the breaking up of slave families as a result of the resale of able-bodied male and female slaves or their transfer into government service. He sadly observed that 'this is a time when slave fathers are sent south, while their sons go north.'[91] A month later an official in the Secretariat-Chancellery (Chung-shu men-hsia) informed the throne of the plight of slaves in the densely populated central region, where, he said, the dispersement of the clergy and the abrupt closing of monasteries left slaves with neither food nor shelter.[92] His memorial warned that these destitute slaves were often being illegally appropriated by corrupt officials and rich merchants and urged that steps be taken to prevent their loss to the government.

Another group of hapless individuals caught up in the dismantlement of Buddhist religious establishments was the aged and infirm who had hitherto been cared for in monastery-operated almshouses called *pei-t'ien* (literally, 'fields of compassion [for reaping merit]').[93] Although we find frequent references after the sixth century to monks and devout laymen who looked after the sick, the poor, the orphaned, and the aged on a private basis, the almshouse as a public institution seems to have emerged only in the last years of the reign of the strongly pro-Buddhist Empress Wu, who provided government funds for their support. In 717 Sung Ching, a chief minister, sent a memorial to Emperor Hsüan-tsung urging that official backing for the almshouses be discontinued since the latter had become a refuge for the indolent as well as for criminals on the run.[94] Sung also pointed out that in view of their Buddhist origins, the administration of almshouses should be left solely in the hands of monks, not government officials.[95] Hsüan-tsung rejected Sung's proposals, probably because he was aware of the social usefulness of these places, which was demonstrated when the decision was made in 734 to clear Ch'ang-an of all beggars by placing them in almshouses, euphemistically redesignated 'sick wards' (*ping-fang*).[96]

Since many monasteries maintained almshouses,[97] Wu-tsung's decrees of the summer of 845 ordering the immediate laicization of the clergy and the closing of all monasteries left the luckless inhabitants of such charitable institutions without any means of support.[98] Recognizing the urgency of this problem, Li Te-yü suggested that since there were no longer any monks available to supervise the almshouses, elderly secretaries (*lu-shih*) of good reputation should be selected by the local authorities to operate these institutions, which were now not to be known by the Buddhistic desigation *pei-t'ien*, but rather as *yang-ping fang*, 'wards for caring for the sick.' A modest proportion of the land confiscated from monasteries was to be allocated for the upkeep of the almshouses: ten *ch'ing* for those in Ch'ang-an and Lo-yang, seven *ch'ing* for those in larger prefectures, and lesser amounts for those in smaller prefectures. Wu-tsung promptly indicated his acceptance of Li's proposals in their entirety.[99]

As the expulsion of monks and nuns from their monasteries was entering its final phase in the fifth month of 845, the commissioners of good works ordered all foreign monks who lacked ordination certificates from the Department of Sacrifices to return to their native countries.[100] Since monks from abroad, who had hitherto been generally exempt from the purge, did not ordinarily hold Chinese ordination certificates, the new decision, as Ennin observed, was tantamount to a mass deportation of the Indian, Central Asian, Korean, and Japanese monks living in China. Ennin received notification on the thirteenth day of the fifth month that he and another Japanese monk resident in the Tzu-sheng ssu who also lacked an ordination certificate from the Department of Sacrifices were to be laicized immediately. Since the order stipulated that any member of the clergy refusing laicization would be subject to summary execution for failure to comply with an imperial edict, Ennin thought it prudent to change to lay clothing the same evening. Two days later he left Ch'ang-an on the first lap of his return journey to Japan.

The dissolution of the Buddhist church in Ch'ang-an and the provinces proceeded with frightening speed. Toward the end of the sixth month Ennin heard from an official who had left Ch'ang-an a month earlier that the laicization of all monks and nuns in the capital had now been completed and that only the three ranking clerical officers (*san kang*) were left in each monastery to prepare an inventory of its property.[101] As soon as the latter passed into the hands of the government, Ennin wrote, the remaining clerical officers were expelled from the monasteries, the buildings of which were then dismantled or put to other use. The Chang-ching ssu, Ch'ing-lung ssu, and An-kuo ssu, which were among the most impressive monasteries in Ch'ang-an, were said to have been converted into imperial gardens. The condition of the Buddhist church in the provinces seemed equally dismal. Ennin reported, for example, that when he reached Ssu-chou (in present-day Kiangsu) on the twenty-second day of the sixth month, he found the P'u-kuang wang ssu deserted; its estates, monetary wealth, and slaves had been seized and the buildings were about to be dismantled. Six days later Ennin described a similar situation in Yang-chou, through which he was then passing. On the sixteenth day of the eighth month he reported from Teng-chou (in the present-day Shantung) that despite the remoteness of the region, the suppression of Buddhism had been as thorough there as in Ch'ang-an: the clergy had been purged, monasteries demolished, scriptures banned,[102] images wrecked, and monastic property confiscated.

With the Buddhist establishment now in shambles, Wu-tsung, at the prompting of the Secretariat-Chancellery, issued a decree in the seventh month of 845 that stipulated the size of the clergy and the geographical distribution of the monasteries that would be allowed to function in the future.[103] Ch'ang-an would be permitted only four monasteries – the Tz'u-en ssu, Chien-fu ssu, Hsi-ming ssu, and Chuang-yen ssu – each with a maximum of thirty resident monks. Lo-yang was, likewise, to be allowed four monasteries with a total of one hundred and twenty monks.

Outside Ch'ang-an and Lo-yang, a single monastery would be permitted in each of forty-one specified provinces (*tao*), with its number of monks and nuns to be determined in accordance with the grade of the province: seventeen provinces would be allowed a maximum of twenty clerics each; fifteen provinces, ten clerics each; eight provinces, five clerics each; and one province, thirteen clerics.[104] All monasteries on the prefectural (*chou*) level were to be closed.[105] Thus in the whole of China only forty-nine monasteries, accommodating approximately 800 monks, would be permitted to operate.[106] Censors (*yü-shih*) were dispatched to the various regions to ensure that the dismantlement of all monasteries other than those sanctioned in this decree proceeded according to a specific schedule.[107]

In line with a proposal from the Secretariat-Chancellery all images and bells made of copper were to be turned over to the commissioner for salt and iron (*yen-t'ieh shih*) for use in the minting of coins.[108] Iron images were to be transferred to the prefectural authorities for recasting as agricultural implements; those images made of gold, silver, and other precious metals were to be melted down into ingots, which would become the property of the Department of Public Revenue (Tu-chih). Individual lay owners of metal images, many of which had been acquired from monasteries when they were being forcibly closed earlier in the year, were ordered to surrender them to the authorities within one month. Even in the small number of monasteries officially sanctioned in Ch'ang-an, Lo-yang, and the provinces no metal images were allowed: only those images made of clay, wood, stone, or other non-metallic substances were to be left undisturbed. Ennin has provided a painful account of the wholesale destruction of Buddhist images in the provinces that he passed through after his expulsion from Ch'ang-an. Arriving in Teng-chou, he observed: '... they have peeled off the gold from the Buddhas and smashed the bronze and iron Buddhas and measured their weight. What a pity! What limit was there to the bronze, iron, and gold Buddhas of the land? And yet, in accordance with the imperial edict, all have been destroyed and have been turned into trash.'[109]

In the eighth month of 845 Wu-tsung issued his Order Regarding the Destruction of Buddhist Monasteries and the Laicization of the Clergy,[110] which provided an *ex post facto* justification for the virtual annihilation of Buddhism in China. After repeating the by now familiar economic, political, moral, and nationalistic arguments against Buddhism, the Emperor declared that he was merely completing the 'reform' (*li-ko*) of Buddhism initiated by his predecessors T'ai-tsung and

Hsüan-tsung. He took evident pride in the thoroughness of the great purge, recording for posterity the achievements thus far: the dismantlement of more than 4,600 monasteries, the defrocking and return to taxable status of 260,500 monks and nuns, the destruction of more than 40,000 chapels and hermitages, the confiscation of 'several tens of millions' of *ch'ing* of fertile land from monastic estates, and the addition of 150,000 ex-slaves to the tax registers.[111] In order to demonstrate clearly the foreign character of the Buddhist church, jurisdiction over the few remaining monks and nuns was transferred from the Department of Sacrifices with which it had rested since 779 to the Office for Overseeing Foreign Visitors (Chu-k'o), which supervised tribute-bearing missions from foreign countries to the court.[112] Even the relatively small Nestorian and Zoroastrian communities were caught in the xenophobic outburst, for, as the imperial order notes, more than 2,000 of their priests were returned to lay status 'so that they might no longer corrupt Chinese customs.'

Li Te-yü, who was one of the principal instigators of the suppression, responded immediately with a highly laudatory memorial couched in Confucian terms congratulating Wu-tsung for his 'heroic decision' to put an end to the Buddhist scourge which had wrought havoc in China since the Han dynasty.[113] Li expressed his sense of indignation toward the Buddhists not only for having obscured the Confucian virtues but also for having contributed to the economic decline of China. He cited with approval the attempt by Kao-tsu, the founder of the T'ang dynasty, to suppress Buddhism, noting that his efforts had failed only because of the machinations of Kao-tsu's trusted minister, Hsiao Yü, who, he was quick to point out, was the scion of the notoriously pro-Buddhist ruling family of the Liang dynasty.[114] Li joined other ministers in a successful proposal submitted to the throne in the eighth month urging that the Imperial Ancestral Hall (T'ai-miao) in Lo-yang, which had burnt down during the An Lu-shan rebellion, be reconstructed with timber from the abandoned Buddhist monasteries in the city.[115]

Despite the harsh penalties with which defrocked members of the clergy were threatened, many preferred to risk their lives rather than return to lay status. Some were clearly motivated by their religious commitments; others dreaded the prospect of being forcibly returned to their native villages which they had not seen for years and being required to work the land as common farmers. As a result large numbers of monks took refuge in the Wei-po, Chao-i, Ch'eng-te and Yu-chou regions where pro-Buddhist military commanders had refused to implement the edicts calling for the dismantlement of monasteries and the purge of the clergy despite repeated orders from the court to do so.[116] Li Te-yü was particularly incensed when reports reached him in the eighth month of 845 that many monks from Wu-t'ai shan were seeking sanctuary in Yu-chou. A blunt warning was dispatched to the military governor of the region, Chang Chung-wu, who, fearing reprisals, subsequently forbade monks from entering the area under his jurisdiction on pain of death.[117]

The problem of ferreting out these 'illegal monks' persisted throughout the remainder of Wu-tsung's reign. Toward the end of the eighth month of 845 all former monks and nuns were ordered to turn over their clerical garb to the local prefectural authorities for burning.[118] In addition, a stern warning was issued to those members of the gentry who, relying on their social status, gave shelter to ex-monks and allowed them to wear their 'black robes' in private. Expelled en masse from their monasteries and deprived of all lay support, the defrocked monks and nuns experienced terrible hardship with the approach of winter. Ennin noted in his diary that bands of ex-monks, lacking food and warm clothing, were frequently apprehended plundering villages.[119] Li Te-yü likewise accused defrocked monks in the Chiang-hsi region of committing acts of brigandage and even murder.[120]

In the ninth month of 845 Wu-tsung is reported to have issued a spate of wildly irrational edicts, possibly drafted under the influence of the elixirs being fed to him.[121] One of these edicts forbade the use of wheelbarrows on the grounds that they would disturb the tranquility of Taoist priests since wheelbarrows tear up 'the center of the road' (*tao chung-hsin*), the latter phrase also connoting 'the heart of Taoism.'[122] Another edict placed a ban on the keeping of black animals, since their color might overwhelm the yellow hue of the garments of Taoist priests.[123] A third edict instructed officials in prefectures close to the seacoast to send live baby otters to the court, presumably for use in medicines. A fourth commanded provincial officials to furnish hearts and livers extracted from the bodies of fifteen year old youths and maidens.[124]

Wu-tsung, in the latter half of 845, began complaining of illness, only to be told by the Taoist quacks surrounding him that this was a sign that he was undergoing 'an exchange of bones' (*huan-ku*), i.e. that he was in the process of ridding himself of his earthly body to become an immortal.[125] His devoted consort, Lady Wang, concluded that his pallid appearance was linked to his daily consumption of drugs and complained that no one other than herself seemed to care.[126] Fearful that his illness might lead to a loss in political power, Wu-tsung made an effort to conceal his weakened physical condition by granting only short audiences with his ministers. At year's end he announced the cancellation of the New Year ceremonies at the court.[127] His health continued to deteriorate, and by the middle of the first month of 846, he stopped attending court altogether and declined audiences even with his chief ministers. Addicted as ever to Taoist superstitions, he came to believe that his affliction was attributable to his personal name Ch'an, which was written with a character that through its radical was associated with water. The T'ang dynasty had been identified with the element earth, which, according to the theory of the five elements (*wu-hsing*), 'conquered' water. Thus in order not to be 'conquered' by the predominant earth element, Wu-tsung, on the first day of the third month, changed his name to Yen, written with a character containing twin fire radicals, since fire 'conquered' earth.[128] All to no avail: carbuncles erupted on his back, he had difficulty breathing, and he finally lost the power of speech.[129] Twenty-two days later this implacable foe of Buddhism was dead, not yet having reached his thirty-second birthday.

The restoration of Buddhism under the reign of Hsuen-tsung (846–859)

When it was realized that Wu-tsung's death was imminent, a group of eunuchs headed by Ma Yüan-chih, the commander of the Shen-ts'e Army of the Left, contrived to issue an edict naming the thirty-five year old Li I, also known as Prince Kuang, heir to the throne. Wu-tsung's four sons were passed over in the succession on the grounds that they were too young to assume the awesome duties of a monarch. The new emperor, posthumously called Hsuen-tsung,[1] was the thirteenth son of Hsien-tsung and was thus the uncle of the three preceding emperors – Ching-tsung, Wen-tsung, and Wu-tsung – who were all sons of Mu-tsung, an elder half-brother to Hsuen-tsung.

Before being called to the throne, Hsuen-tsung scrupulously avoided involvement in court politics. Since he suspected Lady Kuo (Kuo T'ai-hou), the mother of Mu-tsung, of complicity in the murder of his father, it is not surprising that he harbored resentment toward her progeny, i.e. his half-brother and the latter's three sons who ruled before him. Although only a boy of nine when his father died, Hsuen-tsung was strongly attached to his memory and looked back with nostalgia on his father's reign which had ended some twenty-six years earlier. His relationship with Wen-tsung and Wu-tsung was particularly strained; the former ridiculed him in public for his seeming temerity, while the latter, fearing treachery, appears to have plotted his death.[2]

The restoration of Buddhism under Hsuen-tsung (846–859)

Being a devout Buddhist much in the mold of his father, Hsuen-tsung must have been deeply pained to witness the unprecedented assault on the Buddhist church carried out by his despised nephews. Even though there is probably not any truth in the story that Hsuen-tsung, before being called to the throne, had taken the tonsure and lived as an itinerant monk to avoid capture and execution by Wu-tsung,[3] he seems, even in his youth, to have had a genuine interest in Buddhism and to have enjoyed visiting scenic monasteries.[4] Once confirmed as emperor, he lost no time in moving against those ministers and Taoist priests whom he regarded as the principal instigators of the suppression. Since Wu-tsung's anti-Buddhist policies had considerable support within the bureaucracy, the new emperor was compelled to proceed in stages toward his goal of restoring the church to a status similar to that which it had before Wu-tsung's reign.

His first move in this direction, taken a mere month after his enthronement, was the reactivation of the post of commissioner of good works, abolished in the eighth month of 845, when supervision of the few remaining clerics was transferred to the Office for Overseeing Foreign Visitors (Chu-k'o).[5] Perhaps in order not to alarm those officials who might view with suspicion the naming of a eunuch with strong Buddhist sympathies to this potentially powerful post, Hsuen-tsung reappointed the previous incumbent, Yang Ch'in-i.[6] Although, as we have noted, Ennin regarded Yang as an 'irreligious man,' there is no evidence to suggest that he was one of the planners of the purge, even though it was his lot, as a commissioner of good works, to preside over the liquidation of the church between the years 843 and 845 much the way his predecessor, the staunchly pro-Buddhist eunuch Ch'iu Shih-liang, had been compelled under pressure from Wu-tsung to implement various policies which he personally found offensive. As was the rule before the suppression, members of the clergy were ordered to register with the Department of Sacrifices, which in turn would authenticate their status by issuing identification certificates (*tieh*).

No sooner had Yang taken up his commissionership than he was ordered to arrest the chief Taoist instigator of the suppression, Chao Kuei-chen, and eleven other priests, on the charge of 'having brought about the destruction of the Buddhist religion [*hui-ch'u Fo-chiao*] by misleading the previous emperor with false theories.'[7] No Buddhist compassion prevailed in this case: all twelve were condemned to be clubbed to death and their severed heads were put on display. The Confucian culprit – at least from the traditional Buddhist viewpoint[8] – Li Te-yü, who had made many enemies in the factional squabbling over the years and who was roundly despised by Hsuen-tsung for his autocratic behavior during the preceding reign, was dismissed from his office as vice president of the Chancellery (*Men-hsia shih-lang*) in the fourth month of 846 and was demoted through a series of increasingly minor posts in the provinces until he met his death in remote Yai prefecture on Hainan at the close of the year 849. Needless to say, the Buddhists saw his rapid fall from power and humiliating exile as fitting karmic retribution for the evil that he had worked against the church.[9]

Ironically, during the same month that the twelve Taoist priests were being put to a grisly death for their part in the suppression of Buddhism, Hsüan-tsung issued a general amnesty (*ta-she*) that spoke in broad terms of the desirability of achieving harmony after years of discord.[10] To the commissioner of good works this was a clear signal, for he responded in a matter of days with a memorial, immediately approved by the throne, calling for the reopening of sixteen monasteries in Ch'ang-an to augment the four that Wu-tsung had permitted to remain open in his decree issued in the seventh month of the preceding year.[11] Since most of the monasteries that had been closed in 845 had already been dismantled or destroyed, it was proposed, no doubt with a view to curbing expenditures, that only those monasteries that were in a repairable state should be selected for reopening. The inevitable result was that a curious medley of monasteries reappeared – some famous and others that were totally obscure, but had happened somehow to escape destruction. To reduce rivalry among the recommissioned monasteries, seventeen, including some of the best known, were required to drop their former names in favor of new ones, which stressed their mission of affording protection to the state. Thus monasteries with a distinguished tradition like the Pao-ying ssu, the Ch'ing-lung ssu, the Hsi-ming ssu, and the Chuang-yen ssu, although formally reopened, lost their identity in the restoration, resurfacing as new monasteries with patriotic, if bland, names like the Pao-T'ang ssu (Monastery for Protecting the T'ang), T'ang-an ssu (Monastery for the Tranquility of the T'ang), T'ang-ch'ang ssu (Monastery for the Prosperity of the T'ang), and Yen-T'ang ssu (Monastery for the Prolongation of the T'ang).

Together with his general amnesty, which paved the way for increasing the number of monasteries in Ch'ang-an fivefold, Hsuen-tsung issued an edict authorizing all prefectures (*chou*) throughout the empire to open two monasteries, each accommodating fifty monks.[12] In addition, towns in which military governors made their headquarters (*chieh-tu fu*) would be permitted three monasteries each. This action in effect nullified the harsh decree of Wu-tsung issued in the seventh month of 845 which forbade all monasteries on the prefectural level. Hsuen-tsung, for the time being however, still followed a cautious approach with respect to the clergy who were to fill these monasteries, for he stipulated that only persons over fifty years of age who had been ordained before the suppression could take up residence in the reopened monasteries. A bonus of five strings of cash was offered as an inducement to every monk aged eighty or over who would resume his religious calling in one of these monasteries.

Although Hsuen-tsung indicated his desire at this time to permit a limited reopening of monasteries in the provinces and an increase in the number of monasteries in Ch'ang-an and Lo-yang, he was concerned about the effect that this would have on the chronically short supply of metal. He therefore issued a supplementary edict in the eighth month of 846 that stipulated that no metal – gold, silver, copper or iron – or precious stones could be used in the construction of images, which henceforth should be made from clay or wood. Images made from such materials, he pointed out, were wholly adequate for purposes of worship.[13] As a mark of his piety, Hsuen-tsung also ordered the resumption of the longstanding practice – terminated by Wu-tsung at the beginning of 844 – of refraining from slaughter during the three taboo months (*san chai-yüeh*). On the occasion of Hsuen-tsung's birthday in the sixth month of 846, Buddhist monks were once again invited to participate in a vegetarian banquet at the Palace (*nei-chai*) and, along with Taoist priests, were allowed to offer presents to the Emperor as a token of their wish for his longevity.[14] Thus, within a short span of three months the prohibitions against Buddhism, so vigorously enforced by Wu-tsung, began to crumble.

By the intercalary third month of 847, Hsuen-tsung felt sufficiently in control of his newly constituted court to issue an edict calling for the restoration of abandoned monasteries, in which he challenged the hackneyed criticisms of Buddhism frequently repeated during the reigns of his two predecessors.[15] While readily acknowledging that Buddhism was indeed a foreign religion, he declared that it was nevertheless a source of virtue and truth. Since Buddhism had long been adhered to by the people of China, its 'reform' as carried out in the last years of the Hui-ch'ang era had been excessively harsh. He concluded, therefore, that monks of high repute should be permitted to reopen any monasteries closed during the preceding year which they themselves were capable of restoring, regardless of whether these monasteries were situated in sacred mountains, scenic places, or even prefectural capitals, and instructed his officials not to interfere with the activities of these monks.

As the Sung historian Ssu-ma Kuang observed: 'By this time the Emperor and his ministers were making every effort to reverse the policies of the Hui-ch'ang era. Thus did the abuses of the Buddhists recur yet once again!'[16]

To mark the occasion of his second birthday on the throne, Hsuen-tsung pointedly invited Chih-hsüan, one of the most prestigious monks in China at the time, to lecture on Buddhist scriptures.[17] Chih-hsüan, who had first been summoned to the court during the reign of Wen-tsung, had been forced to quit Ch'ang-an and return to lay life in 844 after having incurred the wrath of Wu-tsung in the course of a debate with Taoist priests at the Palace. Almost as if to mock his predecessor, Hsuen-tsung heaped honors on the rehabilitated Chih-hsüan, awarding him the coveted purple robe and granting him the newly created title Doyen of the Three Teachings (San-chiao Shou-tso).[18] In a gesture reminiscent of T'ai-tsung, whom he greatly admired, Hsuen-tsung had a former residence converted into a monastery, which he designated Fa-ch'ien ssu, and assigned one of its pavilions as a residence for Chih-hsüan.

In the first month of 848 Hsuen-tsung proclaimed an amnesty to commemorate his acceptance of an honorific name from his ministers.[19] In his amnesty message he lavished praise on the contributions of the Buddhist religion: its very essence was purity; it brought enlightenment to the ignorant; it lead people to do good works. Hence it was only appropriate that the network of Buddhist monasteries established at the time of his first amnesty of 846 be expanded. Ten additional monasteries were to be opened in Ch'ang-an and five additional ones in Lo-yang. Of these fifteen monasteries, six would be for the exclusive use of nuns. One new monastery and one new convent were to be established in eight specified provinces (*tao*) as well as one additional monastery in each provincial capital in which there was either a military or civil governor. Furthermore, one monastery and one convent were to be built in each prefecture that had hitherto been without a formal community of monks and nuns. Finally, the Buddhist center on Wu-t'ai shan was to be revitalized by the opening of five monasteries, including one nunnery. The monasteries in Ch'ang-an and Lo-yang as well as those on Wu-t'ai shan each were to house fifty monks or nuns, whereas those in the provinces were limited to thirty monks or nuns.[20] Wherever possible pre-existing monasteries were to be repaired and used to fulfill the quotas set in the amnesty message. Officials were advised to proceed slowly in the reconstruction of monasteries in order not to overtax the energies of the people. To ensure the sanctity of the monasteries an order was issued at the suggestion of P'ei Hsiu, a devout Buddhist who at the time was prefect of Hsüan-chou, forbidding officials from using them as hostels.[21] In a separate edict issued during the same year the government authorized the establishment of special 'penitential' Mahāyānist ordination platforms (*hsi-ch'an Fang-teng t'an*) on which ex-members of the clergy could formally repent their transgressions of the *Vinaya* committed during the period of their enforced laicization and reaffirm their precepts.[22]

In the sixth month of 849 the practice of holding debates on the emperor's birthday (*tan-ch'en t'an-lun*) between representatives of Buddhism, Taoism, and Confucianism was resumed after a lapse of six years.[23] Chih-hsüan, who was asked to speak for the Buddhists, used the occasion to petition for a large-scale restoration of the Buddhist church. But the Emperor, for all his piety, was not yet prepared to go this far, and made no response to Chih-hsüan's entreaty other than to order that a portrait of the distinguished monk be installed in the Palace. Even though Chih-hsüan failed to get the sweeping restoration that he sought on this occasion, Buddhist writers are probably correct in attributing to him a major role in bringing about the reopening of monasteries throughout China after the suppression.[24]

By 851, however, Hsuen-tsung was ready to take another far-reaching step toward the total re-establishment of Buddhism. In the first month of that year he issued a decree granting laymen the unrestricted right to build monasteries in villages and to sponsor the ordination of monks and nuns.[25] Meanwhile, at the government level, officials were ordered to resume the memorial services for past emperors (*kuo-chi*), at both Buddhist monasteries and Taoist temples in Ch'ang-an and Lo-yang as well as in the prefectural capitals (*chou-fu*).[26] Wen-tsung had banned such observances at Buddhist monasteries in 839. Personal contacts between Hsuen-tsung and Buddhist monks also grew more frequent: Hsüan-ch'ang, who had been banished by Wu-tsung for his defense of Buddhism in 843, was invited back to the court to participate in the imperial birthday debate;[27] Ting-lan, a thaumaturge who eventually committed religious suicide by burning himself alive, was honored at the Palace and named a teacher to the Emperor;[28] Hung-pien was asked by Hsuen-tsung to lecture on Ch'an.[29]

It is not surprising that officials at the court as well as Confucian scholars were becoming increasingly alarmed by Hsuen-tsung's enthusiastic support of Buddhism. Considerable apprehension was generated by his decision in 851 to allow unrestricted ordination of the clergy and the construction of privately sponsored monasteries in villages, since such policies in the past had had adverse effects on the economy. The opening salvo against Hsuen-tsung's decision to restore the Buddhist church came, appropriately enough, from a *chin-shih* named Sun Ch'iao, who considered himself to be a disciple of Han Yü.[30] Perhaps remembering that Han Yü's denunciations of Hsien-tsung's piety so enraged the Emperor that he sought to have Han Yü put to death, Sun decided to base his memorial, sent to the throne in the sixth month of 851, on economic rather than nationalistic arguments, no doubt in the hope that these would prove less offensive to the Emperor personally.[31] The points in Sun's memorial were all familiar ones: common people had to till the fields and weave the cloth while the clergy sat idly by in luxury, the work of ten households was required to support one monk, etc. Sun asserted that Wu-tsung's indignation at such injustice led him to defrock the clergy, an act which provided a long-needed respite for the common people. 'But since Your Majesty ascended the throne,' Sun observed, 'the sound of axes at the construction sites of monasteries has never stopped! With respect to the ordination of clergy, we have virtually returned to the situation that prevailed before Hui-ch'ang.' Pointing to the lack of funds to complete work on the East Gate of Ch'ang-an, Sun asked whether the government could, in good conscience, spend large sums on the restoration of monasteries. Sun was sufficiently realistic not to ask for another purge of Buddhism, but rather for a ban on any new ordinations or the restoration of monasteries. Hsuen-tsung, at least according to Buddhist sources, angrily rejected the memorial.[32]

One month later a second petition reached the throne – this one drafted at the Secretariat-Chancellery.[33] While refraining from any condemnation of the Buddhist religion *per se*, the petition claimed that the Emperor's enthusiasm for Buddhism had the effect of encouraging the people to squander their resources on the construction of monasteries, which was proving to be a strain on the economy, especially since the country was engaged in a military campaign against the Tanguts. Hsuen-tsung was urged to delay the construction of Buddhist shrines (*Fo-t'ang*) on the village level until the cessation of hostilities and to ascertain through investigations by local officials that only men and women of high moral character were being chosen for ordination lest the clergy fall into disrepute as a haven for miscreants. Hsuen-tsung accepted the main points of the proposal and ordered a moratorium on the construction of Buddhist shrines and hermitages for the duration of the fighting.

In the tenth month of 851, the Secretariat-Chancellery, fearing that the capitulation of the Nan-shan Tanguts two months earlier would result in a deluge of petitions for permission to establish new monasteries, urged that the government adopt unambiguous guidelines regarding the future construction of monasteries, shrines, hermitages, and chapels.[34] It was proposed that all monasteries currently under construction in prefectural capitals should be allowed to be completed only if the people living in the area were willing to provide the labor on a voluntary basis and bear the cost. The building of shrines and hermitages (*Fo-t'ang lan-jo*) would be authorized only after the construction of all monasteries in prefectural capitals had been completed. Large counties (*ta hsien*) that were distant from prefectural capitals might, in certain circumstances, be granted permission to establish a monastery, but the construction of all shrines and hermitages on the village level would be prohibited.

Although Hsuen-tsung gave his approval, he apparently made little effort to ensure that the proposals were actually carried out, for a year later the Department of Sacrifices sent another memorial to him requesting similar curbs on the construction of monasteries.[35] In addition, this new memorial of 852 warned about the great harm that had resulted from the existence of privately ordained monks (*ssu-tu seng*) and urged that this practice be forbidden and such monks, if discovered, be severely punished. The Department of Sacrifices suggested that official ordinations be allowed only when vacancies occur in the allotted number of clergy and that all candidates be screened by a local committee of *Vinaya* masters who were to make certain, before granting ordination, that the prospective monks or nuns were intelligent, pious, and properly trained as novices. All monks and nuns were to be registered with the Department of Sacrifices, which would provide them with certificates of identification (*kao-tieh*). Should members of the Buddhist clergy wish to travel 'in search of the Dharma,' they should be required to carry an official authorization (*kung-yen*) issued by the prefectural authorities, which, it was hoped, would prevent criminals from moving about in the guise of monks.

Hsuen-tsung eventually gave his assent to the memorial from the Department of Sacrifices in 856, after a delay of four years.[36] In the interval, he continued to demonstrate his unflagging support for the restoration of the church and his personal devotion to Buddhism. In 852 he ordered the reconstruction of the Tung-lin ssu, the great monastery on Lu-shan established in 386, and bestowed a posthumous title on its illustrious founder, Hui-yüan.[37] The following year Hsuen-tsung paid a visit to the Chuang-yen ssu to worship its famous relic – a tooth believed to have come from the body of the Buddha.[38] In 854 he issued an edict decreeing the restoration of the Tsung-ch'ih ssu, a magnificent monastery in Ch'ang-an founded by Emperor Yang-ti of the Sui that had been desecrated during the Hui-ch'ang suppression.[39]

During his last years on the throne Hsuen-tsung became increasingly interested in Taoist ideas, particularly the quest for immortality, perhaps as a result of his failing health.[40] In the ninth month of 857 he dispatched an emissary to Lo-fu shan (in the present-day Kwangtung) to escort the Taoist master Hsüan-yüan Chi back to Ch'ang-an. The policy critics voiced strong opposition to the decision to invite Hsüan-yüan to return to the capital since he had been banished from the court in the first days of Hsuen-tsung's reign.[41] The Emperor remained adamant, pointing out that he was well aware that earlier rulers like Ch'in Shih-huang and Han Wu-ti had been manipulated by unscrupulous Taoist priests. He insisted, however, that Hsüan-yüan was a man of high character who had attained longevity through his knowledge of 'inner hygiene' (*she-sheng*). Hsüan-yüan arrived in Ch'ang-an at the New Year of 858, but perhaps recalling the massacre of Taoist priests that took place at the court when Wu-tsung died, refused to stay with the ailing Hsuen-tsung for more than a few months.

Although not widely known, the Emperor was by this time already taking elixirs prepared by Taoist alchemists.[42] Nevertheless his determination to achieve the complete restoration of the Buddhist church remained firm, as can be seen from his order of 858 directing all Buddhist monasteries throughout the empire to repair the halls in which their respective patriarchs were enshrined.[43] By the sixth month of 859 a curious coterie consisting of a court physician, a Taoist priest (*tao-shih*), and a hermit was preparing drugs for the Emperor, who began to suffer from an eruption of carbuncles on his back, as did his predecessor. The Emperor died two months later at the age of forty-nine. It was a strange paradox that Hsuen-tsung, who despised Wu-tsung and made every effort to undo the effects of the brutal suppression of Buddhism carried out by the latter under the influence of Taoist priests, should have ultimately succumbed to the same weakness for their elixirs.

Buddhism in the declining years of the T'ang dynasty

Hsuen-tsung was succeeded on the throne by his twenty-five year old son, Li Ts'ui (known posthumously as I-tsung), who proved to be even more devout than his father.[1] A man of mediocre abilities, I-tsung turned his back on the vexatious world of politics and embraced the Buddhist faith with enthusiasm.[2] He made frequent visits to monasteries, often sending lavish gifts, much to the consternation of his ministers. The Palace Chapel was again filled with monks chanting the scriptures. On the annual imperial birthday celebrations he would regularly invite monks to lecture on Buddhist doctrines. As a further indication of his piety I-tsung held vegetarian feasts for the clergy on the six taboo days of each month,[3] the number of participants sometimes reaching into the thousands. The Emperor on these occasions would compose hymns (*tsan-pai*) for the monks, intone the scriptures himself or transcribe sūtras with his own hand.[4] He also took the unusual step of establishing a convent, known as the Fu-shou ssu, within the Palace grounds to serve as a retreat for women in his entourage.[5] An ordination platform was constructed in the Hsien-t'ai Hall, on which twenty clerics administered the precepts to female palace attendants, who were assigned the task of repairing and copying sets of canon, which at the time comprised 5,461 fascicles.

I-tsung's fervent support of Buddhism promptly drew protests from his ministers. In 861, two years after his enthronement, his grand councillor of the left (*tso san-ch'i ch'ang-shih*), Hsiao Fang, felt compelled to remind him of the virtue of frugality in matters of religion, citing the example of T'ai-tsung's empress, who, when taken ill, refused to allow monks to be ordained on her behalf.[6] Hsiao urged I-tsung to put an end to his discussions with monks at the court so that he could devote himself fully to pressing affairs of state. I-tsung, far from being angered by the blunt warning of dire consequences if he persisted in his support of the alien creed, lauded Hsiao for his memorial, which he nevertheless chose to ignore.[7] The following year an imperial edict was issued ordering the four major monasteries of Ch'ang-an that were permitted by Wu-tsung to continue functioning after the suppression to construct platforms for the performance of penances (*ch'an-fa*) and ordinations. Two additional monasteries, the Ch'ien-fu ssu and the Yen-T'ang ssu, were instructed to allow ordinations, presumably without restriction, for a period of twenty-one days.[8] In 864 a policy critic (*chien-i ta-fu*), P'ei T'an, urged the Emperor to curtail his excessive expenditures on Buddhist projects, since the treasury was desperately short of funds owing to the ongoing military campaigns.[9] The following year another high official, Li Wei, who was executive administrator of the right in the Secretariat of State Affairs (*shang-shu yu-ch'eng*), sent a lengthy memorial to the throne recounting in detail the tragic end of those rulers who squandered the resources of the state on the Buddhist church.[10] On both occasions I-tsung warmly praised his ministers for their solicitude, but failed to act upon their recommendations.

On the contrary, during the last years of his reign, which were marked by the virtual disintegration of the political authority of the emperor, I-tsung spent even greater sums on the Buddhist clergy. In 871, after paying a visit to the An-kuo ssu, he sponsored a vegetarian feast for some 10,000 monks at the Palace.[11] In the third month of 873 I-tsung, once again ignoring the remonstrations of his ministers, dispatched a group of monks to the Fa-men ssu in Feng-hsiang to fetch the famous finger-bone relic of the Buddha.[12] The following month it was carried in a stately procession to the accompaniment of solemn music through the streets of Ch'ang-an, which were elaborately decked out for the occasion, under an escort of soldiers from the Imperial Guard. The splendor of the procession was said to have surpassed even that of 819, when the relic had last been brought to Ch'ang-an. Wealthy families, one vying with the other, erected elegant pavilions along the route providing vegetarian fare for monks and lay worshippers alike. When the procession reached the Palace, I-tsung prostrated himself before the relic, tears reportedly streaming down his face. The sacred bone was held in the Palace Chapel for three days, after which it was installed successively in various monasteries in Ch'ang-an for adoration by the common people, some of whom cut off fingers in the hope of acquiring religious merit.[13] To commemorate the occasion, a limited amnesty was proclaimed.[14] The relic was finally returned to the Fa-men ssu at the end of the year, having been enshrined in Ch'ang-an for eight months.

When I-tsung died in the seventh month of 873, eunuchs proclaimed his eleven year old son, Li Yen (known posthumously as Hsi-tsung), the new emperor. Two years after his enthronement a bandit from Shantung, Wang Hsien-chih, started an insurrection in Honan with a small force of 3,000 men and was soon joined by another malcontent, Huang Ch'ao, who had been an unsuccessful degree-candidate. Within the short span of several months the rebel bands led by these two men had grown into a formidable army that was successfuly defying the imperial forces over a rapidly expanding area in northeast and central China. After the defeat and execution of Wang in 878, Huang Ch'ao absorbed the remnants of his army. By the fifth month of the following year Huang had marched through Kiangsi and Fukien to seize Canton, where he is said to have massacred 120,000 foreigners. After rampaging through Hunan and Ching-chou, the rebels plundered Yang-chou and in the eleventh month of 880 captured Lo-yang. The following month Hsi-tsung abandoned Ch'ang-an, which finally fell to Huang's army in the fifth month of 881. After changing hands briefly in 882, Ch'ang-an was retaken in the following year by loyalist forces, which, after pursuing the rebels through a number of provinces, eventually crushed them in Shantung in the middle of 884, driving their leader, Huang Ch'ao, to commit suicide.

Occurring before the restoration of Buddhism could be adequately carried out, the rebellion by Huang Ch'ao brought to an end the brilliant scholastic traditions of T'ang Buddhism. Unlike the Hui-ch'ang suppression which in its most destructive phase covered a period of approximately two years, Huang Ch'ao's insurrection raged for nine years and devastated almost every major region of China. Although there is no conclusive evidence that the rebels were specifically hostile to Buddhism, the damage suffered by the church proved to be irreversible. While it is true, as the Sung Buddhist historian Tsu-hsiu noted, that the official histories make no mention of the effect that the Huang Ch'ao rebellion had on the established religions,[15] contemporary Buddhist sources leave no doubt that the losses were nothing less than catastrophic and in the long run were probably more detrimental to the maintenance of Buddhist traditions that even the blows of the Hui-ch'ang suppression.

Of the various measures enacted against the Buddhist church by Wu-tsung, the destruction of scriptures – particularly commentaries and treatises by Chinese masters – was potentially the most harmful, since without recourse to these it would not be possible to retain the 'orthodox' interpretations of the canon that had been nurtured over the centuries within each of the schools. Although, as we have seen, Wu-tsung issued the specific order to burn all scriptures in the first month of 846, his antipathy toward Buddhism, evident since his enthronement, suggested the possibility of a full-scale suppression coming later in his reign. Thus some perceptive monks were able to hide sacred texts before the actual closing of their monasteries and their deportation to the countryside. Typical is the case of the T'ien-t'ai scholar Yüan-k'an who, in order to preserve the *Wen-chü* and other commentaries by Chih-i, concealed them in the wall of a house during the Hui-ch'ang purges.[16] Nevertheless the wholesale destruction of monastic libraries and the dispersement of the clergy inevitably led to the loss of large numbers of texts which were not recoverable after the ban on Buddhism was lifted.[17] We can get some idea of how difficult it was to locate a copy of even the basic canon, to say nothing of the commentarial literature, from a eulogy of the monk Shu-yen written in 856, a full ten years after the restoration of Buddhism, which described his efforts to obtain a complete copy of the canon.[18] Unable to find a set in his native T'an-chou (in present-day Hunan), Shu-yen travelled to T'ai-yüan, a region reputed to have a large number of monasteries, in the hope of locating the Buddhist scriptures there. He enlisted the support of the governor, Lu Chün, who, after some months of scouring the area, managed to assemble a set in 5,048 fascicles, which Shu-yen took back to Hunan.

The Buddhist church, while still not yet fully recovered from the disasters of the Hui-ch'ang era, suffered what proved to be a series of irreparable losses during the nine years that the Huang Ch'ao insurgents rampaged through China looting villages, burning towns, and massacring large numbers of innocent people. Buddhist monasteries in virtually every region were affected in one way or another by the incessant warfare and pillaging. As the biographies in the *Sung kao-seng chuan* clearly show, most monks active in the 870s and 880s were forced to abandon their monasteries and flee to what they hoped would be safe areas.[19] Owing to the ever-shifting battlegrounds some unfortunate monks were made refugees two or three times during this relatively short period. The destruction of such major centers of Buddhist learning as Ch'ang-an, Lo-yang, Hang-chou, and T'ai-chou and the scattering of the clergy that occurred with the outbreak of the Huang Ch'ao rebellion and that continued through the remaining two decades of the dynasty resulted in the abrupt termination of many of the prominent exegetical lineages that had existed since the Sui and early T'ang.

The disastrous effects that the Hui-ch'ang suppression and the Huang Ch'ao rebellion had on those schools that stressed textual exegesis, i.e. the so-called 'doctrinal schools' (*chiao-chia*), while not mentioned in the secular literature, is amply attested in Buddhist writings of the time. Monks active in the period of the Five Dynasties and the Sung often were unable to comprehend key concepts appearing in the surviving works of the patriarchs of their own schools. We read, for example, in the biography of the distinguished T'ien-t'ai monk Wu-en that he was forced to deduce for himself the meaning of so basic a T'ien-t'ai term as *shih miao* 'since no explanations of the concept *miao* were available owing to the disappearance of commentaries after the Hui-ch'ang suppression.'[20] Another famous T'ien-t'ai scholar, I-chi (919–987), distressed by the fragmentary nature of the texts remaining after the wars at the end of the T'ang, tried to reassemble the works of Chih-i, the founder of his school, but was able to find only the latter's commentary on the *Wei-mo ching* (*Vimalakīrti Sūtra*).[21] Convinced that without these texts there would be no way for T'ien-t'ai monks to correct the erroneous interpretations already prevalent in their school, I-chi persuaded Ch'ien Hung-shu, the devout ruler of the Wu-yüeh kingdom in which the T'ien-t'ai mountains were situated, to send missions abroad in search of Chih-i's writings, since it was believed at the time that many of the texts lost at the end of the T'ang were circulating in Korea or Japan.[22] In response to a personal letter from Ch'ien carried by one of his emissaries, the king of Koryŏ (Korea), dispatched a T'ien-t'ai scholar, Ch'egwan, to Wu-yüeh with copies of the major commentaries and treatises by Chih-i and Chan-jan.[23] So crucial was Ch'egwan's reintroduction of texts that the Sung T'ien-t'ai historian, Chih-p'an, credited him with having brought about the revival of T'ien-t'ai in China.[24]

Another major T'ang doctrinal school that fell into decline as a result of the incessant warfare during the final decades of the ninth century was the Hua-yen, whose last great patriarch, Tsung-mi, died in 841. As was the case with T'ien-t'ai, Hua-yen, whose chroniclers count five patriarchs during the T'ang, made extensive use of commentaries and treatises for the transmission of its doctrines.[25] Here too the Huang Ch'ao rebellion took its toll. By the time that the Sung dynasty was established, the Hua-yen patriarchal succession had been broken and the major works of the school lost.[26] Although some of the Hua-yen commentaries and treatises were finally reintroduced into China by the Korean monk Ŭich'ŏn who arrived in China in 1085, the full revival of the Hua-yen tradition did not take place until the end of the Ch'ing dynasty when Chinese scholars were able to retrieve from Japan the major Hua-yen treatises that had been missing since the end of the T'ang.

With its transmissions shattered and crucial texts lost, the character of Chinese Buddhism underwent a fundamental transformation after the T'ang. As we have seen, those schools like the T'ien-t'ai and Hua-yen which were heavily dependent on textual exegesis for the explication of their doctrines experienced a sharp decline from which they never fully recovered, while schools such as the Ch'an and Pure Land which were based not so much on mastery of abstract doctrine as on intuitive insights and personal religious experience emerged as the leading expressions of Chinese Buddhism. The Ch'an school was in a particularly strong position to weather the turmoil of the Hui-ch'ang years and the wars at the end of the T'ang, since it held that formal textual study and a thorough acquaintance with a broad range of scripture were not requisites for the attainment of enlightenment, which might occur, depending on the individual, as readily in the give-and-take atmosphere of a marketplace as in the highly disciplined setting of a monastery. Furthermore, by the end of the T'ang Ch'an masters prided themselves on having developed a tradition that was not primarily based on elaborate scriptural exegesis as was the case with doctrinal schools like the Fa-hsiang, T'ien-t'ai, and

Hua-yen, but rather was one that emphasized that the highest spiritual goals of Buddhism could be realized through achieving insight into one's own true nature under the guidance of an awakened teacher.[27] According to this view, monasteries, images, and even scriptures were not necessarily essential for the religious life, a point that is illustrated in countless stories about masters who burn sūtras or chop up wooden images for firewood in order to free their disciples from attachment to external forms.[28] Similarly, Pure Land Buddhism, with its simple message to the common people that Amitābha Buddha would respond to all who invoked his name, had the potential for surviving as a popular faith even though its clerical exponents were dispersed and its theoretical treatises were lost.

Thus when the Hui-ch'ang and Huang Ch'ao disasters overtook the Buddhist world, the Ch'an and Pure Land movements proved far less vulnerable to the dismantlement of monasteries, confiscation of property, laicization of clergy, destruction of images, and loss of commentaries than did the doctrinal schools. Although the Hui-ch'ang suppression and the subsequent warfare attending the collapse of the T'ang were responsible for bringing to an abrupt close an era of unparalleled creativity in Chinese Buddhist intellectual history, they paradoxically opened the way for the Ch'an and Pure Land schools, which sought to give concrete expression to the ideals of Mahāyāna, to establish themselves as the twin pillars of Chinese Buddhism, a position that they have continued to hold down to our own day.

LIST OF ABBREVIATIONS

CKFL	*Chi ku-chin Fo Tao lun-heng. TD*, vol. 52.
CKL	*Shih-shih chi-ku lüeh. TD*, vol. 49.
CSP	*Chi sha-men pu ying pai-su teng shih. TD*, vol. 52.
CTL	*Ching-te ch'uan-teng lu. TD*, vol. 51.
CTS	*Chiu T'ang shu.*
CTW	*Ch'üan T'ang-wen.*
CYL	*Chen-yüan hsin-ting Shih-chiao mu-lu. TD*, vol. 55.
FTLT	*Fo-tsu li-tai t'ung-tsai. TD*, vol. 49.
FTTC	*Fo-tsu t'ung-chi. TD*, vol. 49.
FYCL	*Fa-yüan chu-lin. TD*, vol. 53.
HKSC	*Hsü kao-seng chuan. TD*, vol. 50.
HKYL	*Ta T'ang Chen-yüan hsü K'ai-yüan Shih-chiao lu. TD*, vol. 55.
HTS	*Hsin T'ang shu.*
KHMC	*Kuang hung-ming chi. TD*, vol. 52.
KSC	*Kao-seng chuan. TD*, vol. 50.
KSP	*Tai-tsung chao tseng Ssu-k'ung Ta-pien-cheng Kuang-chih San-tsang Ho-shang piao-chih chi. TD*, vol. 52.
KYL	*K'ai-yüan Shih-chiao lu. TD*, vol. 55.
LFPT	*Lung-hsing Fo-chiao pien-nien t'ung-lun.*
LTSP	*Li-tai san-pao chi. TD*, vol. 49.
NGJK	*Nittō guhō junrei kōki.*
NGJKK	*Nittō guhō junrei kōki no kenkyū*, by Ono Katsutoshi.
PCL	*Pien-cheng lun. TD*, vol. 52.
SFC	*Ta T'ang Ta tzu-en ssu San-tsang Fa-shih chuan. TD*, vol. 50.
SKSC	*Sung kao-seng chuan. TD*, vol. 50.
SS	*Sui shu.*
SSL	*Ta Sung seng-shih lüeh. TD*, vol. 54.
TCTC	*Tzu-chih t'ung-chien.*
TD	*Taishō shinshū daizōkyō.*
TFYK	*Ts'e-fu yüan-kuei.*
THY	*T'ang hui-yao.*
ZZK	*Dai Nihon zokuzōkyō.*

NOTES

Introduction

1 A carefully documented account of the beginnings of Buddhism in China is given in E. Zürcher, *The Buddhist Conquest of China* (Leiden, 1959), vol. 1, pp. 1–43.
2 The first significant challenge to the autonomy of the church in the South was made by Yü Ping 庾冰 in 340. Yü's proposal to require the clergy to do reverence to the throne was rejected. See Zürcher, *Buddhist Conquest*, vol. 1, pp. 106–08. For an overview of the question of the autonomy of the Buddhist clergy in South China see Kenneth K.S. Ch'en, *The Chinese Transformation of Buddhism* (Princeton, N.J., 1973), pp. 67–78.
3 This practice, known as *she-shen* 捨身, 'discarding one's body,' occurred repeatedly during the Liang and Ch'en dynasties; see *FTTC* 37, pp. 350b–353b. For a detailed account of the practice of *she-shen* by the Liang Emperor Wu, see Mori Mikisaburō 森三樹三郎, *Ryō no Butei* 梁の武帝 (Kyoto, 1956), pp. 142–9.
4 On Yang Chien's use of Buddhism for his own political ends see Arthur F. Wright's excellent study, 'The Formation of Sui Ideology, 581–604,' in John K. Fairbank, ed. *Chinese Thought and Institutions* (Chicago, 1957), pp. 71–104.
5 *LTSP* 12, p. 107b. The five sacred mountains (*wu-yüeh* 五嶽) are T'ai-shan 泰山 in Shantung, Heng-shan 衡山 in Hunan, Hua-shan 華山 in Shensi, Heng-shan 恒山 in Shansi, and Sung-shan 嵩山 in Honan. See Mochizuki Shinkō, ed. *Bukkyō daijiten*, vol. 2, pp. 1121c–1122b.
6 *LTSP* 49, pp. 107c–108a.
7 *SS* 35, p. 1099.
8 Ibid.
9 *PCL* 3, p. 508c.
10 The edict, which is entitled *Chao li seng-ni erh ssu chi* 詔立僧尼二寺記 is included in *Chin-shih ts'ui-pien* 金石萃編 (Shih-k'o shih-liao ts'ung-shu 石刻史料叢書 edn, Taipei, 1966) 38, pp. 30a–33a. For a discussion of the dating of the edict see Tsukamoto Zenryū 塚本善隆, *Nisshi Bukkyō kōshōshi kenkyū* 日支佛教交涉史研究 (Tokyo, 1944), pp. 8–9.
11 *PCL* 3, p. 509a.
12 *HKSC* 18, p. 573a–b.
13 *PCL* 3, p. 509b.
14 Kao-tsu, the first T'ang emperor, is described in *FTTC* 19, p. 362c as a man

152

of 'shallow faith.' T'ai-tsung, the second T'ang emperor, bluntly declared in an edict that Buddhism was not a religion that he could follow; see his edict entitled *Pien Hsiao Yü shou-chao* 貶蕭瑀手詔 in *CTW* 8, pp. 7b–8b.
15 *PCL* 4, p. 511b.
16 For a study of the attitudes of the first three T'ang emperors toward the Buddhist church see the valuable article by Yūki Reimon 結城令聞, 'Shotō Bukkyō no shisōshiteki mujun to kokka kenryoku to no kōsaku' 初唐仏教の思想史的矛盾と国家権力との交錯, *Tōyō Bunka Kenkyūjo kiyō* 25 (1961) 1–28.

Reign of Kao-tsu (618–626)
1 *CTS* 192, p. 5125; *HTS* 204, p. 5804.
2 Tu Kuang-t'ing, 杜光庭 *Li-tai ch'ung-tao chi* 歷代崇道記, in *Tao-tsang* 道藏 vol. 329, p. 5a–b.
3 *HTS* 204, p. 5804.
4 *CTS* 1, p. 3.
5 *Li-tai ch'ung-tao chi*, pp. 3b–4b. *THY* 50, p. 865 states that the encounter took place in 620.
6 For an analysis of Fu I's arguments against Buddhism see Arthur F. Wright, 'Fu I and the Rejection of Buddhism,' *Journal of the History of Ideas*, 12 (1951), pp. 33–47. Biographies of Fu I are in *CTS* 79, pp. 2714–17 and *HTS* 107, pp. 4092–62.
7 Summarized from Wright, 'Fu I,' pp. 40–5.
8 *TD* no. 2109. For an account of the polemical literature generated in the various debates see Kubota Ryōon 久保田量遠, *Shina Ju Dō Butsu kōshōshi* 支那儒道佛交涉史 (Tokyo, 1943), pp. 172–81.
9 *FTTC* 39, p. 362c.
10 *FTTC* 39, p. 365c. According to the *Ch'ang-an chih* 長安志 (Ching-hsün-t'ang ts'ung-shu 經訓堂叢書 edn) 8, p. 11a, Kao-tsu built the Sheng-yeh ssu 勝業寺 for Ching-hui 景暉, who had foretold Kao-tsu's rise to power. Note also Tao-hsüan's statement in *HKSC* 11, p. 513b that when the T'ang was founded, 'its intention was to protect Buddhism.'
11 *HKSC* 24, p. 633c.
12 *FTTC* 39, p. 362c.
13 *CKFL* 4, p. 381a.
14 *FTTC* 39, pp. 362c–363a.
15 The text of the edict is given in *CTS* 1, pp. 16–17 and *CTW* 3, pp. 6a–7b.
16 According to *HKSC* 24, p. 637c, the property of all Buddhist monasteries in Ch'ang-an, aside from the three officially permitted, was to be distributed among the aristocratic families. Only one thousand monks were to be allowed to remain in the capital.
17 Wei Shu 韋述, quoted in *Ch'ang-an chih* 7, p. 6a. According to *HTS* 48, p. 1252, a census taken around the year 728 reported the relative sizes of the Buddhist and Taoist churches for the whole of China as follows: 75,524 Buddhist monks, 50,776 Buddhist nuns, 5,358 Buddhist monasteries (*ssu*); 776 Taoist priests (*tao-shih* 道士), 988 Taoist priestesses (*nü-kuan* 女官), 1,687 Taoist temples (*kuan* 觀).
18 *FTTC* 39, p. 363a.

19 For a detailed account of the evolution of the various governmental offices that oversaw the Buddhist church during the period of the Northern and Southern Dynasties see Yamazaki Hiroshi, *Shina chūsei Bukkyō no tenkai* (Tokyo, 1942), pp. 473–537. A short but useful survey of the different organs of government created to exercise control over the Buddhist clergy between the fifth and ninth centuries can be found in Kenneth Ch'en, *The Chinese Transformation of Buddhism*, pp. 114–24.
20 *Wei shu* 114, p. 3040. For the dates for these offices see Yamazaki, p. 499.
21 *SS* 27, p. 758.
22 *SS* 27, p. 756.
23 *SS* 28, p. 777. It is not clear precisely when the Sui abolished the ecclesiastical office of grand controller of the Court for the Illumination of Mysteries. *FTTC* 39, p. 359c notes that the monk T'an-ch'ien 曇遷 was appointed to the position of grand controller of monks in 587, which would indicate that the Court for the Illumination of Mysteries was still in existence at that time.
24 The director held the rank of lower division of the eighth grade (*cheng pa p'in hsia* 正八品下). For a discussion of the functions of the Bureau for the Veneration of Mysteries see *HTS* 48, p. 1252.
25 *HTS* 48, p. 1252. The practice of placing 'overseers' in Buddhist and Taoist religious establishments was begun by Yang-ti, the second Sui emperor. See *SS* 28, p. 802.
26 *SSL* 2, p. 245c.
27 See, for example, the biographies of Pao-kung 保恭 and Chi-tsang 吉藏 in *HKSC* 11, pp. 513a and 514b respectively.
28 For the names of the seven monks see Yamazaki Hiroshi, *Shina chūsei Bukkyō no tenkai*, pp. 603–5, which is the source of my data regarding the Ten Monks of Great Virtue.
29 On the hostility between the partisans of exegesis and those of meditation see S. Weinstein, 'Imperial Patronage in the Formation of T'ang Buddhism,' in Arthur F. Wright and Denis Twitchett, eds. *Perspectives on the T'ang* (New Haven, Conn., 1973), p. 276.
30 Because of the extremely close association of the early T'ien-tai school with the Sui imperial family, T'ien-t'ai monks received virtually no support from early T'ang rulers. See Weinstein, 'Imperial Patronage,' pp. 289–91.

Reign of T'ai-tsung (626–649)
1 In the turmoil that accompanied the disintegration of the Sui and the rise of the T'ang, Buddhist monks and laymen participated in a number of rebellions, often justifying their resort to arms by citing religious motives. Two such uprisings, both unsuccessful, are recorded for the year 613. In one case, a layman, Sung Tzu-hsien 宋子賢, who was reputed to be well versed in the magical arts, proclaimed himself an incarnation of Maitreya, the next Buddha destined to appear in this world. He planned to recruit Buddhist laymen at religious services for an attack on the Emperor, but was killed along with many supporters when his plot was leaked to the authorities. In the second case, a monk, Hsiang Hai-ming 向海明, also claiming to be an earthly manifestation of Maitreya, declared himself

Emperor. He attracted 'several tens of thousands' of followers before being destroyed by the imperial forces. Both incidents are related in *TCTC* 182, pp. 5686–7. In 618, the year in which the T'ang dynasty was established, a monk, Kao T'an-ch'eng 高曇晟, set himself up as Ta-ch'eng Huang-ti 大乘皇帝 (The Mahāyāna Emperor), took a nun as his 'Empress,' and adopted a Buddhist era-name, Fa-lun 法輪 ('Dharmacakra', i.e. 'the wheel of the Dharma'). Government forces managed to kill T'an-ch'eng and his several thousand followers, but only after they had murdered the county magistrate and the local commandant of the military forces (*TCTC* 186, pp. 5833–34). In 619 the rebel general, Liu Wu-chou 劉武周, accompanied by the monk, Tao-ch'eng 道澄, marched into Chieh-chou 介州, 'with Buddhist pennants trailing' (*TCTC* 187, p. 5858). Two years later Li Chung-wen 李仲文, the duke of Chen-hsiang 眞鄉, was accused of plotting a rebellion with 'a strange monk,' Chih-chüeh 志覺 (*TCTC* 188, p. 5904).

2 Arthur F. Wright, 'T'ang T'ai-tsung and Buddhism,' in A.F. Wright and D. Twitchett, eds. *Perspectives on the T'ang*, pp. 246–7. On T'ai-tsung's policy toward Buddhism see also T'ang Yung-t'ung 湯用彤, 'T'ang T'ai-tsung yü Fo-chiao' 唐太宗與佛教, originally published in *Hsüeh-heng* 學衡, 75 (1931), reprinted in T'ang Yung-t'ung, *Wang-jih tsa-kao* 往日雜稿 (Peking, 1962), pp. 8–13.
3 *TCTC* 189, p. 5918.
4 Ibid.
5 *TCTC* 192, p. 6029.
6 *PCL* 4, p. 512a; *FYCL* 100, p. 1027a.
7 *FTTC* 39, p. 363b. The text of the edict ordering the conversion of the T'ung-i Palace into a nunnery is included in *KHMC* 28, p. 329c, where it is dated 630 by Tao-hsüan.
8 *PCL*, p. 512a–b; for the month of the services see *FTTC*, p. 363b. The text of the edict is included in *HKSC* 28, p. 329a.
9 *FTTC*, 363b states that the mass was held at the *Chang-ching ssu* 章敬寺, which must be an error, since this monastery was built in 767. See *THY* 48, p. 847.
10 *PCL*, p. 512a–b; for the precise month see *FTTC*, p. 363b.
11 *PCL*, p. 512b. The *Jen-wang ching*, attributed (falsely) to Kumārajīva, is *TD* no. 245; the *Ta-yün ching*, which, as we shall see, figured prominently in the usurpation of the throne by Empress Wu, is *TD* no. 387.
12 *PCL* 4, p. 514a. *FYCL* 100, p. 1027a reports that more than ten such monasteries were established at former battle-sites. For the text of the edict see *KHMC* 28, pp. 328c–329a.
13 *FTTC* 39, p. 363c.
14 For the names of the authors of the inscriptions see *FTTC*, p. 363c.
15 *HKSC* 24, p. 633a.
16 *HKSC* 24, p. 635a.
17 *HKSC* 22, p. 623c.
18 *HKSC* 25, p. 666a.
19 *HKSC* 20, p. 606a.
20 *Chen-kuan cheng-yao* 貞觀政要 (Tōyō Bunka Kenkyūjo edn, 1962) 7, p. 222.

21 *FTTC* 39, p. 364b.
22 In 631 he converted one of his palaces into a monastery named Tz'u-te ssu 慈德寺 (Monastery of the Virtue of Compassion) in honor of his mother (*PCL* 4, p. 514a; for the precise date see *THY* 48, p. 850). In 632 he established the magnificent Hung-fu ssu 弘福寺 in her memory (*PCL*, p. 514a). The construction of the Hung-fu ssu is dated 634 in *FTTC*, p. 364b, which adds that T'ai-tsung personally took part in the consecration of the Buddha image. In 641 he participated in a memorial service for his mother at the Hung-fu ssu (*CKFL* 3, pp. 385c–386a).
23 *FTTC* 39, p. 364c.
24 The text is included in *KHMC* 28, p. 329a–b.
25 Non-action (*wu-wei* 無爲) is, of course, the basis for the Taoist, *not* Buddhist, precepts.
26 The text of the edict is given in *KHMC* 25, p. 283c.
27 For an account of the ensuing imbroglio see *HKSC* 24, pp. 635b–636a and Yen-tsung 彦琮, *T'ang hu-fa sha-men Fa-lin pieh-chuan* 唐護法沙門法琳別傳 (completed between 640–649) 2, in *TD* 50, pp. 203a–204a.
28 See *HKSC*, p. 635c. Several hundred monks took part in the protest according to *SFC* 9, p. 270a.
29 *HKSC* 15, p. 541a.
30 *T'ang hu-fa sha-men Fa-lin pieh-chuan* 2, p. 204a.
31 *HKSC* 24, p. 636a. *FTTC* 39, p. 364c, however, reports that Chih-shih was defrocked and died in exile in Ling-piao 嶺表, i.e. the region of Kuang-tung and Kuang-hsi provinces.
32 *T'ang hu-fa sha-men Fa-lin pieh-chuan*, p. 203a states that Fa-lin was the author of the memorial presented to T'ai-tsung protesting the inferior status of Buddhism.
33 *HKSC* 24, p. 638a.
34 Ibid.
35 The legal code was in four parts: a penal code (*lü* 律) in 500 articles, administrative statutes (*ling* 令) in 1590 articles, regulations (*ko* 格) in 700 articles, and an unspecified number of ordinances (*shih* 式). See Sogabe Shizuo 曾我部靜雄, *Nitchū ritsuryō ron* 日中律令論 (Tokyo, 1963), pp. 93–6. The *Tao-seng ko* were included among the regulations. For a study of the regulations governing the Buddhist clergy and their relationship to the secular codes see Kenneth K.S. Ch'en, *The Chinese Transformation of Buddhism*, pp. 95–105.
36 The *Yōrō ritsuryō*, which was compiled in the year 718 but not formally promulgated until 757, was made up of a penal code (*ritsu*; Ch. *lü*) and administrative statutes (*ryō*; Ch. *ling*). The *ritsu* section, which had long been lost, was largely restored through the efforts of Ishihara Masaaki 石原正明, who collected fragmentary quotations appearing in various early works. The *ryō*, however, have come down to us virtually intact, only two of its original thirty sections having been lost. These two sections have since been partially restored. The *Sōniryō*, which contains twenty-seven articles, was the seventh of the thirty sections making up the *ryō* portion of the Yōrō code. For the text of the *Sōniryō* see Kuroita Katsumi, ed. *Shintei zōho kokushi taikei* 新訂增補國史大系, vol. 22 (Tokyo, 1939), pp. 81–9.

37 For detailed studies of the *Sōniryō*, including their relationship to the *Tao-seng ko*, see Futaba Kenkō 二葉憲香, *Kodai Bukkyō shisōshi kenkyū* 古代佛教思想史研究 (Kyoto, 1962), pp. 131–301 and Michihata Ryōshū 道端良秀, *Tōdai Bukkyōshi no kenkyū* 唐代仏教史の研究 (Kyoto, 1957), pp. 114–37.

38 The penal code (*lü*) was revised seven times, the administrative statutes (*ling*) ten times; see Niida Noboru 仁井田陞, 'Ritsurei kakushiki' 律令格式 in *Ajiya rekishi jiten*, vol. 9 (Tokyo, 1962), p. 240a. The regulations (*ko*) were amended six times during the seventh century alone. For specifics see Moroto Tatsuo 諸戶立雄, 'Chūgoku ni okeru dochō shoju no nendai ni tsuite' 中国に於ける度牒初授の年代について, *Bunka* 文化, 15.4 (1951) 386–7.

39 The Taihō code (*ritsuryō*) was promulgated in 702 and remained in force until it was superseded by the Yōrō code in 757. Judging from surviving fragments, the Taihō code would appear to have been not very different from the Yōrō code. After an exhaustive study of the available evidence, Futaba concludes that the *Sōniryō* sections of the two codes were almost identical. See Futaba, p. 177.

40 *FTTC* 39, p. 364c; *HKSC* 22, p. 617a.

41 T'ai-tsung's edict of 635, which was issued one month after the Emperor had received Hsüan-wan's appeal, states that officials have been ordered to draw up a list of regulations (*t'iao-chih* 條制) based on 'Buddhist law' (*nei-lü* 內律), i.e. the *Vinaya*, for the control of the clergy. It seems likely that this was done in response to Hsüan-wan's deathbed plea. These regulations, drafted in 635, probably formed the basis of the *Tao-seng ko* (with appropriate additions to cover the Taoist clergy).

42 *SFC* 9, p. 270a–b. In 655 Kao-tsung had decreed that officials might try members of the Taoist and Buddhist clergies according to 'secular law' (*su-fa* 俗法) in certain undefined, dubious cases, thereby suspending the *Tao-seng ko*. Officials apparently had a field-day humiliating monks, which prompted Hsüan-tsang's appeal to Kao-tsung for a return to the *Tao-seng ko*.

43 *Wei shu* 114, p. 3040.

44 *LTSP* 12, p. 108b.

45 *LTSP* 12, pp. 107a and 108b.

46 See for example the biography of Chih-lin 智琳 (*HKSC* 10, p. 504a), who was appointed to this office on the provincial level in 596.

47 On the penalties imposed on monks and nuns see Michihata Ryōshū, *Tōdai Bukkyōshi no kenkyū*, pp. 117–35 and especially pp. 123–4. For a general discussion of the secular restraints on the Buddhist clergy see also Kenneth K.S. Ch'en, *The Chinese Transformation of Buddhism*, pp. 95–105.

48 According to *T'ang-lü su-i* 唐律疏議 (Tai-nan-ko ts'ung-shu 岱南閣叢書 edn) 9, p. 12a, the use of astrological signs and the reading of books on military arts were punishable by two years imprisonment. The penalty for misleading people through stories and books dealing with the supernatural was death by strangulation. See *T'ang-lü su-i* 18, p. 8a.

49 *T'ang-lü su-i* 6, p. 17b.

50 *T'ang-lü su-i*, 19, p. 5a.

51 *T'ang liu-tien* (Wen-hai 文海 edn, Taipei, 1962) 4, p. 46b. We may assume

that these offences in *T'ang liu-tien* are largely drawn from the *Tao-seng ko*, since most of them also occur in the *Sōniryō*.
52 *T'ang liu-tien* 4, p. 47a.
53 *Ssu-fen lü* 四分律 42, in *TD* 22, p. 872b.
54 *Ta-sheng ju leng-ch'ieh ching* 大乘入楞伽經 (*Laṅkāvatāra sūtra*) 6, in *TD* 16, p. 623b–c; *Ta po-nieh-p'an ching* 大般涅槃經 (*Mahāparinirvāṇa sūtra*) 4, in *TD* 12, p. 626a–b; *Fan-wang ching* 梵網經 2, in *TD* 24, p. 1005b.
55 *T'ang liu-tien* 4, pp. 46b–47a.
56 *TD* no. 389.
57 *FTTC* 39, p. 365b. The text of the edict is given in *CTW* 9, p. 9a–b. All of the catalogues of the canon agree in attributing the translation to Kumārajīva, even though there is considerable disagreement regarding the precise title of the sūtra. Critical studies by modern scholars tend to regard this sūtra as a composite work put together from disparate sources rather than as a translation of a single Indian text. See Fukaura Seibun's 深浦正文 introduction to the Japanese translation in *Kokuyaku issaikyō* 國譯一切經, *Kyōshūbu* 經集部, vol. 3 (Tokyo, 1933), pp. 133–39.
58 *Fo i-chiao ching*, in *TD* 12, pp. 1110c–1111a.
59 *Fo i-chiao ching shih-hsing ch'ih* 佛遺教經施行勅, in *CTW* 9, p. 9a.
60 The incident is recounted in two near-contemporary sources: *CKFL* 3, pp. 385c–386a and *FYCL* 100, p. 1027a. *FTTC* 39, p. 365b gives the year as 642.
61 For a partial translation of the vow see Wright, 'T'ang T'ai-tsung and Buddhism,' p. 257.
62 'Bodhisattva precepts' (*p'u-sa chieh* 菩薩戒) refer to the fifty-eight precepts in the Mahāyānist *Fan-wang ching*; see *TD* 24, pp. 1004b–1009b. These precepts were administered to pious laymen as well as monks. There is no indication that T'ai-tsung formally received these precepts.
63 This statement certainly was not true. In 631 T'ai-tsung established the Hsi-hua kuan 西華觀 in Ch'ang-an to effect the recovery of the ailing Crown Prince, Ch'eng-ch'ien 承乾 (*THY* 50, p. 869). Four years later he built the T'ai-shou kuan 太受觀 on Mao-shan 茅山, the center of the Shang-ch'ing school 上清派 of Taoism, in honor of Wang Yüan-chih; see *CTS* 192, p. 5125 and *HTS* 204, p. 5804.
64 *CKFL* 3, p. 386a.
65 The edict, entitled *Pien Hsiao Yü shou-chao* 貶蕭瑀手詔, is included in *CTW* 8, pp. 7b–8b and *CTS* 63, pp. 2403–04.
66 The most detailed account of Hsüan-tsang's relationship with T'ai-tsung and Kao-tsung is found in the last five fascicles of *SFC*, which were completed by Yen-ts'ung 彥悰 in 688, twenty-four years after the death of Hsüan-tsang. An abridged translation will be found in Li Yung-hsi's *The Life of Hsuan-tsang* (Peking, 1958), pp. 161–274. Arthur Waley's *The Real Tripitaka* (London, 1952), pp. 9–130, contains a fascinating description of Hsüan-tsang's travels in India and his activities in China after 645, based largely on *SFC* and Hsüan-tsang's biography in *HKSC*.
67 *SFC* 6, p. 253b.
68 *SFC*, p. 253c.
69 For a full list of the names of the monks who joined Hsüan-tsang at this

time see *SFC*, pp. 253c–254a.
70 The philologist was Hsüan-ying 玄應, who subsequently compiled the *I-ch'ieh-ching yin-i* 一切經音義 in twenty-five fascicles (published in the *Dai-Nihon kōtei daizōkyō* 大日本校訂大藏經, *Ongibu* 音義部, vol. 6), which is the oldest extant Chinese lexicon of Buddhist terminology.
71 The specialist in Indian languages was Hsüan-mu 玄暮 (also known as Hsüan-mo 玄謨 or 玄摸), probably an Indian, who had already translated a number of texts at the beginning of T'ai-tsung's reign. See *Ta T'ang nei-tien lu* 大唐內典錄 (completed in 664) 5, in *TD* 55, p. 281a.
72 *SFC*, p. 254a.
73 *TD* no. 2087. There are two English translations: Samuel Beal, *Si-yu-ki: Buddhist Records of the Western World* (London, 1884) and Thomas Watters, *On Yuan Chwang's Travels in India*, 2 vols. (London, 1904–5).
74 *SFC*, p. 254c.
75 *HKSC* 4, p. 455b. Although the name of Wang Hsüan-ts'e does not appear, the reference is no doubt to his mission to India.
76 *HKSC*, p. 455b–c.
77 *SFC*, p. 255a.
78 *SFC*, pp. 255c–256a. The *Yogācārabhūmi*, known as *Yü-ch'ieh-shih ti lun* 瑜伽師地論 in Chinese, is *TD* no. 1579.
79 The preface, entitled *Ta T'ang san-tsang sheng-chiao hsü* 大唐三藏聖教序, is included in *CTW* 10, pp. 10a–12a and *SFC*, pp. 256b–c.
80 This sūtra has been incorporated into the *Ta pao-chi ching* 大寶積經 (*TD* no. 310) as its twelfth section.
81 *SFC* 7, p. 258b.
82 See Hsüan-tsang's memorial to Kao-tsung dated 656, summarized in *SFC* 9, p. 270a; also *FTTC* 39, p. 367a.
83 *SFC*, p. 259a.
84 *SFC*, p. 259b.
85 *SFC*, p. 260a.

Reign of Kao-tsung (649–683)
1 It should be noted that a Taoist temple, the Tung-ming kuan 東明觀, was also built on this occasion (*SFC* 10, p. 275b and *THY* 50, p. 869). In the same year Kao-tsung had a former mansion converted into a Taoist temple called Hao-t'ien kuan 昊天觀 in memory of his father (*THY* 50, p. 869).
2 For a year-by-year listing of Hsüan-tsang's translations see Fukihara Shōshin 富貴原章信, *Nihon yuishiki shisoshi* 日本唯識思想史 (Kyoto, 1944), pp. 87–94.
3 *SFC*, p. 260b.
4 *SFC*, p. 260c.
5 *SFC* 8, p. 266a.
6 *SFC* 9, p. 269a.
7 *SFC*, p. 269c.
8 *SFC*, p. 270a.
9 The text of the edict, which is entitled *T'ing ch'ih seng-tao fan-tsui t'ung su-fa t'ui-k'an ch'ih* 停勅僧道犯罪同俗法推勘勅, is given in *CTW* 14, pp. 1b–2a and *SFC*, p. 270b.

10 The Emperor, for example, urged Hsüan-tsang to concentrate on translating those texts that were unknown to the Chinese rather than retranslate texts that were already available in unreliable or incomplete versions (*SFC*, p. 272c).
11 Hsüan-tsang appears to have brought some subtle pressure to bear on the Emperor in order to get government support by suggesting that the Indians accompanying him would be scornful if the reburial was carried out in too plain a manner (*SFC*, p. 273a).
12 *SFC* 10, p. 275c.
13 The *Ju o-p'i-ta-mo lun* 入阿毘達磨論 (*TD* no. 1554) was translated at the Ta tz'u-en ssu in the tenth month of 658 (*KYL* 8, p. 557a). According to the same source, Hsüan-tsang completed the translation of three other works in the Ta tz'u-en ssu by the ninth month of 659.
14 *TD* no. 1587. The Sanskrit original no longer survives. For a scholarly French translation of Hsüan-tsang's *Ch'eng wei-shih lun* see Louis de la Vallée Poussin, *Vijñaptimātratāsiddhi: La Siddhi de Hiuan-tsang*, 2 vols. (Paris, 1928–9).
15 *TD* no. 1590. For an English translation of the Chinese text see Clarence H. Hamilton, *Wei Shih Erh Shih Lun* (New Haven, Conn., 1938).
16 *TD* no. 220.
17 Also known under the misnomer, K'uei-chi 窺基. See S. Weinstein, 'A Biographical Study of Tz'u-en,' *Monumenta Nipponica*, 15.1–2 (1959) 119–49.
18 *SFC* 10, p. 276c.
19 *SFC*, p. 278a.
20 Ibid.
21 *KYL* 8, p. 560c. *SFC*, p. 277a attributes seventy-four works to Hsüan-tsang.
22 *SFC* 6, p. 252c.
23 The text of this edict, entitled *Seng-ni pu te shou fu-mo chi tsun-che li-pai chao* 僧尼不得受父母及尊者禮拜詔, is given in *THY* 47, p. 836 and *CTW* 12, p. 5a. *FTTC* 39, p. 367a states that the Taoist clergy also fell within the scope of the edict. For a detailed account of the ensuing controversy see Michihata, *Tōdai Bukkyōshi no kenkyū*, pp. 335–57.
24 The text of this edict, entitled *Ming yu-ssu i sha-men teng chih-pai chün-ch'in ch'ih* 命有司議沙門等致拜君親勅, is given in *CTW* 14, pp. 2b–3a. The basic documents pertaining to the dispute of 662 will be found in *CSP* 3–6, pp. 454c–474c, upon which the following account is based.
25 On Yang-ti's efforts to have the clergy do obeisance to the throne see *KHMC* 25, pp. 280a–281a.
26 *CSP* 3, p. 457b. Tao-hsüan is paraphrasing here the *Sa-che-ni-ch'ien-tzu ching* 薩遮尼乾子經 (*Bodhisattva gocaropāya viṣaya vikurvāṇa nirdeśa sūtra*) 4, in *TD* 9, p. 336a–b.
27 Chung-t'ai was the designation given to the Shang-shu sheng 尚書省 in 662; see *TCTC* 200, p. 6326; also Tu Yu 杜佑, *T'ung-tien* 通典 (Commercial Press edn, Shanghai, 1935) 22, p. 129.
28 *CSP* 6, p. 472a.
29 It is interesting to note that although both Buddhist (*CSP* 6, p. 472b–c and *KHMC* 25, pp. 289c–290a) and non-Buddhist (*CTW* 12, pp. 7b–8a) sources

contain virtually identical texts of the edict, each side provides it with a title suggesting a vindication of its own position. In *CSP* and *HKMC* the edict is entitled *Chin-shang t'ing sha-men pai-chün chao* 今上停沙門拜君詔 (*His Majesty's Order to Buddhist Monks to Cease Doing Obeisance Before the Ruler*); in *CTW* the title reads *Ling seng-tao chih-pai fu-mo chao* 令僧道致拜父母詔 (*An Imperial Order to Members of the Buddhist and Taoist Clergies to Reverence their Parents*). Although the title given in Buddhist sources makes no reference to the Taoist clergy, the text specifically states that the edict applies to the Taoists as well.

30 See, for example, Tao-hsüan's second letter to the mother of Empress Wu, dated the thirteenth day of the eighth month of the year 662 (*CSP* 6, p. 473a–b).
31 See the biography of Wei-hsiu in *SKSC* 17, p. 812b. The date on which the offending edict was withdrawn is not given.
32 *CTS* 8, p. 172; *THY* 47, p. 836.
33 *CTS* 8, p. 172; *FTTC* 40, p. 373b.
34 Hsüan-tsung's edict has come down to us in two conflicting versions, each saying the opposite of the other. In the version of the edict given in the *T'ang ta chao-ling chi* 唐大詔令集 (Commercial Press edn, Peking, 1959) 113, p. 589 the Buddhist clergy is instructed to '*join with* [the Taoists] in reverencing [*chien pai* 兼拜] their parents.' In the *CTW* version (fasc. 30, p. 15a) the Buddhists are ordered '*not to* reverence [*wu pai* 無拜] their parents.' The discrepancy clearly is the result of mistaking the character 兼 *chien* for 無 *wu*, which it resembles in cursive script. The context of the edict as well as the program to curtail the power of the Buddhist church instituted by Hsüan-tsung at this time leave little doubt that the *T'ang ta chao-ling chi* version is the correct one. Regarding the two versions of the edict see further *NGJKK*, vol. 2, pp. 271–2.
35 Both decrees are mentioned in the *T'ung-tien* 通典 68, p. 379.
36 *NGJK*: 840, III.
37 Commentary by Hu San-hsing 胡三省 in *TCTC* 200, p. 6329.
38 *CTS* 5, p. 90.
39 For a description of the monasteries in Yen-chou see *THY* 48, p. 850; for the other prefectural monasteries see *FYCL* 100, p. 1027c.
40 The names are Feng-luan ssu 封巒寺, Fei-yen ssu 非煙寺, and Ch'ung-lun ssu 重輪寺. The names of the first two monasteries would not normally be regarded as Buddhist.
41 *CTS* 5, p. 90, *FTTC* 39, p. 367c. T'ai-tsung, who visited the birthplaces of Confucius and Lao-tzu in 637, was less carried away by the occasion than was his son, Kao-tsung. T'ai-tsung merely assigned twenty households each for the upkeep of the memorial halls dedicated to Confucius and Lao-tzu, but did not confer any posthumous titles nor otherwise accord special privileges to the areas involved. See *CTS* 3, p. 48.
42 *CTS* 192, p. 5127; *HTS* 196, p. 5605.
43 Biographies in *CTS* 192, p. 5126; *HTS* 196, p. 5607.
44 Yoshioka Yoshitoyo 吉岡義豊, *Dōkyō to Bukkyō* 道教と仏教, vol. 1 (Tokyo, 1959), pp. 254 and 262.
45 Stein ms. no. 1513, reproduced in Yoshioka, pp. 254–5.

46 FTTC 39, p. 369a.
47 Ibid. CTS 5, p. 99 attributes the inclusion of the *Tao-te ching* in the civil service examination to Empress Wu, dating the event 674.
48 Tao-hsüan 道宣, *Kan-t'ung lu* 感通錄 (completed in 664), in TD 52, pp. 406c–407b; FYCL 38, pp. 586b–587a.
49 FYCL 14, p. 393a.
50 LFPT 14, P. 278b.
51 FTTC 39, p. 370b.

Interregnum of Empress Wu (684–705)
1 TCTC 200, p. 6322.
2 For a readable and generally reliable biography of Empress Wu, see Toyama Gunji 外山軍治, *Sokuten Bukō* 則天武后 (Tokyo, 1966). Also see C.P. Fitzgerald, *The Empress Wu* (London, 1956), which underplays her involvement with Buddhism. On the manipulation of Buddhist texts by Empress Wu's supporters see the detailed studies by Yabuki Keiki 矢吹慶輝, *Sangaikyō no kenkyū* 三階教の研究 (Tokyo, 1927), pp. 685–761 and Antonino Forte, *Political Propaganda and Ideology in China at the End of the Seventh Century* (Napoli, 1976).
3 See pp. 32–4.
4 SFC 9, pp. 270c–271b.
5 Tsukamoto Zenryū, *Shina Bukkyōshi kenkyū* (Tokyo, 1942), pp. 371–85.
6 Ch'oe Ch'iwŏn 崔致遠, *Pŏpjang Hwasangjŏn* 法藏和尚傳 (completed in 904), in TD 50, p. 281b.
7 In 687 the temple was renamed Wei-kuo ssu 魏國寺 (THY 48, p. 846). After Empress Wu usurped the throne she changed its name to Ta Chou tung ssu 大周東寺, Ta Chou being the designation of her newly founded dynasty. See CYL 13, p. 865c.
8 THY 49, p. 859.
9 Chih-sheng, *Hsü ku-chin i-ching t'u-chi* 續古今譯經圖紀 (completed in 730), in TD 55, p. 386c.
10 The term *chiu-chih* literally signifies 'rescuing [a sentient being] by overcoming [its illusions].'
11 HTS 76, p. 3477.
12 TCTC 203, p. 6421.
13 TCTC 204, p. 6448.
14 For their names see CTS 183, p. 4741.
15 The full title of this sūtra, which was translated by Dharmakṣema in 417, is *Ta fang-teng wu-hsiang ching* 大方等無想經. Its abridged title, *Ta-yün ching* 大雲經, is taken from the name of the chief interlocutor in the sūtra, the Bodhisattva Ta-yün Mi-tsang 大雲密藏. The sūtra is no longer extant in Sanskrit. According to its Tibetan version, the original Sanskrit title was *Ārya Mahāmegha nāma mahāyāna sūtra*. An earlier Chinese translation by Chu Fo-nien 竺佛念 survives in fragments (TD no. 388).
16 There is a considerable discrepancy between the Buddhist and non-Buddhist versions of the incident. CTS 6, p. 121 states that ten monks 'forged' (*wei-chuan* 偽撰) the text, which they then presented to Empress Wu with a statement that she had now received the mandate to assume the

throne. In the biography of Hsüeh Huai-i 薛懷義 (*CTS* 183, p. 4742), about whom more will be said presently, it is likewise reported that Huai-i, Fa-ming 法明, and other monks 'fabricated' (*tsao* 造) the *Ta-yün ching* and presented an oracle (*fu-ming* 符命) declaring Empress Wu to be an incarnation of Maitreya and a World Ruler (*Yen-fu-t'i chu* 閻浮提主). *TCTC* 204, p. 6466 specifically mentions only the name of Fa-ming in connection with the forgery. *HTS* 76, p. 3481, however, states that Empress Wu ordered Huai-i and other unnamed monks to 'compose' (*tso* 作) the sūtra. No Buddhist account of the incident regards the *Ta-yün ching* as a specious work. According to *FTTC* 39, p. 369c, Empress Wu instructed a group of nine monks headed by one Fa-lang 法朗 (presumably a copyist's error for Fa-ming) to 'retranslate' (*ch'ung-i* 重譯) the *Ta-yün ching*. *SSL* 3, p. 248c reproduces almost verbatim the passage in *CTS* 183, but substitutes the word 'retranslated' for 'forged,' pointing out that the *Ta-yün ching* could hardly have been a forgery since a Chinese translation already appeared during the Eastern Chin dynasty. *SSL* suggests that the text might have been wrongly called a forgery because Huai-i tampered with it when it was being retranslated. *LFPT* 14, p. 280a simply notes that ten monks presented a copy of the sūtra at the palace. In fact, it would seem that there is no basis for the traditional view given in non-Buddhist sources that the *Ta-yün ching* is a forgery.

17 *Ta fang-teng wu-hsiang ching* 9, in *TD* 12, pp. 1106a–1107b.
18 It was commonly believed that before a woman could attain Buddhahood she would have to be transformed into a man. As if to foretell Empress Wu's usurpation of the throne and her assumption of the role of a male ruler, there was a rumor in the eighth month of 689 to the effect that a hen had miraculously changed into a rooster. See *HTS* 4, p. 89.
19 The death of the Buddha was commonly said to have occurred in 950 B.C. or 949 B.C. See *HKSC* 50, p. 624b; Fa-lin, *P'o-hsieh lun* 破邪論, in *TD* 52, p. 478b; 'Yüan-Wei Hsiao-ming chao Fo Tao men-jen lun ch'ien-hou' 元魏孝明召佛道門人論前後 in *KHMC* 1, p. 100c.
20 In her preface to Sikṣānanda's translation of the *Hua-yen ching* 華嚴經 dated 699 (*TD* 10, p. 1a–b) Empress Wu declares her assumption of the throne to be the culmination of her past karma in fulfillment of a prophecy of the Buddha. She specifically mentions two sūtras in this connection: the *Ta-yün ching* and the *Pao-yü ching* 寶雨經 (*TD* no. 660). The latter sūtra, translated by Dharmaruci during the reign of Empress Wu, is particularly notable for a passage in which a bodhisattva pretends to commit murder in order to free another person from his delusions (*Pao-yü ching* 3, in *TD* 16, p. 293b).
21 *TCTC* 204, p. 6469; *HTS* 4, p. 91. *CTS* 6, p. 121 states that the Ta-yün ssu were established in the seventh month. It should not be assumed that all of the Ta-yün ssu necessarily were newly constructed monasteries. As Tsukamoto has shown in his *Nisshi Bukkyōshi kenkyū*, pp. 29–30, many of the Ta-yün ssu were existing monasteries whose names were changed to Ta-yün ssu after Empress Wu's edict of 690.
22 *CTS* 183, p. 4742; *TCTC* 204, p. 6469.
23 The commentary, *Wu-hou teng-chi ch'en-shu* 武后登極讖疏 (Stein no.

2658), has been edited by Yabuki and reprinted in his *Sangaikyō no kenkyū*, pp. 686–94, which also contains a detailed analysis of the text. It is interesting to note that the commentary reprinted by Yabuki is, in fact, based upon two works: the *Ta-yün ching* and the *P'u-hsien P'u-sa shuo cheng-ming ching* 普賢菩薩說證明經, the latter being a Chinese forgery already so identified during the Sui dynasty (Fa-ching 法經, *Chung-ching mu-lu* 衆經目錄 [completed in 594] 3, in *TD* 55, p. 126c). The *Cheng-ming ching* (*TD* no. 2879) was drawn upon by Empress Wu's supporters because of its advocacy of the worship of Maitreya.

24 *CTS* 6, p. 121.
25 See her edict entitled *Shih-chiao tsai Tao-fa shang chih* 釋教在道法上制, in *CTW* 95, p. 4a.
26 *CTS* 6, p. 122 and p. 130.
27 *CTS* 6, p. 123. Her new title was a curious mixture of Indian and Chinese terminology. Chin-lun is a contraction of Chin-lun wang 金輪王 (Suvarṇacakravartin), 'Ruler with the Golden Wheel,' the highest of the four types of rulers according to traditional Indian Buddhist cosmology. See *O-p'i-ta-mo chü-she lun* 阿毘達磨俱舍論 12, in *TD* 29, p. 64b–c.
28 *HTS* 48, p. 1258.
29 *FTTC* 39, pp. 369c–370a. *THY* 59, p. 1028 states that jurisdiction over the Taoist clergy also was transferred at this time to the Department of Sacrifices (*Tz'u-pu*).
30 *HTS* 4, p. 95.
31 The only prominent translator during this entire period, aside from Hsüan-tsang, was Prabhākaramitra. He translated three works between 627, the year that he arrived in Ch'ang-an, and 633, the year that he died.
32 *KYL* 9, p. 564a.
33 *CTW* 97, p. 5b. The sūtra is *TD* no. 187.
34 *KYL* 9, p. 570a.
35 *KYL* 9, p. 568b.
36 *KYL* 9, p. 568c. The text of the preface is found in *TD*, vol. 15, p. 706a–b and *CTW* 97, pp. 7b–8b.
37 *KYL* 9, p. 566a.
38 See her preface to the *Hua-yen ching*, in *TD* 10, p. 1a–b.
39 For a detailed account of the practice of meditation in China through the sixth century see the excellent study by Mizuno Kōgen, 'Zenshū seiritsu izen no Shina no zenjō shisōshi josetsu,' *Komazawa daigaku kenkyū kiyō*, 15 (1957) 15–44.
40 The Ch'an center on Mt Huang-mei can be traced back to Tao-hsin 道信, the Fourth Patriarch of the Ch'an school. It was the first permanent Ch'an community in China and had already in Tao-hsin's time some 500 monks in residence. See *HKSC* 20, p. 606b.
41 The settlement on Mt Niu-t'ou, which held more than 100 monks, was founded by Fa-jung 法融 in the year 634. Traditional Ch'an sources regard Fa-jung as a disciple of Tao-hsin, although Fa-jung's biography in *HKSC* 20, p. 603c does not mention this.
42 *CTL* 4, p. 232c. According to this source, which is not very reliable despite the great veneration in which it is held by the Ch'an school, when Jen-chien

was brought into the presence of the Empress, he simply glared at her in silence. After some time the monk asked the Empress whether she understood what was on his mind. When she said that she did not and sought an explanation, Jen-chien stalked out muttering, 'I am upholding my vow not to speak!' It will be recalled that this was the year that Empress Wu had her pseudo-monk lover, Huai-i, pummeled to death.

43 *CTL* 4, p. 231c; *CKL* 3, 821c.
44 *Li-tai fa-pao chi* 歷代法寶紀 (completed during the latter half of the eighth century), in *TD* 51, p. 184a.
45 On the history of the Ch'an school through the eighth century see the excellent monograph by Philip Yampolsky, *The Platform Sutra of the Sixth Patriarch* (New York, 1967), pp. 1–121.
46 The earliest biography of Shen-hsiu is the stele inscription written by Chang Yüeh 張說, a high-ranking official who was Shen-hsiu's lay disciple. The biography is included in *CTW* 231, pp. 1b–4a. See also Shen-hsiu's biography in *SKSC* 8, pp. 755c–756b.
47 The 'Three Rulers' refer to Empress Wu and her two sons, Chung-tsung and Jui-tsung.
48 Dōchū Mujaku 道忠無著, *Zenrin shōkisen* 禪林象器箋 (Baiyō shoin edn, Kyoto, 1909), p. 166.
49 The other two monks so honored are Hsüan-tsang and I-hsing 一行 (683–727), a Tantric master and expert in calendric science who served at the court of Hsüan-tsung. The biographies of the three monks are included in *CTS* 191, pp. 5108–13.
50 The earliest full length biography of Fa-tsang is Ch'oe Ch'iwŏn, *Pŏpjang Hwasangjŏn*, in *TD* 50, pp. 280c–286b. For a detailed biography based on various sources and arranged in chronological order see Hsü-fa 續法, *Fa-chieh tsung wu-tsu lüeh-chi* 法界宗五祖略紀 (completed in 1680), in *ZZK*, ser. 2B, case 7, vol. 3, p. 273a–275a.

Reign of Chung-tsung (705–710)

1 *TCTC* 208, p. 6583.
2 For the text of the edict, entitled *Chin hua-hu ching ch'ih* 禁化胡經勅, see *CTW* 17, pp. 2b–3a. The date of the edict is given in *CTS* 7, p. 140.
3 *FTTC* 39, p. 370b. The reference to Lao-tzu's transformation into the Buddha occurs in a memorial by Hsiang K'ai 襄楷 presented to Emperor Huan in 166 (*Hou Han Shu* 30b, p. 1082).
4 *TFYK* 51, pp. 18b 19a.
5 See, for example, the entries under the Lo-yang Lung-hsing ssu and Ch'ang-an Lung-hsing ssu in *THY* 48, pp. 845 and 847.
6 *THY* 48, p. 847.
7 For the text of the edict see *CTW* 17, p. 3a–b. The date is given in *TCTC* 208, p. 6610.
8 *CTS* 7, p. 141.
9 *SKSC* 8, p. 757c.
10 *KYL* 9, p. 568c.
11 *FTTC* 40, p. 371b. *CKL* 3, p. 822c, which dates this order 706, states that the ordination of monks through examination (*shih-ching tu-seng* 試經度

僧) began at this time. In fact, however, there is at least one earlier instance of acolytes being required to pass an examination before being admitted to ordination. In 658 candidates for ordination at the Hsi-ming ssu had to take qualifying examinations. See *SFC* 10, p. 275c. It may be that the examinations at the Hsi-ming ssu were a strictly local affair. In any event, after the An Lu-shan rebellion ordination through examination was widely practiced.
12 *FTTC* 40, p. 372b–c.
13 *KYL* 9, p. 566b.
14 *SKSC* 14, p. 792a; *SKSC* 18, p. 822a.
15 *FTTC* 40, p. 372c; *CTS* 7, p. 149.

Reign of Jui-tsung (710–712)

1 For the text of the edict, entitled *Ling seng-tao ping-hsing chih* 令僧道並行制, see *CTW* 18, pp. 9b–10a. The date of the edict is taken from the *SSL* 2, p. 247a.
2 *FTTC* 40, p. 372c; *LFPT* 15, p. 284a. Jui-tsung's prohibition against illegally ordained monks and nuns is mentioned in his edict entitled *Shen-ch'üan li-su chih* 申勸禮俗勅 in *CTW* 19, p. 3a. For an example of the legitimation *en masse* of 'illicit monks' see *SSL* 2, p. 247c.
3 *THY* 48, pp. 850–51.
4 Monks were exempt from most civil obligations such as payment of taxes and military service.
5 *THY* 48, p. 851.
6 *CTW* 19, p. 3b.
7 The *ming-o*, more commonly known as *pien-o* 扁額, *ssu-o* 寺額, or simply *o* 額, was a large rectangular wooden tablet that hung over the main gate to a monastery. It bore the name of the monastery and signified formal government recognition. Such tablets were occasionally granted by the emperor as a mark of respect. See, for example, *SSL* 3, p. 251a.
8 *SKSC* 26, p. 874c. *FTTC* 40, p. 373a enters this under the year 713, which it erroneously includes within Jui-tsung's reign.

Reign of Hsüan-tsung (712–756)

1 *THY* 50, p. 878.
2 The merit cloister was an officially sanctioned private temple erected at the site of the family grave at which resident monks offered prayers for the ancestors of the patron's family. Since all lands assigned to the cloister were tax-exempt, wealthy families could evade taxes on lands nominally placed under the jurisdiction of the cloister. The earliest concrete reference to such cloisters occurs in an entry for the year 711 in *FTTC* 40, p. 373a, which states that imperial consorts and princes were permitted for the first time to establish merit cloisters.
3 *THY* 47, pp. 836–37. This is only a rough estimate. *HTS* 48, p. 1252 and *THY* 49, p. 863 puts the size of the clergy about the year 728, when the first registration of the samgha took place, at 75,524 monks and 50,576 nuns. These figures refer to the clergy at the 5,358 'recognized' monasteries. We have no way of knowing the number of monks and nuns who resided in

village temples, supposedly abolished in 727 (see below, p. 52). It should be noted that the precise number of monks and nuns defrocked in 714 is also in dispute. *TCTC* 211, p. 6695 and *FFTC* 40, p. 373b both put the figure at twelve thousand. Although Buddhist sources do not mention it, Hsüan-tsung states in an edict dated 731 quoted in *THY* 49, p. 861 that he has not allowed any ordinations since coming to the throne.

4 *TCTC* 211, p. 6696. For the text of the edict, entitled *Chin ch'uang-tsao ssu-kuan chao* 禁創造寺觀詔, which includes a ban on the construction of Taoist temples as well, see *CTW* 26, p. 17b.
5 *TCTC* 211, p. 6703. The edict, entitled *Chin pai-kuan yü seng-tao wang-huan chih* 禁百官與僧道往還制, is included in *CTW* 21, p. 1a–b.
6 *TCTC* 211, p. 6703. The edict, entitled *Chin fang-shih chu-fo hsieh-ching chao* 禁坊市鑄佛寫經詔, is included in *CTW* 26, pp. 9b–10a and, under a variant title, in *T'ang ta chao-ling chi* 113, p. 588.
7 *Chin fang-shih chu-fo hsieh-ching chao*, in *CTW* 26, p. 10a.
8 For details see the edicts entitled *Chin seng-t'u lien-ts'ai chao* 禁僧徒斂財詔, in *CTW* 30, pp. 10a–11a and *Chin seng-tao pu shou chieh-lü chao* 禁僧道不守戒律詔, in *CTW* 29, p. 5b.
9 This was, no doubt, a deliberate misreading of the *Vinaya*. The post-midday prohibitions in the latter pertain to eating, not religious activities.
10 *THY* 59, p. 1028.
11 *FFTC* 40, p. 374a.
12 Ibid.
13 *FFTC* 40, p. 374b. The Buddhist sources may be in error here, however, since the legal code issued in 719 already required the registration of the clergy every third year. See Niida Noboru 仁井田陞, *Tōrei shūi* 唐令拾遺 (Tokyo, 1933), p. 859.
14 *T'ang liu-tien* 4, p. 46b. *THY* 49, p. 863 states that only two copies of the register were required – one for the local authority and the other for the Department of Sacrifices.
15 See his edict entitled *Kuo-chien seng-ni chao* 括檢僧尼詔, in *CTW* 30, p. 6a–b.
16 *THY* 49, p. 859–60; *FFTC* 40, p. 375a.
17 *THY* 49, p. 860 indicates that although the Buddhist clergy was formally reattached to the Department of Sacrifices in 743, this latter department had already been made responsible for 'investigating' (*chien-chiao* 檢校) monks and nuns some six years earlier, in 737. See also *THY* 59, p. 1028. It should be noted that *SSL* 2, p. 245c contains an apparent copyist's error, as a result of which the years 736 and 737 appear as 726 and 727.
18 Although Hsüan-tsung did not commission any great monasteries or order mass ordinations as his predecessors had done, he is the first T'ang emperor alleged to have produced a commentary on a Buddhist text – the *Diamond Sūtra* (*Chin-kang po-jo ching* 金剛般若經 [*Vajracchedikā prajñāparamitā sūtra*], *TD* nos. 235–39). The commentary was written in 735 or 736 in collaboration with the monk Tao-yin 道氤, who had been brought to the Emperor's notice by I-hsing (see below). Hsüan-tsung's commentary is now lost, but a purported 'subcommentary' by Tao-yin was discovered in Tun-huang and has been published in *TD* 85, pp. 8c–52b (*TD* no. 2733). This

'subcommentary,' which is evidently a work of considerable scholarship, provides a line-by-line exegesis of the sūtra itself, but does not treat Hsüan-tsung's commentary other than to eulogize it in the preface. For references to Hsüan-tsung's commentary see *CYL* 14, p. 878c; *SKSC* 5, p. 735a; *SKSC* 14, p. 795b; *FTTC* 40, p. 375a.

19 *THY* 50, p. 879. *FTTC* 40, p. 375a, which also mentions the event, reports erroneously that the Lung-hsing monasteries were established at this time.

20 *THY* 48, p. 850 states categorically that *all* Ta-yün ssu were converted to K'ai-yüan ssu. Elsewhere (fasc. 50, p. 879), however, *THY* quotes Hsüan-tsung's edict as stipulating simply that an imposing monastery in each prefecture should be designated as a K'ai-yüan ssu. There is evidence that some Ta-yün ssu continued to exist throughout Hsüan-tsung's reign despite their association with Empress Wu's usurpation of the throne. Hui-ch'ao 慧超 reported visiting Ta-yün monasteries in Kansu and Kashgar in 727 (*Wang wu-t'ien-chu kuo chuan* 往五天竺國傳, in *TD* 51, p. 979b); Chien-chen 鑑眞, a prominent monk of the Lü (Vinaya) school, likewise stayed in several Ta-yün monasteries between 748 and 750 while en route to Japan (*Tō Daiwajō tōseiden* 唐大和上東征傳 [completed in 779], in *TD* 51, p. 991a and c).

21 *FTTC* 40, p. 375a.

22 *FTTC* 40, p. 374c.

23 *FTTC* 40, p. 375b.

24 I use the term 'Esoteric Buddhism' to refer to that form of Buddhism that based itself on the tantras, i.e. the so-called 'ritual texts' rather than on the sūtras. Although the Buddhist tantra literature covers a very wide spectrum of materials, we may say in very general terms that the tantras emphasize the use of spells, incantations, mystical hand signs, sacred diagrams, and certain unconventional types of meditation to achieve either material goals such as the curing of illness and the defeat of one's enemies or spiritual goals such as the attainment of higher states of consciousness or enlightenment.

25 It should be noted that esoteric practices within Buddhism can be traced back to the first century of the Western era, if not earlier. It was, however, only in the late seventh and early eighth centuries with the appearance of such systematic tantras as the *Ta-jih ching* and the *Chin-kang-ting ching* (*TD* no. 865; see n. 34 below) that esotericism came to be recognized as one of the major traditions within Buddhism.

26 A few of the pro-Taoist measures adopted during the reign of Hsüan-tsung might be briefly noted here. In 733 each household was ordered to keep a copy of the *Tao-te ching*, which replaced the *Book of Documents* (*Shang-shu* 尚書) and the *Analects of Confucius* (*Lun-yü* 論語) in the examinations (*CTS* 8, p. 199). Hsüan-tsung himself wrote a commentary on the *Tao-te ching*, which is included in the Taoist canon (*Tao-tsung* no. 679). In 741 the Emperor decreed that temples to be known as Hsüan-yüan Huang-ti Miao 玄元皇帝廟 to honor Lao-tzu should be erected in the two capital cities and in each of the prefectures (*CTS* 9, p. 213). In addition, schools for Taoist studies called Ch'ung-hsüan hsüeh 崇玄學, where candidates could be trained for the newly instituted

examination in Taoism (*tao-chü* 道舉), were to be opened at each of these temples dedicated to Lao-tzu (*THY* 77, p. 1404). In 747 the *Tao-te ching* was formally ranked first among the classics. Honorary titles were repeatedly bestowed on Lao-tzu (743, 748, 754), each more grandiose than the preceding. A series of eminent Taoist priests including Ssu-ma Ch'eng-chen 司馬承禎 and Wu Yün 吳筠 were invited to the court and presented with various honors. For general surveys of Hsüan-tsung's policy toward Taoism see Ichimura Sanjirō 市村瓚次郎, *Tōyō shitō* 東洋史統, vol. 2 (Tokyo, 1940), pp. 204–9 and Kubo Noritada 窪德忠, *Dōkyōshi* 道教史 (Tokyo, 1977), pp. 231–34.

27 For the biographies of the three great tantric masters, Śubhakarasiṃha, Vajrabodhi, and Amoghavajra see Chou Yi-liang, 'Tantrism in China,' *Harvard Journal of Asiatic Studies*, 8 (1945) 241–332.

28 Li Hua 李華 (fl. 760), *Shan-wu-wei San-tsang ho-shang pei-ming* 善無畏三藏和尚碑銘, in *TD* 50, pp. 290a–291c. Li Hua claims that Śubhakarasiṃha was already known in China by reputation during the reign of Jui-tsung, which may explain the prompt invitation to the court.

29 *TD* no. 848. *Ta-jih ching*, i.e. '*Mahāvairocana sūtra*,' is the common designation of the work; its full title is *Ta p'i-lu-che-na ch'eng-fo shen-pien chia-ch'ih ching* 大毘盧遮那成佛神變加持經.

30 *SKSC* 2, p. 716a.

31 In addition to the biography of Vajrabodhi in *SKSC* 1, pp. 711b–712a see also the biographical notice by a lay disciple in *CYL* 14, pp. 876b–877a.

32 The Tzu-sheng ssu was founded by Kao-tsung in 663 as a memorial to his mother. The Ta chien-fu ssu was established in 684 by Empress Wu in memory of Kao-tsung, who had died during the previous year. For brief accounts of the establishment of both monasteries see *THY* 48, p. 846.

33 One curious incident, not attested elsewhere, deserves mention. It seems that at one point during the K'ai-yüan era officials ordered the expulsion of all 'barbarian' (=Central Asian?) monks (*fan-seng* 蕃僧) from China 'in accordance with the wishes of the Emperor.' Vajrabodhi protested that the order did not apply in his own case since he was an Indian monk (*fan-seng* 梵僧). Nevertheless he decided to leave, but was restrained by the personal intervention of the Emperor. Tsan-ning attributed the order to expel foreign monks to Hsüan-tsung's partiality toward Taoism and lack of interest in Buddhist doctrine. See *SKSC* 1, p. 711c.

34 *TD* no. 866. There are two other Chinese translations of the text: one by Pu-k'ung 不空 (*TD* no. 865) and the other, a greatly expanded version, by Shih-hu 施護 (*TD* no. 882).

35 On I-hsing see the detailed monograph by Osabe Kazuo 長部和雄, *Ichigyō Zenji no kenkyū* 一行禪師の研究 (Kobe, 1963).

36 His Taoist studies are described in his biography in *CTS* 191, pp. 5111–13, but not in his biography in *SKSC* 5, pp. 732c–733c.

37 Pu-k'ung, *Chin-kang-ting ching i-chüeh* 金剛頂經義訣 1, in *TD* 39, p. 808b.

38 The *Ta p'i-lu-che-na ch'eng-fo ching shu* 大毘盧遮那成佛經疏, twenty fascicles, *TD* no. 1796.

39 The text of the inscription, which is the earliest extant biography of I-hsing, has been preserved in Japan. It is included in Kūkai 空海, *Shingon fuhōden*

眞言付法傳 (completed in 821), published in *Dai-Nihon Bukkyō zensho* 106, pp. 28–9.

40 Pu-k'ung's formal biography is in *SKSC* 1, pp. 712a–714a. For a critical study of Pu-k'ung see Osabe Kazuo, *Tōdai Mikkyōshi zakkō* 唐代密教史雜考 (Kobe, 1971).

41 *FTTC* 40, p. 375b. This story must be regarded as suspect, since it does not occur in the earlier biographies by Fei-hsi 飛錫 (in *KSP* 4, p. 848c) and Chao Ch'ien 趙遷 (*Pu-k'ung San-tsang hsing-chuang*, 不空三藏行狀 in *TD* p. 292c). The entries in *FTTC* regarding Pu-k'ung often contain chronological errors; for example, *FTTC* 40, p. 375b states that Pu-k'ung returned from Sri Lanka to China in 741, when in fact he arrived back in 746 (biography by Chao Ch'ien in *TD* 50, p. 293a; biography in *SKSC* 1, p. 713a).

42 *CYL* 15, p. 881b.
43 *SKSC* 1, p. 712c.

Reign of Su-tsung (756–762)

1 Fei-hsi's biography of Pu-k'ung in *KSP* 4, p. 849a. The *homa* originated as a Vedic sacrifice involving the kindling of a sacred fire. It was later adopted by followers of Esoteric Buddhism, who gave a symbolic meaning to the ritual. In practice, however, the *homa* was performed to bring about worldly benefits.
2 *FTTC* 40, p. 375c.
3 *FTTC* 40, p. 376a.
4 *CTS* 111, p. 3327.
5 *FTTC* 40, p. 376a.
6 *SSL* 3, p. 252b.
7 *TCTC* 222, pp. 7115–16.
8 *CTS* 10, p. 260.

The effects of the An-lu Shan rebellion on the Buddhist church

1 *HTS* 51, p. 1347; *CTS* 48, p. 2087.
2 *HTS* 51, p. 1347; *CTS* 48, p. 2087.
3 *FTLT* 13, p. 598b–c. Both this source and the earlier *FTTC* 40, p. 376a state that laymen who could recite from memory five hundred pages of sūtra texts – a substantial amount of scripture – were entitled to be ordained without payment of any fee. According to *SKSC* 15, p. 803c, however, a layman had to be conversant (*t'ung* 通) with seven hundred pages of sūtra texts to qualify for ordination.
4 *TCTC* 209, p. 6623 states in an entry for the year 708 that an ordination could be arranged for thirty thousand cash. Judging from a memorial by Wei Hsüan-chung 魏玄忠, it would seem that money paid to secure ordinations ended up not in the treasury but in the pockets of corrupt officials (*HTS* 122, p. 4346). For an example of the practice during the reign of Jui-tsung see the memorial from Hsin T'i-p'i quoted on p. 50.
5 The memorial, entitled *Wang Chih-hsing tu seng-ni chuang* 王智興度僧尼狀, is included in *CTW* 706, pp. 1b–2a.
6 *SSL* 2, p. 247c; *FTTC* 42, p. 385a.

7 According to *HTS* 48, p. 1252, the Buddhist clergy numbered 126,100 monks and nuns around the year 728 when the first clerical registers were compiled (see note 258). In 845, when Emperor Wu-tsung ordered the dismantlement of the Buddhist church, a total of 260,500 monks and nuns were defrocked (see below n. 111, p. 194 and also p. 134).
8 *SSL* 3, p. 252b.
9 The destruction of Buddhist scripture was not limited to materials kept in monasteries in Ch'ang-an and Lo-yang. Many of the most important treatises of the T'ien-t'ai school, which had its headquarters in Chekiang, were also lost at this time. See *FTTC* 8, p. 190c.
10 For a detailed study of the life and thought of Ch'eng-kuan see Kamata Shigeo 鎌田茂雄, *Chūgoku Kegon shisōshi no kenkyū* 中国華嚴思想史の研究 (Tokyo, 1965).
11 *FTTC* 41, p. 380a; *FTLT* 14, p. 609c. The title Grand Recorder of Monks was probably more honorific than substantive. The designation Recorder of Monks was formally recognized as an ecclesiastical rank only in 807. See p. 101.
12 *FTTC* 41, p. 381a. This title was conferred on only one other monk under the T'ang, Wei-ying 惟英, in 806. See *SSL* 2, p. 243c. It would appear that the title was an honorary one, its holder not exercising any real authority; see Yamazaki Hiroshi, *Shina chūsei Bukkyō no tenkai*, p. 631.
13 *LFPT* 25, p. 335b. The seven emperors were Tai-tsung, Te-tsung, Shun-tsung, Hsien-tsung, Mu-tsung, Ching-tsung, and Wen-tsung.
14 His biography in *SKSC* 5, p. 737a–c mentions his relationship with two military governors and a civil governor. *FTLT* 14, p. 609c speaks of his connection with still another military governor and various high-ranking officials.
15 Virtually no attention was paid to Pure Land Buddhism by the 'elitist' schools before the An Lu-shan rebellion, even though this was probably the predominant form of Buddhism among the common people. There is no indication that any of the leading monks of the philosophical schools (Fa-hsiang, Hua-yen, T'ien-t'ai) were in the least influenced by the writings of, say, Shan-tao 善導, the great systematizer and proselytizer of Pure Land, who lived in Ch'ang-an for some thirty years.
16 Ch'eng-kuan studied under no less than four Ch'an masters. One belonged to the Northern Ch'an tradition of Shen-hsiu, one was a follower of Southern Ch'an through Shen-hui, and two belonged to the Niu-t'ou lineage. Ch'eng-kuan seems to have been closest to the Niu-t'ou line, which did not survive the collapse of the T'ang. For the Ch'an influence on Ch'eng-kuan see Kamata Shigeo, 'Chōkan ni okeru Zen shisō no keisei' 澄観における禅思想の形成, *Indogaku Bukkyōgaku kenkyū*, 9–2 (1961) 73–8.
17 For his biography as a Hua-yen patriarch see *Fa-chieh tsung wu-tsu lüeh-chi*, in *ZZK*, ser. 2B, case 7, vol. 3, pp. 277a–278a; his biography as a Ch'an master is given in *CTL* 13, pp. 305c–308b.
18 Although for convenience sake I refer simply to 'Ch'an ideas', it should be noted that Ch'an at this time was divided into a number of competing lines, Tsung-mi himself supplying the names of ten such lines (*Ch'an-yüan chu*

ch'üan-chi tu-hsü 禪源諸詮集都序 1, in *TD* 48, p. 400c). Tsung-mi belonged to the lineage of Shen-hui, which died out by the end of the T'ang, despite the fact that its founder, Shen-hui, was responsible for bringing Hui-neng's 'Southern Ch'an' into prominence. The Lin-chi 臨濟 and Ts'ao-tung 曹洞 branches of Ch'an which were subsequently to become so famous in China and Japan (as well as in the West) are traditionally said to have arisen from two other lines of the Southern school – those of Nan-yüeh Huai-jang 南嶽懷讓 (677–744) and Ch'ing-yüan Hsing-ssu 青原行思. Both men appear in later sources as disciples of Hui-neng, as was Shen-hui; in fact, however, we have little reliable information about them.

19 *Shen-hui yü-lu* 神會語錄 3, reprinted in Hu Shih, *Shen-hui Ho-shang i-chi* 神會和尚遺集 (Shanghai, 1930), p. 176.
20 On Hui-neng's life and ideas see Philip B. Yampolsky, *The Platform Sūtra of the Sixth Patriarch* (New York, 1967).
21 Shen-hui's denunciation of Shen-hsiu is the subject of the *P'u-t'i-ta-mo Nan-tsung ting shih-fei lun*. 菩提達摩南宗定是非論. A copy of this long-lost work was discovered in Tun-huang. The text has been edited and published by Hu Shih in the revised edition of his *Shen-hui Ho-shang i-chi* (Taipei, 1968), pp. 258–319. For Shen-hui's refutation of Northern Ch'an see Hu Shih's pioneering article, 'The Development of Zen Buddhism in China,' *The Chinese Social and Political Science Review*, 15-4 (1932), pp. 475–505.
22 *Ting shih-fei lun*, pp. 261–2. This is the first occurrence of the well known story of the confrontation between Bodhidharma and Emperor Wu of the Liang dynasty. In fact, it is highly unlikely that the two men, although contemporaries, ever met. See Ui Hakuju 宇井伯壽, *Zenshūshi kenkyū* 禪宗史研究, vol. 1 (Tokyo, 1939), pp. 8–11.
23 *Ting fei-shih lun*, p. 284.
24 Tsung-mi, *Yüan-chiao ching ta-shu ch'ao* 圓覺經大疏鈔 3B, in *ZZK*, ser. 1, case 14, vol. 3, p. 277a.
25 *SKSC* 8, pp. 756c–757a.
26 According to *SSL* 3, p. 251c, Su-tsung dispatched an emissary in the year 760 to Ts'ao-hsi 曹谿, where Hui-neng had lived, to fetch the robe and bowl of the latter so that it could be venerated at the court. *SKSC* 9, p. 762c reports that during the following year Hui-chung 慧忠, a former disciple of Hui-neng, was invited to become an imperial preceptor. Su-tsung's interest in Hui-neng's line of Ch'an was no doubt attributable to the influence of Shen-hui.
27 *Yüan-chiao ching ta-shu ch'ao* 3B, in *ZZK*, ser. 1, case 14, vol. 3, p. 277b.

The growth of Pure Land Buddhism
1 Although the term *ching-t'u* 淨土, 'Pure Land,' occurs with great frequency in Chinese translations of Indian Buddhist texts, it has no fixed Sanskrit equivalent. In some cases *ching-t'u* is used as a translation of *Buddha kṣetra*, 'Buddha Land,' or simply of *kṣetra* itself. In other instances the word *ching-t'u* is supplied by the translator on the assumption that the context implies some such term despite the fact that the Sanskrit text does not contain any corresponding word.
2 Mochizuki Shinkō 望月信亨, *Jōdokyō no kigen oyobi hattatsu* 浄土教の起

源及発達 (Tokyo, 1930), p. 302. For a comprehensive list of the sūtras that mention Amitābha see Yabuki Keiki 矢吹慶輝, *Amida Butsu no kenkyū* 阿弥陀仏の研究 (Tokyo, 1911; revised edn., 1937), pp. 450–74.

3. The two earliest Chinese versions of the *Pan-chou san-mei ching* are *TD* no. 418, attributed to Lokakṣema, who is also said to be the translator of what appears to be an abridged version of the same text (*TD* no. 417), and *TD* no. 419, which is an anonymous translation dating from the Han period. See Fujita Kōtatsu 藤田宏達, *Genshi Jōdo shisō no kenkyū* 原始浄土思想の研究 (Tokyo, 1970), p. 229. The two earliest versions of the *Wu-liang-shou ching* are *TD* no. 362, translated by Chih Ch'ien 支謙 (fl. 250), and *TD* no. 361, traditionally attributed to Lokakṣema. As modern studies have shown, the latter attribution is incorrect; in all likelihood the translation was made by Po Yen 帛延, a monk from Kucha, between 256 and 259. See Fujita, p. 49. Although the *Wu-liang-shou ching* and *O-mi-t'o ching* are different works, they share the same Sanskrit title, *Sukhāvatīvyūha*. The Sanskrit originals of both the *Wu-liang-shou ching* and *O-mi-t'o ching* have been preserved. They have been translated into English by F. Max Müller and published in the *Sacred Books of the East*, vol. 49 (Oxford, 1894). The same volume also contains an English translation by J. Takakusu of the Chinese text of the *Kuan Wu-liang-shou Fo ching* under the reconstructed Sanskrit title *Amitāyurdhyāna sūtra*. Sanskrit originals do not survive for either the *Pan-chou san-mei ching* or the *Kuan Wu-liang-shou Fo ching*.

4. *Pan-chou san-mei ching* 1, in *TD* 13, p. 905b.

5. There are two Chinese translations, each one fascicle in length: *TD* no. 366, translated by Kumārajīva in 402 and *TD* no. 367, translated by Hsüan-tsang in 650. The former is the version customarily used.

6. Although this sūtra is often referred to by a reconstructed Sanskrit title, *Amitāyurdhyāna sūtra*, most contemporary scholars believe that it is not a translation of an Indian text, but of a text originating in Central Asia. There is strong evidence of Chinese influence on the *Kuan Wu-liang-shou Fo ching* as it has come down to us today, which has led a few scholars to argue that the text was composed in China. For a comprehensive discussion of the various problems relating to this sūtra see Fujita Kōtatsu, *Genshi Jōdo shisō no kenkyū*, pp. 116–36.

7. On Hui-yüan see E. Zürcher, *The Buddhist Conquest of China*, vol. 1, pp. 204–53.

8. Biography of Hui-yüan in *KSC* 6, pp. 358c–359a. For an English translation of the vow see E. Zürcher, *The Buddhist Conquest of China*, vol. 1, pp. 244–5.

9. Chia-ts'ai, Preface to *Ching-t'u lun* 淨土論, in *TD* 47, p. 83b.

10. The development of Pure Land Buddhism in South China is carefully documented in Mochizuki Shinkō, *Shina Jōdo kyōrishi* (Tokyo/Kyoto, 1942), pp. 49–59.

11. Tsukamoto Zenryū, *Shina Bukkyōshi kenkyū* 支那佛教史研究 (Tokyo, 1942), p. 379.

12. Mochizuki Shinkō, *Shina Jōdo kyōrishi*, pp. 57–8.

13. Tsukamoto Zenryū, *Shina Bukkyōshi kenkyū*, pp. 377–8.

14. Biographies in *HKSC* 6, p. 470a–c; Chia-ts'ai, *Ching-t'u lun* 3, in *TD* 47,

pp. 97c–98a.
15 T'an-luan, *Wang-sheng lun chu* (also known as *Wu-liang-shou ching yu-p'i-t'i-she yüan-sheng chieh chu* 無量壽經優婆提舍願生偈註) 1, in *TD* 40, p. 862a–b; ibid. 2, pp. 835a–836a.
16 Biographies in *HKSC* 20, pp. 593c–594b; Chia-ts'ai, *Ching-t'u lun* 3, in *TD* 47, p. 98b.
17 Tao-ch'o, *An-lo chi* 安樂集 1, in *TD* 47, p. 13c.
18 Tao-ch'o, *An-lo chi* 1, p. 4b.
19 Biographies in *HKSC* 27, p. 684a; *Wang-sheng hsi-fang Ching-t'u jui-ying shan-chuan* 往生西方淨土瑞應刪傳 (compiled by Wen-shen 文諗 and Shao-k'ang 少康 c. 800), in *TD* 51, p. 105b–c; Chieh-chu 戒珠, *Ching-t'u wang-sheng chuan* 淨土往生傳 (completed between 1068 and 1077) 2, in *TD* 51, p. 119a–b.
20 Shan-tao, *Kuan Wu-liang-shou Fo ching shu* 觀無量壽佛經疏 4, in *TD* 37, pp. 271a–272b.
21 Tsukamoto Zenryū, *Shina Bukkyōshi kenkyū*, pp. 377–8. It should be noted that these figures apply only to images bearing dated inscriptions.
22 *FTTC* 26, p. 260c. For the belief that Shan-tao was an earthly transformation (*hua-shen* 化身) of Amitābha see Tz'u-yün Tsun-shih 慈雲遵式, *Ching-t'u lüeh-chuan* 淨土略傳, cited in *FTTC* 26, p. 263b and Hōnembō Genkū 法然房源空 (1133–1212), *Senchaku hongan nembutsu shū* 選擇本願念佛集, in *TD* 83, p. 19c.
23 The lack of interest in Pure Land Buddhism by the court is clearly illustrated in the case of Tao-ch'o, who, although born and active in T'ai-yüan, the 'Northern Capital' of the T'ang where the imperial clan had its origins, was not singled out for any special honors. According to an inscription preserved in *Chin-shih ts'ui-pien* 84, p. 13a, T'ai-tsung met Tao-ch'o while on a visit to T'ai-yüan and requested him to pray for the recovery of the ailing Empress. Since the Empress died in 636, the meeting must have taken place before that date. The silence of Buddhist sources regarding this meeting would suggest that it produced no lasting ties between Tao-ch'o and the imperial clan. In any case, Tao-ch'o was not granted any honorary titles by T'ai-tsung. Perhaps his prayers failed.
24 For a detailed study of the fragmentary materials relating to Fa-chao see Tsukamoto Zenryū, *Tō chūki no Jōdokyō* 唐中期の淨土教 (Kyoto, 1933), pp. 114–348. Although Ennin notes in his diary (*NGJK*: 840, IV, 29) that Fa-chao died in 838, Ono Katsutoshi concluded after a careful study of all available evidence that Fa-chao's death occurred about 820. See his *Nittō guhō junrei kōki no kenkyū* 入唐求法巡禮行紀の研究, vol. 2 (Tokyo, 1966), pp. 432–3.
25 Wang Jih-hsiu 王日休 (died 1173), *Lung-shu tseng-kuang Ching-t'u wen* 龍舒增廣淨土文 5, in *TD* 47, p. 267a; Tsung-hsiao 宗曉, *Lo-pang wen-lei* 樂邦文類 (completed 1200) 3, in *TD* 47, p. 193a.
26 The earliest biographies of Ch'eng-yüan are two funerary inscriptions: Lü Wen 呂溫 (772–811), *Nan-yüeh Ta-shih Yüan-kung t'a-ming chi* 南嶽大師遠公塔銘記, in *Lü Heng-chou chi* 呂衡州集 (Yüeh-ya-t'ang ts'ung-shu 粵雅堂叢書 edn, case 20) 6, pp. 15b–19b; Liu Tsung-yüan 柳宗元 (779–819). *Nan-yüeh Mi-t'o Ho-shang pei* 南嶽彌陀和尚碑, in *Liu Ho-tung chi* 柳河東

集 (Kuo-hsüeh chi-pen ts'ung-shu 國學基本叢書 edn, Shanghai, 1933) 6, vol. 2, pp. 17–18.

27 Fa-chao, *Ching-t'u wu hui nien-fo sung-ching kuan-hsing i* 淨土五會念佛誦經觀行儀 2, in *TD* 85, p. 1253b–c. The *wu hui nien-fo* seems to have been derived from a practice known as *yin-sheng nien-fo* 引聲念佛 in which the devotee lengthened the sound of each syllable in the name of Amitābha as he intoned it. This peculiar style of invoking Amitābha's name was transmitted within the Ch'an lineage of Chih-hsien 智詵, which was based in Szechwan. It seems likely that Fa-chao, who himself was probably from this region, learned of the practice of *yin-sheng nien-fo* from his teacher, Ch'eng-yüan, who had studied under Ch'u-chi 處寂, the successor to Chih-hsien. For the practice of *yin-sheng nien-fo* in Szechwan by followers of the Nan-shan nien-fo men Ch'an tsung 南山念佛門禪宗, as Chih-hsien's lineage is called, see Tsung-mi, *Yüan-chüeh ching ta-shu ch'ao* 3B, in *ZZK* ser. 1, case 14, vol. 3, p. 279b. Chih-hsien's lineage is discussed in Philip Yampolsky, *The Platform Sūtra of the Sixth Patriarch*, pp. 42–4.

28 *Wu-liang-shou ching* 2, in *TD* 12, p. 273c, which states: '... the wind spontaneously arises in all four directions to blow through the jewelled trees [of Pure Land], making them produce the five sounds.' This passage, which does not occur in the Sanskrit text of the sūtra, appears to be a Chinese interpolation. The term 'five sounds' (*wu yin-sheng* 五音聲) is also found in ibid. 1, p. 271a, where it is specifically identified with the notes of the Chinese pentatonic scale. See Ching-ying Hui-yüan 淨影慧遠 (523–592), *Wu-liang-shou ching i-shu* 無量壽經義疏 2, in *TD* 37, p. 105c. The corresponding Sanskrit passage makes no mention of 'five sounds,' but speaks only of 'a sweet and delightful sound' that proceeds from the trees when they are moved by the wind. See F. Max Müller, tr. *The Larger Sukhāvatī-vyūha*, p. 35, in *The Sacred Books of the East*, vol. 49.

29 According to Fa-chao's biography in *SKSC* 21, p. 844b, in 770 he had a vision of the future Chu-lin ssu, which consisted of 120 halls spread out over a wide area that had a circumference of twenty *li* (approximately seven miles). The construction of the Chu-lin ssu was begun sometime after 777 and seems to have been completed by 796 (Yen-i 延一, *Kuang Ch'ing-liang chuan* 廣清涼傳 [compiled 1060] 2, in *TD* 51, pp. 1115c–1116a). When the Japanese monk Ennin visited the Chu-lin ssu in 840, it consisted of six halls with forty monks in residence and was not subject to the control of the hierarchs of Wu-t'ai shan (*NGJK*: 840, V, 2). Ennin reports elsewhere in his diary that the Chu-lin ssu was only one of the two monasteries in China at which ordinations could be legally performed. The other monastery was the Hui-shan ssu 會善寺 on Mt Sung 嵩山 to the east of Lo-yang (*NGJK*: 838, x, 19). For a detailed discussion of the dates for the construction of the Chu-lin ssu see Tsukamoto Zenryū, *Tō chūki no Jōdokyō*, pp. 171–81.

30 *Ching-t'u wu hui nien-fo sung-ching kuan-hsing i* 3, in *TD* 85, p. 1266a.
31 *NGJK*: 840, IV, 29.
32 *NGJK*: 841, II, 8.

Reign of Tai-tsung (762–779)

1 *CTS* 118, p. 3417; *TCTC* 224, p. 7196. Tai-tsung's initial antagonism

toward Buddhism and Taoism is reflected in an edict calling for a purge of the clergies of both religions that was promulgated in the eighth month of the year 762, i.e. four months after Tai-tsung ascended the throne. In this edict he forbade outsiders, either government officials or private individuals, to stay in Buddhist or Taoist monasteries – a prohibition that was to be reissued during the reign of his son, Te-tsung. He further instructed all clergy living in Buddhist and Taoist monasteries, with the exception of the aged, the infirm, and those charged with administrative responsibilities, to participate in religious services twice daily and decreed punishment of those monks who were lax in the performance of their religious duties. Both clergies were specifically prohibited from discussing supernatural phenomena. In addition, all unscheduled religious gatherings were forbidden. For the text of this edict, which was entitled *T'iao-kuan seng-ni ch'ih* 條貫僧尼勅 see *T'ang ta chao-ling chi* 113, p. 590. This edict also appears in an abridged format under the title *Chin-tuan kung-ssu chieh ssu-kuan chü-chih chao* 禁斷公私借寺觀居止詔 in *CTW* 46, pp. 12b–13a.

2 *TD* nos. 944A and 944B. For the text of the memorial and Tai-tsung's reply see *KSP* 1, pp. 829c–830a. Pu-k'ung translated a number of tantras dedicated to the worship of Marīci (*TD* nos. 1254, 1255, 1258, etc.).

3 *CYL* 15, p. 884a.

4 *TFYK* 52, p. 2a.

5 For the text of Pu-k'ung's memorial see *KSP* 1, p. 831b–c. Although the T'ang catalogues of the canon follow *LTSP* 8, p. 78a in attributing the earlier 'translation' to Kumārajīva, the *Ch'u san-tsang chi chi* 出三藏記集 (compiled by Seng-yu 僧祐 c. 518) puts it in the category of texts whose translators are unknown (see *TD* 55, p. 29c). A preface to the *Ta-p'in ching* 大品經 written by Emperor Wu of the Liang, which is contained in the *Ch'u san-tsang chi chi*, states (p. 54b) that the *Jen-wang ching* was commonly regarded as a 'sūtra of doubtful authenticity' (*i-ching* 疑經). Fa-ching 法經 notes in his catalogue of the canon, the *Chung-ching mu-lu* 衆經目錄 completed in 594, that viewed from the standpoint of style and content, the *Jen-wang ching* does not appear to have been translated by Kumārajīva (*TD* 55, p. 126b) and hence includes it in the section listing dubious works (*i-huo lu* 疑惑錄). Tz'u-en likewise doubts its authenticity, pointing out that Hsüan-tsang was unable to locate a copy of the original text in India (*Yü-ch'ieh-shih ti lun lüeh-tsuan* 瑜伽師地論略纂 10, in *TD* 43, p. 129c).

6 *Jen-wang ching* 2, in *TD* 8, p. 833b. The terminology employed in the text likewise suggests a Chinese origin for the work. Its anonymous author was apparently attempting to dissuade Northern Wei rulers from interfering with the autonomy of the church.

7 *CYL* 15, p. 885a.

8 Pu-k'ung's 'new translation' is *TD* no. 246.

9 Both prefaces by Tai-tsung are preserved in *CTW* 49, pp. 22a–24b. Pu-k'ung's letter of thanks to the emperor is included in *KSP* 1, p. 832b–c.

10 *CYL* 15, pp. 885b–886c; *CTS* 11, p. 280.

11 *CTS* 118, p. 3417. The date is given in *FTTC* 41, p. 378a.

12 *CYL* 15, p. 886c. For the texts of the imperial decrees see *KSP* 1, p. 832b–c.

13 *CTS* 118, p. 3417.

14 As an example of Tu Hung-chien's piety *HTS* 126, p. 4424 notes that he feted one thousand monks after his return to Ch'ang-an from Szechwan in 767.
15 *THY* 48, p. 847.
16 *TCTC* 224, p. 7196. See also Wang Chin's biography in *CTS* 118, p. 3417.
17 *TCTC* 224, pp. 7196–7.
18 Pu-k'ung's petition, upon which much of the following account is based, is included in *KSP* 2, p. 834a–b.
19 The *Hua-yen ching* (*Avataṃsaka sūtra*), which had been brought to China from Khotan in 418, states that Wen-shu permanently dwells in the Ch'ing-liang 清涼 mountains in the northeastern region with his retinue of ten thousand bodhisattvas (fasc. 29, in *TD* 9, p. 590a). It is not clear whether the compilers of the *Hua-yen ching* had Wu-t'ai shan in mind when they spoke of Ch'ing-liang shan as the abode of Wen-shu. The identification between the two names was certainly made by the year 516, when the Hua-yen scholar (and devotee of Wen-shu) Ling-pien 靈辨 began writing his monumental commentary on the *Hua-yen ching* at the Ch'ing-liang ssu in Wu-t'ai shan. See *Hua-yen ching chuan-chi* 華嚴經傳記 1, in *TD* 51, p. 157b.
20 The *Wen-shu fa-tsang ching* 文殊法藏經 (*TD* no. 1185), supposedly translated into Chinese in 710 by Bodhiruci, has the Buddha prophesy: 'After my Parinirvāṇa [i.e. demise], there shall arise a country named Mahā Cīna [*Ta Chen-na* 大振那], 'Great China'] to the northeast of Jambudvīpa [India]. In that country there will be a group of mountains known as the Five Peaks [Wu Ting 五頂], where Wen-shu shall take up residence and preach the Dharma to all sentient beings' (*TD* 20, p. 791c). Although the *K'ai-yüan lu*, which was completed twenty years after the translation of this sūtra is said to have taken place, unhesitatingly accepts it as an authentic scripture of Indian origin (fasc. 9, in *TD* 55, p. 569c), the text, as we now have it, contains a number of clearly Chinese interpolations, as, for example, its reference to the 'disarray of the five elements [*wu hsing* 五行] and the commingling of the *yin* and *yang*' (p. 791c). With regard to Wen-shu's connection with China, I-ching reported that Indians believed that he was presently dwelling in Ping-chou 并州, i.e. the vicinity of Wu-t'ai shan (*Nan-hai chi-kuei nei-fa chuan* 南海寄歸內法傳 4, in *TD* 54, p. 228b). For another reference to this belief see ibid., p. 224c. It should also be remembered that the Indian translator Prajñā (Po-jo San-tsang 般若三藏), who arrived in Ch'ang-an in 782, was motivated to undertake the perilous journey from India by his conviction that Wen-shu was then living in China. See *CYL* 17, p. 891c.
21 *CTS* 118, p. 3418.
22 Biography of Tao-i in *SKSC* 21, p. 844a.
23 Ibid.
24 *KSP* 3, p. 844b. Han-kuang was later visited here by Chan-jan (711–782), the 'restorer' of the T'ien-t'ai school under whom the Han-lin scholar Liang Su studied Buddhist doctrine. See *SKSC* 27, p. 879b.
25 For a detailed description of the Chin-ko ssu at this time see *NGJK*: 840, VI, 2.
26 For a study of the role of Wen-shu in East Asian Esoteric Buddhism see

Raoul Birnbaum, *Studies on the Mysteries of Mañjuśrī*, Society for the Study of Chinese Religions Monograph No. 2 (n. p., 1983).
27 *Fang-po-ching* 放鉢經, in *TD* 15, p. 451a, which was translated into Chinese sometime during the Western Chin dynasty (265–316). It should be noted that Pu-k'ung likewise refers to Wen-shu as the 'progenitor and teacher' (*tsu-shih* 祖師) of all Buddhas. See *KSP* 3, p. 841c.
28 I-hsing, *Ta p'i-lu-che-no ch'eng-fo ching shu* 大毘盧遮那成佛經疏 10, in *TD* 39, p. 682b.
29 Fei-hsi's biographical stele inscription in *KSP* 4, p. 849a.
30 *TD* nos. 319, 1171, 1172, 1174–7, 1195, 1276, and 1299.
31 For the text of Pu-k'ung's memorial see *KSP* 2, p. 837a–b.
32 For an early version of the legend see the *Shih-sung lü* 十誦律 37, in *TD* 23, pp. 268c–269b. The ritual of offering food to Pin-t'ou-lu is described in detail in *Ch'ing Pin-t'ou-lu fa* 請賓頭盧法, in *TD* 32, p. 784a–b.
33 *KSC* 5, p. 353b.
34 Tao-hsüan 道宣, *Kan-t'ung lu* 感通錄, in *TD* 52, p. 437b.
35 Fa-tsang states that in the 'Western lands,' i.e. India and Central Asia, monasteries belonging to the Hīnayāna regard Pin-t'ou-lu as the 'elder' (*shang-tso* 上座), i.e. guardian, whereas Mahāyāna monasteries assign this position to Wen-shu (*Fan-wang ching p'u-sa chieh-pen shu* 梵網經菩薩戒本疏 1, in *TD* 40, p. 605b).
36 *NGJK*: 840, IV, 28. In some monasteries at this time, however, Pin-t'ou-lu still continued to occupy the seat of the 'elder'. See for example the biography of Ts'ung-chien 從諫 in *SKSC* 12, p. 779b.
37 *KSP* 3, p. 841c.
38 *KSP* 3, p. 842a.
39 *KSP* 3, p. 842b.
40 Chao Ch'ien 趙遷, *Pu-k'ung San-tsang hsing-chuang* 不空三藏行狀, in *TD* 50, p. 293c.
41 His memorials abound in phrases such as 'I respectfully make these detailed translations for the benefit of the state' (*feng wei kuo-chia hsiang-i* 奉爲國家詳譯), 'I have translated these sūtras for the benefit of the state and thus help to proclaim the Imperial Way' (*wei kuo i-ching chu hsüan huang-hua* 爲國譯經助宣皇化); 'The Mahāyāna scriptures that I have translated will be of benefit to the state and eliminate disasters' (*tzu pang-kuo hsi-mieh tsai-o* 資邦國息滅災厄); 'By relying on the power of the Buddha, we contribute to the consolidation of the empire' (*fu ch'eng kuo-chia* 輔成國家); 'Through the recitation of the mantra the Imperial Person will be afforded everlasting protection' (*ch'ang hu sheng-kung* 長護聖躬); etc. The preceding examples are all taken from the catalogue of translations presented to Tai-tsung on his birthday in 771 by Pu-k'ung (text in *KSP* 3, p. 840a–b). For Pu-k'ung's promotion of Esoteric Buddhism as a state cult see Yamazaki Hiroshi, *Zui Tō Bukkyōshi no kenkyū* (Kyoto, 1967), pp. 239–50.
42 *KSP* 3, p. 840b.
43 *LFPT* 17, p. 297a. *FTTC* 41, p. 378c, following *TCTC* 224, pp. 7201–02, places this event in 768. *CTS* 118, p. 3418 contains an account of the ceremony that differs in some details, but does not supply a precise date.
44 *SSL* 3, p. 248b. The feasting of the clergy by the emperor was known as *nei-*

chai 內齋, 'palace banquet'. The practice was discontinued in 833.
45 *Pu-k'ung San-tsang hsing-chuang*, in *TD* 50, p. 293b.
46 Ibid., p. 293c.
47 For Tai-tsung's edict authorizing the service see *KSP* 2, p. 837b–c.
48 *KSP*, p. 837c.
49 *KSP*, p. 837c–838a.
50 *Pu-k'ung San-tsang hsing-chuang*, in *TD* 50, p. 293c.
51 *CTS* 184, p. 4764. Tai-tsung's mother had been given the name Chang-ching posthumously in 762 (*THY* 3, p. 28).
52 See Arthur Waley, *The Life and Times of Po Chü-i* (London, 1949), pp. 18 and 23.
53 *TCTC* 224, pp. 7195–6.
54 *TCTC*, p. 7196.
55 *TFYK* 52, p. 3a.
56 For the size of the monastery see *Ch'ang-an chih* 10, p. 12a. The date of completion is given in *TFYK*.
57 Among the monks who lived here were Huai-hui 懷暉 and Fa-ch'in 法欽, both noted Ch'an masters; Liang-pen 良賁, the great commentator and collaborator of Pu-k'ung; Fa-chao, the popularizer of Pure Land; Wu-k'ung 悟空, the last major T'ang traveller to India; Hsi-chao 希照 and P'u-chen 普震, both *Vinaya* scholars; Tao-ch'eng 道澄, who administered the precepts to Emperor Te-tsung; and the Japanese monk, Ennin. For biographical details as well as the names of other monks who lived here see Tsukamoto, *Tō chūki no Jōdokyō*, pp. 35–6.
58 There is some confusion regarding the precise date. *FTTC* 41, p. 378a gives 765; *SSL* 3, p. 250b, and again on p. 252a, states simply that the edict was issued during the Yung-t'ai 永泰 period (765–6). *SSL*, however, notes elsewhere (p. 249c) that the date for the edict was 771.
59 *TFYK* 52, p. 3a–b. *SSL* 2, p. 246a states that K'uo-ch'ing was appointed commissioner of good works during the reign of Chung-tsung, which is clearly an error, since *TFYK*, p. 3a–b identifies K'uo-ch'ing as a resident of the Hsing-t'ang ssu 興唐寺, which was not built until 732 (see *THY* 48, p. 846). Furthermore, a contemporary source, Fei-hsi's 飛錫 biography of Pu-k'ung (included in *KSP* 4, p. 849b), indicates that K'uo-ch'ing (whom it refers to by his honorary ecclesiastical title of Ta-chi Ch'an-shih 大濟禪師) held the posts of permanent commissioner of good works and honorary director of the Department of Palace Affairs (*ch'ang hsiu kung-te shih chien-chiao tien-chung chien* 常修功德使檢校殿中監) at the time of Pu-k'ung's burial in the seventh month of 774. K'uo-ch'ing continued to occupy these two posts for at least one more year (see the biography of Hui-chung 慧忠 in *SKSC* 9, p. 763b). K'uo-ch'ing was alive and still politically active as late as 779 when he provided funds for a religious observance at the New Year festival (see *HKYL* 2, p. 761a). For an account of the evolution of the post of commissioner of good works see the detailed study by Tsukamoto Zenryū, 'Tō chūki irai no Chōan no kudokushi,' *Tōhō gakuhō* (Kyoto), 4 (1933) 368–406, reprinted in *Tsukamoto Zenryū chosaku shū*, vol. 3 (Tokyo, 1975), pp. 251–84.
60 *CYL* 17, p. 891a. It is not clear how K'uo-ch'ing's post of commissioner of

good works differed in jurisdiction from the newly established and more precisely defined office of commissioner of good works for Buddhist monasteries and Taoist temples in the capital. It is unlikely that K'uo-ch'ing, a Buddhist monk, would have been asked to oversee the construction or administration of Taoist temples, which was one of the responsibilities of the newly created post. Since K'uo-ch'ing was affiliated with two monasteries in Ch'ang-an (the Hsing-t'ang ssu and the Ta hsing-shan ssu) and concurrently held a palace office, it would appear that the 'good works' for which he had jurisdiction were probably located in the capital region. One possibility is that K'uo-ch'ing was appointed commissioner of good works to oversee the construction of a specific, but now unidentifiable, monastery in the capital. That such *ad hoc* appointments were made from time to time during the reign of Tai-tsung can be surmised from the nomination of Pu-k'ung's disciple, Hui-hsiao 惠曉, to serve as commissioner of good works for the supervision of construction projects on Wu-t'ai shan (*Wu-t'ai shan hsiu kung-te shih*) during the years 777 and 778 (see his two memorials to the throne in *KSP* 6, pp. 858c–859b).

61 *CYL* 17, p. 891a.
62 Pu-k'ung states that Li Yüan-ts'ung had been a devout disciple for over thirty years (*KSP* 3, p. 844b). In 754, Li received an esoteric consecration from Pu-k'ung while the latter was accepting the patronage of the Ho-hsi military governor, Ko-shu Han (Fei-hsi's biography of Pu-k'ung in *KSP* 4, p. 848c). It should be noted that Pu-k'ung's leading clerical disciple, Han-kuang, also received his consecration at the same time. Pu-k'ung's affection for Li Yüan-ts'ung is clearly shown by his decision to bequeath to Li a number of his own liturgical implements used in Tantric rituals (*KSP*, p. 844b).
63 Hui-lang's memorial dated the twelfth month of 776, in *KSP* 5, p. 853b.
64 *HKYL* 2, p. 760b.
65 The title first occurs in a letter to Tai-tsung dated the fifteenth day of the fourth month of 778 (see *KSP* 6, p. 860a).
66 *KSP* 3, p. 844b.
67 See, for example, *KSP*, pp. 838b, 840c, 843b, 843c, 846b, 846c, etc.; also *CYL*, pp. 750b, 755b, etc. Li Hsien-ch'eng's name first appears in a memorial from Pu-k'ung dated the thirteenth day of the sixth month of 768 (*KSP*, p. 836b).
68 For Li Hsien-ch'eng's full title see *KSP* 6, pp. 855c and 856b.
69 *Chung-shih* was not a specific rank, but rather a generic term denoting a eunuch attached to the Inner Palace (see Robert des Rotours, *Traité des fonctionnaires et traité de l'armée*, vol. 2 (Leiden, 1948), p. 844, n. 3).
70 The designation *chien-shih* does not appear in any of the standard lists of official positions under the T'ang, although it occurs frequently as Li Hsien-ch'eng's title in memorials to the throne written by monks (see *KSP*, pp. 836b, 843b, 846b, 853b, etc.). Pu-k'ung implies in his will (*KSP*, p. 844b) that the primary responsibility of Li Hsien-ch'eng as *chien-shih* was to oversee (*chien*) Buddhist affairs at the court. For his title as *chung-shih* see *CYL*, pp. 750b, 755b, 760b, 761b, etc.

71 HKYL 2, p. 760a.
72 The full title is *Ssu-fen lü shu*. 四分律疏. This work, which is in twenty fascicles, is included in ZZK, ser. 1, case 65, vols. 3–5.
73 The full title is *Ssu-fen lü k'ai-tsung chi*. 四分律開宗記. This commentary, also in twenty fascicles, is included in ZZK, ser. 1, case 66, vol. 5 through case 67, vol. 1.
74 Biography of Huai-su in SKSC 14, p. 792c.
75 HKYL 2, p. 760b.
76 LFPT 17, p. 297a; FTTC 41, p. 377c.
77 Biography of Tao-hsüan in SKSC 14, p. 791a–b. FTTC 41, p. 379a places this incident in the year 776, which seems to be the result of a careless reading of Tao-hsüan's biography by the compiler of the FTTC.
78 TFYK 52, p. 5a.
79 TFYK 52, pp. 4b–5a. Tai-tsung's edict refers specifically to the ordination of Buddhist monks (*seng*), Buddhist nuns (*ni*), and Taoist priests (*tao-shih*). I have used the word 'cleric' to include these three categories.
80 HKYL 2, p. 760b.
81 SSL 3, p. 252a.
82 Biography of Ch'ung-hui 崇惠 in SKSC 17, p. 816.
83 Biography of Wang Chin in CTS 118, p. 3417.

Reign of Te-tsung (779–805)

1 HKYL 2, p. 761c.
2 *Mo-chih*, literally 'an imperial order in black ink,' refers to an *ad hoc* decree prepared in the Inner Palace, in theory by the emperor himself, that is issued without going through the usual departmental channels. Cf. *mo-ch'ih* 墨勅, in Morohashi Tetsuji, *Dai Kanwa jiten*, vol. 3, p. 259c, entry 161.
3 HKYL 2, pp. 761c–762a.
4 CTS 12, p. 321.
5 CTS 12, p. 326. For the removal of the Palace Chapel see SSL 2, p. 247c.
6 The Taoist Wang Yü 王璵, who first made a name for himself at the court of Hsüan-tsung by offering prayers that involved the burning of paper money (*chih-ch'ien* 紙錢), was appointed prefect (*tz'u-shih*) and military governor of P'u-chou 蒲州 and several other prefectures by Su-tsung in 760 in recognition of his magical prowess. He subsequently was awarded the court posts of vice president of the Secretariat (*Chung-shu shih-lang* 中書侍郎) and chief minister (*t'ung chung-shu men-hsia p'ing-chang-shih* 同中書門下平章事) (biography of Wang Yü in CTS 130, p. 3617). The biography of Li Mi 李泌 in CTS 130, p. 3623 states that in the opening years of his reign Te-tsung held thaumaturges and tellers of fabulous stories in extreme contempt and banned their activities at the court.
7 Biographies in CTS 122, pp. 3506–07; HTS 147, pp. 4757–59. Elsewhere (the biography of P'eng Yen 彭偃 in CTS 127, p. 3579) Li is referred to as the civil governor (*kuan-ch'a shih*) of Chien-nan Tung-ch'uan. The text of his memorial, entitled *Ch'ing shan-t'ai seng-tao shu*, 請刪汰僧道疏 is included in CTW 394, p. 1a–b. THY 47, p. 837 dates the memorial 778, which would place it in the reign of Tai-tsung. Both CTS (biography of P'eng Yen) and HTS (biography of Li Shu-ming), however, clearly indicate

Notes to pages 90–93

that the memorial was received by Te-tsung. The *terminus ad quem* for its presentation is 783, the year when P'eng Yen who had participated in the discussion of the proposals at the court, joined the rebel government of Chu Tz'u 朱泚.

8 Since there were fewer Taoist temples, they were to be divided into only two grades – upper and lower – and would be permitted to house fourteen monks in the case of the former and seven in the case of the latter.
9 Biography of P'eng Yen in *CTS* 127, p. 3579.
10 Biography of Li Shu-ming in *HTS* 147, p. 4758.
11 The text of his memorial, entitled *Shan-t'ai seng-tao i* 刪汰僧道議 is included in *CTW* 445, pp. 22b–24a.
12 *CTW* 445, p. 23a.
13 According to a memorial in *CTW* 855, p. 1 1a–b by Li Ch'in-ming 李欽明 entitled *Ch'ing t'ai seng-jen shu*, 請汰僧人疏 a monk consumed one *sheng* 升 (.594 liters) of rice a day and required five *p'i* 匹 (one *p'i* = 12.1 meters; cf. 'bolt') of silk (*chüan* 絹) and fifty *liang* 兩 (one *liang* = 37.3 grams) of silk floss (*mien* 綿) for his robes every year. (The metric equivalents are based on figures given in Edwin O. Reischauer, tr. *Ennin's Diary* [New York, 1955], p. 33, n. 127; p. 44, n. 192; p. 50, n. 217.) In 780 the price of one *tou* 斗 (i.e. ten *sheng*) of rice was two hundred cash, while a bolt of silk sold for approximately 4,000 cash. Thus a year's supply of rice and silk for one monk cost 27,300 cash (365 *sheng* of rice at twenty cash per *sheng* and five bolts of silk at 4,000 cash per bolt). To this sum, of course, must be added the price of fifty *liang* of silk floss, tailoring charges, and the enormous cost of maintaining the monk's monastery, with its halls, altars, library, and cells. For the price of commodities I have used the figures in Kenneth Ch'en, 'The Economic Background of the Hui-ch'ang Suppression of Buddhism,' *Harvard Journal of Asiatic Studies*, 19 (1956), 84.
14 P'eng (*CTW* 445, p. 23b) quotes the well-known words of Confucius: 'At fifty, I knew the decrees of Heaven' (James Legge, *The Chinese Classics*, vol. 1, pp. 146–7) and paraphrases a line from the *Lieh-tzu*: 'If a man is not advanced in years, he cannot know the Way' (Yang Po-chün 楊伯峻, *Lieh-tzu chi-shih* 列子集釋 [Hong Kong, 1965], p. 154).
15 P'ei's proposals are recorded in the biography of Li Shu-ming in *HTS* 147, p. 4758 and reproduced in *CTW* 616, p. 4b under the title *T'ai seng-tao i* 汰僧道議. *CTW*, however, erroneously attributes the document to P'ei Chi 裴坰 who was made a Han-lin scholar during the reign of Hsien-tsung. There is no indication in the biographies of P'ei Chi (*CTS* 148, pp. 3989–92; *HTS* 169, pp. 5147–50) that he ever held a post of auxiliary secretary in the Ministry of Justice (*Hsing-pu yüan-wai-lang*), which is the title that P'ei Po is given in the biography of Li Shu-ming.
16 The text of the edict is in *CTS* 12, pp. 339–40.
17 Biography of P'eng Yen in *CTS* 127, p. 3581.
18 *SSL* 2, p. 246b. The precise date is given in *FTTC* 41, p. 379b.
19 *FTTC* 41, p. 379b. For a general discussion of the disposition of the property of deceased monks see J. Gernet, *Les aspects économiques du Bouddhisme dans la société chinoise* (Saigon, 1956), pp. 70–90; also Michihata Ryōshū, *Tōdai Bukkyōshi no kenkyū*, pp. 502–13.

20 The *Ta po-nieh-p'an ching* 大般涅槃經 (*TD* 12, pp. 641a and 805b) speaks of 'eight impure things' (*pa pu-ching wu* 八不淨物), i.e. objects which a monk may not own or occupations in which he may not engage. According to Kuan-ting 灌頂, the eight prohibitions are: (1) accumulating gold and silver, (2) holding slaves (*nu-pi* 奴婢), (3) keeping livestock, (4) owning warehouses, (5) engaging in commerce, (6) working in the fields, (7) preparing one's own food, and (8) eating food that has not been given to one (see his *Ta po-nieh-p'an ching shu* 疏 10, in *TD* 38, p. 98b). Ch'eng-kuan gives a somewhat different list which includes bans against owning paddy land, buildings, and objects made of precious materials (*Hua-yen yen-i ch'ao* 華嚴演義鈔, as quoted in Chi-chao 寂照, *Ta-tsang fa-shu* 大藏法數 [Kōmeisha edn, Tokyo, 1899] 45, vol. 2, pp. 1020–1). That monks in India did in fact own land, houses, slaves, etc. is apparent from I-ching's discussion of how such property is to be disposed of after the death of its owner (see his *Nan-hai chi-kuei nei-fa chuan* 4, in *TD* 54, p. 230b).
21 *Wei-shu* 114, p. 3041.
22 A monk named Hui-fan 慧範 who was executed during the reign of Chung-tsung is said to have accumulated property valued at an incredible 13,000,000 strings of cash (Li Ch'o 李綽, *Shang-shu ku-shih* 尚書故實 [*Chi-fu ts'ung-shu* 畿輔叢書 edn, vol. 37], p. 2a).
23 For a discussion of the types of property that may be distributed to individual monks, i.e. to the 'visible clergy' (*hsien-ch'ien seng-ch'ieh* 現前僧伽) as opposed to property that must be turned over to the collective ownership of the Buddhist church as a whole, i.e. to the 'clergy of the ten directions' (*shih-fang seng-ch'ieh* 十方僧伽), see *Ssu-fen lü* 41, in *TD* 22, p. 589b–c. The importance of the question of the disposition of the property of deceased monks, technically known as *wang pi-ch'iu wu* 亡比丘物, can be seen from the fact that Tao-hsüan, the *de facto* founder of the Lü (or *Vinaya*) school, wrote a work solely devoted to this subject (the *Liang-ch'u ch'ing-chung i* 量處輕重儀 in two fascicles, in *ZZK*, ser. 2, case 10, vol. 1, pp. 49a–64a).
24 For the texts of two such wills see Niida Noboru 仁井田陞, *Tō-Sō hōritsu bunsho no kenkyū* (Tokyo, 1937), pp. 638–49. Both wills have been translated by Gernet, pp. 77–9. One of the wills, drawn up in 865 by a nun, bequeaths a female slave (*pi-tzu* 婢子) to her niece. The other will, undated but thought by Niida to be no later than the eleventh century and possibly earlier, does in fact bequeath substantial amounts of property in the category of 'heavy objects' to his monastery, although clerical and lay acquaintances and relatives receive some objects of value such as a slave girl, fifteen *liang* of silver, and an ox.
25 Biography of Ch'eng-ju in *SKSC* 15, p. 801c; also *SSL* 3, p. 249c.
26 *FTTC* 41, p. 379b.
27 Biographies in *CTS* 184, pp. 4766–7; *HTS* 207, pp. 5866–8. *CTS* states that when Huo became ill in 796, Te-tsung ordered that prayers be offered in all Buddhist monasteries in Ch'ang-an for his recovery. T'ou Wen-ch'ang is reported to have sponsored annual masses on Wu-t'ai shan in which as many as ten thousand monks participated to commemorate the Emperor's birthday (Yen-i 延一, *Kuang ch'ing-liang chuan* 廣清涼傳 2, in *TD* 51, p. 1116a).

Notes to pages 95–98   184

28 Biography of Tao-ch'eng in *SKSC* 16, p. 806b.
29 *CKL* 3, p. 829c.
30 Ibid.
31 *SKSC*, p. 806b.
32 *FTTC* 41, p. 379c.
33 Ibid.
34 *HTS* 48, p. 1253.
35 T'ou Wen-ch'ang is identified as commissioner of good works for the left half of Ch'ang-an in a memorial dated 789 reproduced in *HKYL* 2, p. 764b.
36 Neither *CTS* nor *HTS* contains a biography of Wang Hsi-ch'ien. He is mentioned as commissioner of good works for the right half of Ch'ang-an in a memorial dated 788 included in *HKYL* 2, pp. 762c–763a. His full title is given in *CYL* 17, p. 892a–b.
37 It is not known when Huo succeeded Wang. Huo is referred to as commissioner of good works in a document dated 798, the year of his death, included in *CYL* 17, p. 895b.
38 *CYL* 19, p. 909c.
39 *HTS* 48, p. 1253.
40 The text of this edict, which is entitled *Hsiu-ch'i ssu-kuan chao*, 修葺寺觀詔, is included in *CTW* 52, p. 3a. The date of the edict is given in *FTTC* 41, p. 379c. It will be recalled that Te-tsung's father, Tai-tsung, similarly prohibited outsiders from staying in monasteries (see above, p. 175, n. 1.)
41 *TFYK* 52, p. 6a.
42 Note, for example, his visits to the Chang-ching ssu in 791 (*CTS* 13, p. 372) and to the An-kuo ssu in 799 (*FTTC* 41, p. 380c).
43 *CTS* 13, p. 369; *TFYK* 52, p. 6b; *TCTC* 233, p. 7520; *FTTC* 41, p. 379c.
44 *FTTC* 41, p. 379a.
45 *CYL* 17, p. 892b.
46 *CYL* 17, p. 892a. For a comprehensive study of the life and teachings of Prajñā see Yoritomi Motohiro 賴富本宏, *Chūgoku Mikkyō no kenkyū* (Tokyo, 1979), pp. 1–109.
47 For an account of the activities of Ching-ching or 'Adam' in China see P. Y. Saeki, *The Nestorian Monument in China* (London, 1916) and the same author's *Nestorian Documents and Relics in China* (Tokyo, 1937).
48 *CYL*, p. 892a.
49 *TD* no. 261. Te-tsung's preface is included in *CTW* 55, pp. 6a–8a.
50 *CYL*, p. 893c.
51 The full Chinese title of Prajñā's translation of the *Gaṇḍavyūha* is *Ta fang-kuang Fo hua-yen ching ju pu-k'o-ssu-i chieh-t'o ching-chieh P'u-hsien yüan-hsing p'in* 大方廣佛華嚴經入不可思議解脫境界普賢願行品 (*TD* no. 293), which, because of its unwieldiness, is rarely used. Ordinarily this text is simply called the *Ssu-shih hua-yen ching* 四十華嚴經, i.e. the *Hua-yen Sūtra in Forty Fascicles*. Considerably shorter versions of the *Gaṇḍavyūha* were included in the translations of the *Hua-yen ching* by Buddhabhadra in 420 (as Chapter 34) and by Śikṣānanda in 699 (as Chapter 39). For an account of the *Gaṇḍavyūha* and its influence in East Asian art see Jan Fontein, *The Pilgrimage of Sudhana* (The Hague, 1967).
52 The circumstances relating to the translation of the *Gaṇḍavyūha* are given in detail in the colophon to Prajñā's version of the *Hua-yen ching* (*TD* 10,

pp. 848b–851c) and also in *CYL* 17, pp. 894a–896b.
53 Prajñā translated a total of eight texts which together filled seventy-four fascicles. Although we know of several translators who were active after the death of Prajñā c. 810, their output was in all cases limited to short, one-fascicle works.
54 According to the preface by Ching Shen 景審 (*TD* 54, p. 311c), Hui-lin began compiling the *I-ch'ieh-ching yin-i* in 784 and completed the project in 807, i.e. two years after the death of Te-tsung.
55 The tenth-century Buddhist historian Tsan-ning observed that during the century and a half in which the court ceased providing support for translation activities, i.e. the period from 810 [a reference to the death of Prajñā] to the end of the Later Chou dynasty, nothing of significance was accomplished (*SKSC* 3, p. 725a).

Reigns of Shun-tsung (805) and Hsien-tsung (805–820)
1 Biography of Ch'eng-kuan in *SKSC* 5, p. 737b–c.
2 Buddhist sources (the biography of Tuan-fu in *SKSC* 6, p. 741b; *SSL* 2, p. 243c; *FTTC* 41, p. 380a) uniformly depict the relationship between the two men as being as close as that between brothers.
3 *FTTC*, p. 380a.
4 *SSL* 2, p. 247c.
5 Biography of Pao-hsiu attached to the biography of Wei-k'uan 惟寬 in *SKSC* 10, p. 768b.
6 *FTTC*, p. 380b.
7 *CTL* 7, p. 253a. For Shih-li's attainment of enlightenment under Shih-t'ou see ibid. 14, p. 310b. Another Ch'an master supported by Shun-tsung at this time was Ju-man 如滿, the spiritual preceptor of Po Chü-i.
8 For the names of the monks who were summoned to the court between 806 and 810 and a brief description of the exchanges that took place see *FTTC*, pp. 380b–381a.
9 *FTTC*, p. 380b.
10 *CTS* 14, p. 420; *HTS* 48, p. 1253.
11 See the biography of Seng-lüeh 僧䂮 in *KSC* 6, p. 363b. According to *SSL* 2, p. 244a, the *seng-lu* was referred to under the Northern Wei as *lu-kung* 錄公, 'supervisor of records.' The term *seng-lu* seems to have subsequently fallen into disuse until it was revived by Hsien-tsung as an appellation for the chief clerical officers of the empire. *Yüeh-chung* is a Chinese translation of the monastic office known in Sanskrit as *karmadāna*, 'assigner of duties,' usually rendered in Chinese as *chih-shih* 知事 or *wei-no* 維那 (*SSL* 2, p. 242b). The term *seng-chu*, 'head of the clergy,' is of Chinese origin, a centralized hierarchy being unknown in Indian Buddhism. For a detailed account of the evolution of the office of *seng-lu* see Yamazaki Hiroshi, *Shina chūsei Bukkyō no tenkai*, pp. 637–56.
12 There is some disagreement regarding the precise date of the appointment. Both *Shih-shih tzu-chien* 釋氏資鑑 7, in *ZZK*, ser. 2B, case 5, vol. 1, p. 68b and *CKL* 7, p. 831b, claiming to base themselves on *CTS*, give the year as 807. *FTTC* 41, p. 380b, however, puts the year at 806. I have followed the former date since it coincides with the year given in both *CTS* and *THY* for

the broadening of the jurisdiction of the commissioners of good works. It might also be noted here that the *Shih-shih tzu-chien*, which was compiled in 1336, contains a passing reference to a monk, otherwise unknown, named Shen-kuang 神光, whom it cryptically identifies in an entry pertaining to the year 714 as the *tso-chieh seng-lu* (p. 61b). Since this title is not mentioned in any earlier work, it must be regarded as dubious.

13　*SSL* 2, p. 243c.
14　In a petition to Te-tsung dated 799 in *CYL* 1, p. 773c Ling-sui identifies himself as chief of the office of the commissioner of good works for the right half of Ch'ang-an (*kou-tang yu-chieh kung-te so* 勾當右街功德所), which suggests that the commissioners of good works relied on monks for the conduct of the day-to-day operations of their office.
15　*NGJK*: 839, I, 18.
16　See, for example, the entry in *NGJK* for 843, VI, 11.
17　*NGJK*: 839, I, 18.
18　*THY* 50, p. 881.
19　*FTTC* 41, p. 380b–c. See also Hsien-tsung's *Nan-chiao she-wen* 南郊赦文 in *CTW* 63, pp. 8b–9a.
20　See p. 60 above.
21　*CTS* 14, p. 435.
22　*TFYK* 52, p. 8a.
23　*THY* 48, p. 853: *TFYK* 52, p. 8b.
24　See the reigns of Kao-tsung, Chung-tsung, Su-tsung, and Te-tsung above for details. In 767, as we have already noted, Tai-tsung had two alleged relics of the Buddha – a tooth and a lump of flesh – brought to the Palace so that he could reverence them.
25　*TCTC* 240, p. 7756.
26　Biography of Han Yü in *CTS* 160, p. 4198.
27　*THY* 47, p. 838.
28　The essay is included in his collected works, *Han Ch'ang-li chi* 韓昌黎集 (Kuo-hsüeh chi-pen ts'ung-shu edn) 11, *ts'e* 3, pp. 59–63.
29　It will be recalled that essentially the same ideas were put forward by Fu I in 621. Han Yü's contempt for the clergy is evident from the phrase that he uses to convey the idea of 'laicization,' viz. *jen ch'i jen* 人其人, 'to humanize its members.'
30　The only extant Buddhist work of the T'ang period that attacks Han Yü's ideas is Tsung-mi's *Yüan-jen lun* 原人論 (*TD* no. 1886), which is clearly a reply to Han Yü's essay that bears an almost identical title (*Yüan-jen*), although Han Yü is never mentioned by name in Tsung-mi's work.
31　For the text of the memorial see the biography of Han Yü in *CTS* 160, pp. 4198–4200; *THY*, pp. 839–40; and *Han Ch'ang-li chi* 39, *ts'e* 7, pp. 34–7.
32　Translation by James Hightower (with minor changes) in Edwin O. Reischauer, *Ennin's Travels in T'ang China* (New York, 1955), pp. 223–4.
33　*TCTC* 240, p. 7759.
34　*THY*, p. 840.

Reigns of Mu-tsung (820–824) and Ching-tsung (824–826)

1　The 'Annals' (*pen-chi* 本紀) portion of *CTS* 14 (p. 472) states that the

sudden manner of Hsien-tsung's death led people to say that he had been murdered by the eunuch Ch'en Hung-chih 陳弘志. Elsewhere (biography of the eunuch Wang Shou-ch'eng 王守澄 184, p. 4769) the murder of Hsien-tsung is reported as an unequivocal fact.
2. Biography of Fa-chen 法眞 in *SKSC* 29, p. 894a. For secular references to Mu-tsung's piety see the citations of *CTS* and *TFYK* below.
3. Biography of Wu-yeh in *SKSC* 11, p. 773a. According to this source, Ling-chun held the especially exalted rank of recorder of monks for both halves of Ch'ang-an (*liang-chieh seng-lu*). Other Buddhist historical works (*LFPT* 23, p. 327b and *FTTC* 42, p. 384b) give the name of the envoy as Ling-fu 靈阜 and date the incident 822. *LFPT* identifies Ling-fu as the recorder of monks for the left half of Ch'ang-an.
4. Biography of Fa-chen in *SKSC*, p. 894a.
5. *CTS* 16, p. 500.
6. *CTS* 16, p. 503.
7. *TFYK* 52, p. 9a.
8. *CTS* 16, p. 503.
9. *TFYK* 52, p. 9a.
10. *TCTC* 243, p. 7828.
11. *TCTC* 242–43, pp. 7822–31.
12. Ichimura Sanjirō, *Tōyō shitō*, vol. 2 (Tokyo, 1944), pp. 318–20.

Reign of Wen-tsung (826–840)

1. *CTS* 17B, p. 580.
2. *CTS* 17A, pp. 523–24.
3. *CTS*, pp. 523–24. *FTLT* 16, pp. 628c–629a, which erroneously places this incident in the fifth month of 826, states that twenty-eight Taoist priests and one Buddhist monk ('the sycophant Wei-chen' 惟眞, otherwise unknown) were arrested, defrocked, and sent into exile by Wen-tsung. In fact, as *CTS* indicates, three Buddhist monks, including Wei-chen, were expelled from the court at this time. Chao Kuei-chen had been a priest at the T'ai-ch'ing kung 太清宮, which was the main Taoist temple in Ch'ang-an dedicated to Lao-tzu. Founded by Hsüan-tsung in 742, it was originally named Hsüan-yüan Huang-ti miao 玄元皇帝廟 and renamed T'ai-ch'ing kung the following year (*CTS* 9, pp. 214–16; *THY* 50, pp. 865–6). In the eleventh month of 826 Emperor Ching-tsung placed Chao at the head of the Taoist clergy in Ch'ang-an, granting him the title Chief Scholar and Master of the Taoist Clergy for Both Halves of Ch'ang-an (*Liang-chieh Tao-men tu chiao-shou po-shih* 兩街道門都教授博士); see *CTS* 17A, p. 521.
4. See p. 60 above.
5. *CTS* 17A, p. 533; *TFYK* 699, p. 16a. *FTTC* 42, p. 385a, which dates the event 828, gives Shen's position as civil governor and places the site of the ordination platform at Hung-chou. The incident, in fact, may have occurred in the opening year of Wen-tsung's reign, when many of his reforms were instituted in rapid succession, since the biography of Shen in *CTS* 149, p. 4037 indicates that he died in 827.
6. There was apparently a tradition among the civil governors (*kuan-ch'a shih*) assigned to Hung-chou to enrich themselves by authorizing private

Notes to pages 106–110

ordinations at the Pao-li ssu 寶曆寺, a famous monastery in that region, several times renamed, that dated from the early fifth century (see the biography of the monk Yu-hsüan 幽玄 in *SKSC* 27, p. 881a). In the third month of 826 Shen Chuan-shih's predecessor as civil governor of Hung-chou, Yin Yu 殷侑, was fined three months' salary for 'having arbitrarily established a platform for ordinations' (*CTS* 17A, p. 519; *TFYK* 699, pp. 15b–16a).

7 Biography of Sung Shen-hsi in *CTS* 167, pp. 4370–1.
8 The memorial, entitled *Ch'ing shen-chin seng-ni tsou* 請申禁僧尼奏 (*A Memorial Requesting a Reimposition of the Ban on the Buddhist Clergy*), is included in *CTW* 966, pp. 7b–9b.
9 This decree by Hsüan-tsung is mentioned only in the memorial from the Department of Sacrifices dated 830. Originally Hsüan-tsung proposed that clerical registers, like household registers (*hu-chi* 戶籍), be compiled every three years (see p. 52 above).
10 The amnesty, entitled *T'ai-ho san-nien nan-chiao she* 太和三年南郊赦 is found in the *T'ang ta chao-ling chi* 71, pp. 397–98.
11 During the 820s the eunuch general Liang Shou-ch'ien 梁守謙, who together with the eunuch Wang Shou-ch'eng arranged for Mu-tsung's enthronement, held the post of commissioner of good works for the right half of Ch'ang-an in addition to his various military offices (see the *Pin-kuo kung kung-te ming* 邠國公功德銘 in *Chin-shih ts'ui-pien* 金石萃編 107, p. 29b.
12 *TCTC* 244–5, pp. 7894–5.
13 *SSL* 2, pp. 247c–248a; *FTTC* 42, p. 385a.
14 *SSL* 3, p. 248b.
15 Biography of Li Hsün in *CTS* 169, pp. 4395–6.
16 *LFPT* 25, p. 334a; *FTTC*, p. 385b; *SSL*, p. 247c.
17 This story, which is repeated in various Buddhist sources (*LFPT* 25, p. 334a; *FTTC* 42, p. 385b), also appears in substantially the same form in the 'Monograph on the Five Elements' (*Wu-hsing chih* 五行志) in *CTS* 37, pp. 1362–63. *TCTC* 245, p. 7909 alone attributes the suspension of the purge to the intercession of Cheng Chu 'who wanted to preserve the honor of the Buddhist clergy.'
18 *TCTC*, p. 7906.
19 *FTTC*, p. 385b.
20 Chung-tsung was the first emperor to require candidates for ordination to pass an examination in the scripture (see p. 49 above). In 757, when ordination certificates were being openly sold for 100 strings of cash, laymen who either could recite 500 pages of scripture from memory or were able to read 700 pages were eligible for ordination without payment of any fee (see above, p. 170, n. 3). In 773 the devout emperor Tai-tsung ordered that all neophytes (*t'ung-hsing* 童行) who could pass an examination in the three divisions of the canon were to be issued ordination certificates (see the biography of Shen-ts'ou 神湊 in *SKSC* 16, p. 807b; also see *FTTC* 41, p. 379a). Another instance of ordination through examination before the reign of Wen-tsung occurred in 825 in response to a personal appeal to Ching-tsung by the court monk Fa-chen, who claimed that owing to the

endless warfare in the northeast, the only monks who could be found in the area were 'old and decrepit' (*lao-hsiu* 老朽), because the ordination platforms had been closed down for some time. To remedy the situation, the two commissioners of good works were instructed to open up the ordination platforms in their respective halves of the city for a period of exactly one month so that aspiring candidates could present themselves for examination by clerical elders (*ta-te* 大德). To qualify for ordination a male novice had to recite 150 pages of scripture from memory, a female novice only 100 pages (see *TFYK* 52, p. 9b; *FTTC* 42, p. 384c; and the biography of Fa-chen in *SKSC* 29, p. 894a–b). For a full discussion of the examination system as applied to the Buddhist clergy see Michihata Ryōshū, *Tōdai Bukkyōshi no kenkyū* (Kyoto, 1957), pp. 34–9.

21 *THY* 49, p. 861.

22 The importance attached in this period to sūtra chanting as the principal religious activity of the monk is clearly indicated in Hsüan-tsung's decree which stipulates that a monk could not substitute his alleged meditative skills (*tso-ch'an* 坐禪) for the requirement of reciting a specified number of pages of scripture.

23 The edict, entitled *T'iao-liu seng-ni ch'ih* 條流僧尼勅 (*Edict for the Purge of the Clergy*), is included in the *T'ang ta chao-ling chi* 113, p. 591: *CTW* 74, pp. 12b–14b. It is also referred to in *CTS* 17B, p. 559 and *TCTC* 245, p. 7906, which gives its precise date.

24 According to a widely accepted tradition dating back to the third century, the Han emperor Ming (57–75 C.E.) dreamed that a radiant deity (*shen-jen* 神人) descended into his courtyard. When he asked his minister to interpret the dream, he was told that the deity was none other than the Indian Buddha. Subsequently the emperor is said to have dispatched an embassy to India, which ultimately brought the first Buddhist scriptures to China. For a detailed analysis of this legend see T'ang Yung-t'ung 湯用彤, *Han Wei Liang-Chin Nan-pei-ch'ao fo-chiao shih* 漢魏兩晉南北朝佛教史 (Shanghai, 1938), vol. 1 pp. 16–23. The Western scholarly literature on the subject is summarized in E. Zürcher, *The Buddhist Conquest of China* vol. 1, p. 22 and accompanying notes. The legend is also discussed critically in Kenneth K. S. Ch'en, *Buddhism in China* (Princeton, N. J., 1964), pp. 29–31.

25 The three taboo months, which refer to the first, fifth, and ninth months of the year, are so designated because all killing, including the slaughter of animals and the execution of convicts, was forbidden on specified days of each of these months. Although commonly believed to be Buddhist in origin, the practice of observing three taboo months seems to be based primarily on Taoist cosmological notions that were incorporated into a 'sūtra' known as the *T'i-wei po-li ching* 提謂波利經 that was forged in the fifth century (see *Ch'u san-tsang chi chi* 出三藏記集 5, in *TD* 55, p. 39a). The passage describing the three taboo months in this now lost 'sūtra' is quoted in *FYCL* 88, pp. 932b–933a.

26 We can get some idea of how arduous a task it must have been to memorize 300 pages of scripture if we bear in mind that according to the T'ang catalogue, *KYL* (fasc. 19, p. 682b), the full Chinese text of the *Lotus Sūtra*

covered only 152 pages. The corresponding English version translated by Murano Senchū under the title *The Sutra of the Lotus Flower of the Wonderful Law* (Tokyo, 1974) fills 310 printed pages.

27 Biography of Tsung-mi in *SKSC* 6, p. 742a; biography of Li Hsün in *CTS* 169, p. 4398; also *TCTC*, fasc. 245, pp. 7915–16.
28 *FTTC* 42, p. 385b.
29 Biography of Ch'iu Shih-liang in *HTS* 207, p. 5872. For the date of Ch'iu's appointment as commander of the Shen-ts'e Palace Army of the Left see *TCTC* 245, p. 7904.
30 *FTTC*, p. 385b.
31 Ibid.
32 *CTS* 17B, p. 571.
33 *TFYK* 699, p. 16b.
34 Biography of Ts'ui Li in *CTS* 117, p. 3403. The text of the memorial, entitled *Ch'ing t'ing kuo-chi hsing-hsiang tsou* 請停國忌行香奏, is included in *CTW* 718, pp. 16b–17a.

The suppression of Buddhism under the reign of Wu-tsung (840–846)

1 *NGJK*: 840, II, 22.
2 Hsien-tsung and Mu-tsung are both said to have taken elixirs. See *CTS* 15, p. 471 and 16, p. 504.
3 *CTS* 18A, p. 585.
4 *NGJK*: 884, III. *FTLT* 16, p. 636a likewise notes that 'Wu-tsung disliked Buddhism since his youth.'
5 *TFYK* 54, pp. 22a–b; *CTS* 18A, p. 584; *THY* 50, p. 868. *CTS* states that the suspension of government functions was limited to a single day. *TFYK* gives the fifteenth day of the third month as Lao-tzu's birthday; *CTS* and *THY* both give the fifteenth day of the second month, which is the usual date for observances in Taoist temples (see Yoshioka Yoshitoyo 吉岡義豊, *Dōkyō no kenkyū* [Kyoto, 1952], pp. 314 and 324). It should be noted that Buddhists regard the latter date as the day on which the Buddha died (see *Ta po-nieh-p'an ching* 大般涅槃經 1, in *TD* 12, p. 365c).
6 *CTS* 18A, pp. 585–6 states simply that the ceremony was held in the autumn of 840. The precise month is given in the [*Wu-tsung*] *Shih-lu*, quoted in *TCTC k'ao-i* (*TCTC* 246, p. 7952) and also in *CKL* 3, p. 837c. *TCTC* follows *THY* 50, p. 868, in placing the event in the sixth month of 841, which is specifically rejected in Hu's commentary.
7 *Wei-shu* 114, p. 3053.
8 The number eighty-one is particularly significant in Taoism both as a multiple of nine (*chiu-chiu* 九九), which figures prominently in Chinese numerology, and as a reference to the *Tao-te ching*, which contains eighty-one chapters. On the importance of this number to Taoists see Fukui Kōjun 福井康順, *Dōkyō no kisoteki kenkyū* (Tokyo, 1952), pp. 310–20.
9 For a description of the altar set up for the *chin-lu* ritual see Henri Maspero, *Le Taoïsme* (Paris, 1950), pp. 161–2. On the use of *chin-lu* as an imperial rite see Ōfuchi Ninji 大淵忍爾, *Dōkyōshi no kenkyū* (Okayama, 1964), pp. 517–18, and Kubo Noritada 窪德忠, *Chūgoku no shūkyō kaikaku* (Tokyo, 1967) pp. 36 and 202.

10 CKL 3, p. 837c. CTS 18A (p. 586), THY 50 (p. 868), and TCTC 246 (p. 7952) characterize the platform as a *chiu t'ien t'an* 九天壇, 'a platform for [sacrificing to] the nine divisions of Heaven.' For the concept of *chiu t'ien* in Taoism see Ōfuchi, p. 360. FTLT 16, p. 636a describes the Mysterious Platform as one used for making offerings to the Nine Immortals (*chiu hsien* 九仙).
11 TCTC, p. 7952. The [*Wu-tsung*] *Shih-lu* adds that Wang Che unsuccessfully petitioned the Emperor not to allow candidates who passed the *chin-shih* or *ming-ching* 明經 examinations to be ordained as Taoist priests. Wang apparently feared that Wu-tsung's partiality toward Taoism would induce many opportunistic degree holders to seek a Taoist ordination to curry favor with the throne.
12 NGJK: 841, I, 4. The mass was probably performed at the request of Wen-tsung's mother, Empress Dowager Hsiao 蕭太后, who two months earlier had been moved into the Hsing-ch'ing Palace 興慶宮 and granted the honorific title Empress Dowager Chi-ch'ing 積慶太后 (TCTC 246, p. 7947). The only other vaguely pro-Buddhist act by Wu-tsung was his willingness in the ninth month of 840 to grant permission to his grandmother to have a monastery established in Ch'ang-an in memory of her mother (see NGJK 840, IX, 6 and NGJKK, vol. 3, pp. 294–5).
13 HTS 8, p. 240; NGJK: 841, I, 7.
14 NGJK: 841, I, 9. For a useful survey of the role of 'popular lectures' in Chinese Buddhism see Kenneth K.S. Ch'en, *The Chinese Transformation of Buddhism*, pp. 240–55. Wu-tsung formally terminated the practice of 'popular lectures' in 843 (see NGJK: 844, x).
15 Hu San-hsing noted that those monks who specialized in 'popular lectures,' unlike regular monks, were unable to discuss abstract philosophical questions, but rather sought to entertain their audiences with interesting stories in the hope of attracting large donations (commentary for 825, IV, *chi mao* 己卯 day [TCTC, p. 7850], on which Ching-tsung is reported to have visited the Hsing-fu ssu 興福寺 to listen to a 'popular lecture' by the monk Wen-hsü 文溆, a master of the art). 'Popular lectures' were often held for the specific purpose of raising funds for a worthy project. Ennin, for example, records in his diary (839, I, 6–7) that officials especially authorized monks to lecture at the Hsiao-kan ssu 孝感寺 in order to collect money for the repair of a monastery building. A total of 10,000 strings of cash was said to have been contributed on that occasion.
16 According to an edict issued in 784, 'popular lectures' were to be given only during the three taboo months (*san chai-yüeh* 三齋月) (see below) and were limited to one Buddhist monastery and one Taoist temple in each area under the jurisdiction of a civil or military governor (*kuan-ch'a shih chieh-tu chou* 觀察使節度州); see TFYK 52, p. 8a. The reason given for the restriction was the fear that the crowds that gathered at such lectures might cause disturbances.
17 NGJK: 841, I, 9.
18 The first such debate occurred in 624, only six years after the establishment of the T'ang, when Emperor Kao-tsu ordered the Confucian scholar Hsü Wen-yüan 徐文遠 to lecture on the *Classic of Filial Piety* (*Hsiao ching* 孝經), the Buddhist monk Hui-ch'eng 惠乘 to lecture on the *Prajñāpāramitā*

sūtra (*Po-jo ching* 波若經), and the Taoist priest Liu Chin-hsi 劉進喜 to lecture on the *Lao-tzu*. Lu Te-ming 陸德明, a scholar attached to the Imperial College (T'ai-hsüeh 太學), put critical questions to each of the participants, much to the delight of Kao-tsu, who rewarded him with fifty bolts of silk (biographies of Lu Te-ming in *CTS* 189A, p. 4945 and *HTS* 198, p. 5640; *FTTC* 39, p. 362b; *CKFL* 4, pp. 381a–382b, which dates the debate 625). For a survey of these debates throughout the T'ang see Lo Hsiang-lin 羅香林, 'T'ang-tai san-chiao chiang-lun k'ao' 唐代三教講論考 in his *T'ang-tai wen-hua shih* 唐代文化史 (Taipei, 1968), pp. 159–76.

19 *SSL* 3, p. 248b, and *FTTC* 42, p. 384c. Despite his pro-Buddhist sentiments Po Chü-i did not hesitate to write a highly critical essay on Buddhism in 806 in order to pass the palace examination. For a partial translation see Kenneth Ch'en *The Chinese Transformation of Buddhism*, pp. 191–2. An illuminating analysis of the 'birthday debate' of 827 will be found in Arthur Waley, *The Life and Times of Po Chü-i*, pp. 169–71.

20 *NGJK*: 841, VI, 11.

21 *SSL*, pp. 248c–249a. The practice of bestowing purple robes on monks is said to have originated with Empress Wu who presented robes of this color to the ten monks who forged the texts that legitimized her reign. The idea of granting a monk a purple robe as a mark of distinction, unknown in India, was patterned after the traditional Chinese practice of presenting high ranking officials with a gold seal attached to a purple cord (*tzu-shou chin-chang* 紫綬金章). See *SSL*, p. 248c.

22 In the imperial birthday debates of 842 and 843 the Buddhist participants were again denied the purple robe (see the entries in *NGJK* for these dates).

23 *CTS* 18A, p. 587. *TCTC* 246, p. 7952 states that Wu-tsung personally received the talismans, an act signifying his formal initiation into Taoism.

24 *NGJK*: 842, III, 3. The term *pao-wai*, literally 'outside of the *pao*,' probably refers to those monks who were not affiliated with a *pao*, i.e. a group of approximately five persons who shared collective responsibility for the actions of any member of the group. See *NGJKK*, vol. 3, p. 423.

25 Ennin (*NGJK*: 842, III, 3) calls him simply Li Tsai-hsiang 李宰相, 'Chief Minister Li,' which is ambiguous since there were two chief ministers at this time surnamed Li: Li Te-yü and Li Shen 李紳. While the latter evidently was not well disposed toward Buddhism (note Ennin's accusation in *NGJK*: 842, x, 9 that he instigated the murder of the monk Hsüan-hsüan 眩玄), Li Te-yü actively argued for its total suppression and openly lauded Wu-tsung for this (see below). Li Te-yü's writings contain frequent attacks on Buddhism from a Confucian standpoint: it is a barbarian religion; it ignores fundamental social relationships; it is a drain on the economy, etc. (See, for example, his *Wu-tsung kai-ming kao t'ien-ti wen* 武宗改名告天地文 in *CTW* 711, p. 18b and his *Ch'i-chi hsi-yüeh wen* 祈祭西嶽文 in *CTW* 711, p. 19b. The most thorough study of the suppression of Buddhism is in Ono Katsutoshi's superb commentary on Ennin's diary, *Nittō guhō junrei kōki no kenkyū*, 4 vols. (Tokyo, 1964–9), to which I am much indebted.

26 Biography of Li Te-yü in *CTS* 174, p. 4511; also see *CTS* 16, p. 503. It should be noted that the 'shrines' and 'cloisters' were not exclusively Buddhist.

27 *CTS*, p. 4516. The text of the letter, entitled *Po-chou sheng-shui chuang* 亳州

聖水狀, is included in *CTW* 706, p. 1a–b.
28 See the document from the office of the commissioner of good works reproduced in full in *NGJK*: 842, III, 12.
29 *NGJK*: 842, V, 29.
30 There is some confusion regarding the precise date. Ennin provides a summary of the decree, which he says, in an entry for 842, X, 13, was issued on the ninth day of the tenth month. The latter portion of the entry, however, contains a reference to a decree for a purge issued on the 'seventh day of the tenth month of the preceding year,' which would be 841. As Ono has shown (*NGJKK*, vol. 3, p. 469), this portion of the entry properly belongs to the events described under 843, I, 17. Hence the words 'preceding year' point to 842, not 841. The discrepancy between the 'seventh' and 'ninth' days is probably the result of a copyist's error, since the characters for 'seven' and 'nine' bear a close resemblance to each other.
31 *NGJK*: 842, X, 13.
32 *NGJK*: 843, I, 18.
33 A number of important Buddhist texts specifically prohibit individual monks or nuns from acquiring slaves or accepting them as 'donations' from lay patrons (see for example the *Fo i-chiao ching* 佛遺教經, in *TD* 12, p. 1110c and Tao-hsüan's definitive commentary on the *Vinaya* entitled *Ssu-fen lü hsing-shih ch'ao* 四分律行事鈔 6, in *TD* 40, p. 70a–b). The practice, nevertheless, was widespread, which prompted the censor (*shih-yü-shih* 侍御史) Ch'eng Shu-ch'ing 鄭叔清 to urge Emperor Su-tsung in 757 to deny monks the right to own slaves, land, or other property (see his memorial entitled *Yü-chüeh t'iao-ko tsou* 裛爵條格奏 in *CTW* 432, p. 6a; for the date, see *T'ung-tien* 11, p. 61c).
34 Summary of the decree in *NGJK*: 842, X, 13.
35 The ordination of slaves was generally forbidden in India (see I.B. Horner, trans. *Book of the Discipline*, Part 4 (London, 1951), p. 120.
36 *NGJK*: 843, I, 17.
37 *NGJK*: 843, II, 1.
38 *FTTC* 39, p. 370a, which calls Manichaeism 'the false doctrine of the *Scripture of the Two Principles*' (*Erh-tsung-ching wei-chiao* 二宗經偽教), the 'two principles' referring to the key Manichaean concepts of light and darkness.
39 *T'ung-tien* 40, p. 229c.
40 *Tōyō rekishi daijiten*, vol. 8, p. 86a–b; ibid., vol. 9, p. 86c; David Bivar, 'Sasanians and Turks in Central Asia', in Gavin Hambly, ed. *Central Asia* (London, 1969), pp. 60–1.
41 *T'ang-shu hui-yao* 唐書會要 19, quoted in Hu San-hsing's commentary for the entry for 806, XI in *TCTC* 237, p. 7638.
42 *SSL* 3, p. 253c. Manichaean temples in China all bore the designation Ta kuang-ming ssu 大光明寺, 'Temples of Great Light', in honor of their chief deity Ch'ing-ching Kuang-ming Shih-chieh Ming-tsun 清淨光明世界明尊, 'the Brilliant Divinity of the World of Purity and Light.'
43 *FTTC* 41, p. 378c.
44 See, for example, the description of the Uighurs in *HTS* 217A, p. 6126, which links the annual visit to Ch'ang-an by Manichaean priests with the

illicit trade in the western market of the city conducted by the Uighur merchants 'with their leather bags,' presumably filled with smuggled contraband.

45 See his *Tz'u Hui-hu k'o-han shu-i* 賜回鶻可汗書意, in *CTW* 699, pp. 18b–19b. In this document Li reminded the *qaghan* that Manichaeism, which had been banned in China before the T'ien-pao era (742–56), was tolerated subsequently only as a concession to the Uighurs.

46 The text of the edict is given in *CTS* 18A, p. 594 and in somewhat fuller form in the *T'ang ta chao-ling chi* 130, p. 707, which places it in the first month of 843. The precise meaning of *hsiu kung-te Hui-hu*, which I translate as 'Uighur priests' is unclear. The term *hsiu kung-te* normally signifies one who undertakes religious acts such as the construction of temples or the making of images and hence could apply either to clerics or laymen. In the present case it would appear to refer only to the former, since the edict speaks of their laicization (*le kuan-tai* 勒冠帶).

47 The reference to the burning of Manichaean scriptures and holy objects (*hsiang* 象) is found only in *HTS* 217B, p. 6133.

48 *NGJK*: 843, IV. *SSL*, p. 253c and *FTTC* 42, p. 385c, which also mention the edict that ordered the closing of all Manichaean temples, report that seventy (seventy-two in *SSL*) Manichaean priestesses were killed in Ch'ang-an alone. The resettlement of the Uighurs in the countryside, according to both sources, turned out to be a death march, with more than half of the participants dying en route.

49 *SSL* 2, pp. 243c–244a; *FTTC* 42, p. 385c.

50 Biography of Hsüan-ch'ang in *SKSC* 17, p. 818a–b.

51 *NGJK*: 843, VI, 3; *TCTC* 247, p. 7985. Ennin (*NGJK*: 845, V, 14) characterized Yang as a man who lacked religious faith (*wu tao-hsin* 無道心).

52 *TCTC*, p. 7983, states that although Wu-tsung went through the outward motions of showing respect for Ch'iu, he actually despised him, a fact of which Ch'iu was well aware. Gradually isolated, Ch'iu sought to preserve his wealth by seeking voluntary retirement in the sixth month of 843, pleading poor health. He in fact died later the same month. *CTS* 18A, p. 600 reports that the year after his death an edict was issued stripping him posthumously of his rank and decreeing confiscation of his property on the pretext that weapons had been discovered in his house. Ennin (*NGJK*: 844, IX) repeats what was probably a current rumor in Ch'ang-an, i.e. that the wealth of the Ch'iu family in gold, silver, ivory, precious stones, and cash was so vast that it was not possible to remove it all from Ch'iu's mansion within the span of a month even though thirty carts were dispatched daily to carry away the treasure.

53 *NGJK*: 843, VI, 13, which also provides a summary of the edict issued on this occasion.

54 The incident is recounted in *NGJK*: 843, IX, 13.

55 It is not clear precisely how this decree differed from the one issued in the third month of 842. The decree of 843 specifies that unregistered monks are to be defrocked (*huan-su* 還俗), whereas the decree of 842 speaks only of their expulsion (*fa-ch'ien* 發遣) from monasteries, which is technically not

Notes to pages 122–124

the same as laicization, since the latter signifies a change in one's legal status.
56 *CTS* 18A, p. 599. Ennin (*NGJK*: 844, III) attributes the decree specifically to a memorial from these two men. *THY* 41, p. 733, which erroneously places the decree in the fourth month, probably because of a copyist's error due to the similarity between the characters *cheng* 正 and 四 *ssu*, states simply that the memorial originated with the Secretariat-Chancellery. The full text of the decree, entitled *Ch'u chai-yüeh tuan-t'u ch'ih* 除齋月斷屠勅, is given in *CTW* 77, p. 1a. For the dubious scriptural basis of the three taboo months see above, p. 189, n. 25.
57 *LTSP* 12, p. 108a.
58 *THY* 41, p. 731. The ten taboo days of each month on which slaughter was forbidden were the 1st, 8th, 14th, 15th, 18th, 23rd, 24th, 28th, 29th and 30th. Although generally said to be of Indian Buddhist origin – the dubious *Ti-tsang p'u-sa pen-yüan ching* 地藏菩薩本願經 is cited as the source – the concept of ten taboo days in each month appears to have developed in China. The relevant passage in this sūtra appears in fasc. 1, *TD* 13, p. 783b–c.
59 Niida Noboru 仁井田陞, *Tōrei shūi* 唐令拾遺 (Tokyo, 1933), p. 847.
60 *TFYK* 53, pp. 15b–16a. The *Wei-shu* 114, p. 3055 mentions the seventh day of the first month, the seventh day of the seventh month, and the fifteenth day of the tenth month as sacred to the Taoists.
61 *THY*, p. 733.
62 *Ch'u chai-yüeh tuan-t'u ch'ih* in *CTW* 77, p. 1a.
63 *NGJK*: 844, III.
64 *CTS* 18A, p. 600. Chao was popularly referred to by the simple designation *Tao-shih-chang* 道士長, 'Chief of the Taoist Priests' (see, for example, *NGJK* 845, I, 3).
65 *TCTC* 247, p. 8000. Li Te-yü's intense distrust of Taoist priests like Chao became well known while he was serving as the civil governor of Che-hsi. In 826 Emperor Ching-tsung was persuaded by Chao and others to conduct a search for an 'unusual man' (*i-jen* 異人) who could teach the secret of immortality. Eventually a report reached the throne that a hermit reputed to be several hundred years old had been discovered in Che-hsi. The Emperor dispatched a ranking official to escort the hermit back to the Palace and instructed Li to provide the transportation. Li availed himself of the occasion to warn Ching-tsung of the dangers of following the advice of Taoist priests to search for 'unusual men' or to imbibe their elixirs in the hope of attaining immortality. See the biography of Li Te-yü in *CTS* 174, p. 4517. For Li's warning to Ching-tsung see his *Chien Ching-tsung sou-fang tao-shih shu* 諫敬宗搜訪道士疏, in *CTW* 701, pp. 1b–2b. Li's hostility toward alchemists can be gleaned from his *Fang-shih lun* 方士論, in *CTW* 709, pp. 22b–23b.
66 *CTS* 18A, p. 603, which reports Li's protest in an entry for the first month of 845.
67 *CTS*, p. 600.
68 See the 'Monograph on the Five Elements' (*Wu-hsing chih*) in *HTS* 35, p. 913. The relationship between the number eighteen and the surname Li

derives from a pun on the character used to write the surname. The character consists of three elements, *shih* (ten), *pa* (eight), and *tzu* (child), which when read in sequence mean eighteen children, hence eighteenth generation.

69 *NGJK*: 844, III.
70 *KHMC* 6, p. 124a; *KHMC* 8, p. 136a; *CKFL* 2, p. 372a. For the use of apocryphal texts to justify the suppression of Buddhism under the Northern Chou see Nomura Yōshō 野村耀昌, *Shū-Bu hōnan no kenkyū* 周武法難の研究 (Tokyo, 1968), pp. 149–52 and Tsukamoto Zenryū, 'Hokushū no haibutsu' 北周の廃仏, pp. 467–76, published as an appendix to his *Gisho Shakurōshi no kenkyū* 魏書釋老志の研究 (Kyoto, 1961), in which he questions whether Wu-ti's suppression of Buddhism in 574 was in fact influenced by apocryphal texts as is stated in Buddhist sources.
71 For a summary of the decrees see *NGJK*: 844, III.
72 At least four monasteries in Ch'ang-an – the Ch'ung-sheng ssu 崇聖寺, the Chuang-yen ssu 莊嚴寺, the Chien-fu ssu 薦福寺, and the Hsing-fu ssu 興福寺 – claimed to possess authentic tooth-relics from the body of the Buddha. See *NGJKK*, vol. 3, p. 364 for the provenance of these relics.
73 Wu-tsung's particular aversion to this monastery may be related to the foreign origins of its founder. It was built during the Lung-shuo 龍朔 period (661–3) by the Central Asian thaumaturge Seng-ch'ieh 僧伽, who after his death in 710 was widely venerated as a bestower of good fortune. Shrines dedicated to him, known as Seng-ch'ieh Ho-shang t'ang 僧伽和尚堂 or, more simply, Ssu-chou t'a 泗州塔, sprung up in various parts of China during the T'ang and Sung dynasties. For an account of Seng-ch'ieh in popular Chinese legend see Henry Doré, *Researches into Chinese Superstitions*, English translation by M. Kennelly, vol. 7 (Shanghai, 1922), pp. 447–56.
74 Ennin (*NGJK*: 844, III) reports that services had been conducted day and night at the Palace Chapel by three alternating groups of seven monks who were selected from monasteries in Ch'ang-an. The closing of the Palace Chapel at this time is also mentioned in *SSL* 3, p. 248b.
75 *NGJK*: 844, VII, 15.
76 *NGJK*: 844, VII, 15.
77 The precise meaning of *chai-t'ang* is not clear. The word normally refers to the refectory in a large monastery (see *FTTC* 45, p. 412c). Here it may signify a small village chapel at which one or two monks are maintained.
78 Ennin appears to be using a unit of Japanese measurement here. One *ken* in the Heian period was approximately 10 feet, according to the *Nihon kokugo daijiten*, vol. 7 (Tokyo, 1974), p. 267c. Reischauer states that one *ken* was equivalent to six feet (*Ennin's Diary*, p. 347, fn. 1331).
79 Tu Mu 杜牧 reported that before the suppression entered its final phase in 845 forty thousand chapels, hermitages, and other small places of worship situated in villages or mountains were dismantled, with close to 100,000 of their clergy laicized. See his *Hang-chou hsin-tsao nan-t'ing tzu chi* 杭州新造南亭子記 in his collected works entitled *Fan-ch'uan wen-chi* 樊川文集 (Ssu-pu ts'ung-k'an edn) 10, p. 91b.
80 *Tsun-sheng* is an abbreviation of *Fo-ting tsun-sheng t'o-lo-ni* 佛頂尊勝陀羅

尼 (Uṣṇīṣa-vijaya-dhāraṇī), which in T'ang times was a widely used incantation that was believed to have an extraordinary range of miraculous powers, including the ability to transform one into a Taoist immortal. For an account of some of the miracles associated with this incantation see the T'ang work *Chia-chü ling-yen Fo-ting tsun-sheng t'o-lo-ni chi* 加句靈驗佛頂尊勝陀羅尼記 in *ZZK*, ser. 2, case 9, vol. 4, pp. 334b–337a.

81 As we have seen, in the year 727 Hsüan-tsung ordered the dismantlement of all village chapels and small shrines. The memorial sent to Wen-tsung in 830 from the Department of Sacrifices similarly proposed ending the autonomy of village chapels, shrines, monastery hostels, and hermitages on private estates. In his edict of 835 Wen-tsung placed a ban on any new construction of buildings in these categories as well as on monasteries in general.

82 *NGJK*: 844, VIII. Ennin identifies Kuo T'ai-hou as an empress of Wen-tsung, which is not confirmed by *CTS*, *HTS*, or *THY*. Hsien-tsung had an empress with this surname, but she died in 848 (*THY* 3, p. 30).

83 *NGJK*: 844, IX.

84 *NGJK*: 844, IX. Chao's memorial is alluded to in *CTS* 18A, p. 600.

85 *NGJK*: 844, X. *CTS* 18A, p. 603 and *TCTC* 248, p. 8013 both state that the order to build the terrace was issued in the first month of 845. Tall 'terraces' or towers on which the ruler could come into direct contact with immortals (*hsien*) had been erected periodically, the earliest ones dating back at least to the second century B.C. The *Feng-shan shu* 封禪書 in *Shih chi* 28, pp. 1400–2 mentions several such terraces built by the Han emperor Wu-ti, including one called the Shen-ming t'ai 神明臺, which is said to have reached a height of almost 400 feet.

86 *NGJK*: 844, X.

87 The message, entitled *Chia tsun-hao hou chiao-t'ien she-wen* 加尊號後郊天赦文, is included in *CTW* 78, p. 16a-b. For the date see the text of the message (p. 10b) and *TCTC* 248, p. 8013.

88 The following account is based on *NGJK*: 845, III, 3 ff.

89 The original has *li ch'i yüeh-che ai yü hsien-tao*, which Reischauer translates '... *li* and *ch'i* are in excess, blocking the way of the immortal' (*Ennin's Diary*, p. 357). Reischauer arrives at this translation by taking the character *li* (village) that occurs in the diary to be an error for *li* ('noumenon,' as opposed to *ch'i*, 'phenomenon'; Reischauer's note 1368). My interpretation follows Ono's suggestion that the character *li* (village) in the original should be emended to *hc* (black) which is similar in form (*NGJKK*, vol 4, p. 126). Cf. the entry for 845, IX discussed below, where Ennin specifically refers to the Taoist fear that an abundance of black (= Buddhism) would overwhelm yellow (= Taoism) causing it to disappear.

90 *NGJK*: 845, IV-V.

91 *NGJK*: 845, III, 3. Regarding the disposition of monastery slaves, Tu Mu wrote that they were each granted one hundred *mou* of land and entered into the registers as farmers (*Hang-chou hsin-tsao nan-t'ing tzu chi*, p. 91b). According to *HTS* 52, p. 1361, able-bodied monastery dependents (*ssu-chia* 寺家) and both male and female slaves were each provided with ten *mou* of middle or inferior grade land that had been confiscated from monastic

estates. Tu estimated that the number of monastery dependents equalled that of the clergy. The unlikelihood of female slaves and dependents receiving land from the state is discussed in D.C. Twitchett, 'The Monasteries and China's Economy in Medieval Times,' *Bulletin of the School of Oriental and African Studies*, 19.3 (1957) 547–8.

92 *THY* 86, p. 1572.
93 For the evolution of Buddhist almshouses in China see Michihata Ryōshū, *Tōdai Bukkyōshi no kenkyū*, pp. 388–406, and Kenneth Ch'en, *The Chinese Transformation of Buddhism*, pp. 295–300.
94 See the memorial dated 717 by Sung Ching 宋璟 in *THY* 49, p. 863.
95 The memorial by Sung Ching and Su T'ing 蘇頲, as quoted by Li Te-yü in his *Lun liang-ching chi chu-tao pei-t'ien chuang* 論兩京及諸道悲田狀 in *CTS* 704, pp. 3b–4a.
96 *TCTC* 214, p. 6809; Li Te-yü, pp. 3b–4a.
97 Hu San-hsing, commenting on the prohibition against beggars in Ch'ang-an in 734, noted that 'at the time "sick wards" were attached to all monasteries' (*TCTC*, p. 6809).
98 Li Te-yü observed in his memorial (p. 4a): 'Since all monks and nuns throughout the provinces have now been laicized, there are no longer any people to supervise the almshouses. I cannot but fear that the sick and the poor, having no one to turn to, will experience still greater hardships.'
99 Memorial of Li Te-yü in *CTW* 704, p. 4a; *HTS* 52, p. 1361; *CTS* 18A, p. 607; *CTW* 77, p. 2b.
100 *NGJK*: 845, IV–V.
101 *NGJK*: 845, VI, 23.
102 Although economic motives were an important factor in the suppression of Buddhism, it should not be forgotten that religious bias was at least of equal significance, as is shown by the ban on scriptures, holy paintings, and other devotional articles that had little or no economic value. While none of the decrees that survive in Chinese compendia mention a ban on scriptures as such, Ennin makes it clear that it was extremely perilous to move about with scriptures or religious objects. He reports (*NGJK*: 845, IV–V) that since the government intended to 'eliminate Buddhism' (*tuan Fo-chiao* 斷佛教), anyone apprehended with scriptures in his possession might be charged with disobedience to an imperial decree, which carried the death penalty. So great was Ennin's fear that after reaching Ch'u-chou 楚州 in the seventh month of 845, he entrusted the various Buddhist texts, maṇḍalas, and other religious articles that he was hoping to take back to Japan to a Korean interpreter who could use his official status to smuggle them through the prefectural checkpoints. In the first month of 846 an edict was finally issued decreeing the death penalty for anyone who kept Buddhist sūtras, altar decorations, robes, or monks' utensils (*NGJK*: 846, I, 9).
103 *CTS* 18A, pp. 604–5; *TCTC* 248, pp. 8015–16; [*Wu-tsung*] *Shih-lu*, quoted in *TCTC k'ao-i* (*TCTC*, p. 8016).
104 For a list of the provinces see the [*Wu-tsung*] *Shih-lu* in *TCTC*, p. 8016. Tu Mu, however, states that one monastery was allowed for each of thirty-four provinces (*Hang-chou hsin-tsao nan-t'ing tzu chi*, p. 91b).
105 Tu Mu (p. 91b). The memorial from the Secretariat-Chancellery originally

Notes to pages 133–134

proposed that Ch'ang-an and Lo-yang each be allowed twenty monasteries, and the large provincial commands (*ta fan-chen* 大藩鎮) each one monastery (*Shih-lu* in *TCTC*, p. 8016). According to *CTS*, the Secretariat-Chancellery proposed that each 'higher prefecture' (*shang-chou* 上州) should be permitted one monastery, whereas 'lower prefectures' (*hsia-chou* 下州) should not be allowed any monasteries.

106 *TCTC*, p. 8018 states that the number of monks was further reduced in the eighth month. Those provinces that had been allotted twenty monks would have that number cut by half; provinces with ten monks were to be allowed only seven; provinces with five monks would not be permitted to retain any monks; the city of Lo-yang was to reduce the number of its clergy from 120 to twenty monks.

107 *TCTC*, p. 8016.

108 *CTS* 18A, p. 605; *THY* 49, p. 861. Ennin mentions this order to melt down metal images in an entry for the twenty-eighth day of the sixth month.

109 *NGJK*: 845, VIII, 16, as translated by Edwin Reischauer, *Ennin's Diary*, p. 382.

110 The text of the order, entitled *Hui Fo-ssu le seng-ni huan-su ch'ih* 毀佛寺勒僧尼還俗勅, is included in *CTW* 76, pp. 9b–10b; *T'ang ta chao-ling chi* 113, pp. 591–2; *CTS* 18A, pp. 605–6; *THY* 47, pp. 840–1. A free – and in part inaccurate – English translation appears in Edwin Reischauer, *Ennin's Travels in T'ang China*, pp. 225–7.

111 Virtually identical figures are given in *CTS*, p. 604 (in an entry for the fourth month of 845); *HTS* 52, p. 1361; *TCTC*, p. 8015 (in an entry for the fifth month); and *FTTC* 42, p. 386a. The figure of 260,500 defrocked monks and nuns is somewhat puzzling in view of the statements in *FTTC* and *SSL* cited earlier that 700,000 ordination certificates were issued by the Department of Sacrifices in 830. Some scholars have sought to explain the discrepancy by suggesting that the 700,000 figure is an exaggeration, since it does not occur in secular sources. There need not necessarily be a contradiction between these two figures, however, if one interprets the 260,500 figure as referring only to those monks and nuns laicized in response to Wu-tsung's sweeping edict against the clergy issued in the third month of 845. As we have noted, the defrocking of the clergy began in 842. Speaking of the period prior to 845, Tu Mu mentions the laicization by Wu-tsung of 100,000 monks and nuns who had been attached to mountain cloisters and village chapels. Ennin likewise frequently refers to monks and nuns who 'voluntarily' left the order before the suppression of 845 although they were not yet subject to expulsion. It is likely, therefore, that by 845 the Buddhist clergy had dwindled to a figure approaching the 260,500 mentioned in the edict. We also know (see below) that some monks, rather than submit to laicization, fled to areas under the control of military officers who were deemed sympathetic to the Buddhist faith. It might also be noted here that the figure given for the amount of land confiscated from the Buddhist church at this time should be read rhetorically rather than literally (see Denis Twitchett, 'Monastic Estates in T'ang China,' *Asia Major*, New Series, 5.2 (1956), pp. 141–42.

112 *HTS* 48, p. 1253 states that the Buddhist clergy was placed under the

jurisdiction of the Office for Overseeing Foreign Visitors in 842, which is evidently incorrect, since an edict was issued as late as the fourth month of 845 directing the Department of Sacrifices to determine the number of monasteries and size of the clergy (*CTS* 18A, p. 604). In fact the plan to remove the clergy from the jurisdiction of the Department of Sacrifices originated with the Secretariat-Chancellery and was presented to the Emperor in the seventh month of 845 along with a suggestion that the Court for State Ceremonials (Hung-lu ssu) be made responsible for Buddhist affairs (*CTS* 18A, p. 605). After some discussion it was decided that it would be inappropriate to allow either the Department of Sacrifices or the Court for State Ceremonials to be concerned with Buddhism, which, because of its foreign provenance, should be dealt with by those officials who handled the affairs of tributary countries (*THY* 49, p. 860 and *SSL* 2, p. 245c).

113 See his memorial entitled *Ho fei-hui chu-ssu te-yin piao* 賀廢毀諸寺德音表 in *CTW* 700, pp. 21a–22b.
114 There is no evidence to suggest that Hsiao Yü prevented Kao-tsu from carrying out a suppression of Buddhism, although, as we have already noted, his decision to return to lay life after having retired to a monastery provoked T'ai-tsung into a diatribe against Buddhism.
115 *TCTC* 248, pp. 8017 and 8020.
116 *NGJK*: 845, XI, 3.
117 *TCTC* 248, pp. 8018–19.
118 *NGJK*: 845, IX.
119 Ibid.
120 See his letter entitled *Ch'ing Huai-nan teng wu-tao chih yu-i-ch'uan chuang* 請淮南等五道置遊奕船狀 in *CTW* 704, pp. 2b–3b.
121 *TCTC*, p. 8020 notes in an entry for this month that Wu-tsung was becoming increasingly short-tempered as a result of the elixirs (*chin-tan* 金丹) that he was then taking.
122 This edict and the three following ones are mentioned in *NGJK*: 845, IX.
123 It will be remembered that a warning against the predominance of the color black was given to Wu-tsung by Taoist priests in the third month of 845.
124 Ennin (*NGJK*: 845, IX) claims that Wu-tsung was duped by Taoist priests into issuing this edict. Although secular sources make no mention of cannibalism by Wu-tsung, Ennin's report here cannot be totally ignored, since it was believed in T'ang times that the eating of human flesh could cure serious illnesses, an idea attributed to the T'ang physician, Ch'en Ts'ang-ch'i 陳藏器 (see *HTS* 195, p. 5577). *HTS* (biography of Yang Yü-ch'ing 楊虞卿 175, p. 5249) reports that in 835 a rumor was circulating in Ch'ang-an that Wen-tsung was being given elixirs made from the livers of young children.
125 *TCTC* 248, p. 8021.
126 Biography of Lady Wang in *HTS* 77, p. 3509.
127 *TCTC*, pp. 8021.
128 Commentary of Hu San-hsing in *TCTC* 248, p. 8022; see also *CTS* 18A, p. 610.
129 *FTTC* 42, p. 386a and collation note 5; *CTS*, p. 610. Ennin, who learned of

Wu-tsung's death on the fifteenth day of the fourth month, likewise reported that when the Emperor died, his body was covered with festering sores.

The restoration of Buddhism under the reign of Hsuen-tsung (846–859)

1 Although written with different characters, the posthumous names of this emperor and his predecessor, Hsüan-tsung, have the same romanization. To distinguish between them, I have used the altered romanization Hsuen-tsung when referring to the emperor discussed in this chapter.
2 *TCTC* 248, p. 8022; Wei Chao-tu 韋昭度, *Hsü Huang-wang pao-yün lu*, 續皇王寶雲錄 quoted in *K'ao-i* in *TCTC*, p. 8022.
3 The earliest reference to this story occurs in the *Chung-ch'ao ku-shih* 中朝故事 written by Yü-ch'ih Wo 尉遲偓 shortly after the collapse of the T'ang (*Sui-an Hsü-shih ts'ung-shu* 隨盦徐氏叢書 edn, pp. 1a–2b). The story is amplified in Buddhist sources, which make Prince Kuang a disciple of several eminent Ch'an masters. See for example *FTTC* 42, pp. 387a–b and 388c.
4 See his edict entitled *Ch'ung-chien Tsung-ch'ih ssu ch'ih* 重建總持寺勅 (*CTW* 81, p. 12a) praising the *Chuang-yen ssu*, which he says he visited before ascending the throne. Hsuen-tsung claimed that he was so impressed by the *Chuang-yen ssu* that he decided to order the reconstruction of its sister-temple, the Tsung-ch'ih ssu, which was devastated during the suppression.
5 *THY* 49, p. 860; *TCTC* 248, p. 8024; *HTS* 48, p. 1253. The subordinate clerical office of recorder of monks (*seng-lu*) was allowed to lapse under the reign of Wu-tsung, the last reference to it occurring in the year 843 (see *SSL* 2, p. 243c). It was filled again in 849 with the appointment of the monk Ling-yen 靈晏 as recorder of monks for both halves of Ch'ang-an (*FTTC* 42, p. 387a). The office, occasionally subdivided into recorders for each of the two 'halves' of Ch'ang-an, was occupied by a succession of monks throughout the remaining years of the T'ang.
6 *FTTC*, p. 386b. *SSL* 2, p. 246a states that Yang was appointed commissioner for the left half of Ch'ang-an, not for 'both halves' as *FTTC* has it.
7 *FTTC*, p. 386b; *SSL*, p. 246a; *CTS* 18B, p. 615; *TCTC*, p. 8024. *CTS* erroneously lists the famed Taoist adept Liu Hsüan-ching 劉玄靖 as one of the priests executed at this time. Although Liu had ministered to Wu-tsung since 841, he wisely decided in the tenth month of 845 to decline the directorship of the College for Taoist Learning (Ch'ung-hsüan kuan 崇玄館) offered to him by the Emperor, who was by then consuming large doses of drugs, and to return to Heng-shan 衡山, perhaps to wait out the upheaval that he saw coming with the death of Wu-tsung (see *TCTC*, p. 8020). After the enthronement of Hsuen-tsung, Liu briefly reappeared at the court to persuade the new emperor to issue a ban on slaughter for a period of eight days in the tenth month, which was one of the Taoist holy months, and to present him with talismans (*THY* 50, p. 869; *TCTC*, p. 8028).
8 See the comments by the Buddhist historian Tsu-hsiu 祖琇 in *LFPT* 25, p. 338a–b.

9   *FTTC*, p. 386c.
10 *HTS* 8, p. 246. For the text of the amnesty, entitled *Chi-wei she-wen* 即位赦文, see *CTW* 82, pp. 2b–3a and *T'ang ta chao-ling chi* 3, pp. 13–14, which dates the amnesty the fifth day of the fifth month of 846, as does *CTS* 18B, p. 615 and *TCTC*, p. 8024. The latter source alone places the execution of the Taoist priests in the fourth month, i.e. before the declaration of the amnesty. All other sources say that the executions occurred sometime in the fifth month, most likely after the amnesty had been proclaimed.
11 The most complete version of the memorial appears in *THY* 48, pp. 853–4 under the incorrect date of the first month of 846. This error is probably attributable to the slip of a copyist, since the character *cheng* (first month) resembles the character *wu* (fifth month). The memorial in an abridged form is also included in *CTS* 18B, p. 615.
12 *NGJK*: 846, v, 22. The edict that Ennin refers to here does not survive in any Chinese compilation, but it is alluded to at the end of Hsuen-tsung's amnesty message issued on the third day of the first month of 848 (see below, p. 140).
13 *THY* 49, P. 862.
14 *SSL* 3, p. 248b. The custom of inviting Buddhist monks to the Palace to celebrate the emperor's birthday was formally abolished by Wu-tsung in the sixth month of 844 (*SSL*, p. 248b).
15 For the text of the edict, which is entitled *Fu fei-ssu ch'ih* 復廢寺勑, see *CTW* 81, p. 2b; *CTS* 18B, p. 617; and *THY* 49, p. 854.
16 *TCTC* 248, pp. 8029–30.
17 *FTTC* 42, p. 386c and the biography of Chih-hsüan in *SKSC* 6, p. 774b.
18 This title was created during the reign of Hsuen-tsung and was conferred for the first time on the monk Pien-chang 辯章 in recognition of his efforts in assisting in the reconstruction of abandoned monasteries (*SSL* 2, p. 244b). Since Chih-hsüan was granted the title in 847, Pien-chang probably received it during the preceding year.
19 For the text of the amnesty, entitled *Shou tsun-hao she-wen* 受尊號赦文, see *CTW* 82, pp. 14b–20a and *THY* 48, p. 854, which provides the precise date.
20 The biography of Chih-chün 智頵 (*SKSC* 27, p. 881b), which also mentions this edict, makes it clear that government funds were used to reopen the monasteries on Wu-t'ai shan and also that the limit of five monasteries was exceeded.
21 *FTTC* 42, p. 387a. As we have noted above, Tai-tsung issued a similar order in 789.
22 *SSL* 2, pp. 250c and 252b; *FTTC*, p. 387a. Special platforms were necessary for the reordinations, since certain offences committed by a laicized monk or nun would have automatically precluded readmission to the Order. Hence ordinary ordination platforms (*chieh-t'an* 戒壇) could not be used without doing violence to the traditions of the *Vinaya*.
23 *FTTC*, p. 387a.
24 See the comments of Tsan-ning in his biography of Chih-hsüan in *SKSC* 6, p. 744a.
25 *THY* 48, p. 854.
26 *SSL* 2, p. 242a; *THY* 23, p. 451.
27 Biography of Hsüan-ch'ang in *SKSC* 17, p. 818b.

28 Biography of Yu-yüan 有緣 in *SKSC* 12, p. 781c; biography of Ting-lan in *SKSC* 23, p. 856b. After Ting-lan's suicide Hsuen-tsung bestowed an honorary name on him and built a pagoda in his memory.
29 *LFPT* 26, p. 340b; *CTL* 9, p. 269a.
30 See Edwin G. Pulleyblank, 'Neo-Confucianism in T'ang Intellectual Life,' in Arthur F. Wright, ed. *The Confucian Persuasion* (Stanford, 1960), p. 113 and p. 334, n. 164.
31 The text of the memorial, entitled *Fu Fo-ssu piao* 復佛寺表, is included in *CTW* 794, pp. 6b–8b and *TCTC* 249, p. 8047.
32 *FTTC* 42, p. 387b.
33 *THY* 48, p. 854 and *TCTC* 249, p. 8048.
34 *TCTC* 249, p. 8048. For the text of the memorial see *THY* 48, pp. 854–5.
35 The text of this lengthy memorial, dated the twelfth month of 852, is included in *THY* 48, pp. 843–4. Summaries of it will be found in *TCTC* 249, p. 8052 and *FTTC* 42, p. 387b–c.
36 Formal approval was given in the eleventh month of 856. For a summary of the edict of assent see *TCTC* 249, p. 8061 and *FTTC*, p. 388b.
37 *LFPT* 26, p. 341a.
38 Biography of Hui-ling 慧靈 in *SKSC* 16, p. 807b. For the history of the relic see *KYL* 6, p. 536a–b.
39 *SSL* 2, p. 244a. For the text of the edict, entitled *Ch'ung-chien Tsung-ch'ih ssu ch'ih*, see *CTW* 81, p. 12a.
40 *TCTC* 249, p. 8065; *CTS* 18b, p. 640.
41 *TCTC* 248, p. 8024.
42 *TCTC* 249, p. 8069.
43 *FTTC* 42, p. 388b.

Buddhism in the declining years of the T'ang dynasty
1 See Tsan-ning's assessment of I-tsung in his biography of Seng-ch'e 僧徹 in *SKSC* 6, pp. 744c–745a.
2 Biography of Hsiao Fang 蕭倣 in *CTS* 172, p. 4480; *SKSC*, p. 744c.
3 The six taboo days fall on the 8th, 14th, 15th, 23rd, 29th, and 30th of each month. On these days monks within a given area are required to assemble and preach the Dharma (see *Shih-sung lü* 十誦律 57, in *TD* 23, p. 420c). Tsan-ning terms the taboo days *pa chai-jih* 八齋日, which refers to the eight types of abstinence required of laymen on these days.
4 *TCTC* 250, p. 8097; *SKSC*, p. 745a.
5 The establishment of a convent within the Palace grounds had occurred only once before, when T'ai-tsung allowed a female attendant, who was the daughter of the Sui minister Hsüeh Tao-heng 薛道衡, to take the precepts from ten monks summoned to the Palace for this purpose (*SSL* 3, p. 252a).
6 For the text of Hsiao's memorial, entitled *Chien I-tsung feng-Fo shu* 諫懿宗奉佛疏, see *CTW* 747, pp. 18b–19b. The date of the memorial is given in *THY* 48, p. 844.
7 *TCTC*, p. 8098.
8 *SSL*, p. 252b. *SKSC*, p. 745a states that the four major Ch'ang-an monasteries were also ordered to carry out ordinations for a period of twenty-one days.

9 *CTS* 19A, p. 655.
10 The text of Li's memorial is included in his biography in *CTS* 178, pp. 4625–27. For the date see *THY*, p. 844.
11 *FTTC* 42, p. 389a. *TCTC* 252, p. 8162 indicates that the feast was held at the An-kuo ssu.
12 *CTS* 19A, p. 683; *LFPT* 27, p. 348a; *TCTC* 252, p. 8165; *TFYK* 52, p. 11a–b; *FTTC*, p. 389a.
13 Biography of Li Wei 李蔚 in *HTS* 181, p. 5354.
14 The text of the amnesty, entitled *Ying Feng-hsiang chen-shen te-yin* 迎鳳翔眞身德音, is included in the *T'ang ta chao-ling chi* 113, p. 592, and in *CTW* 85, p. 29a–b.
15 *LFPT* 28, p. 349b.
16 Biography of Chih-en 志恩 in *SKSC* 7, p. 745c.
17 A random check of the biographies of 'eminent monks' who lived through the suppression indicates that a surprisingly large number went into hiding during the last years of Wu-tsung's reign rather than submit to laicization. Wen-chih 文賁, for example, took refuge in the mountains (*SKSC* 27, p. 881c), as did Chih-chün 智頵 (p. 881b); Ch'u-nan 楚南 fled to the forests (*SKSC* 17, p. 817c); Jih-chao 日照 and Shou-liang 守亮 both lived in caves (*SKSC* 12, p. 778b, and *SKSC* 27, p. 881c); etc.
18 The text of the eulogy of Shu-yen, written by Li Chieh 李節, is included in *LFPT* 26, pp. 342b–343b.
19 Some examples culled at random from *SKSC* follow: Bands of brigands (*ch'ün-k'ou* 群寇), during the Ch'ien-fu 乾符 era (874–9), forced Ch'an monks to abandon their monastery in Che-hsi (biography of Tsang-i 藏廙 in *SKSC* 12, p. 780b); Wen-hsi 文喜 was forced by the 'Ch'ao bandits' 巢寇 to flee from Hang-chou to Hunan in 879 (*SKSC* 12, p. 784a); during the Kuang-ming 廣明 era (880–1) Hsü-shou 虛受 fled to the Yüeh 越 region from Ch'ang-an when the latter was occupied by rebels (*SKSC* 7, p. 747b); Hui-tse 慧則, in 880, fled from Hua-chou 華州 when the 'Ch'ao bandits' invaded (*SKSC* 16, p. 809a); Hung-hsiu 鴻休, in the Kuang-ming era, miraculously escaped execution at the hands of the 'Ch'ao bandits' during their occupation of Fukien (*SKSC* 23, p. 856b); Ch'i-yin 棲隱 in the Kuang-ming era, took refuge in Lu-shan to escape the 'Ch'ao bandits' (*SKSC* 30, p. 896b); Heng-t'ung 恒通, in the period c. 884–5, was forced to flee with his followers from Anhwei to Chekiang (*SKSC* 12, p. 783a); etc.
20 *SKSC* 7, p. 752a.
21 *SKSC*, p. 752b; *FTTC* 8, p. 191a.
22 *Shih-men cheng-t'ung* 釋門正統 (completed 1237) 3, in *ZZK*, ser. 2B, case 3, vol. 5, p. 390a. Although Korea was thought to have preserved the most complete collection of T'ien-t'ai materials (see the biography of Te-shao 德韶 in *CTL* 25, p. 407c), missions were sent to Japan as well as to Korea (*FTTC* 43, pp. 394c–395a).
23 *FTTC* 10, p. 206a.
24 *FTTC* 8, p. 191a.
25 See, for example, Hsü-fa 續法, *Fa-chieh tsung wu-tsu lüeh-chi* 法界宗五祖略紀, in *ZZK*, ser. 2B, case 7, vol. 3, pp. 271b–278a.
26 *FTTC* 29, p. 294a.

27 The Ch'an position is conveniently summarized in the often quoted verse: 'Ch'an is a separate transmission outside the formal doctrines of Buddhism – one that does not depend upon texts. It points directly to the mind of man so that he may see his true nature and thereby attain Buddhahood.' See for example the *Tsu-t'ing shih-yüan* 祖庭事苑 5, in *ZZK*, ser. 2, case 18, vol. 1, p. 66b.
28 Typical examples are the story of Te-shan 德山, who, after being ridiculed for his mechanical adherence to scripture by an old lady cake-peddler, burned his commentaries on the *Diamond Sutra* (see *Lien-teng hui-yao* 聯燈會要 20, in *ZZK*, ser. 2B, case 9, vol. 4, p. 378a–b) and the story of Tan-hsia 丹霞 who, much to the astonishment of other monks in his monastery, set fire to a wooden image of the Buddha to keep warm (*CTL* 14, in *TD* 51, p. 310c).

GLOSSARY OF CHINESE CHARACTERS

An, Prince of 安王
An-kuo ssu 安國寺
An Lu-shan 安祿山
chai 齋
chai-jih 齋日
Chan-jan 湛然
Ch'an 禪 (Buddhist school)
Ch'an 澶 (personal name)
ch'an-fa 懺法
Chang-ching ssu 章敬寺
Chang Chung-wu 張仲武
Chang–hsin ssu 章信寺
Chang Tsun-liu 張遵騮
Chang Yüeh 張說
Ch'ang-an 長安
ch'ang-chu-t'ien 常住田
ch'ang hsiu kung-te shih chien-chiao tien–chung chien 常修功德使檢校殿中監
ch'ang hu sheng-kung 長護聖躬
Chao-ch'eng ssu 昭成寺
Chao-hsüan ssu 昭玄寺
Chao-hsüan ts'ao 昭玄曹
chao-hsüan t'ung 昭玄統
Chao-i 昭義
Chao Kuei-chen 趙歸眞
Chao Lien-shih 趙練師
Ch'ao bandits 巢寇
Ch'ao-chou 潮州
ch'ao-san ta-fu 朝散大夫
Ch'egwan 諦觀
Chen-hsiang 眞鄉
chen-kuan lü 貞觀律
Chen-kuo 鎭國
Chen-yüan hsien 眞源縣
Ch'en, Prince of 陳王

ch'en 臣 (subject)
Ch'en-chou 陳州
Ch'en Hung-chih 陳弘志
Ch'en Ts'ang-ch'i 陳藏器
cheng 正 (first month)
Cheng-chou 鄭州
Cheng Chu 鄭注
cheng-i 證義
cheng pa p'in hsia 正八品下
Cheng Shu-ch'ing 鄭叔清
cheng-ting chih yeh 正定之業
Ch'eng-chien 承乾
Ch'eng-ju 乘如
Ch'eng-kuan 澄觀
Ch'eng-te 成德
Ch'eng-yüan 承遠
chi 籍
Chi-ch'ing 積慶
chi mao 己卯
chi-mieh 寂滅
chi-mo 籍沒
Chi Shan-hsing 吉善行
Chi-tsang 吉藏
Chi-ts'ui Palace 積翠宮
ch'i 氣
Ch'i-chou 蘄州
Ch'i-yin 棲隱
Chia-ts'ai 迦才
Chiang, Prince 絳王
chiang-sheng chieh 降聖節
Chiang Sun 畺孫
chiao-chia 教家
chiao-shou ho-shang 教授和尚
chieh-ch'an 戒懺
Chieh-chou 介州
chieh-t'an 戒壇

206

Glossary of Chinese characters

chieh-tu fu 節度府
chien 間 (bays)
chien 兼 (join with)
chien 監 (overseer)
chien-chiao 檢校
Chien-fu ssu 薦福寺
Chien-fu ts'ao 監福曹
chien-i ta-fu 諫議大夫
chien-kuan 諫官
Chien-nan Tung-ch'uan 劍南東川
chien pai 兼拜
chien-shih 監使
Chien-wen-ti 簡文帝
Ch'ien-fu 乾符
Ch'ien-fu ssu 千福寺
Ch'ien Hung-shu 錢弘俶
Chih Ch'ien 支謙 (monk)
chih-ch'ien 紙錢 (paper money)
Chih-chüeh 志覺
Chih-chün 智頵
Chih-hsien 智詵
Chih-hsüan 知玄
Chih-i 智顗
Chih-lin 智琳
chih-shih 知事 (monastic office)
Chih-shih 智實 (monk)
Chih-te ssu 至德寺
Chih-yen 智儼
chin-chung ching-she 禁中精舍
Chin-hsien kuan 金仙觀
Chin-kang-chih 金剛智
Chin-kang shen-wang 金剛神王
Chin-ko ssu 金閣寺
chin-lu 金籙
Chin-lun Sheng-shen Huang-ti 金輪聖神皇帝
Chin-lun wang 金輪王
chin-ping 禁兵
chin-shih 進士
chin-tan 金丹
Chin-yang 晉陽
Ching-chao yin 京兆尹
ching-ch'eng ssu-kuan hsiu kung te shih 京城寺觀修功德使
Ching-ching 景淨
Ching-chou 荊州
Ching-hui 景暉
Ching-kuang T'ien-nü 淨光天女

Ching-pao tseng-chang 淨寶增長
Ching Shen 景審
Ching-shuang 鏡霜
Ching-tsung 敬宗
Ching-t'u 淨土
Ching-t'u lüeh-chuan 淨土略傳
Ching-t'u men 淨土門
ch'ing 頃
ch'ing-ching 清淨
Ch'ing-ching Kuang-ming Shih-chieh Ming-tsun 清淨光明世界明尊
Ch'ing-liang 清涼
Ch'ing-liang Fa-shih 清涼法師
Ch'ing-lung ssu 青龍寺
Ch'ing-T'ang kuan 慶唐觀
ch'ing-wu 輕物
Ch'ing-yüan Hsing-ssu 青原行思
chiu-chih 救治
chiu-chiu 九九
chiu chou 九州
chiu-ch'u 救除
chiu hsien 九仙
chiu ko 舊格
Chiu shu 舊疏
chiu t'ien t'an 九天壇
Ch'iu Shih-liang 仇士良
cho-pi 灼臂
chou 州
chou-fu 州府
Chu Fo-nien 竺佛念
Chu-k'o 主客
Chu-lin ssu 竹林寺
Chu Tz'u 朱泚
Ch'u-chi 處寂
Ch'u-chou 楚州
Ch'u-kuo kung 楚國公
ch'u-mo-ch'ien 除陌錢
Ch'u-nan 楚南
ch'uan 釧
Chuang-yen ssu 莊嚴寺
chui-wen 綴文
Chung-ching fa-shih 衆經法式
Chung-hsing kuan 中興觀
Chung-hsing ssu 中興寺
Chung-nan shan 終南山
Chung-shu men-hsia 中書門下
chung-wu 重物

Glossary of Chinese characters

chung-shih 中使
Chung-shu shih-lang 中書侍郎
Chung-t'ai tu-t'ang 中臺都堂
Chung-tsung 中宗
Chung-yüan chieh 中元節
Ch'ung-hsüan hsüeh 崇玄學
Ch'ung-hsüan kuan 崇玄館
Ch'ung-hsüan shu 崇玄署
Ch'ung-hui 崇惠
ch'ung-i 重譯
Ch'ung-lun ssu 重輪寺
Ch'ung-sheng ssu 崇聖寺
Ch'ung-T'ang kuan 崇唐觀
Ch'ü-chiang Pavilion 曲江亭館
chüan 絹
ch'ün-k'ou 羣寇
Dōgen Zenji 道元禪師
Ennin 圓仁
Erh-tsung-ching wei-chiao 二宗經偽教
Fa-ch'ang 法常
Fa-chao 法照
Fa-chen 法真
fa-ch'ien 發遣
Fa-ch'ien ssu 法乾寺
Fa-hsiang 法相
Fa-jung 法融
Fa-lang 法朗
Fa-li 法蠣
Fa-lin 法琳
fa-lu 法籙
Fa-lun 法輪
Fa-men ssu 法門寺
Fa-ming 法明
Fa-tsang 法藏
fa-wang 法王
Fan-ching yüan 翻經院
fan-seng 蕃僧 (barbarian monk)
fan-seng 梵僧 (Indian monk)
Fan Wen 樊文
Fan Wen-lan 范文瀾
fang-shih 方士
Fei-hsi 飛錫
fei-lien 飛鍊
Fei-yen ssu 非煙寺
Fen-chou 汾州
Feng-hsiang 鳳翔
Feng-luan ssu 封巒寺
feng-shan 封禪

Feng-shan shu 封禪書
Feng-t'ien 奉天
feng wei kuo-chia hsiang i 奉爲國家詳譯
Fo-kuang wang 佛光王
Fo shou-chi ssu 佛授記寺
Fo-t'ang 佛堂
Fo-ting tsun-sheng t'o-lo-ni 佛頂尊勝陀羅尼
Fo-ya 佛牙
fu ch'eng kuo-chia 輔成國家
Fu-feng 扶風
Fu-hsi 伏羲
Fu I 傅奕
Fukaura Seibun 深浦正文
fu kuan-ssu k'o-tsui 付官司科罪
fu-jui 符瑞
fu-ming 符命
fu-seng 富僧
Fu-shou ssu 福壽寺
fu-ssu 富寺
fu-yeh 福業
Han-kuang 含光
Han-kuo kung 韓國公
Han Yü 韓愈
Han Yüeh 韓約
Hao-t'ien kuan 昊天觀
Hao-t'ien Shang-ti 昊天上帝
he 黑
Heng-shan 衡山 (Hunan)
Heng-shan 恒山 (Shansi)
Heng-t'ung 恒通
Hirakawa Akira 平川彰
Hosaka Gyokusen 保坂玉泉
Ho-tse ssu 荷澤寺
hsi-ch'an Fang-teng t'an 洗懺方等壇
Hsi-chao 希照
Hsi-hu 西胡
Hsi-hua kuan 西華觀
Hsi-ming ssu 西明寺
Hsi-tsung 僖宗
hsia chou 下州
hsiang 象
hsiang-fa 鄉法
Hsiang Hai-ming 向海明
Hsiang K'ai 襄楷
hsiang-shui ch'ien 香水錢
Hsiao 蕭 (Empress Dowager)

Glossary of Chinese characters

Hsiao-ching 孝經
Hsiao Fang 蕭倣
Hsiao-kan ssu 孝感寺
hsiao-ssu 小寺
Hsiao Yü 蕭瑀
Hsieh Ling-yün 謝靈雲
hsien 縣
hsien-ch'ien seng-ch'ieh 現前僧伽
Hsien-shou 賢首
Hsien-t'ai 仙臺
Hsien-t'ai Hall 咸泰殿
hsien-tan 仙丹
Hsien-t'ien T'ai-hou 先天太后
Hsien-tsung 憲宗
Hsien-yang 咸陽
Hsin shu 新疏
Hsin T'i-p'i 辛替否
Hsing-ch'ing Palace 興慶宮
Hsing-fo ssu 興佛寺
Hsing-fu ssu 興福寺
Hsing-pu 刑部
Hsing-pu shih-lang 刑部侍郎
Hsing-pu yüan-wai-lang 刑部員外郎
Hsing-T'ang Kuan 興唐觀
Hsing-T'ang ssu 興唐寺
hsiu kung-te 修功德
hsiu kung-te Hui-hu 修功德回鶻
hsiu kung-te shih 修功德使
Hsü-chou 徐州
Hsü-shou 虛受
Hsü Wen-yüan 徐文遠
Huüan-ch'ang 玄暢
Hsüan-chou 宣州
Hsüan-chung ssu 玄忠寺
Hsüan-hsüan 眩玄
Hsüan-mo 玄謨 / 玄摸
Hsüan-mu 玄暮
hsüan-t'an 玄壇
Hsüan-tsang 玄奘
Hsüan-tsung 玄宗 (reigned 712–756)
Hsüan-tsung 宣宗 (reigned 846–859)
Hsüan-wan 玄琬
Hsüan-ying 玄應
Hsuan-yüan Chi 軒轅集
Hsüan-yüan Huang-ti 玄元皇帝
Hsüan-yüan Huang-ti Miao 玄元皇帝廟
Hsüeh Huai-i 薛懷義
Hsüeh Tao-heng 薛道衡
hu-chi 戶籍
hu-fa p'u-sa 護法菩薩
hu-mo 護摩
Hu San-hsing 胡三省
Hua-ch'ing Palace 華清宮
Hua-chou 華州
Hua-shan 華山
hua-shen 化身
Hua-t'ai 滑臺
Hua-tu Monastery 化度寺
Hua-yen 華嚴
Huai-hui 懷暉
Huai-su 懷素
huan-ku 換骨
huan-su 還俗
Huang Ch'ao 黃巢
Huang-mei 黃梅
Hui-an 慧安
Hui-ch'ang 會昌
Hui-ch'ao 慧超
Hui-ch'eng 惠乘
hui-ch'u Fo-chiao 毀除佛教
Hui-chung 慧忠
Hui-fan 慧範
Hui-hsiao 慧曉
Hui-lang 慧朗
Hui-ling 慧靈
Hui-neng 慧能
Hui-shan ssu 會山寺
Hui-tse 慧則
Hui-yüan 慧遠
Hung-chou 洪州
Hung-fa Yüan 弘法院
Hung-fu ssu 弘福寺
Hung-hsiu 鴻休
Hung-jen 弘忍
Hung-lu ssu 鴻臚寺
Hung-pien 弘辨
Huo 霍
Huo Hsien-ming 霍仙鳴
I-chi 義寂
I-ching 義淨 (monk)
i-ching 疑經 (sutra of dubious authenticity)
i-ching 義井 (well)
I-ching Yüan 譯經院
I-fu 義福

Glossary of Chinese characters

I-hsing 一行
i-hsing tao 易行道
i-huo lu 疑惑錄
i-jen 異人
I-tsung 懿宗
Ikku no on nao hōsha subeshi 一句の恩なほ報謝すべし
Ishihara Masaaki 石原正明
i-tao 異道
I-yang 弋陽
jen ch'i jen 人其人
Jen-chien 仁儉
Jih-chao 日昭
Ju-ching 如淨
Ju-kuan 儒館
Ju-man 如滿
Jui-tsung 睿宗
Jung-kuo, Lady 榮國夫人
K'ai-chou 開州
k'ai-fu i-t'ung san-ssu 開府儀同三司
K'ai-yüan monasteries 開元寺
Kan-lu chih pien 甘露之變
Kao T'an-ch'eng 高疊晟
kao-tieh 告牒
Kao-tsu 高祖
Kao-tsung 高宗
Kao Ying 高郢
ken 間
ko 格
ko-chu 閣主
Ko-shu Han 哥舒翰
kou-tang yu-chieh kung-te so 勾當右街功德所
k'u-i 苦役
k'u-shih 苦使
kuan 觀
kuan-ch'a shih 觀察使
kuan-ch'a shih chieh-tu chou 觀察使節度州
kuan-ting 灌頂 (consecration)
Kuan-ting 灌頂 (monk)
kuan-ting tao-ch'ang 灌頂道場
Kuang, Prince 光王
Kuang-chou 廣州
Kuang-ming 廣明
Kuang-ming ssu 光明寺
Kuang-shun Gate 光順門
kung 宮

kung-te yüan 功德院
kung-yen 公驗
k'ung 空
k'ung-ming kao-shen 空名告身
K'ung-tzu shuo 孔子說
kuo-chi 國忌
Kuo-hsüeh 國學
kuo-hui 國諱
Kuo-i 國一
Kuo P'eng 郭朋
kuo-shih 國師
Kuo T'ai-hou 郭太后
Kuo-tzu chi-chiu 國子祭酒
K'uo-ch'ing 郭清
lan-jo 蘭若
lan-ssu 濫賜
lan-tu seng 濫度僧
Lao-chün 老君
lao-hsiu 老朽
Lao-tzu hua-hu ching 老子化胡經
le kuan-tai 勒冠帶
li 理 ("noumenon")
Li 李 (surname)
li 里 (village)
Li Chan 李湛
Li Ch'an 李瀍
Li Chi 李勛
li ch'i yüeh-che ai yü hsien-tao 理氣越著礙於仙道
Li Chieh 李節
Li Chih 李治
Li Ch'in-ming 李欽明
Li Ching-yeh 李敬業
Li Ch'un 李純
Li Chung-wen 李仲文
Li Han 李涵
Li Heng 李恆
Li Hsi-lieh 李希烈
Li Hsien-ch'eng 李憲誠
Li Hsün 李訓
Li Hung 李弘
Li I 李怡
li-ko 釐革
Li Lung-chi 李隆基
Li Mi 李泌
Li Pao-ch'en 李寶臣
Li-pu 禮部
li-pu shih-lang 禮部侍郎

Glossary of Chinese characters

Li Shen 李紳
Li Shih-min 李世民
Li Shu-ming 李叔明
Li Sung 李誦
Li Tan 李旦
Li Te-yü 李德裕
Li Tsai-hsiang 李宰相
Li Ts'ui 李漼
Li Wei 李蔚
Li Wei-yüeh 李惟岳
Li Yen 李儼
Li Ying 李穎
Li Yüan 李淵
Li Yüan-ts'ung 李元琮
liang 兩
liang-chieh seng-lu 兩街僧錄
Liang-chieh Tao-men tu chiao-shou po-shih 兩街道門都教授博士
liang-ching fa-chu san ti kuo-shih 兩京法主三帝國師
Liang-pen 良賁
Liang Shou-ch'ien 梁守謙
Lin-chi 臨濟
Lin-kao 臨皋
lin-t'an ta-te 臨壇大德
Lin-te calendar 麟德曆
Lin-te Hall 麟德殿
ling 令
Ling-chun 靈準
Ling-fu 靈阜
Ling-piao 嶺表
Ling-pien 靈辨
Ling-sui 靈邃
Ling-yen 靈晏
Liu Chen 劉稹
Liu Chin-hsi 劉進喜
Liu Ch'ung-hsün 劉崇訓
Liu Hei-t'a 劉黑闥
Liu Hsüan-ching 劉玄靖
Liu Tao-ho 劉道合
Liu Wu-chou 劉武周
Liu Yen-mo 劉彥謨
Lo-fu shan 羅浮山
lo-han 羅漢
Lo river 洛水
Lo-yang 洛陽
Lu I 盧弈
Lu Chün 盧鈞

lu-kung 錄公
Lu-shan 廬山
lu-shih 錄事
Lu Te-ming 陸德明
Lung-shuo 龍朔
Lun-yü 論語
lung-hsing 龍興
Lung-men 龍門
Lung-wu Palace Army 龍武軍
Lü 律
Masunaga Reihō 增永靈鳳
Ma Yüan-chih 馬元贄
Mao-shan 茅山
Men-hsia shih-lang 門下侍郎
mi-chiao 密教
Mi-le 彌勒
mien 綿
Ming-chan 明瞻
ming-ching 明經
ming-o 名額
mo-chih 墨制
mo-ch'ih 墨勅
Mo-li-chih 摩利支
mou 畝
Mou-yü k'o-han 牟羽可汗
mu 牧
Mu-tsung 穆宗
Nan-shan nien-fo men Ch'an-tsung 南山念佛門禪宗
Nan-shan Tanguts 南山黨項
nan-hsing-tao 難行道
Nan-yüeh 南嶽
Nan-Yüeh Huai-jang 南嶽懷讓
nei-chai 內齋
nei-chi-shih 內給事
nei kung-te shih 內功德使
nei-lü 內律
nei-shih 內侍
nei-tao-ch'ang 內道場
ni 尼
nien-hao 年號
Niu-t'ou 牛頭
nu-pi 奴婢
nü-kuan 女官
o 額
pa chai-jih 八齋日
pa pu-ching wu 八不淨物
P'an Shih-cheng 潘師正

Glossary of Chinese characters

Pao-hsiu 寶修
Pao-kung 保恭
Pao-li ssu 寶曆寺
Pao-T'ang ssu 保唐寺
pao-t'u 寶圖
pao-wai wu-ming seng 保外無名僧
Pao-ying ssu 寶應寺
pei-t'ien 悲田
P'ei, Prince of 沛王
P'ei Chi 裴洎
P'ei Hsiu 裴休
P'ei Mien 裴冕
P'ei Po 裴伯
P'ei T'an 裴坦
P'ei Tu 裴度
pen-chi 本紀
pen-yüan li 本願力
P'eng-lai Palace 蓬萊宮
P'eng Yen 彭偃
pi 婢 (female slave)
pi-tzu 婢子
p'i 匹 / 疋
P'i-sha-men 毘沙門
p'iao-chi ta chiang-chün 驃騎大將軍
Pien-chang 辮章
pien-o 扁額
Pin-t'ou-lu 賓頭盧
Ping-chou 并州
ping-fang 病坊
Ping-pu shih-lang 兵部侍郎
Po-chou 亳州
Po-jo San tsang 般若三藏
po-lo-i 波羅夷
Po Yen 帛延
pu-ch'üeh 補闕
Pu-k'ung 不空
P'u-chen 普震
P'u-chi 普寂
P'u-chou 蒲州
P'u-hsien 普賢
P'u-hsien P'u-sa shuo cheng-ming ching
  普賢菩薩說證明經
P'u-ku Huai-en 僕固懷恩
P'u-kuang wang ssu 普光王寺
p'u-sa chieh 菩薩戒
p'u-t'ung 普通
san chai-yüeh 三齋月
san ch'ang-chai yüeh 三長齋月

san-chiao chiang-lun 三教講論
San-chiao Shou-tso 三教首座
san kang 三綱
san yüan-yüeh 三元月
seng 僧
Seng-ch'e 僧徹
seng-cheng 僧正
seng-ch'i pu 僧祇部
Seng-ch'ieh 僧伽 (monk)
seng-ch'ieh 僧伽 (Buddhist clergy)
Seng-ch'ieh Ho-shang t'ang
  僧伽和尚堂
seng chih 僧制
seng-chu 僧主
seng-lu 僧錄
Seng-lüeh 僧㽞
seng-ni chi 僧尼籍
seng-ni chi-chang 僧尼籍帳
seng-t'ung 僧統
sha-men t'ung 沙門統
sha-mi 沙彌
shan-fang 山房
Shan-tao 善導
Shan-ts'ai 善財
Shan-wu-wei 善無畏
Shan-yin ssu 善因寺
Shang-ch'ing 上清
shang-chou 上州
shang-teng ssu 上等寺
Shang-shih chü 尚食局
Shang-shu 尚書
Shang-shu sheng 尚書省
shang-shu yu-ch'eng 尚書右丞
shang-tso 上座
Shao-lin ssu 少林寺
shao-ting 燒頂
she-shen 捨身
she-sheng 攝生
Shen Chuan-shih 沈傳師
shen-fu 神府
Shen-hsiu 神秀
Shen-hui 神會
shen-jen 神人
Shen-kuang 神光
Shen-ming t'ai 神明臺
Shen-ts'e Army 神策軍
Shen-ts'ou 神湊
sheng 升

Glossary of Chinese characters

sheng-li 聖理
Sheng-mu 聖母
Sheng-mu Shen-huang 聖母神皇
Sheng-tao 聖道
Sheng-tsun 勝尊
Sheng-yeh ssu 勝業寺
shih 式
Shih Ch'ao-i 史朝義
shih-ching tu-seng 試經度僧
shih-fang seng-ch'ieh 十方僧伽
Shih-hu 施護
shih-i 拾遺
Shih-li 尸利
shih miao 十妙
shih-pa tzu 十八子
Shih ssu-ming 史思明
shih ta-te 十大德
Shih-t'ou 石頭
Shih-tsun 世尊
shih-yü-shih 侍御史
Shōbōgenzō gyōji 正法眼藏行持
Shou-liang 守亮
Shu-yen 疏言
shui-chien-chia 稅間架
Shun 舜
Shun-tsung 順宗
Sōniryō 僧尼令
ssu 寺
ssu-chia 寺家
Ssu-chou 泗州
Ssu-chou t'a 泗州塔
Ssu-feng 司封
Ssu-ma Ch'eng-chen 司馬承禎
Ssu-men hsüeh 四門學
ssu-o 寺額
Ssu-pin ssu 司賓寺
ssu-seng kung-an 寺僧公案
ssu-tu 私度
su-chiang 俗講
su-fa 俗法
Su-kuo 肅國
su-ti 觫滌
Su T'ing 蘇頲
Su-tsung 肅宗
Suan-shan 蒜山
Sun Ch'iao 孫樵
Sung chih-wen 宗之問
Sung Ching 宋璟

Sung Lao-sheng 宋老生
Sung-shan 嵩山
Sung Shen-hsi 宋申錫
Sung Ting 宋鼎
Sung Tzu-hsien 宋子賢
Sung-yang 嵩陽
Ta-chi Ch'an-shih 大濟禪師
Ta Chen-na 大振那
Ta chien-fu ssu 大薦福寺
Ta Chou tung ssu 大周東寺
ta fan-chen 大藩鎮
ta hsien 大縣
Ta hsing-kuo ssu 大興國寺
Ta hsing-shan ssu 大興善寺
Ta-hui Ch'an-shih 大慧禪師
Ta-kuang-chih San-tsang 大廣智三藏
Ta kuang-ming ssu 大光明寺
Ta-ming Palace 大明宮
ta seng-lu 大僧錄
ta-she 大赦
Ta-sheng Huang-ti 大聖皇帝
Ta-sheng Wen-shu chen-kuo chih ko
　　大聖文殊鎮國之閣
ta-ssu 大寺
ta-te 大德
Ta tsung-ch'ih ssu 大總持寺
ta t'ung 大統
Ta-t'ung Ch'an-shih 大通禪師
Ta tz'u-en ssu 大慈恩寺
Ta-wu Ho-shang 大悟和尚
Ta-yen li 大衍曆
Ta-yün kuang-ming ssu 大雲光明寺
Ta-yün Mi-tsang 大雲密藏
Ta-yün monasteries 大雲寺
t'a-li 他力
Taihō 大寶
Tai-tsung 代宗
t'ai-ch'ang ch'ing 太常卿
T'ai-ch'ing kung 太清宮
T'ai ch'ung-fu ssu 太崇福寺
T'ai-hou 太后
T'ai-hsüeh 太學
T'ai-i kuan 太一觀
t'ai-miao 太廟
T'ai-po shan 太白山
T'ai-shan 泰山
T'ai-shang Hsüan-yüan Huang-ti
　　太上玄元皇帝

Glossary of Chinese characters

T'ai-shang Lao-chün 太上老君
T'ai-shih 太師
t'ai-shih ling 太史令
T'ai-shou kuan 太受觀
T'ai-tsung 太宗
T'ai-tzu chan-shih 太子詹事
T'ai-yüan 太原
T'ai-yüan ssu 太原寺
tan-ch'en t'an-lun 誕辰談論
Tan-hsia 丹霞
T'an-chou 潭州
T'an-luan 曇鸞
T'ang-an ssu 唐安寺
T'ang-ch'ang ssu 唐昌寺
T'ang-shu hui-yao 唐書會要
T'ang T'ung-t'ai 唐同泰
tao 道
Tao-an 道安
tao-ch'ang 道場
Tao-ch'eng 道澄
Tao-ch'o 道綽
tao chung-hsin 道中心
tao-chü 道舉
tao-hsiang 道像
Tao-hsin 道信
Tao-hsüan 道宣
Tao-i 道意 (abbot of Hung-fu ssu)
Tao-i 道義 (monk at Chin-ko ssu)
Tao-in 道氤
tao-jen t'ung 道人統
Tao-seng ko 道僧格
tao-shih 道士
Tao-shih-chang 道士長
tao-shu 道術
Tao-te ching 道德經
Te-shan 德山
Te-shao 德韶
Te-tsung 德宗
t'e-chin shih hung-lu ch'ing 特進試鴻臚卿
Teng-chou 登州
teng-hsia 登霞
Ti-wu Shou-liang 第伍守亮
T'i-wei po-li ching 提謂波利經
t'iao-chih 條制
t'iao-liu 條流
tieh 牒
Tien-chung chien 殿中監

Tien-ssu shu 典寺署
T'ien-hou 天后
T'ien-t'ai 天台
T'ien-tsun 天尊
ting 丁
Ting-lan 定蘭
tou 斗
Tou Wen-ch'ang 竇文場
tsa-se i 雜色役
Tsan-ning 贊寧
tsan-pai 讚唄
Tsang-i 藏廙
tsao 造
Ts'ao-tung 曹洞
Ts'ao-hsi 曹谿
tso 作
tso-ch'an 坐禪
tso-chieh 左街
tso-chieh seng-lu 左街僧錄
tso-chieh ta kung-te shih 左街大功德使
tso san-ch'i ch'ang-shih 左散騎常侍
Tso-yu-chieh Tao-men chiao-shou hsien-sheng 左右街道門教授先生
tsu-shih 祖師
Ts'ui Ch'ün 崔羣
Tsu-hsiu 祖琇
Ts'ui Li 崔蠡
Ts'ui-wei Palace 翠微宮
Tsun-sheng shih-ch'uang 尊勝石幢
ts'un-fang 村坊
ts'un-i chai-t'ang 村邑齋堂
Tsung-cheng ssu 宗正寺
Tsung-ch'ih ssu 總持寺
Tsung-mi 宗密
Ts'ung-chien 從諫
Tu Cheng-lun 杜正倫
Tu-chih 度支
Tu Hung-chien 杜鴻漸
Tu-kuan 都官
Tu-men lan-jo 度門蘭若
T'u-t'u Ch'eng-ts'ui 吐突承璀
tuan Fo-chiao 斷佛教
Tuan-fu 端甫
tuan-shih sha-men 斷事沙門
tung-chieh ta kung-te shih 東街大功德使
Tung-lin ssu 東林寺
Tung-tu kung-te shih 東都功德使

Glossary of Chinese characters

t'ung 通
t'ung chung-shu men-hsia p'ing-chang-shih 同中書門下平章事
t'ung-hsing 童行
T'ung-hua Gate 通化門
T'ung-i Palace 通義宮
t'ung-kuan 統官
Tung-ming kuan 東明觀
t'ung-p'ing-chang-shih 同平章事
T'ung-tao Academy 通道觀
t'ung-tzu sha-mi 童子沙彌
tzu-chih t'ung-chien k'ao-i 資治通鑑考異
tzu-li 自力
tzu-hsüeh 字學
tzu pang-kuo hsi-mieh tsai-o 資邦國息滅災厄
Tzu-sheng ssu 資聖寺
tzu-shou chin-chang 紫綬金章
Tzu-wei Palace 紫微宮
Tz'u-en 慈恩
Tz'u-en ssu 慈恩寺
Tz'u-pu 祠部
tz'u-shih 刺史
Tz'u-te ssu 慈德寺
Tz'u-yün Tsun-shih 慈雲遵式
Ŭich'ŏn 義天
wan-jen chai 萬人齋
wang 王
Wang Che 王哲
Wang Chih-hsing 王智興
Wang Chin 王縉
Wang Hsi-ch'ien 王希遷
Wang Hsien-chih 王仙芝
Wang-hsien t'ai 望仙臺
Wang Hsüan-ts'e 王玄策
wang pi-ch'iu wu 亡比丘物
Wang Shou-ch'eng 王守澄
Wang Wei 王維
Wang Yü 王璵
Wang Yüan-chih 王遠知
Wei 韋
Wei Chao-tu 韋昭度
Wei-chen 惟眞
wei-chuan 僞撰
wei-hsin 維新
Wei-hsiu 威秀
Wei Hsüan-chung 魏玄忠
Wei-k'uan 惟寬

wei kuo i-ching chu hsüan huang-hua 為國譯經助宣皇化
Wei-kuo ssu 魏國寺
wei-no 維那
Wei-po 魏博
Wei Shu 韋述
Wei Tsung-ch'ing 韋宗卿
Wei-ying 惟英
Wen-chih 文質
Wen-hsi 文喜
Wen-hsü 文漵
Wen-shu 文殊
Wen-shui 汶水
Wen-te, Empress 文德皇后
Wen-tsung 文宗
Wu, Empress 武后
wu 五 (fifth month)
wu 無 (not to)
Wu Chao 武昭
wu-che seng-chai 無遮僧齋
Wu Ch'eng-ssu 武承嗣
wu-chu 巫祝
Wu-en 晤恩
Wu-hou teng-chi ch'en-shu 武后登極讖書
wu hsing 五行
Wu-hsing chih 五行志
wu hui nien-fo 五會念佛
Wu-k'ung 悟空
wu pai 無拜
Wu-shang Shen-hsien 無上神仙
Wu Shih-huo 武士彠
Wu-t'ai shan 五臺山
Wu-t'ai shan hsiu kung-te shih 五臺山修功德使
wu tao-hsin 無道心
Wu-ti 武帝
Wu Ting 五頂
Wu-tsung shih-lu 武宗實錄
wu-wei 無為
Wu-yeh 無業
wu yin-sheng 五音聲
Wu-yüeh 吳越 (region)
wu yüeh 五嶽 (five peaks)
Wu Yün 吳筠
Yai-chou 崖州
Yang-chiao 羊角
Yang Chien 楊堅

Glossary of Chinese characters

Yang Ch'in-i 楊欽義
Yang-chou 揚州
Yang Hsiung 楊雄
yang-hua 陽化
Yang Kuo-chung 楊國忠
yang-ping fang 養病坊
Yang-ti 煬帝
Yang Yü-ch'ing 楊虞卿
Yao 堯
Yao Ch'ung 姚崇
Yen 炎
Yen-chou 兗州
yen-fu-t'i chu 閻浮提主
Yen Shang-wen 顏尚文
Yen-T'ang ssu 延唐寺
yen-t'ieh shih 鹽鐵使
Yen-ts'ung 彥悰
yin-sheng nien-fo 引聲念佛
Yin-t'ai Gate 銀臺門
yin-tz'u 淫祠
Yin Yu 殷侑
Yokoyama Kōitsu 橫山紘一
Yōrō ritsuryō 養老律令
yu-chieh 右街
yu-chieh ta kung-te shih 右街大功德使
Yu-chou 幽州
Yu-hsüan 幽玄
Yūki Reimon 結城令聞
Yu-yüan 有緣
Yung-ch'ang 永昌
Yung-chou 雍州
Yung-t'ai 永泰
Yü 禹
Yü Ch'ao-en 魚朝恩
Yü-ch'üan ssu 玉泉寺
Yü-hua Palace 玉華宮
Yü-hua ssu 玉華寺
Yü Hung-chih 魚弘志
Yü-lan-p'en hui 盂蘭盆會
Yü Ping 庾冰
yü-shih 御史
Yü-wen Hsüan 宇文炫
yüan 院
Yüan-chao 圓照
Yüan-k'an 元堪
Yüan-tao 原道
Yüan Tsai 元載
yüan-wen 願文
Yüeh 越
yüeh-chung 悅眾
Yün-kang 雲崗

BIBLIOGRAPHY

1. Standard Dynastic Histories
The Standard Dynastic Histories are cited from the punctuated edition published by the Chung-hua Shu-chü, Peking, 1971–.

Chiu T'ang shu 舊唐書, by Liu Hsü 劉昫 et al., 945.
Hou Han shu 後漢書, by Fan Yeh 范曄 (398–445).
Hsin T'ang shu 新唐書, by Ou-yang Hsiu 歐陽修 et al., 1060.
Sui shu 隋書, by Wei Cheng 魏徵 et al., 656.
Wei shu 魏書, by Wei Shou 魏收, 554.

2. Collections of source materials, traditional encyclopaedias, legal compendia

Chin-shih ts'ui-pien 金石萃編, by Wang Ch'ang 王昶, 1805. Shih-k'o shih-liao ts'ung-shu 石刻史料叢書 edition. Taipei, 1966.
Ch'üan T'ang wen 全唐文, by Tung Kao 董誥 et al., 1814. Citations are from the 1965 Taiwan reprint.
Dai Nihon zokuzōkyō 大日本續藏經, Ed. Nakano Tatsue 中野達慧 750 vol. in 150 cases. Kyoto: Zōkyō Shoin, 1905–1912.
Taishō shinshū daizōkyō 大正新修大藏經. Ed Takakusu Junjirō and Watanabe Kaigyoku 渡辺海旭. 85 vol. Tokyo: Taishō Issaikyō Kankōkai, 1924–1932.
T'ang hui-yao 唐會要, by Wang P'u 王溥 et al., 961. Kuo-hsüeh chi-pen ts'ung-shu 國學基本叢書 edition.
T'ang liu-tien 唐六典. Completed c. 739. Wen-hai 文海 edition. Taipei, 1962.
T'ang-lü su-i 唐律疏議, by Li Lin-fu 李林甫 et al., 737. Tai-nan-ko ts'ung-shu 岱南閣叢書 edition.
T'ang ta chao-ling chi 唐大詔令集, by Sung Min-ch'iu 宋敏求, 1070. Peking: Commercial Press, 1959.
Ts'e-fu yüan-kuei 册府元龜, by Wang Ch'in-jo 王欽若 et al., 1013. Citations are from the 1642 edition.
T'ung-tien 通典, by Tu Yu 杜佑, 801. Shanghai: Commercial Press, 1935.

3. Primary sources: chronicles, sūtras, treatises, commentaries, historical works

An-lo chi 安樂集, by Tao-ch'o (562–645). *TD*, vol. 47, no. 1958.
Ch'an-yüan chu ch'üan-chi tu-hsü 禪源諸詮集都序, by Tsung-mi (780–841). *TD*, vol. 48, no. 2015.
Ch'ang-an chih 長安志, by Sung Min-ch'iu, c. 1079. Ching-hsün-t'ang ts'ung-shu

Bibliography

經訓堂叢書 edition.

Chen-kuan cheng-yao 貞觀政要, by Wu Ching 吳兢, c. 742. Toyō Bunka Kenkyūjo edition. Tokyo, 1962.

Chen-yüan hsin-ting Shih-chiao mu-lu 貞元新訂釋教目錄, by Yüan-chao, c. 800. *TD*, vol. 55, no. 2157.

Ch'eng wei-shih lun 成唯識論. *TD*, vol. 31, no. 1585.

Chi ku-chin Fo Tao lun-heng 集古今佛道論衡, by Tao-hsüan, 664. *TD*, vol. 52, no. 2104.

Chi sha-men pu ying pai-su teng shih 集沙門不應拜俗等事, by Yen-ts'ung, c. 662. *TD*, vol. 52, no. 2108.

Chia-chü ling-yen Fo-ting tsun-sheng t'o-lo-ni chi 加句靈驗佛頂尊勝陀羅尼記. *ZZK*, ser. 2, case 9, vol. 4.

Chin-kang po-jo ching 金剛般若經. *TD*, vol. 8, no. 235.

Chin-kang-ting ching i-chüeh 金剛頂經義訣, by Pu-k'ung (705–774). *TD*, vol. 39, no. 1798.

Chin kuang-ming ching 金光明經. *TD*, vol. 16, nos. 663–665.

Ching-te ch'uan-teng lu 景德傳燈錄, by Tao-yüan 道原, c. 1004. *TD*, vol. 51, no. 2076.

Ching-t'u lun 淨土論, by Chia-ts'ai, c. 648. *TD*, vol. 47, no. 1524.

Ching-t'u wang-sheng chuan 淨土往生傳, by Chieh-chu 戒珠, (completed between 1068–1077). *TD*, vol. 51, no. 2071.

Ching-t'u wu hui nien-fo sung-ching kuan-hsing i 淨土五會念佛誦經觀行儀, by Fa-chao, 774. *TD*, vol. 85, no. 2827.

Ch'ing pin-t'ou-lu fa 請賓頭盧法. *TD*, vol. 32, no. 1689.

Ch'u san-tsang chi chi 出三藏記集, by Seng-Yu 僧祐, c. 518. *TD*, vol. 55, no. 2145.

Chung-ch'ao ku-shih 中朝故事, by Yü-ch'ih Wo 尉遲偓. Sui-an Hsü-shih ts'ung-shu 隨盦徐氏叢書 edition.

Chung-ching mu-lu 衆經目錄, by Fa-ching 法經 et al., 594. *TD*, vol. 55, no. 2146.

Fa-chieh tsung wu-tsu lüeh-chi 法界宗五祖略紀, by Hsü-fa 續法, 1680. *ZZK*, ser. 2B, case 7, vol. 3.

Fa-yüan chu-lin 法苑珠林, by Tao-shih 道世, 668. *TD*, vol. 53, no. 2122.

Fan-wang ching 梵網經. *TD*, vol. 24, no. 1484.

Fan-wang ching p'u-sa-chieh-pen shu 梵網經菩薩戒本疏, by Fa-tsang (643–712). *TD*, vol. 40, no. 1813.

Fang-kuang ta chuang-yen ching 方廣大莊嚴經. *TD*, vol. 3, no. 187.

Fang-po ching 放鉢經. *TD*, vol. 15, no. 629.

Fo i-chiao ching 佛遺教經. *TD*, vol. 12, no. 389.

Fo-tsu li-tai t'ung-tsai 佛祖歷代通載, by Nien-ch'ang 念常, 1341. *TD*, vol. 49, no. 2036.

Fo-tsu t'ung-chi 佛祖統紀, by Chih-p'an 志磐, 1269. *TD*, vol. 49, no. 2035.

Hsi-yü chi 西域記. Full title: *Ta T'ang hsi-yü chi* 大唐西域記, by Hsüan-tsang. Edited by Pien-chi 辯機, 645. *TD*, vol. 51, no. 2087.

Hsü kao-seng chuan 續高僧傳, by Tao-hsüan, c. 660. *TD*, vol. 50, no. 2060.

Hsü ku-chih i-ching t'u-chi 續古今譯經圖紀, by Chih-sheng 智昇, 730. *TD*, vol. 55, no. 2152.

Hsüan-tsung ch'ao fan-ching san-tsang Shan-wu-wei tseng hung-lu ch'ing hsing-chuang 玄宗朝翻經三藏善無畏贈鴻臚卿行狀, by Li Hua 李華 (fl. 760). *TD*, vol. 50, no. 2055.

Hua-yen ching 華嚴經. *TD*, vol. 9, no. 278; *TD*, vol. 10, no. 279.
Hua-yen ching chuan-chi 華嚴經傳記, by Fa-tsang (643–712). *TD*, vol. 51, no. 2073.
Hua-yen yen-i ch'ao 華嚴演義鈔, by Ch'eng-kuan (738–839). *TD*, vol. 36, no. 1736.
I-ch'ieh-ching yin-i 一切經音義, by Hsüan-ying 玄應, c. 650. *Dai-Nihon kōtei daizōkyō ongibu* 大日本校訂大藏經音義部, vol. 6.
I-ch'ieh-ching yin-i 一切經音義, by Hui-lin 慧琳, 807. *TD*, vol. 54, no. 2128.
Jen-wang ching 仁王經. *TD*, vol. 8, nos. 245 and 246.
Ju o-p'i-ta-mo lun 入阿毘達磨論. *TD*, vol. 28, no. 1554.
K'ai-yüan Shih-chiao lu 開元釋教錄, by Chih-sheng 智昇, 730. *TD*, vol. 55, no. 2154.
Kan-t'ung lu 感通錄, by Tao-hsüan, 664. *TD*, vol. 52, no. 2107.
Kao-seng chuan 高僧傳, by Hui-chiao 慧皎, 519. *TD*, vol. 50, no. 2059.
Kuan Wu-liang-shou Fo ching 觀無量壽佛經. *TD*, vol. 12, no. 365.
Kuan Wu-liang-shou Fo ching shu 觀無量壽佛經疏, by Shan-tao (613–681). *TD*, vol. 37, no. 1753.
Kuang Ch'ing-liang chuan 廣清涼傳, by Yen-i 延一, 1060. *TD*, vol. 51, no. 2099.
Kuang hung-ming chi 廣弘明集, by Tao-hsüan, c. 664. *TD*, vol. 52, no. 2103.
Li-tai ch'ung-tao chi 歷代崇道記, by Tu Kuang-t'ing 杜光庭, (850–933?). Tao-tsang 道藏 edition.
Li-tai fa-pao chi 歷代法寶紀, latter half of the eighth century. *TD*, vol. 51, no. 2075.
Li-tai san-pao chi 歷代三寶紀, by Fei Ch'ang-fang 費長房, 597. *TD*, vol. 49, no. 2034.
Liang-ch'u ch'ing-chung i 量處輕重儀, by Tao-hsüan, 667. *ZZK*, ser. 2, case 10, vol. 1.
Lien-teng hui-yao 聯燈會要, by Wu-ming 悟明, 1183. *ZZK*, ser. 2B, case 9, vols. 3–5.
Lo-pang wen-lei 樂邦文類, by Tsung-hsiao 宗曉, 1200. *TD*, vol. 47, no. 1969A.
Lung-hsing Fo-chiao pien-nien t'ung-lun 隆興佛教編年通論, by Tsu-hsiu 祖琇, 1164. *ZZK*, ser. 2B, case 3, vols. 3–4.
Lung-shu tseng-kuang Ching-t'u wen 龍舒增廣淨土文, by Wang Jih-hsiu 王日休, 1160. *TD*, vol. 47, no. 1970.
Lüeh-ch'u nien-sung ching 略出念誦經. *TD*, vol. 18, no. 866.
Mi-yen ching 密嚴經. *TD*, vol. 16, nos. 681 and 682.
Nan-hai chi-kuei nei-fa chuan 南海寄歸內法傳, by I-ching, 691. *TD*, vol. 54, no. 2125.
Nieh-p'an ching 涅槃經. See *Ta po-nieh-p'an ching*.
Nittō guhō junrei kōki 入唐求法巡禮行記, by Ennin 圓仁, 847. Citations are from the text edited by Ono Katsutoshi and published in his *Nittō guhō junrei kōki no kenkyū*.
O-mi-t'o ching 阿彌陀經. *TD*, vol. 12, nos. 366 and 367.
O-p'i-ta-mo chü-she lun 阿毘達磨俱舍論. *TD*, vol. 29, nos. 1558 and 1559.
Pan-chou san-mei ching 般舟三昧經. *TD*, vol. 13, nos. 416–419.
Pao-yü ching 寶雨經. *TD*, vol. 16, no. 660.
Pien-cheng lun 辯正論, by Fa-lin 法琳, c. 626. *TD*, vol. 52, no. 2110.
P'o-hsieh lun 破邪論, by Fa-lin 法琳, 622. *TD*, vol. 52, no. 2109.

Pŏpjang Hwasang jŏn 法藏和尚傳, by Ch'oe Ch'iwŏn 崔致遠, 904. *TD*, vol. 50, no. 2054.
Pu-k'ung San-tsang hsing-chuang 不空三藏行狀, by Chao Ch'ien 趙遷, 774. *TD*, vol. 50, no. 2056.
P'u-sa-tsang ching 菩薩藏經. *TD*, vol. 11, no. 310 (12).
P'u-t'i-ta-mo nan-tsung ting shih-fei lun 菩提達摩南宗定是非論, by Shen-hui (670–762). In Hu Shih ed. *Shen-hui Ho-shang i-chi*.
Ryō no gige 令義解, by Kiyohara no Natsuno 清原夏野 et al., 833. *Shintei zōho kokushi taikei* 新訂增補國史大系, vol. 22.
Ryō no shūge 令集解, by Koremune Naomoto 惟宗直本, c. 859–876. *Shintei zōho kokushi taikei*, vols. 23–24.
Sa-che-ni-ch'ien-tzu ching 薩遮尼乾子經. *TD*, vol. 9, no. 272.
Senchaku hongan nembutsushū 選擇本願念佛集, by Hōnembō Genkū 法然房源空, 1198. *TD*, vol. 83, no. 2608.
Shan-wu-wei San-tsang ho-shang pei-ming 善無畏三藏和尚碑銘. See *Hsüan-tsung ch'ao fan-ching san-tsang Shan-wu-wei tseng hung-lu ch'ing hsing-chuang*.
Shang-shu ku-shih 尚書故事, by Li Ch'o 李綽, late T'ang. Chi-fu ts'ung-shu 畿輔叢書 edition.
Shen-hui yü–lu 神會語錄, attributed to Shen-hui (670–762). In Hu Shih ed. *Shen-hui Ho-shang i-chi*.
Shih-men cheng-t'ung 釋門正統, by Tsung-chien 宗鑑, 1237. *ZZK*, ser. 2B, case 3, vol. 5.
Shih-shih chi-ku lüeh 釋氏稽古略, by Chüeh-an 覺岸, c. 1354. *TD*, vol. 49, no. 2037.
Shih-shih tzu-chien 釋氏資鑑, by Hsi-chung 熙仲, 1336. *ZZK*, ser. 2B, case 5, vol. 1.
Shih-sung lü 十誦律. *TD*, vol. 23, no. 1435.
Shingon fuhōden 眞言付法傳, by Kūkai 空海, 821. *Dai Nihon Bukkyō zensho* 大日本佛教全書, vol. 106.
Ssu-fen lü 四分律. *TD*, vol. 22, no. 1428.
Ssu-fen lü hsing-shih ch'ao 四分律行事鈔, by Tao-hsüan, 630. *TD*, vol. 40, no. 1804.
Ssu-fen lü k'ai-tsung chi 四分律開宗記, by Huai-su, 682. *ZZK*, ser. 1, case 66, vol. 5 through case 67, vol. 1.
Ssu-fen lü shu 四分律疏, by Fa-li, 626. *ZZK*, ser. 1, case 65, vols. 3–5.
Ssu-shih hua-yen ching 四十華嚴經. Formal title: *Ta fang-kuang Fo hua-yen ching* 大方廣佛華嚴經. *TD*, vol. 10, no. 293.
Sung Kao-seng chuan 宋高僧傳, by Tsan-ning et al., 988. *TD*, vol. 50, no. 2061.
Ta fang-kuang Fo hua-yen ching ju pu-k'o-ssu-i chieh-t'o ching-chieh P'u-hsien yüan-hsing p'in 大方廣佛華嚴經入不可思議解脫境界普賢願行品. *TD*, vol. 10, no. 293.
Ta fang-teng wu-hsiang ching 大方等無想經. *TD*, vol. 12, no. 387.
Ta Fo-ting t'o-lo-ni 大佛頂陀羅尼. *TD*, vol. 19, nos. 944A and 944B.
Ta-jih ching 大日經. See *Ta P'i-lu-che-na ch'eng-fo shen-pien chia-ch'ih ching*.
Ta-kuang-chih San-tsang Ho-shang chih pei 大廣智三藏和上之碑, by Fei-hsi, 779. *KSP* 4, pp. 848b–849c.
Ta pao-chi ching 大寶積經. *TD*, vol. 11, no. 310.
Ta P'i-lu-che-na ch'eng-fo shen-pien chia-ch'ih ching 大毘盧遮那成佛神變加持經.

TD, vol. 18, no. 848.
Ta P'i-lu-che-na ch'eng-fo ching shu 大毘盧遮那成佛經疏, by I-hsing, 725. *TD*, vol. 39, no. 1796.
Ta-p'in ching 大品經. Formal title: *Mo-ho po-jo po-lo-mi ching* 摩訶般若波羅蜜經. *TD*, vol. 8, no. 223.
Ta po-jo ching 大般若經. *TD*, vols. 5–7, no. 220.
Ta po-nieh-p'an ching 大般涅槃經. *TD*, vol. 12, nos. 374 and 375.
Ta po-nieh-p'an ching shu 大般涅槃經疏, by Kuan-ting, 619. *TD*, vol. 38, no. 1767.
Ta Sung seng-shih lüeh 大宋僧史略, by Tsan-ning, 999. *TD*, vol. 54, no. 2126.
Ta-sheng ju Leng-ch'ieh ching 大乘入楞伽經. *TD*, vol. 16, no. 672.
Ta-sheng li-ch'ü liu po-lo-mi-to ching 大乘理趣六波羅蜜多經. *TD*, vol. 8, no. 261.
Ta T'ang Chen-yüan hsü K'ai-yüan Shih-chiao lu 大唐貞元續開元釋教錄, by Yüan-chao, 794. *TD*, vol. 55, no. 2156.
Ta T'ang nei-tien lu 大唐內典錄, by Tao-hsüan, 664. *TD*, vol. 55, no. 2149.
Ta T'ang Ta tz'u-en ssu San-tsang Fa-shih chuan 大唐大慈恩寺三藏法師傳, by Hui-li 慧立 and Yen-ts'ung, 688. *TD*, vol. 50, no. 2053.
Ta-tsang fa-shu 大藏法數, by Chi-chao 寂照, c. 1658. Tokyo: Kōmeisha, 1899.
Ta-yün ching 大雲經. See *Ta fang-teng wu-hsiang ching*.
Tai-tsung ch'ao tseng Ssu-k'ung Ta-pien-cheng Kuang-chih San-tsang Ho-shang piao-chih chi 代宗朝贈司空大辨正廣智三藏和尚表制集, by Yüan-chao, completed between 778–800. *TD*, vol. 52, no. 2120.
T'ang hu-fa sha-men Fa-lin pieh-chuan 唐護法沙門法琳別傳, by Yen-tsung 彥琮, completed between 640–649. *TD*, vol. 50, no. 2051.
Ti-tsang p'u-sa pen-yüan ching 地藏菩薩本願經. *TD*, vol. 13, no. 412.
Tō Daiwajō tōseiden 唐大和上東征傳, by Mahito Genkai 眞人元開, also known as Ōmi no Mifune 淡海三船, 779. *TD*, vol. 51, no. 2089.
Tsu-t'ing shih-yüan 祖庭事苑, by Mu-an Shan-ch'ing 睦庵善卿, c. 1108. *ZZK*, ser. 2, case 18, vol. 1.
Tzu-chih t'ung-chien 資治通鑑, by Ssu-ma Kuang 司馬光, 1084. Hong Kong: Chung-hua Shu-chü, 1971.
Wang-sheng hsi-fang ching-t'u jui-ying shan-chuan 往生西方淨土瑞應刪傳, by Wen-shen 文諗 and Shao-k'ang 少康, c. 800. *TD*, vol. 51, no. 2070.
Wang-sheng lun chu 往生論註. See *Wu-liang-shou ching yu-p'i-t'i-she yüan-sheng chieh chu*.
Wang wu-t'ien-chu kuo chuan 往五天竺國傳, by Hui-chao 慧超, c. 727. *TD*, vol. 51, no. 2089.
Wei-mo ching 維摩經. *TD*, vol. 14, no. 475.
Wei-shih erh-shih lun 唯識二十論, *TD*, vol. 31, no. 1590.
Wen-chü 文句. Full title: *Miao-fa lien-hua ching wen-chü* 妙法蓮華經文句, by Chih-i, 587. Edited by Kuan-ting, 629. *TD*, vol. 34, no. 1718.
Wen-shu fa-tsang ching 文殊法藏經. *TD*, vol. 20, nos. 1185A and 1185B.
Wu-liang-shou ching 無量壽經. *TD*, vol. 12, no. 360.
Wu-liang-shou ching i-shu 無量壽經義疏, by Ching-ying Hui-yüan 淨影慧遠 (523–592). *TD*, vol. 37, no. 1745.
Wu-liang-shou ching yu-p'i-t'i-she yüan-sheng chieh chu 無量壽經優婆提舍願生偈註, by T'an-luan (died c. 555). *TD*, vol. 40, no. 1819.
Yü-ch'ieh-shih ti lun 瑜伽師地論. *TD*, vol. 30, no. 1579.

Yü-ch'ieh-shih ti lun lüeh-tsuan 瑜伽師地論略纂, by Tz'u-en, also known as K'uei-chi 窺基 (632–682). *TD*, vol. 43, no. 1829.

Yü-chu chin-kang po-jo po-lo-mi ching hsüan-yen 御注金剛般若波羅蜜經宣演, by Tao-in 道氤, c. 736. *TD*, vol. 85, no. 2733.

Yüan-chüeh ching ta-shu ch'ao 圓覺經大疏鈔, by Tsung-mi (780–841). *ZZK*, ser. 1, case 14, vols. 3–5; case 15, vol. 1.

Yüan-jen lun 原人論, by Tsung-mi (780–841). *TD*, vol. 45, no. 1886.

Yüan-Wei Hsiao-ming chao Fo Tao men-jen lun ch'ien-hou 元魏孝明召佛道門人論前後. In *KHMC* 1.

Yüeh-tsang ching 月藏經. Full title: *Ta fang-teng ta-chi yüeh-tsang ching* 大方等大集月藏經. *TD*, vol. 13, no. 397 (15).

Zenrin shōkisen 禪林象器箋, by Dōchū Mujaku 道忠無著, 1741. Kyoto: Baiyō Shoin, 1909.

4. Primary sources: edicts, decrees, memorials, letters, inscriptions

Chao li seng-ni erh ssu chi 詔立僧尼二寺記, by Sui Wen-ti. In *Chin-shih ts'ui-pien* 38.

Chi-wei she-wen 即位赦文, by Hsüan-tsung (reigned 846–859). In *T'ang ta chao-ling chi* and *CTW* 82.

Ch'i-chi hsi-yüeh wen 祈祭西嶽文, by Li Te-yü. *CTW* 711.

Chia tsun-hao hou chiao-t'ien she-wen 加尊號後郊天赦文, by Wu-tsung. *CTW* 78.

Chien Ching-tsung sou-fang tao-shih shu 諫敬宗搜訪道士疏, by Li Te-yü. *CTW* 701.

Chien I-tsung feng-Fo shu 諫懿宗奉佛疏, by Hsiao Fang. *CTW* 747 and *THY* 48.

Chin ch'uang-tsao ssu-kuan chao 禁創造寺觀詔, by Hsüan-tsung. *CTW* 26.

Chin fang-shih chu-fo hsieh-ching chao 禁坊市鑄佛寫經詔, by Hsüan-tsung. *CTW* 26 and *T'ang ta chao-ling chi* 113.

Chin hua-hu ching ch'ih 禁化胡經勅, by Chung-tsung. In *CTW* 17.

Chin pai-kuan yü seng-tao wang-huan chih 禁百官與僧道往還制, by Hsüan-tsung. *CTW* 21.

Chin seng-tao pu shou chieh-lü chao 禁僧道不守戒律詔, by Hsüan-tsung. *CTW* 29.

Chin seng-t'u lien-ts'ai chao 禁僧徒斂財詔, by Hsüan-tsung. *CTW* 30.

Chin-shang t'ing sha-men pai-chün chao 今上停沙門拜君詔, by Kao-tsung. *CSP* 6 and *KHMC* 25.

Chin-tuan kung-ssu chieh ssu-kuan chü-chih chao 禁斷公私借寺觀居止詔, by Tai-tsung. *CTW* 46.

Ch'ing Huai-nan teng wu-tao chih yu-i-ch'uan chuang 請淮南等五道置遊奕船狀, by Li Te-yü. *CTW* 704.

Ch'ing shan-t'ai seng-tao shu 請刪汰僧道疏, by Li Shu-ming. *CTW* 394 and *THY* 47.

Ch'ing shen-chin seng-ni tsou 請申禁僧尼奏. *CTW* 966.

Ch'ing t'ing kuo-chi hsing-hsiang tsou 請停國忌行香奏, by Ts'ui Li. *CTW* 718.

Ch'u chai-yüeh tuan-t'u ch'ih 除齋月斷屠勅, by Wu-tsung. *CTW* 77.

Ch'ung-chien Tsung-ch'ih ssu ch'ih 重建總持寺勅, by Hsüan-tsung (reigned 846–859). *CTW* 81.

Fang-shih lun 方士論, by Li Te-yü. *CTW* 709.

Fo i-chiao ching shih-hsing ch'ih 佛遺教經施行勅, by T'ai-tsung. *CTW* 9.

Fu fei-ssu ch'ih 復廢寺勅, by Hsüan-tsung (reigned 846–859). *CTW* 81.

Bibliography

Fu Fo-ssu piao 復佛寺表, by Sun Ch'iao. *CTW* 794 and *TCTC* 249.
Hang-chou hsin-tsao nan-t'ing tzu chi 杭州新造南亭子記, by Tu Mu. In *Fan-ch'uan wen-chi* 樊川文集 (Ssu-pu ts'ung-k'an edition) 10.
Ho fei-hui chu-ssu te-yin piao 賀廢毀諸寺德音表, by Li Te-yü. *CTW* 700.
Hsiu-ch'i ssu-kuan chao 修葺寺觀詔, by Te-tsung. *CTW* 52.
Hui Fo-ssu le seng-ni huan-su ch'ih 毀佛寺勒僧尼還俗勅, by Wu-tsung. In *T'ang ta chao-ling chi* 113, *THY* 47, *CTW* 76, and *CTS* 18A.
K'uo-chien seng-ni chao 括檢僧尼詔, by Hsüan-tsung. *CTW* 30.
Ling seng-tao chih-pai fu-mo chao 令僧道致拜父母詔, by Kao-tsu. *CTW* 12.
Ling seng-tao ping-hsing chih 令僧道並行制, by Jui-tsung. *CTW* 18.
Lun Fo-ku piao 論佛骨表, by Han Yü, 819. *CTS* 160, *THY* 47, and *Han Ch'ang-li chi* 韓昌黎集 (Kuo-hsüeh chi-pen ts'ung-shu edition) 39.
Lun liang-ching chi chu-tao pei-t'ien chuang 論兩京及諸道悲田狀, by Li Te-yü. *CTW* 704.
Ming yu-ssu i sha-men teng chih-pai chün-ch'in ch'ih 命有司議沙門等致拜君親勅, by Kao-tsung. *CTW* 14.
Nan-chiao she-wen 南郊赦文, by Hsien-tsung. *CTW* 63.
Nan-yüeh Mi-t'o Ho-shang pei 南嶽彌陀和尚碑, by Liu Tsung-yüan 柳宗元 (779–819). In *Liu Ho-tung chi* 柳河東集 (Kuo-hsüeh chi-pen tsung-shu edition).
Nan-yüeh Ta-shih Yüan-kung t'a-ming chi 南嶽大師遠公塔銘記, by Lü Wen 呂文 (772–811). In *Lü Heng-chou chi* 呂衡州集 (Yüeh-ya-t'ang ts'ung-shu 粵雅堂叢書 edition).
Pien Hsiao Yü shou-chao 貶蕭瑀手詔, by T'ai-tsung. *CTW* 8 and *CTS* 63.
Pin-kuo kung kung-te ming 邠國公功德銘. In *Chin-shih ts'ui-pien* 107.
Po-chou sheng-shui chuang 亳州聖水狀, by Li Te-yü. *CTW* 706.
Seng-ni pu te shou fu-mo chi tsun-che li-pai chao 僧尼不得受父母及尊者禮拜詔, by Kao-tsung. *THY* 47 and *CTW* 12.
Sha-t'ai Fo Tao chao 沙汰佛道詔, by Kao-tsu. *CTW* 3.
Shan-t'ai seng-tao i 刪汰僧尼議, by P'eng Yen. *CTW* 445.
Shen-ch'üan li-su ch'ih 申勸禮俗勅, by Jui-tsung. *CTW* 19.
Shih-chiao tsai Tao-fa shang chih 釋教在道法上勅, by Empress Wu. *CTW* 95.
Shou tsun-hao she-wen 受尊號赦文, by Hsüan-tsung (reigned 846–859). *CTW* 82 and *THY* 48.
Ta Chou hsin-fan san-tsang sheng-chiao hsü 大周新翻三藏聖教序, by Empress Wu. *TD*, vol. 15, p. 706; *CTW* 97.
T'ai-ho san-nien nan-chiao she 太和三年南郊赦, by Wen-tsung. In *T'ang ta chao-ling chi* 71.
T'ai seng-tao i 汰僧道議, by P'ei Chi. *CTW* 616.
T'iao-kuan seng-ni chih 條貫僧尼勅, by Tai-tsung. In *T'ang ta chao-ling chi* 113.
T'iao-liu seng-ni ch'ih 條流僧尼勅, by Wen-tsung. In *T'ang ta chao-ling chi* 113 and *CTW* 74.
T'ing ch'ih seng-tao fan-tsui t'ung su-fa t'ui-k'an ch'ih 停勅僧道犯罪同俗法推勘勅, by Kao-tsung. *CTW* 14.
Tz'u Hui-hu K'o-han shu-i 賜回鶻可汗書意, by Li Te-yü. *CTW* 699.
Wang Chih-hsing tu seng-ni chuang 王智興度僧尼狀, by Li Te-yü. *CTW* 706.
Wu-tsung kai-ming kao t'ien-ti wen 武宗改名告天地文, by Li Te-yü. *CTW* 711.
Ying Feng-hsiang chen-shen te-yin 迎鳳翔眞身德音, by I-tsung. In *T'ang ta chao-*

ling chi 113 and *CTW* 85.

Yü-chüeh t'iao-ko tsou 翼爵條格奏, by Ch'eng Shu-ch'ing. *CTW* 432.

5. Modern reference works: dictionaries, encyclopaedias, indices

Ajiya rekishi jiten アジア歴史事典. Ed. Shimonaka Kunihiko 下中邦彥. 10 vols. Tokyo: Heibonsha, 1959–1962.

Bukkyō daijii 佛教大辭彙. Ed. Ryūkoku Daigaku 龍谷大學. 6 vols. Tokyo: Fuzambō, 1914–1922.

Bukkyō daijiten 佛教大辭典. Oda Tokunō 織田得能, 1917. Revised and enlarged edition, Tokyo: Daizō Shuppan, 1954.

Bukkyō daijiten 佛教大辭典. Ed. Mochizuki Shinkō 望月信亨. Revised and enlarged edition. 10 vols. Tokyo: Sekai Seiten Kankō Kyōkai, 1958–1963.

Bussho kaisetsu daijiten 佛書解說大辭典. Ed. Ono Gemmyō 小野玄妙. 12 vols. Tokyo: Daitō Shuppansha, 1932–1936.

Dai kanwa jiten 大漢和辭典. Ed. Morohashi Tetsuji 諸橋轍次. 13 vols. Tokyo: Taishūkan Shoten, 1955–1960.

Shih-shih i-nien lu 釋氏疑年錄, by Ch'en Yüan 陳垣, 1939; rpt. Peking: Hsin-hua Shu-tien, 1964.

Sō kōsōden sakuin 宋高僧傳索引. Ed. Makita Tairyō 牧田諦亮 et al. 3 vols. Kyoto: Heirakuji Shoten 1976–1978.

Taishō shinshū daizōkyō sakuin 大正新修大藏經索引. Ed. Daizōkyō Gakujutsu Yōgo Kenkyūkai. 38 vols. to date. Tokyo: Taishō Shinshū Daizōkyō Kankōkai, 1962–.

Tō kōsōden sakuin 唐高僧傳索引. Ed. Makita Tairyō et al. 3 vols. Kyoto: Heirakuji Shoten, 1973–1975.

Tōyō rekishi daijiten 東洋歷史大辭典. Ed. Shimonaka Yasaburō 下中彌三郎. 9 vols. Tokyo: Heibonsha, 1937–1939.

6. Secondary studies in Chinese and Japanese

Fujita Kōtatsu 藤田宏達. *Genshi Jōdo shisō no kenkyū* 原始淨土思想の研究. Tokyo: Iwanami Shoten, 1970.

Fukaura Seibun 深浦正文, 'Bussui hatsunehan ryakusetsu kyōkaikyō kaidai' 佛垂般涅槃略說教誡經解題, in *Kokuyaku issaikyō kyōshūbu* 國譯一切經經集部, vol. 3, pp. 133–39. Tokyo: Daitō Shuppansha, 1933.

Fukihara Shōshin 富貴原章信. *Nihon yuishiki shisōshi* 日本唯識思想史. Kyoto: Taigadō, 1944.

Fukui Kōjun 福井康順 et al., ed. *Dōkyō* 道教. 3 vols. Tokyo: Hirakawa Shuppansha, 1983.

———. *Dōkyō no kisoteki kenkyū* 道教の基礎的研究. Tokyo: Shoseki Bumbutsu Ryūtsūkai, 1952.

Futaba Kenkō 二葉憲香. *Kodai Bukkyō shisōshi kenkyū* 古代佛教思想史研究. Kyoto: Nagata Bunshōdō, 1962.

Hu Shih 胡適, ed. *Shen-hui Ho-shang i-chi* 神會和尚遺集. 1930; rev. ed. Taipei: Hu Shih Chi-nien-kuan, 1968.

Ichimura Sanjirō 市村瓚次郎. *Tōyō shitō* 東洋史統. Vol. 2. Tokyo: Fuzambō, 1940.

Kamata Shigeo 鎌田茂雄. "Chōkan ni okeru zen shisō no keisei" 澄觀に於ける禪思想の形成. *Indogaku Bukkyōgaku kenkyū* 印度學佛教學研究, 9-2

(1961) 73-78.

———. *Chūgoku Kegon shisōshi no kenkyū* 中国華嚴思想の研究. Tokyo: Tōkyō Daigaku Tōyō Bunka Kenkyūjo, 1965.

Kubo Noritada 窪德忠. *Chūgoku no shūkyō kaikaku* 中国の宗教改革. Kyoto: Hōzōkan, 1967.

———. *Dōkyōshi* 道教史. Tokyo: Yamakawa Shuppansha, 1977.

Kubota Ryōon 久保田量遠. *Shina Ju Dō Butsu Kōshōshi* 支那儒道佛交渉史. Tokyo: Daitō Shuppansha, 1943.

Lo Hsiang-lin 羅香林. "T'ang-tai san-chiao chiang-lun k'ao" 唐代三教講論考. In his *T'ang-tai wen-hua shih* 唐代文化史. Taipei: T'ai-wan Shang-wu Yin-shu-kuan, 1968.

Michibata Ryōshū 道端良秀. *Tōdai Bukkyōshi no kenkyū* 唐代仏教史の研究. Kyoto: Hōzōkan, 1957.

Mizuno Kōgen 水野弘元. "Zenshū seiritsu izen no Shina no zenjō shisōshi josetsu" 禪宗成立以前のシナの禪定思想史序說. *Komagawa Daigaku kenkyū kiyō*, 15 (1957) 15-44.

Mochizuki Shinkō 望月信亨. *Jōdokyō no kigen oyobi hattatsu* 淨土教の起源及發達. Tokyo: Kyōritsusha, 1930.

———. *Shina Jōdo kyōrishi* 支那淨土教理史. Tokyo: Hōzōkan, 1942.

Mori Mikisaburō 森三樹三郎. *Ryō no Butei* 梁の武帝. Kyoto: Heirakuji Shoten, 1956.

Moroto Tatsuo 諸戶立雄. "Chūgoku ni okeru dochō shoju no nendai ni tsuite" 中国に於ける度牒初授の年代について. *Bunka* 文化, 15.4 (1951) 376-392.

Niida Noboru 仁井田陞. "Ritsuryō kakushiki" 律令格式. *Ajiya rekishi jiten*.

———. *Tō Sō hōritsu bunsho no kenkyū* 唐宋法律文書の研究. Tokyo: Tōhō Bunka Gakuin, 1937.

———. *Tōrei shūi* 唐令拾遺. Tokyo: Tōyō Bunka Gakuin, 1933.

Nomura Yōshō 野村耀昌. *Shū-Bu hōnan no kenkyū* 周武法難の研究. Tokyo: Azuma Shuppan, 1968.

Ōfuchi Ninji 大淵忍爾. *Dōkyōshi no kenkyū* 道教史の研究. Okayama: Okayama Daigaku Kyōsaikai Shosekibu, 1964.

Ono Katsutoshi 小野勝年, *Nittō guhō junrei kōki no kenkyū* 入唐求法巡禮行記の研究. 4 vols. Tokyo: Suzuki Gakujutsu Zaidan, 1964-1969.

Osabe Kazuo 長部和雄. *Ichigyō Zenji no kenkyū* 一行禪師の研究. Kobe: Kōbe Shōka Daigaku Gakujutsu Kenkyūkai, 1963.

———. *Tōdai Mikkyōshi zakkō* 唐代密教史雜考. Kone: Kōbe Shōka Daigaku Gukujutsu Kenkyūkai, 1971.

Shigenoi Shizuka 滋野井恬. *Tōdai Bukkyōshi ron* 唐代佛教史論. Kyoto: Heirakuji Shoten, 1973.

Sogabe Shizuo 曾我部靜雄. *Nitchū ritsuryō ron* 日中律令論. Tokyo: Yoshikawa Kōbunkan, 1963.

T'ang Yung-t'ung 湯用彤. *Han Wei Liang-chin Nan-pei-ch'ao Fo-chiao shih*. 漢魏兩晉南北朝佛教史. 2 vols. Shanghai: Shang-wu Yin-shu-kuan, 1938.

———. "T'ang T'ai-tsung yü Fo-chiao" 唐代宗與佛教. *Hsüeh-heng* 學衡, 75 (1931). Reprinted in T'ang Yung-t'ung, *Wang-jih tsa-kao* 往日雜稿. Peking: Chung-hua Shu-chü, 1962.

Toganoo Shōun 栂尼祥雲. *Mandara no kenkyū* 曼荼羅の研究. Kōyasan: Kōyasan Daigaku Shuppambu, 1927.

Toyama Gunji 外山軍治. *Sokuten Bukō* 則天武后. Tokyo: Chūō Kōronsha, 1966.
Tsukamoto Zenryū 塚本善隆. "Hokushū no haibutsu" 北周の廃仏. In his *Gisho Shakurōshi no kenkyū* 魏書釋老志の研究. Kyoto: Bukkyō Bunka Kenkyūjo Shuppambu, 1961.
———. *Nisshi Bukkyō kōshōshi kenkyū* 日支佛教交渉史研究. Tokyo: Kōbundō Shobō, 1944.
———. *Shina Bukkyōshi kenkyū: Hokugi hen* 支那佛教史研究北魏篇. Tokyo: Kōbundō Shobō, 1942.
———. "Tō chūki irai no Chōan no kudokushi" 唐中期以來の長安功德使. *Tōhō gakuhō* 東方学報 (Kyoto), 4 (1933) 368–406; rpt. in *Tsukamoto Zenryū chosakushū* 著作集, vol. 3, pp. 251–84. Tokyo: Daitō Shuppansha, 1975.
———. *Tō Chūki no Jōdokyō* 唐中期の淨土教. Kyoto: Tōhō Bunka Gakuin Kyōto Kenkyūjo, 1933.
Ui Hakuju 宇井伯壽. *Zenshūshi kenkyū* 禪宗史研究. Vol. 1. Tokyo: Iwanami Shoten, 1939.
Yabuki Keiki 矢吹慶輝. *Amida Butsu no kenkyū* 阿弥陀佛の研究. 1911; rev. ed. Tokyo: Meiji Shoin, 1937.
———. *Sangaikyō no kenkyū* 三階教の研究. Tokyo: Iwanami Shoten, 1927.
Yamazaki Hiroshi 山崎宏. *Shina chūsei Bukkyō no tenkai* 支那中世仏教の展開. Tokyo: Shimizu Shoten, 1942.
———. *Zui Tō Bukkyōshi no kenkyū* 隋唐仏教史の研究. Kyoto: Hōzōkan, 1967.
Yoritomi Motohiro 賴富本宏. *Chūgoku Mikkyō no kenkyū* 中国密教の研究. Tokyo: Daitō Shuppansha, 1979.
Yoshioka Yoshitoyo 吉岡義豊. *Dōkyō no kenkyū* 道教の研究. Kyoto: Hōzōkan, 1952.
———. *Dōkyō to Bukkyō* 道教と佛教. Vol. 1. Tokyo: Nihon Gakujutsu Shinkōkai, 1959.
Yūki Reimon 結城令聞. "Shotō Bukkyō no shisōshiteki mujun to kokka kenryoku to no kōsaku" 初唐仏教の思想的矛盾と国家権力との交錯. *Tōyō Bunka Kenkyūjo kiyō* 東洋文化研究所紀要, 25 (1961) 1–28.

7. Secondary studies in European languages

Beal, Samuel, trans. *Si-yu-ki: Buddhist Records of the Western World*. 2 vols. London: Trübner and Co., 1884; rpt. 4 vols. Calcutta: Susil Gupta (India) Limited, 1957–1958.
Birnbaum, Raoul. *Studies on the Mysteries of Mañjuśrī*. Society for the Study of Chinese Religions Monograph No. 2. [United States]: n.p., 1983.
Bivar, David. 'Sasanians and Turks in Central Asia'. In *Central Asia*, edited by Gavin Hambly. London: Widenfeld and Nicolson, 1969.
Ch'en Kenneth, K.S. *Buddhism in China: A Historical Survey*. Princeton: Princeton University Press, 1964.
———. *The Chinese Transformation of Buddhism*. Princeton: Princeton University Press, 1973.
———. 'The Economic Background of the Hui-ch'ang Suppression of Buddhism'. *Harvard Journal of Asiatic Studies*, 19 (1956), pp. 67–105.
Chou, Yi-liang. 'Tantrism in China'. *Harvard Journal of Asiatic Studies*, 8 (1945), pp. 241–332.
Doré, Henry, S.J. *Researches into Chinese Superstitions*. Translated by M.

Kennelly, S.J. 11 vols. Shanghai: T'usewei Printing Press, 1914–38.
Fitzgerald, C.P. *The Empress Wu*. London: The Cresset Press, 1956; 2nd ed., 1968.
Fontein, Jan. *The Pilgrimage of Sudhana*. The Hague: Mouton & Co., 1967.
Forte, Antonino. *Political Propaganda and Ideology in China at the End of the Seventh Century*. Napoli: Istituto Universitario Orientale, 1976.
Gernet, Jacques. *Les aspects économiques du bouddhisme dans la société chinoise du Ve au Xe siècle*. Saigon: École Française d'Extrême-Orient, 1956.
Hamilton, Clarence, trans. *Wei Shih Erh Shih Lun*. New Haven: American Oriental Society, 1938.
Horner, I.B., trans. *The Book of the Discipline (Vinaya Piṭaka)*. 6 vols. London: Luzac and Co., 1938–1966.
Hu Shih. 'The Development of Zen Buddhism in China'. *The Chinese Social and Political Science Review*, 15–4 (1932), pp. 475–505.
Jan, Yün-hua, trans. *A Chronicle of Buddhism in China 581–960 A.D.* Santiniketan: Visva-Bharati, 1966.
La Vallée Poussin, Louis de, trans. *Vijñaptimātratāsiddhi: La Siddhi de la Hiuan-tsang*. 2 vols. Paris: Librairie Orièntaliste Paul Guenther, 1928–1929. Index, Paris: Librairie Orièntaliste Paul Guenther, 1948.
Legge, James, trans. *The Chinese Classics*. Vol. 1. 2nd rev. ed. Oxford: Clarenden Press, 1893.
Li, Yung-hsi. *The Life of Hsuan-tsang*. Peking: The Chinese Buddhist Association, 1958.
Maspero, Henri. *Le Taoïsme*. Paris: Publications du Musée Guimet, 1950.
Müller, F. Max, trans. 'The Larger Sukhāvatī-vyūha', in *Buddhist Mahāyāna Texts*. Ed. E.B. Cowell et al. *Sacred Books of the East*, vol. 49. Oxford: Oxford University Press, 1894.
Pulleyblank, Edwin G. 'Neo-confucianism in T'ang Intellectual Life'. In *The Confucian Persuasion*, edited by Arthur F. Wright. Stanford: Stanford University Press, 1960.
Reischauer, Edwin O., trans. *Ennin's Diary: The Record of a Pilgrimage to China in Search of the Law*. New York: The Ronald Press Co., 1955.
———. *Ennin's Travels in T'ang China*. New York: The Ronald Press Co., 1955.
Rotours, Robert des. *Traité des fonctionnaires et Traité de l'armée*. 2 vols. Leiden: E.J. Brill, 1948.
Saeki, Paul Y. *Nestorian Documents and Relics in China*. Tokyo: The Maruzen Co., 1937.
———. *The Nestorian Monument in China*. London: Society for Promoting Christian Knowledge, 1916.
Twitchett, Denis C. 'The Monasteries and China's Economy in Medieval Times'. *Bulletin of the School of Oriental and African Studies*, 19.3 (1957), pp. 526–49.
———. 'Monastic Estates in T'ang China'. *Asia Major*, new series, 5.2 (1956), pp. 123–46.
Waley, Arthur. *The Life and Times of Po Chü-i*. London: George Allen and Unwin Ltd., 1947.
———. *The Real Tripitaka*. London: George Allen and Unwin, 1952.
Watters, Thomas, trans. *On Yuan Chwang's Travels in India, A.D. 629–645*. 2 vols.

London: Royal Asiatic Society, 1904–1905; rpt. 1 vol. Delhi: Munshi Ram Manohar Lal, 1961.
Weinstein, Stanley. 'A Biographical Study of Tz'u-en'. *Monumenta Nipponica*, 15.1–2 (1959), pp. 119–49.
——. 'Imperial Patronage in the Formation of T'ang Buddhism'. In *Perspectives on the T'ang*, edited by Arthur F. Wright and Denis Twitchett. New Haven: Yale University Press, 1973.
Wright, Arthur F. 'Fu I and the Rejection of Buddhism'. *Journal of the History of Ideas*, 12 (1951), pp. 33–47.
——. 'T'ang T'ai-tsung and Buddhism', in *Perspectives on the T'ang*, edited by Arthur F. Wright and Denis Twitchett. New Haven: Yale University Press, 1973.
——. 'The Formation of the Sui Ideology, 581–604', in *Chinese Thought and Institutions*, edited by John K. Fairbank. Chicago: Chicago University Press, 1957.
Yampolsky, Philip, trans. *The Platform Sutra of the Sixth Patriarch*. New York: Columbia University Press, 1967.
Zürcher, Erik. *The Buddhist Conquest of China*. 2 vols. Leiden: E.J. Brill, 1959.

INDEX

almshouses, 131
Amitābha, 66–74 *passim*
 images of, 69, 72
 see also Pure Land
Amoghavajra: *see* Pu-k'ung
An-kuo ssu, 87, 132, 146
An Lu-shan rellion, 59–65
animals and fish, ban on killing, of 43, 114, 123, 201, n.7; *see also* taboo days; taboo months
appointment, blank letters of, 60
astrology, ban on practice of, 20

birthdays, imperial, 61, 140, 145
 celebrated at Buddhist monasteries, 54
 debates on, 117, 141
 slaughter of animals banned on, 114
 vegetarian banquets for clergy held on, 83, 139
 vegetarian banquets for clergy discontinued on, 110
 see also vegetarian banquets; palace debates
black, superstitions regarding color, 125, 129, 135; *see also* superstitions
Bodhiruci, 44, 49
Buddha, traditional date of death of, 163, n.19
Buddha's Light, Prince of: *see* Chung-tsung
Buddhism
 criticized as foreign religion by Kao-tsu, 8; by T'ai-tsung, 16
 defense of, by Chih-shih, 16; by Fa-ch'ang, 16, 17; by Fa-lin, 7; by Hsiao Yü, 8; by Hsüan-ch'ang, 121; by Hsüan-tsang, 28–29; by Tao-hsüan, 32–3
 edicts critical of, 8 (621, 625), 8–9 (626); 14 (631); 15 (635); 16 (637); 23 (646); 29 (655); 32 (657); 31 (664); 49 (710); 50 (by Jui-tsung); 34, 51–2 (714); 52 (722, 727, 729); 34 (733); 53 (736); 175, n.1 (762); 101 (807); 118, 119 (826); 111–12 (835); 117–18 (842); 122 (843); 123, 125, 127 (844); 128, 129, 132, 133, 134 (845)
 given equal status with Taoism, 39, 49–50
 memorials critical of, 193, n.33 (757); 102 (811); 108–9 (830); 110 (835); 118 (842); 134 (845); 142 (851); 143 (852); 145 (861, 862, 864); by Fu I, 7–8; by Han Ÿ, 104; by Hsin T'i-pi, 50; by Kao Ying, 84; by Li Ch'in-ming, 182, n.13; by Li Shu-ming, 90; by P'ei Po, 92; by P'eng Yen, 91; by Ts'ui Li, 114, by Yao Ch'ung, 51
 ranked above Taoism, 43
 ranked below Taoism, 16
 ranked below Taoism and Confucianism, 8
 suppression of, under Northern dynasties, 3–4, 70, 125; under Wu-tsung, 115–36
 Taoist view of, 37
Buddhist church
 supervision of, under Sui, 10; under Kao-tsu 10
 wealth of, 50, 89
 see also clergy; hierarchy; monasteries
Bureau for the Veneration of Mysteries, 10

cakravartin: *see* Universal Monarch
cannibalism, 200, n.124
certificates of identification, 108, 137, 143
chai-yüeh: *see* taboo months
Chan-jan, 177, n.24
Ch'an Master (Ch'an-shih), first use of title, 46
Ch'an school, 45–6, 62–65, 99, 100, 149, XIX.27, 150, XI.27
Chang-ching ssu, 74, 84, 100, 132
Chang-hsin ssu, 95
Chao-ch'eng ssu, 88
Chao-hsüan ssu (Bureau for the Veneration of Mysteries), 10
Chao-hsüan ts'ao (Office for the Illumination of Mysteries), 9, 10, 19

229

Index

Chao-hsüan t'ung (controller of the Office for the Illumination of Mysteries), 9
Chao Kuei-chen, 107, 116, 117, 124, 127, 128
chapels, cloisters, hermitages, mountain temples, shrines, 5, 142, 143
   dismantlement of, 52, 118, 126
   number of, dismantled, 196, n.79, 134
Cheng Shu-ch'ing, 60, 193, n.33
Ch'eng-ju, 94
Ch'eng-kuan, 62, 63, 99
Ch'eng-yüan, 73, 74
Chi Shan-hsing, 6
chien (overseer of a monastery), 10
Chien-fu ssu: *see* Ta chien-fu ssu
Chien-fu ts'ao (Office for Overseeing Meritorious Works), 9
chien-shih (commissioner for overseeing Buddhist affairs), 86
Ch'ien-fu ssu, 145
Chih-hsien, 45, 64, 175, n.27
Chih-hsüan, 140, 141
Chih-lin, 157, n.46
chih-shih (chief administrator), 185, n.11
Chih-shih (monk), 16, 17
Chih-te ssu, 83
Chih-yen, 46
Chin-hsien kuan, 123, 124
Chin-kan-chih: *see* Vajrobodhi
Chin-o ssu, 80
Chin-lu (golden talisman) ritual, 116
Ching-ching, 97
Ching-hui, 7
Ching-shuang, 74
Ching-tsung, 106
   interest in Taoism, 195, n.65
Ching-t'u, 172, n.1; *see also* Pure Land
Ch'ing-liang ssu, 177, n.19
Ch'ing-lung ssu, 132, 138
Ch'iu Shih-liang, 113, 114, 115, 118, 119, 121
Chu-k'o: *see* Office for Overseeing Foreign Visitors
Chu-lin ssu, 74
Ch'u-chi, 175, n.27
Chuang-yen ssu, 132, 138, 143, 196, n.72, 201, n.4
Chung-hsing kuan, 48
Chung-hsing ssu, 48
Chung-tsung, 38, 40, 47–9, 60
Ch'ung-hsüan hsüeh, 168, n.26
Ch'ung-hsüan kuan, 201, n.7
Ch'ung-hsüan shu, 10
Ch'ung-lun ssu, 161, n.40
Ch'ung-sheng ssu, 88, 196, n.72
Ch'ung-T'ang kuan, 36
clergy, Buddhist
   activities forbidden to, 20, 21, 22, 175, n.1, 183, n.20
   autonomy of, under Southern dynasties, 4
   burning of robes of, 135
   clothing of, regulations regarding, 20
   contacts with laymen by, discouraged, 125
   credentials for, 108
   criticism of, 15, 16
   denunciation of offending, to authorities, 20
   donations to, banned, 125
   execution of, 122, 125, 130, 132
   expulsion of foreign, 131–2, 169, n.33;
   of corrupt, from court, 107
   fleeing persecution, 134, 204, n.17, 148
   fraudulent, 53, 101, 102
   illegally ordained, 50, 108, 109, 143; recognition of, under Sui, 5; 700,000 seek legitimation in 830, 61
   investigation of, 14, 16, 130
   jurisdiction over, assigned to Department of Sacrifices, 43; assigned to Bureau for the Veneration of Mysteries, 10, 36; returned to Department of Sacrifices, 90; transferred to Office for Overseeing Foreign Visitors, 134
   laicization of, 119, 121, 128, 130, 132; 30,000 in 714; 51 166, n.3; 100,000 in 844; 196, n.79; as punishment, 20; in Lo-yan by T'ai-tsung, 12; in 845, 134; proposed in 826, 9; under age 40, 129; under age 50, 129
   maintenance of, annual cost for, 91
   moneylending by, prohibited, 93
   not considered subjects of throne, 58
   officials forbidden to associate with, 51
   of the ten directions. 183, n.23
   ordered to adhere to *Fo i-chiao ching*, 21
   participation in rebellions, 154, n.1
   preaching to laymen by, considered offense, 21
   property of, 93–4; confiscated, 119
   proposal to collect data on, 108
   proselytization in villages by, forbidden, 52
   punishment of, 18–21, 157, n.42, 29
   purges of, 14 (627); 17 (640); 51 (714); 175, n.1 (762); 108–9 (830); 111–12 (835); 117–36 (842–846); Li Shu-ming's proposal for, 90; P'ei Po's proposal for, 92; P'eng Yen's proposal for, 91–2
   registration of, 166, n.3
   regulations regarding behavior of, 18–19, 157, n.41
   size of, 17, 166, n.3, 133; restrictions on, 8, 153, n.16, 143

Index

undesirable, defined, 119
unaffiliated, 117, 118
visits to homes of parishioners by, forbidden, 11
wealthy, 93
wills of, 94
see also Buddhist church; clerical registers; monastic property; ordination; parents; ruler
clergy, Taoist: see Taoist priests
clerical registers, 52, 53, 110, 122
compilation of, 52
denounced by *Jen-wang ching*, 78
maintained by commissioners of good works, 96; by recorders of the clergy, 100
Taoist, 100
see also clergy, registration of
commissioners of good works (*kung-te shih*)), 85–9 *passim*, 100, 102, 103, 113, 119, 121, 122, 128, 131, 138
abolished in 779, 89; revived in 788, 95–6
abolished in 845, 137; revived in 846, 137, 188, n.20
Confucius, imperial visits to birthplace of, 35, 161, n.41
Court for State Ceremonials (Hung-lu ssu), 10, 36, 43, 52, 53, 200, n.112
Court in Charge of Foreign Visitors (Ssu-pin ssu), 43
Court of Imperial Clan Affairs (Tsung-cheng ssu), 36, 53

Department of Sacrifices (Tz'u-pu), 43, V.29, 52, 53, 167, n.17, 61, 90, 93, 100, 108, 109, 134, 137, 143
Divākara, 44
divination, ban on, 20, 21

edicts: see Buddhism, edicts critical of; Taoism, edicts concerning
elixirs, 36, 106, 115, 127, 129, 135, 144, 195, n.65
Ennin, 34, 115–35 *passim*
Esoteric Buddhism (Mi-chiao;, 54–9 *passim*, 77–83 *passim*
esoteric consecrations, 56, 57, 83
examinations for ordination, 49, 170, n.3, 110, 188, n.20, 111, 112
executions, restrictions on, 123

Fa-ch'ang, 16, 17
Fa-chao, 73–4
Fa-chen, 105, 188, n.20
Fa-ch'ien ssu, 140
Fa-hsiang school, 62, 63, 149
Fa-jung, 164, n.41, 64
Fa-li, 87

Fa-lin, 17
Fa-men ssu, 37, 46, 58
pilgrimages to, banned, 125
Fa-ming, 162, n.16
Fa-tsang, 44, 46–7, 63
Fan-wang ching, 33
Fei-yen ssu, 161, n.40
Feng-luan ssu, 161, n.40
five sacred mountains, (*wu yüeh*), 152, n.5
Fo i-chiao ching, 21, 22
Fo-kuang wang: see Chung-tsung
Fo shou-chi ssu, 44, 45
Fu I, 7–8, 12
Fu-shou ssu, 145

Gaṇḍavyūha, 98
gender change as an omen, 163, n.18

Han-kuang, 80, 180, n.62
Han Yü, 103–5
Hao-t'ien kuan, 159, n.1
hermitages: see chapels
hierarchy under Northern and Southern dynasties, 4, 9, 10, 101
Ho-tse ssu, 65
homa, 58
Hsi-hua kuan, 158, n.63
Hsi-ming ssu, 28, 30, 32, 33, 165, n.11, 78, 98, 102, 132, 138
Hsi-tsung, 146
hsiang-shui ch'ien, 60
Hsiao Fang, 145
Hsiao-kan ssu, 191, n.15
Hsiao Yü, 8, 134
hsien-ch'ien seng-ch'ieh (visible clergy), 183, n.23
Hsien-tsung, 62, 99–105, 190, n.2
Hsin T'i-p'i, 50
Hsing-fo ssu, 102
Hsing-fu ssu, 102, 191, n.15, 196, n.72
Hsing-T'ang kuan, 124, 126
Hsing-T'ang ssu, 179, n.59, 179, n.60
hsiu kung-te shih: see commissioners of good works
Hsüan-ch'ang, 121, 141
Hsuan-chung ssu, 70, 71
Hsüan-mu (Hsüan-mo), 159, n.71
Hsüan-tsang, 18, 24–31 *passim*, 38, 165, n.49
Hsüan-tsung (reigned 712–56), 51–9, 110–11, 120, 123
Hsüan-tsung (reigned 846–59); see Hsuen-tsung
Hsüan-wan, 18
Hsüan-yüan Chi, 144
Hsüan-yüan Huang-ti, 35, 47
Hsüan-yüan Huang-ti miao, 168, n.26, 187, n.3
Hsüeh Huai-i, 162, n.16, 43, 44

Hsuen-tsung, 136–44
Hua-tu ssu, 49
Hua-yen ching, 45, 47, 177, n.19, 184, n.51, 99
Hua-yen monasteries, 47
Hua-yen school, 45, 46, 47, 62, 63, 149, 150
Huai-su, 87
Huang Ch'ao, 146–9 *passim*
Huang-mei shan, 45
Hui-an, 45, 49
Hui-ch'ang suppression of Buddhism, 115–36
Hui-ch'eng, 191, n.18
Hui-chung, 172, n.26
Hui-hsiao, 180, n.60
Hui-lang, 85
Hui-neng, 64, 65
Hui-shan ssu, 175, n.29
Hui-yüan, 68, 69, 73, 81, 143
Hung-fu ssu, 156, n.22, 22, 24, 25, 26, 33, 106
Hung-jen, 64
Huo Hsien-ming, 95, 96

I-ch'ieh-ching yin-i 159, n.70, 98–9
I-ching, 44, 45
I-ching yüan, 97
I-hsing, 165, n.49, 55–6
I-tsung, 144–6
images, Buddhist
    ban on manufacture of, 51
    ban on use of metal for, 139
    bearing likeness of Hsüan-tsung, 54
    bearing likeness of kao-tsung, 37
    disposition of, after purge of 845, 133
    production of, under Yang Chien, 4, 5
    see also Amitābha, Lung-men, Maitreya, Śākyamuni
images, Taoist, 6

Jen-chien, 45
Jen-wang ching, 12, 78
Ju-ching, 87
Ju-man, 185, n.7
Jui-tsung, 40, 49–50, 60

K'ai-yüan ssu, 54
Kao-tsu, 152, n.14, 5–11, 123
Kao-tsung, 26, 27–37, 159, n.1, 38, 117
Kao Ying, 84
k'u-i (hard labor), 19
Kuan wu-liang-shou Fo ching, 66, 67, 70
Kuang-ming ssu, 72
K'uei-chi, 30
kung-te shih: *see* commissioners of good works
kung-te yüan, (merit cloisters), 51
K'ung-tzu shuo, 124

Kuo-hsüeh, 8
K'uo-ch'ing, 85

Lao-chün, 125: *see also* T'ai-shang Lao-chün; Lao-tzu
Lao-tzu
    belief that, went to India, 37
    birthday of, declared festival day, 116
    birthplace of, imperial visits to, 35, 161, n.41
    Buddhist view of, 17
    honorific titles conferred on, 35, 168, n.26
    honorific titles of, revoked, 47
    memorial hall of, in Po-chou, 7
    paintings of, converting barbarians banned, 47
    T'ang ruling family claims descent from, 6, 16
    see also Lao-chün; T'ai-shang Lao-chün
Lao-tzu hua-hu ching, 48
law, secular, 157, n.42, 29
legal codes, 17, 18, 156, n.35; *see also Tao-seng ko*; *Vinaya*
Li (ruling family of T'ang), 6, 16
    superstitions regarding name, 195, n.68
Li Ch'in-ming, 182, n.13
Li Hsien-ch'eng, 86, 87
Li Hsün, 110, 112, 113
Li Hung, 28, 36
Li Lung-chi, 49, 50; *see* Hsüan-tsang
Li Shen, n.25, 119, 122, 192
Li Shih-min: *see* T'ai-tsung
Li Shu-ming, 90
Li Te-yü, 60, 61, 118, 119, 120, 122, 124, 195, n.65, 131, 134, 135, 137–8
Liang Wu-ti, 23, 82
lin-t'an ta-te (ordination preceptors), 85
Ling-chun, 105
Ling-fu, 187, n.3
Ling-pien, 177, n.19
Ling-sui, 101
Ling-yen 201, n.5
Liu Ch'ung-hsün, 86, 87, 89
Liu Hsüan-ching, 117, 201, n.7
Liu Tao-ho, 36
Li Yüan, *see* Kao-tzu
Li Yüan-ts'ung, 85, 86
Lung-hsing kuan, 48
Lung-hsing ssu, 48, 54
Lung-men, 38–39, 48, 69, 72
Lü school, 63; *see also Vinaya*
Lüeh-ch'u nien-sung ching, 55, 57

Maitreya, 70
    earthly manifestations of, 154, n.1
    Empress Wu identified with, 41, 42, 43
    images of, 69, 72
Manichaeism, 120, 121

Index

Mañjuśrī: *see* Wen-shu
Marīci, 77
masses: *see* services, Buddhist
meat, ban on eating, 20–1, 99
memorials: *see* Buddhism, memorials critical of
merit cloisters, 51
military governors, 57, 62–3, 80, 138
Ming-chan, 13
monasteries, Buddhist
  construction of, banned, 51, 90, 112; allowed in villages, 141; on battlefields, 5, 13; under Sui, 5; at the five sacred mountains, 4, 58
  destruction of, in An Lu-shan rebellion, 61
  dismantlement of small, 128
  established in each province by Kao-tsung, 35; by Empress Wu, 42–43; by Chung-tsung, 48; by Hsüan-tsung, 53–4
  guests not to be invited to, 20
  investigation of, 52, 128
  land held by, restrictions on, 52
  may not be used as hostels, 96, 141
  merging of small, with large ones, 128
  number of, in Ch'ang-an, 9; in China, 153, n.17, 166, n.3; dismantled in 845, 134; to be allowed after Hui-ch'ang suppression, 132–3; restrictions imposed on, 8, 9
  officials may not stay at, 175, n.1
  renaming of, 138
  reopening of, after 846, 138–9, 141
  repair of dilapidated, ordered, 96
  required to install image of Wen-shu, 81
  restoration of abandoned, 139
  restrictions on oversized, 102
  supervision of, 85
  tablets granting recognition to, 50
  see also Chung-hsing ssu, K'ai-yüan ssu, Lung-hsing ssu, Ta-yün ssu
monastic property, confiscation of, 153, n.16, 50, 52, 128, 134; *see also* clergy, property of
monks and nuns; *see* Buddhist church; clergy; parents; ruler
mountain temples: *see* chapels
mourning, period of, changed for mother, 40
Mu-tsung, 105–6, 190, n.2

nei kung-te shih (commissioner of good works for the palace), 86
nei-tao-ch'ang; *see* palace chapel
Nestorians, 97, 98, 134
Niu-t'ou school, 171, n.16, 64
Niu-t'ou shan, 45
Northern school: *see* Ch'an school

novices, ban on accepting, 117, 118
nuns: *see* clergy

Office for Overseeing Foreign Visitors (Chu-k'o), 134
Office for Peerage Ranks (Ssu-feng), 53, 100
Office for the Illumination of Mysteries: *see* Chao-Hsüan ts'ao
omens: *see* oracles and prophecies
O-mi-t'o ching, 66, 67, 68, 72
oracles and prophecies, 6, 41, 00, n.18, 50, 82
ordination certificates, 109, 129, 130
  sale of, 59–61, 65
  sent to authorities upon death of monk, 93
ordination platforms, 141, 145
ordination preceptors, 141, 145
ordinations
  banned by Hsüan-tsung, 166, n.3; by Te-tsung, 90; in 835, 111
  ban on, lifted by Sui, 4
  for defrocked monks, 202, n.22,
  illegal, punishable by death, 14
  locally authorized, banned in 807, 60
  local, 187, n.6
  local, official punished for allowing, 107
  mass, 14, 15, 26, 50
  number of, under Sui, 5
  officially sanctioned sites for, 175, n.29
  permitted in order to replenish clergy, 188, n.20
  screening of clergy for, 143
  selection of candidates for, 15
  sponsored by Tai-tsung, 78–88
  unrestricted, allowed in 851, 141
  see also clergy, Buddhist; examinations for ordination

palace chapel, 78, 82, 97, 118, 125, 145, 146
  converted into Taoist shrine, 125
  dismantled in 780, 90
  esoteric altar in, 57
  establishment of, 58
  housed spirit tablets of imperial family, 82
  reopened under Shun-tsung, 99
palace debates, 37; *see also* birthdays, imperial
palaces, conversion of, into monasteries of nunneries, 12, 156, n.22
Pan-chou san-mei ching, 66, 67, 68
P'an Shih-cheng, 36
Pao-hsiu, 99
Pao-T'ang ssu, 138
pao-t'u (precious chart), 41
Pao-ying ssu, 79, 138

Index

Pao-yü ching, 163, n.20
pārājika offenses, 19, 20
parents
  clergy criticized for receiving homage of, 14
  question whether clergy should reverence, 32–4
P'ei Mien, 60
P'ei Po, 92
P'ei T'an, 145
P'eng Yen, 91–2
Pien-chang, 202, n.18
pilgimages, 125
Pin-t'ou-lu, 81
Po Chü-i, 117
popular lecutres (*su-chiang*), 111, 116
Prajñā (Po-jo San-tsang), 97, 98, 177, n.20
prophecies: *see* oracles and prophecies
Pu-k'ung, 56–8, 62, 77–83 *passim*, 180, n.62, 85
P'u-chi, 64, 65
P'u-ku Huai-en, 77, 78
P'u-kuang wang ssu, 125
Pure Land, 67–74 *passim*
Pure Land Buddhism, 11, 66–74, 149, 150
purple robe, 192, n.21

rebellions, participation of monks in 154, n.1
recorders of the clergy (seng-lu), 100, 101, 105, 121, 201, n.5
relic
  finger bone, 37, 46, 49, 58, 96, 102, 103, 104, 146
  tooth, 88, 125, 143
revelations: *see* oracles and prophecies
ruler
  as guardian of the Dharma, 22, 82
  attempts to compel clergy to reverence, 32, 33
  clergy exempted from reverencing, 34
  monk praised for not rising in presence of, 3
  ransoming of, from clergy, 4
  receives bodhisattva precepts, 49
  subordination of clergy to, under Northern dynasties, 4
  woman as, 40, 41

Śākyamuni, 66
  images of, 69, 72
saṃgha: see clergy, Buddhist
san chai-yüeh: *see* taboo months
san yüan-yüeh, 123; *see also* taboo months
Sanskrit manuscripts, 27, 28, 31, 44, 58
scriptures, Buddhist
  banned, 132
  catalogues of, 98
  imperial prefaces to, 25, 26, 44, 49, 78, 98
  institutes for translation of, 26, 27, 97
  laymen forbidden to copy, 51
  loss of, 61, 147, 148, 149
  translation of, 24, 30, 31, 44, 55, 57, 78, 81, 97–98
self-mutilation, 15, 103, 146
seng-cheng (rectifier of the clergy), 101
Seng-ch'i pu (Department for the Buddhist Clergy), 10
Seng-ch'ieh, 49, 196, n.73
seng-chu (head of the clergy), 101
seng-lu: *see* recorders of the clergy
seng-t'ung (controller of monks), 62
services, Buddhist, 12, 54
  annual, for Te-tsung's father, 96
  for deceased emperors, 141
  for war dead, 5
  officials barred from participating in, 114
  sponsored by T'ai-tsung, 12, 15
sha-men t'ung (controller of monks), 9
Shan-tao, 00, n.15, 71–2, 73
Shan-wu wei, 54
Shan-yin ssu, 105
Shao-lin ssu, 24, 29
Shen Chuan-shih, 107
Shen-hsiu, 45, 46, 49, 63, 64, 65
Shen-hui, 45, 63, 64, 171, n.18, 65
Shen-kuang, 185, n.12
Sheng-yeh ssu, 153, n.10
shih-ching tu-seng (ordination by examination), 165, n.11
shi-fang seng-ch'ieh (clergy of the ten directions), 183, n.23
Shih-li, 99
shih ta-te: *see* Ten Monks of Great Virtue
Shih-t'ou, 99
shrines: *see* chapels
Śikṣānanda, 45, 47, 49
Shun-tsung, 99
slaves
  clergy forbidden to own, 21
  confiscation of, 128, 129, 134
  number of, owned by monasteries, 130
  owned by clergy, 119
Sōniryō, 18
Southern school: *see* Ch'an school
Sri Lanka, 55, 57, 80
Ssu-feng: *see* Office for Peerage Ranks
Ssu-ma Ch'eng-chen, 168, n.26
Ssu-pin ssu (Court in Charge of Foreign Visitors), 43
su-chiang; *see* popular lectures
Su-tsung, 57–9, 65, 172, n.26, 123
Śubhakarasiṃha, 54, 55, 56
Sui Wen-ti (Yang Chien), 4, 5, 7, 19, 123
Sui Yang-ti (Yang Kuang), 32

suicide, 72, 141
Sukhāvatī, 66, 67
see also Ching-t'u; Pure Land
Sun Ch'iao, 142
Sung Shen-hsi, 108
superstitions, 135, 136, 163, n.18, 195, n.68
use of, against Buddhism, 124, 125, 129

Ta chien-fu ssu, 55, 116, 132, 196, n.72
Ta Chou tung ssu, 162, n.7
Ta hsing-kuo ssu, 5
Ta hsing-shan ssu, 57, 78, 82, 83, 85, 179, n.60
Ta-jih ching, 55, 56, 168, n.25
ta seng-lu (grand recorder of the clergy), 62
Ta tsung-ch'ih ssu, 17, 144, 201, n.4
ta t'ung (grand controller), 10
Ta tz'u-en ssu, 26–33 *passim*, 55, 72, 88, 132
Ta yün ching, 12, 41–3
Ta-yün ssu
changes in name, 48, 54
established in each prefecture, 42–3
tablets at monastery gates, 50, 126
taboo characters, 39–40
taboo days, 195, n.58, 145
taboo months, 111, 116, 191, n.16, 122, 123, 139
Tai-tsung, 74, 77–89
T'ai-ching kung, 187, n.3, 116
T'ai ch'ung-fu ssu, 83
T'ai-i kuan, 36
T'ai-shang Hsüan-yüan Huang-ti, 35
T'ai-shang Lao-chün (Grand Lord Lao), 7; see also Lao-chün, Lao-tzu
T'ai-shou kuan, 158, n.63
T'ai-tsung, 152, n.14, 11–27, 28–9, 157, n.41, 203, n.5
T'ai-yüan ssu, 39, 46
Taihō ritsuryō 157, n.7
talismans, 116, 117, 127, 201, n.7
T'an-ch'ien, 154, n.23
T'an-luan, 69–70
T'ang-an ssu, 138
T'ang-ch'ang ssu, 138
Tao-ch'eng, 95
Tao-ch'o, 70–1, 174, n.23
Tao-hsin, 164, n.40
Tao-hsüan, 32
Tao-i (abbot of Hung-fu ssu), 22, 23
Tao-i (founder of Chin-ko ssu), 80
Tao-yin, 167, n.18
tao-jen t'ung (controller of the religious), 9
Tao-seng ko, 17–22 *passim*, 29, 32
Tao-shih-chang, 195, n.64

Tao-te ching
accorded status of classic by Kao-tsung, 37
households required to keep copy of, 168, n.26
translation into Sanskrit, 25
Taoism
accorded first place among the three teachings, 13
Buddhist critiques of, 17
edicts concerning, 8–9, 16
imperial support for, 35, 168, n.26, 115, 116, 117, 144
Taoist canon, 36
Taoist priests, 5, 9, 12, 39, 100, 116
ban on ordination of, 90
Buddhist criticism of, 17
criticized for not reverencing parents, 14
degree holders forbidden to become, 191, n.11
exempt from reverencing emperor, 34
explusion of, from court, 107
fraudulent, 101
imperial patronage of, 6, 36
jurisdiction over, assigned to commissioners of good works, 100; to Court of Imperial Clan Affairs, 36, 53; to Department of Sacrifices, 164, n.29
number of, 153, n.17
officials forbidden to associate with, 51
ordination of, ordered by Tai-tsung, 50, 88
proposal for purge of, 90, 175, n.1
purchase of ordination certificates by, 60
raising money through ordination of, 60
Taoist temples
ban on construction of, 90
established in each province, 35, 48, 53–4, 168, n.26
founded by emperors, 158, n.63, 159, n.1, 36
given bells confiscated from Buddhist monasteries, 128
imperial birthdays celebrated at, 54
investigation of, 52
may not be used as hostels, 96
memorial services for deceased emperors at, 141
number of, in Ch'ang-an, 9; in China, 153, n.17
officials forbidden to stay at, 176, n.1
supervision of, 85
Te-shan, 205, n.28
Te-tsung, 62, 65, 74, 175, n.1, 89–99
temples, Buddhist: *see* monasteries, Buddhist
temples, Taoist: *see* Taoist temples

Index

Ten Monks of Great Virtue, 10, 11, 13
Terrace for the Immortals, 127, 129
thaumaturges, 90
Ti-wu Shou-liang, 96
Tien-ssu shu (Bureau for Temple Administration), 10
T'ien-t'ai school, 11, 171, n.9
   loss of texts of, 147–8, 149
T'ien-tsun, 125, 126
Tou Wen-ch'ang, 95, 96
Ts'ui Li, 114
Tsun-sheng incantation, 126
Tsung-cheng ssu (Court of Imperial Clan Affairs), 36, 53
Tsung-mi, 62, 63, 171, n.18, 113
Tu Hung-chien, 79
Tu-men Lan-jo, 45
T'u-t'u Ch'eng-ts'ui, 100
Tuan-fu, 99, 101
tuan-shih sha-men (adjudicator), 19
Tung-ming kuan, 159, n.1
Tzu-sheng ssu, 55, 78, 120, 132
Tz'u-en, 30
Tz'u-pu: *see* Department of Sacrifices
Tz'u-en ssu: *see* Ta tz'u-en ssu
Tz' u-te ssu, 156, n.22

Uighurs, 120, 121
Universal Monarch, 43, 58, 78: *see also* World Ruler

Vajrabodhi, 55, 78
vegetarian banquets, 49, 83, 88, 102, 114, 139, 145, 146
Vinaya, 18–22, 24, 52, 111
   forbids clergy to reverence ruler, 33
   new commentary on, 86–8, 97
   on disposition of property of clergy, 93, 94
Vinaya school, 63

Wang Che, 116
Wang Chih-hsing, 60
Wang Chin, 79, 80
Wan Hsi-ch'ien, 96, 97, 98
Wang Shou-ch'eng, 108, 109, 110, 113
Wang Yü, 181, n.6
Wang Yüan-chih, 6, 36, 158, n.63

Wei-hsiu, 32
Wei Hsüan-chung, 170, n.4
Wei-kuo ssu, 162, n.7
wei-no, 185, n.11
Wei Tsung-ch'ing, 121–2
Wei-ying, 171, n.12
Wen-hsü, 191, n.15
Wen-shu (Mañjuśrī), 80–3 *passim*
Wen-shu fa-tsang ching 177, n.20
Wen-tsung, 106–14
woman as ruler, 40
   Ta-yün ching used to justify, 41–2
World Ruler, 162, n.16, 43; *see also* Universal Monarch
Wu Chao: *see* Wu, Empress
Wu, Empress, 28, 37–47, 48, 131
wu hui nien-fo (five rhythm intonation of the Buddha's name), 73, 74
Wu-liang-shou ching, 66, 67, 68, 73, 175, n.28
Wu-t'ai shan, 37, 47, 74, 80, 83, 135, 140, 179, n.60, 183, n.27
   pilgrimages to, banned, 125
Wu-tsung, 114–36
Wu-yeh, 105
Wu Yün, 168, n.26

Yang Chien: *see* Sui Wen-ti
Yang Ch'in-i, 121, 137
Yang Kuang: *see* Sui Yang-ti
Yang Kuo-chung, 60
Yao Ch'ung, 51
Yen-T'ang ssu, 138, 145
yin-sheng nien-fo (drawled invocation of the Buddha's name), 175, n.27
Yōrō ritsuryō, 156, n.36, 157, n.39
Yü Ch'ao-en, 83, 84
Yu'-ch'üan ssu, 45
Yü-hua ssu, 30, 31
Yü-lan-p'en, 82, 84, 90, 95, 126
Yü-wen Hsüan, 95
Yüan-chao, 86, 88, 97, 98
Yüan-k'an, 147
Yüan Tsai, 79
Yüeh-chung, 101

Zoroastrians, 134

Made in the USA
Lexington, KY
24 February 2018